Bridge of Hope

JEWL

Bridge of Hope

JEWL

Introduction

BRIDGE OF HOPE is a publication conceived and undertaken by JEWL—
the Japanese Executive Women's League. The founding members of
JEWL arrived in Southern California well after the end of World War II.
Some became executives in already-established companies. Others went
into business for themselves. In 1985, a group of seven decided to enter
into an organization that would foster personal growth and networking,
whereupon JEWL was born.

At the outset, challenges were everywhere to be found—the English
language, the legal system in all of its complexity, the world of business
practices and relationships. As women, we faced the additional hurdle of
getting beyond convention and stereotype. However, we persevered, in
spite of the many obstacles we faced, and we managed to succeed. In due
course, though, we came to realize that our path to success had in fact
been paved by many exemplary individuals who had preceded us—
pioneering Japanese-Americans who struggled so hard to earn the full
entitlements of citizenship that we now take for granted.

These early pioneers selflessly strove to adapt to their new lives in a
strange new land. They endured much hardship and managed to
overcome the many obstacles and setbacks that threatened their
livelihoods and their very survival. Despite tremendous odds, their
communities took root and flourished. These forerunners cultivated the
soil that would later harbor and nurture our own dreams and ambitions,
which have yielded such a rich harvest over a century later.

This, then, was the legacy of those who came before, a legacy that has
indeed become a noteworthy chapter of American history. It is to these
individuals, and what they stood for, that we proudly dedicate this
book, this *BRIDGE OF HOPE.*

Bridge of Hope/The Road Traveled by Japanese-Americans

Published in 2007 by JEWL (Japanese Executive Women's League)
3538 Carson Street, Suite 125, Torrance, California 90503 U.S.A.

Editor-in-Chief:	Mami Mizuguchi
Senior Editor:	Fujimi Fujimura
Assistant Editor:	Hiroko Nishikawa Naumann

Writer and Researcher:	Yumi Mitani
DTP Design:	Hidenori Ito
Jacket Design:	Masako Boissonnault
Historical Gallery:	Mami Mizuguchi & Akemi Nakamori
Children's Life in the Camps:	Masako Boissonault & Akemi Nakamori
Chronology:	Mami Mizuguchi

English Translation Supervisor and Editor: Marvin Marcus
Associate Professor of Japanese
Washington University

Translators: Joseph Brewster Dreher
Aaron Hames
Shiho Takai
Graduate students in Japanese literature,
Washington University

First Edition Printed in November, 2007

ISBN13: 978-0-9790933-0-2
ISBN10: 0-9790933-0-9

Printed in the United States of America
J&L Press, Inc. Glendale, California 91201 U.S.A.

Editor's Preface

Being a U.S. non-profit organization comprised of Japan-born women entrepreneurs, our task of publishing a major historical study has been a significant undertaking. During the two and a half years that have gone into this project, we have benefited immensely from many volunteers who generously devoted their time and talents to our collective effort.

The text was first written in Japanese and then translated into English. We are especially grateful to Professor Marvin Marcus of Washington University and his group of graduate students for their work on the English translation. Every attempt has been made to produce a bilingual volume in which the Japanese and English textual "halves" mirror each other. However, the fact of this book's being published in the U.S with English-language readers in mind, more information has been included in the English text than in the Japanese text. We have tried to remain as faithful as possible to the Japanese text, and we beg your indulgence in the event of any minor shortcomings or discrepancies.

Bridge of Hope bears the mark of many individuals who have contributed unstintingly to its construction. Our heartfelt thanks go out to Aileen Willoughby, Nancy Jacobson, Karen Matsumoto Copeland, Pam Eisenberg, and all those who kept their faith in us and our mission.

Special thanks go to the Japan Camera Museum, Yokosuka City Museum, Nagasaki Prefecture Museum, and the Tozenji Temple in Takasaki-shi for providing us with rare archival materials that we have included in the Historical Gallery. Our sincere appreciation goes to the staff of the Bancroft Library, University of California, Berkeley, for their encouragement and generosity in providing many valuable photographs from their archives, and to the Lighthouse/Takuyo Corporation for allowing us to include a number of relevant columns from their publications.

We hope that the reading of this book provides you with some insight into the cultural growth and transition of Japanese-Americans over the last 150+ years, and an appreciation for their efforts and significant achievements.

NOTE TO THE READER:

* All photograph captions and quotations have been rendered as in the original sources.

* Every possible effort has been made to obtain permission from all reference sources, and any omissions are unintended and/or unavoidable.

* We have chosen to hyphenate "Japanese-American." However, we have elected not to require other writers to conform to this practice. Hence, any inconsistencies in this regard are not the result of oversight.

Table of Contents

NOTE TO THE READER:

In the Prologue only, Japanese names are written according to the Japanese system. Surnames follow the given name.

Prologue

Around the time American pioneers first crossed the Rocky Mountains in covered wagons and looked to settle the West, a spate of isolationist proclamations calling for an end to all contact with foreign countries was promulgated in Japan. Despite the fact that Japanese authorities had outlawed the construction of large sea-going vessels and the nation had become a secluded archipelago, there were those who, through various twists of fate, ended up setting foot on American soil. These castaways, shipwrecked off the coast of Japan, either managed to ride the ocean currents and safely come ashore in America or were rescued by American ships. These few resilient individuals later strived to make new livelihoods in a strange, new land. In their own way, these castaways made very substantial contributions to United States-Japan relations and to the modernization of Japan.

Otokichi (John Matthew Ottoson): 1817-1867
Adrift on the Pacific Ocean for 14 Months
Buried under Foreign Soil

Otokichi, who hailed from the town of Mihama in Aichi prefecture, is known as one of the first Japanese to set foot on the continental United States. At age 14, Otokichi joined the crew of the *Hōjun-maru* as an apprentice sailor. In November of 1832 the vessel, loaded with rice and pottery, set sail for Edo (Tokyo). The crew of 14 included a sailor named Iwakichi (age 28) and an apprentice, Kyūkichi (age 15). Their ship had disappeared after stopping at the port of Toba. Relatives assumed that the ship was lost in the storm-tossed wintry seas and erected tombstones for the lost sailors. In reality, ocean currents had carried the *Hōjun-maru* to the northwest away from the Japanese coast and out into the Pacific Ocean. After drifting for 14 months, the *Hōjun-maru* finally came ashore at Flattery Point near Cape Alava in Washington.

The *Hōjun-maru* was an extraordinarily sturdy ship, built for sailing in coastal waters. It had a capacity of approximately 150 tons of freight.[1] The fact that the crew was able to endure over a year adrift on the Pacific Ocean after being damaged was due to two factors. First, they managed to produce fresh water with the use of a device for distilling seawater. Second, the ship carried a cargo of rice.[2] Although a surprising number of individuals managed to survive despite damage to their vessel, there were no nautical charts for the coastal areas, nor were there any Japanese sailors capable of open-sea navigation at this time. If a ship lost its mast in a storm at sea, there was nothing the crew could do except to let the wind and ocean currents carry the ship to its fate.

During the *Hōjun-maru*'s long odyssey across the Pacific Ocean, the crew succumbed, one by one. By the time the ship reached Flattery Point in Washington Territory, only three remained alive—Otokichi, Kyūkichi, and Iwakichi. Washington was still a vast undeveloped territory and not yet a state in the American Union. It was home to a number of Native-American tribes. Members of the local Makah tribe rescued the three Japanese survivors who soon came to the attention of an English employee of the fur-trading Hudson's Bay Company.

The men were then taken to Fort Vancouver, a trading outpost some 200 kilometers to the south, where they received instructions in English. Hoping to use the castaways in an effort to open trade with Japan, the company officials transported the survivors to London, stopping first in Hawaii. The British government would not consent to a long stay, so after 10 days, the men were sent to Macao. In Britain they received permission to disembark for one day, thus becoming the first Japanese on record to visit London.[3]

Otokichi's Odyssey (1832~1867)

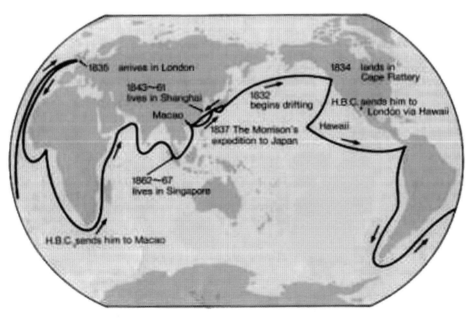

Otokichi's Odyssey. Source: Hudson's Bay Company.

At that time, the only area in China where foreigners were allowed to reside was in Macao, so the three castaways awaited their chance to return to Japan. In the interim, they came under the care of a missionary named Charles Gutzlaff. It was over the course of a year that Gutzlaff, with the help of his three native informants, managed to produce the first Japanese translation of the Gospel of John and the Epistles of John.[4]

During their stay in Macao, the castaways met four Japanese sailors, including Captain Shōzō and Rikimatsu, who had suffered a similar fate. Captain Shōzō's group from Kumamoto was brought to Macao aboard a Spanish ship after coming ashore on Luzon Island in the Philippines. As this case illustrates, Japanese sailors adrift in the Pacific Ocean experienced landfall in places other than the continental United States. Indeed, there are records of men turning up as far north as the Kamchatka Peninsula in Russia and the Aleutian Islands. They also ended up in Taiwan, Vietnam, Central America, Luzon, and on any number of islands in the South Pacific.[5]

It was in July of 1837, that the opportunity arrived for the seven castaways in Macao to finally return home. Looking to establish trade ties with Japan, an American trading company in Canton took Otokichi and the others aboard the *Morrison* and set sail for Japan. It had already been five years since Otokichi had left his hometown of Mihama. This was to be their long-awaited homecoming, but fate proved otherwise.

When the *Morrison* entered the waters of Edo Bay near Uraga, it was suddenly met with cannon fire. This attack, now known as "The *Morrison* Incident," was encouraged by the Edo Shogunate and duly recorded in the annals of Japanese history. Its root cause is traced to 1825 when the Shogunate, responding to Europe's growing colonial ambitions in Asia, issued a decree calling for the repulsion of all foreign ships. Therefore, despite having raised a white flag, the *Morrison* was relentlessly fired upon and forced to retreat. They headed south and entered Kagoshima Bay on August 8, 1825. Unfortunately, negotiations with the ruling Satsuma Clan were unsuccessful and the long-awaited journey home of the *Hōjun-maru*'s survivors ended in failure.[6]

The Shogunate's *Sakoku* policy of national seclusion, together with its strict ban on Christianity, prohibited all foreign trade and outlawed travel to foreign countries. A death sentence awaited former Japanese citizens if they re-entered Japan after residing abroad. The timing of the castaways' return proved to be ill-fated. After the

The *Morrison* Anchored at Uraga Bay, Japan in 1837. Drawing by a Japanese Artist. Source: National Archives of Japan.

Morrison incident, the castaways abandoned all hopes of repatriation and resolved to live out their days in foreign lands. Several years later, following China's defeat in the 1840 Opium War, the Shogunate realized the potential danger that could ensue from reckless attacks on foreign ships and slightly relaxed its policy of national seclusion. A new decree was issued which allowed the provisioning of firewood and water for foreign ships.

In 1838, Otokichi worked as a sailor on the *Morrison* and sailed to New York City. He stayed at a boarding house on the East River in Manhattan.[7] Later that year, he moved to Macao where he was christened and adopted the name John Matthew Ottoson. Soon after, he found employment with a British trading company and was transferred to a new operation in Shanghai. Although Otokichi vowed never to return to Japan, an ironic twist of fate brought him back to Japan against his will.

When England joined the Crimean War to support the Turks against Russia, Otokichi accompanied Admiral James Stirling's fleet of the British Royal Navy throughout the seas of Asia in search of Russian ships. In 1854, a year after Commodore Matthew Perry arrived in Uraga, Admiral Stirling's fleet entered Nagasaki harbor. Otokichi had no choice but to serve as an interpreter. He interpreted skillfully and almost single-handedly negotiated with the Japanese government to open trade at the Nagasaki port. His contribution to the first treaty between Japan and England (the historic Peace and Amity Treaty) earned him British citizenship and a handsome reward from the British government.[8]

After obtaining British citizenship, Otokichi settled in the affluent British quarter of Shanghai. He visited Japan twice but no longer sought permanent residence in his native land. Whenever a Japanese castaway appeared in Shanghai, Otokichi would devote himself to helping that person return to Japan. He married an English woman in Shanghai and raised three children—two girls and a boy named John William. After his wife passed away, Otokichi married a Malaysian woman. In 1862, the couple moved to her birthplace, Singapore. According to the memoirs of Fukuzawa Yukichi, when Japan's first delegation to Europe stopped in Singapore, Otokichi paid them a visit.[9]

Traveling with the delegation as an interpreter was Moriyama Einosuke, who had studied English under Ranald MacDonald in Nagasaki. MacDonald was the son of a Scottish trader and a Native-American woman. He originally traveled to Japan due to Otokichi's influence. MacDonald was born in Fort Vancouver, the same outpost where Otokichi and the other castaways had been taken after they came ashore. At the time, the group of castaways hailing from a strange land in the Far East was surely the talk of the town. Their fate left a deep impression on MacDonald and instilled in him an interest in Japan.

MacDonald conceived a plan whereby he himself would "wash ashore." In 1848, while aboard a whaling vessel off the Japanese coast, He defied the ship's captain and set adrift in a small boat. He eventually

Japanese Drawing of Otokichi. In 1849, Otokichi visited Japan dressed as a Chinese man. Source: National Archives of Japan.

came ashore on Rishiri, a small island off Hokkaidō. MacDonald was immediately sent to a prison in Nagasaki, as common practice of the time dictated. However, his affable personality quickly charmed his captors and before long, he was teaching English to them. Since Japanese interpreters at that time were able to function only in the Dutch language, a good number of them regularly visited MacDonald's jail cell for the opportunity to learn English from a native speaker. After a year of conducting his language tutorials through the grating of a Nagasaki prison cell, MacDonald was deported.[10]

In 1867, one year before the Meiji Restoration, Otokichi passed away in Singapore at the age of 50. He had a Christian burial. In 1970, an urban renewal project converted the cemetery into a park. Otokichi's remains were moved, but their whereabouts were unknown for decades. It was in 2004, through the joint effort of the Japanese Association of Singapore and the Singapore Land Authority, that the location of Otokichi's remains became known—a grave in the Choa Chu Kang National Cemetery.

In February 2005, 173 years after the *Hōjun-maru* set sail, Otokichi's ashes were finally returned to his hometown.[11] John William, Otokichi's son, carried out his father's wishes and moved to Japan in 1879. He applied for naturalization in Japan but he was unable to become a Japanese citizen since such legislation was not in force at that time. Records show that he took the name Yamamoto Otokichi and worked for a private company in Kobe.[12] Nothing further is known of the man.

Manjirō (John Manjirō): 1827-1898
From Fisherman to University Professor
A Fortuitous Life

John Manjirō. Circa 1880. Courtesy of Tenjin-cho, Tosashimizu-shi, Kōchi-ken.

In 1841, four years after the *Morrison* incident, a small fishing boat left Tosa, Kōchi-ken. In the waters near Ashizuri, the boat was caught in a winter storm. There were five young fishermen aboard, one of whom was John Manjirō of Nakanohama. Fourteen years of age at the time, Manjirō was the youngest of the group. His father died when he was a child so he had to work in order to help his mother.[13]

After 10 days of buffeting by strong winds, the severely damaged boat drifted ashore on Torishima, an uninhabited island. The five fishermen barely escaped the storm with their lives. For the next five months, they lived on the meat of albatross that frequented the island. Luckily, an American whaling vessel, the *John Howland*, happened upon the island and rescued the stranded fishermen.

Castaways who drifted ashore on islands such as Torishima were common in those days. Records from the Edo period indicate one castaway who spent 20 years on an uninhabited island and others who built rafts and made perilous voyages' back home. It also lists 100 to 200 individuals who managed to return home after the shipwrecks. Those are only the successful cases; the number of those who lived out their days in foreign lands without ever seeing Japan again is undoubtedly far greater.

Manjirō's rescue after five months was indeed a stroke of luck—only the first, as it turned out, in a lifetime marked by good fortune. However, it was the man's own initiative and enterprising spirit that enabled him to exploit his good fortune as he went on to transform himself from a humble fisherman to a significant historical figure.

Due to the Shogunate's isolation policy, the *John Howland* was unable to return the stranded fishermen to their homeland. Instead, the ship set sail for the island of Oahu in Hawaii. Four of the fishermen elected to remain in Hawaii, but Manjirō chose to part from his compatriots and make the voyage to the United States. The young man's eagerness and courage impressed the crew of the whaling ship, and they developed a liking for him. He became known affectionately as "John Mung," being christened with the ship's first name. It took two years for the *John Howland* to return to New Bedford, Massachusetts, the center of the American whaling industry, whereupon Manjirō became the first Japanese to set foot on the East Coast of the United States.

William Whitfield, captain of the *John Howland*, brought Manjirō to his hometown of Fairhaven. Captain Whitfield treated Manjirō as a son and provided for his education. Attending school for the first time in his life, young Manjirō studied subjects such as English, mathematics, navigation, and surveying. His own family had been too poor to afford any formal education; hence, Manjirō was indeed fortunate to have been given this opportunity. He did not let Captain Whitfield down, and eagerly took to his studies, rapidly absorbing the newfound knowledge. Unbeknownst to Manjirō himself, the education he received in Fairhaven not only benefited him personally, but it would become a resource that would help promote Japan's advancement toward modernization.

Captain William Whitfield.
Courtesy of Millicent Library.

After graduation, Manjirō joined the crew of the *Franklin* as a navigation officer. In the course of the next 40 months spent circumnavigating the globe, Manjirō was appointed First Mate.[14] Upon returning to Fairhaven, he found the town abuzz with the news that gold had been discovered in California. The Gold Rush was on! Here was an unparalleled opportunity for Manjirō who wasted no time in making his way to California. Within two months he had accumulated $600 with which he purchased a ship and set sail for Hawaii.[15] His erstwhile compatriots, Denzō and Goemon, joined Manjirō in Hawaii and the threesome set out for their long-awaited journey back to Japan. They ventured home knowing that a potential death sentence could be waiting for them. Nonetheless, they took this gamble and history turned out to be on Manjirō's side.

In 1851, 10 years after leaving Tosa, the three men landed in Ryūkyūs (Okinawa). From there, they were dispatched to Satsuma and interrogated. Manjirō's return to Japan, 14 years after the *Morrison*'s failed attempt to land, came at a time when the Shogunate was entering its final decline. The timing could not have been more propitious. It was Manjirō's good fortune that the ruling clan of Satsuma had been championing the overthrow of the Shogunal regime. Foreign ships were regularly plying the waters around the Satsuma domain which meant that Manjirō's experience overseas, combined with his expertise in navigation and shipbuilding, made him a valuable asset.

In Manjirō's home province of Tosa, Sakamoto Ryōma was a leading opponent of the Shogunate and had risen to prominence. After hearing about the man's various exploits, Sakamoto summoned Manjirō to Tosa and bestowed upon him the status of samurai. Manjirō became an instructor at the *Kyojukan*, a school for elite samurai located near Kōchi Castle. The following year the Shogunate summoned

Sakamoto Ryōma (1835-1867). Source: © 2004 National Diet Library, Japan.

him to Edo and made him a direct retainer of the Shogun. Thus, after braving the threat of capital punishment upon his return to a *Sakoku*-dominated Japan, Manjirō met with extraordinary success. At age 26, he was granted the right to carry a sword and bear a surname. Manjirō chose as his surname the name of his hometown—a privilege normally reserved for the Japanese social elite. He was now known as Nakahama Manjirō. That same year, Commodore Perry and his fleet of Black Ships arrived in Japan.

Manjirō produced the first Japanese language text on navigation through his translation of the *New American Practical Navigator*. He also served on the faculty of the Japanese Naval Academy and published the first English conversation textbook in Japan. In 1860, Manjirō sailed to the United States aboard the *Kanrin-maru*. This ship accompanied the first official Japanese delegation to the United States. The purpose of this important diplomatic mission was to exchange instruments of ratification for the U.S.-Japan Treaty of Amity and Commerce. At sea, the *Kanrin-maru* met with a fierce storm and were it not for the navigational skills of Captain John Brooke and First Mate Manjirō, the voyage may well have ended in disaster. It was during this visit to the United States that Fukuzawa Yukichi and Manjirō made their famous purchase of a Webster's Dictionary.

John Manjirō and Family in Later Years. Courtesy of Tenjin-cho, Tosashimizu-shi, Kōchi-ken.

After returning to Japan, Manjirō received an appointment by the Meiji government to teach at *Kaisei* Academy (forerunner of Tokyo University), the nation's most prestigious educational institution. In his later years, Manjirō continued to serve as a bridge between Japan and the international community. His contributions are truly legendary.

Manjirō spent his final days in Okayama in the home of his son, who had become a doctor and professor of medicine at Okayama University. He passed away at the age of 71.

The amazing tale of Manjirō's life has been the subject of many published accounts over the years, and his story proved deeply inspirational to the people of Japan during the Shogunate's last days. As part of the celebration of the American bicentennial in 1976, Manjirō was one of 29 historical figures, together with Charles Dickens who penned *American Notes*, included in the Smithsonian exhibition *Abroad in America: Visitors to a New Nation*.[16]

Hamada Hikozō (Joseph Heco): 1837-1897
Shaking Hands with Three U.S. Presidents
The First Japanese-American Citizen

The Shogunate's *Sakoku* Policy (1635-1854) banned foreign ships from entering all Japanese ports and Japanese castaways were prohibited from returning home. However, in the 1800s many foreign ships began to appear in the waters around Japan and demanded the opening of the ports for the supply of food and fuel and the humane treatment of shipwrecked foreigners. In 1846, Commodore James Biddle was sent by the U.S. government to open trade with Japan but was ultimately refused by the Shogunal authorities.

In 1854, Commodore Perry was aboard the famous Black Ships, whose arrival in Japanese waters triggered the end of the country's long feudal epoch. A Japanese castaway named Sentarō was aboard one of the ships, the *Susquehanna*, and hoped to return to his homeland. However, when the ships arrived at Uraga, he refused to set foot on Japanese soil. He feared the Shogunate's severe punishment even though the Uraga officials tried to persuade him to leave the ship. Instead, Sentarō chose to return to America.[17]

Among the many Japanese sailors who left Japan and were unable to return for fear of the Shogunate's stern treatment was a castaway named Hamada Hikozō. He later became the first Japanese–American citizen and was privileged to have met three American Presidents.

During the winter of 1851, when Hikozō was a lad of 13 years old, his vessel, the *Eiriki-maru*, was damaged in a severe storm. After being adrift for over seven weeks, the 17 Japanese castaways were rescued by an American ship, the *Auckland*, and finally disembarked in San Francisco. The U.S. government was already making plans to dispatch Commodore Perry to Japan, and officials believed these men could be used to diplomatic advantage. Thus, after spending a year in San Francisco, Hikozō and his shipmates were sent aboard the *St. Mary* to Macao, and then aboard the *Susquehanna* to Hong Kong where they awaited the arrival of Commodore Perry's fleet. It was in Hong Kong that Hikozō met the aforementioned Rikimatsu and heard about the *Morrison* incident from him. He reconsidered a return to Japan. Manjirō's successful return to Japan was a strong indication that the tides of change were sweeping over his native land. However, Hikozō opted to return to San Francisco where fortune would smile upon him in unexpected ways.

Upon his return to San Francisco, Hikozō was regularly called upon to interpret for other castaways. In this capacity, he encountered the chief customs officer, a local notable named Beverly Sanders. Just as Manjirō's relationship with Captain Whitfield proved so fortuitous, the contact with Sanders would have a profound effect on Hikozō's life. Sanders took Hikozō into his care and brought him to New York and Washington, D.C. Hikozō marveled at the steam locomotives in New York and the gas lamps in Washington. There he was introduced to President Franklin Pierce and thus became the very first Japanese to have met with an American President. Hikozō expressed amazement at the fact that the great White House lacked any imposing fortifications or gateways, and that the President himself dressed like a commoner in quite ordinary clothing.[18]

Joseph Heco Courtesy of Harima-chō, Hyōgo-ken.

Hikozō, like Manjirō, would contribute to Japan's modernization after returning home. Their lives intersected in interesting ways. They were both castaways at an early age (Manjirō, 14; Hikozō, 13). Each had an American benefactor who was instrumental in providing a fine education. With the support of Sanders, Hikozō was able to attend a Catholic school in Baltimore where he studied English, mathematics, and the Bible. In 1854, encouraged by Sanders' wife, Hikozō was baptized and took the name Joseph Heco. He then gained employment in the Washington office of Senator William Gwin, a close friend of Sanders. Senator Gwin introduced Heco to President James Buchanan. In 1858, through Sanders' sponsorship, Heco became the first Japanese to acquire U.S. citizenship.[19]

Joseph Heco became a naturalized American citizen in the year of Japan's official "opening," with the signing of the U.S.-Japan Treaty of Amity and Commerce. The following year he returned to his native land for the first time in nine years. Through his acquaintanceship with U.S. Consul General Townsend Harris in Japan, Heco worked in Kanagawa as an interpreter for the newly appointed Consul, E.M. Dorr. While working at the consulate, Heco bade farewell to his friend, Captain Brooke, who was on board the *Kanrin-maru*. This ship was bound for the United States with the first Japanese delegation. Manjirō, who shared a similar fate with Heco, was on the *Kanrin-maru* as well. Interestingly, Heco would happen to meet Manjirō face to face on this occasion.[20]

In 1861, after a barrage of attacks on foreigners, Heco decided to make his third trip to the United States. This trip coincided with the outbreak of the Civil War. During his stay, and in the midst of this critical period in American history, Heco was given the opportunity to have an encounter with President Abraham Lincoln, the third president he would meet during his remarkable career. At age 25, Heco returned to Yokohama to serve once again as a consular interpreter. With the looming

Meiji Restoration and the dawn of Japan's modern era, Heco would distinguish himself through his involvement in drafting the National Bank Ordinance and in helping establish the Osaka Mint Bureau.

In addition, as publisher of Japan's first newspaper, the *Kaigai Shimbun,* he achieved distinction as the father of Japanese journalism. It bears noting that the sixth issue of the *Kaigai Shimbun* covered President Lincoln's assassination.[21] Heco remained in Japan until his death at the age of 60. He is interred in the Aoyama Cemetery in Tokyo.

The *Kanrin-maru* Delegation and its Aftermath

In January 1860, the Tokugawa Shogunate, with the encouragement of U.S. Consul General Townsend Harris, dispatched an official delegation of 77 men to the United States, to exchange instruments of ratification for the U.S.-Japan Treaty of Amity and Commerce. The delegation, led by Foreign Magistrate Shinmi Masaoki, included Muragaki Narimasa as Vice Envoy and Lord Oguri Kōzukenosuke (also known as Oguri Tadamasa) as Inspector. This was the first such visit by the nation of Japan. The delegation crossed the Pacific Ocean aboard an American steamship, the

Commodore Perry's Flagship "*Powhatan.*" Watercolor and ink on paper by a Japanese artist. Courtesy of Yokosuka City Museum.

Powhatan, which had previously served as Commodore Perry's flagship. The *Kanrin-maru,* whose members included Manjirō, accompanied the *Powhatan* as far as San Francisco, serving as escort. Captain John Brooke, an American Navy Officer and Manjirō were onboard the *Kanrin-maru* and offered nautical training to the crew.

The Japanese delegation members were received as official guests of state, with Congress having appropriated a budget of $50,000 to cover expenses.[22] They first stopped at Hawaii and San Francisco, then on to Panama to traverse the Atlantic Ocean. The canal project would not be completed for decades so the delegation traveled cross-country by steam locomotive. Recounting his first ride aboard a train, Vice Envoy Muragaki wrote:

> The roar of the train boomed like thunder, and the plants and trees appeared as lines at first glance. It was a captivating sight. But there was so much noise that I couldn't hear anyone speak — it was more than one could bear.[23]

The rush and roar of the train evidently proved overwhelming for the samurai accustomed to the relatively tranquil life inside the castle walls. Departing Panama, the delegation arrived in Washington, D.C., on May 15, some five months after its departure from Uraga. In Washington, the delegates spent three weeks at the Willard Hotel. The appearance of the samurai in topknots quickly created a national sensation. Large crowds appeared in front of the hotel for days on end, hoping to catch a glimpse of the strange visitors from the far-off land of Japan. Witnessing the Americans' astonished reception upon their arrival at the hotel, Vice Envoy Muragaki remarked in his diary:

> It reminded me of a festival in Edo. Such a din and clamor! I simply cannot fathom why these people conduct themselves without the least bit of restraint. Truly laughable. [24]

A local newspaper reported that the visitors from Japan were "... quiet and dignified, expressing neither surprise nor admiration in their demeanor or speech." [25] To say the least, the sense of cultural contrast was mutually apparent.

The delegation also visited Philadelphia and New York where the members received warm and enthusiastic welcomes. Banquets, balls, and parades were held in their honor, but it was the spectacle of ballroom dancing that elicited the greatest shock. Vice Envoy Muragaki wrote about the attire of women in his diary:

> Women uncover their shoulders. Most of them wear thin white garments with the widespread bottoms just like *hakama* (Japanese man's formal divided skirt).

He described Americans dancing at the balls as follows:

> Men and women in each other's grasp busily took steps together as if they were little mice circling around and around. Many couples just went around the dance floor. To me, it was not appealing. Women's skirts flipped as they circled, which was quite comical. They seemed to enjoy dancing the night away, but I was amazed and couldn't believe my eyes. [26]

Ballroom dancing was obviously an alien practice in the eyes of these Shogunal emissaries.

In Washington, the delegation met with President Buchanan and formally ratified the U.S.-Japan Treaty of Amity and Commerce. Their return voyage was via the Cape of Good Hope, Jakarta, and Hong Kong. The group arrived back in Edo on November 10, 1860. [27] The *Kanrin-maru*, having sustained damage to its hull, remained in San Francisco to undergo repairs. When it was once again seaworthy, the ship crossed the Pacific Ocean to return to Japan.

The delegation's formal mission was to ratify the treaty; there were no further political objectives. However, much was gained during the visit to the United States through the day-to-day experiences of the samurai contingent. For one, they learned first-hand about America's extensive iron-steel based industries, which included railroads, ship-building, urban construction, and the like. Upon returning to Japan, several of them endeavored to introduce these industries to Japan, together with a fiscal system based on private investment. Lord Oguri, who had become Magistrate of the Treasury, made an appeal in 1867 to tradesmen and merchants and founded Japan's first stock company, *Hyōgo Shōsha*. In the same manner, he approached private contractors to build a hotel for foreigners in the Tsukiji district of Tokyo by establishing a stock company. Lord Oguri also promoted the construction of a shipbuilding yard in an effort to spur Japan's modernization. He fully understood the necessity for Japan to move away from its "wood and paper" past and emulate nations like America, which was "overflowing with iron." It was Lord Oguri's leadership that led to the founding of the Yokosuka Iron Works which began operation as a full-fledged shipyard in 1869.[28]

Lord Oguri Tadamasa. Source: © 2004 National Diet Library, Japan.

Traveling to San Francisco aboard the *Kanrin-maru* were two individuals who fully comprehended the differences between Japanese feudalism and American democracy. They emerged as leading figures of the Meiji era: Katsu Kaishū and Fukuzawa Yukichi. Katsu was known for his involvement in the anti-Shogunal movement. Fukuzawa Yukichi wrote the well-known treatise entitled *An Encouragement of Learning*, which contains the famous epigram, "Heaven has created no man above or below another man." Katsu, when asked to compare Japan and the United States, is said to have responded to a high-ranking official as follows:

> Unlike the situation in our own land, Americans in high office are as wise as their positions require them to be.[29]

Fukuzawa Yukichi. Source: © 2004 National Diet Library, Japan.

Katsu Kaishū. Source: © 2004 National Diet Library, Japan.

Katsu's eldest son, Koroku, graduated from the U.S. Naval Academy in Annapolis. After returning to Japan, Koroku advanced to the rank of lieutenant commander but died of an illness while still a young man. Koroku's half brother, Kaji Umetarō, married Clara Whitney. She was the daughter of William Whitney whom the Japanese government invited to help establish Hitotsubashi University in Tokyo. Umetarō and Clara had six children together.[30]

Many young erstwhile samurai flocked to schools in the eastern United States for specialized training and to broaden their knowledge and experience. Upon returning home, they helped introduce modern values and democratic ideals to what had long been a reclusive and feudalistic land. Through the efforts of men like Lord Oguri Kōzukenosuke, Fukuzawa Yukichi and Katsu Kaishū, a cherished notion of America as the embodiment of modern nationhood emerged among virtually all Japanese. These men, as well as the remarkable overseas experiences of Manjirō and Heco, would exert a strong influence on the Meiji era in Japan.

Japanese Students at Rutgers College. New Jersey. Circa 1870. Courtesy of Rutgers College.

One must finally recall the benevolence and solicitude shown by those generous Americans who fostered young Japanese castaways such as Manjirō and Heco. These, too, were gifts that would benefit so many Japanese. Manjirō never forgot the kindness of his benefactor, Captain William Whitfield, and over the course of five generations, the two families have maintained a warm relationship.[31] In 2005, the descendants of the *Kanrin-maru*'s crew traveled to Lexington, Virginia, to express their gratitude and strengthen their friendship with the descendents of Captain John Brooke—the man who saved their ancestors from that perilous sea voyage of long ago.[32]

Chapter 1

from the 1890s~

The Beginning of Emigration

Sugarcane Workers Using a Steam Plow. In the 1880s, the steam plow replaced plows drawn by horses or oxen. The plows worked in pairs, with one on each side of a field and usually more than a 1,000 feet apart. One engine pulls a gangplow across the field, as the other draws it back. Double mould-board plows created shallow trenches for planting seed cane. Circa 1900. Courtesy of Bishop Museum.

CONTENTS

With the arrival of Commodore Matthew Perry's "Black Ships" and the spectacular opening of Japan, many young people bound their hopes and dreams to their wicker trunks and crossed the Pacific. However, once in America, they would confront the harsh reality of discrimination and exclusion. Faced with adversity, these young people struggled earnestly and helped one another in the spirit of cooperation. Before long, they established roots in this foreign soil and built the foundation of a thriving Japanese-American community.

Hawaii's First Japanese Settlers

In 1853, upon the order of President Millard Fillmore, Commodore Perry's Black Ships arrived at Uraga, Japan. This would ultimately come to symbolize the beginning of a new era and the dawn of Japan's modernization. In the years that followed, Japan quickly put an end to over two centuries of feudal reign and isolation from the world with the U.S.-Japan Treaty of Peace and Amity in 1854. This treaty brought about opportunities for ordinary Japanese citizens to join the larger, international community.

15

Chapter 1

In 1868, with the advent of the new era of Emperor Meiji, people of strong will and determination made the voyage overseas. On May 17 of that year, 153 Japanese set sail from Yokohama and arrived in Hawaii aboard the steamship, *Scioto*. They were called the *Gannenmono*—"People of the New Era."[1]

With the transition from the Shogunal rule to the modern nation-state, those who left Japan without approval from the new government would face a harsh reality upon their arrival in Hawaii—namely, day labor in the sugarcane fields. For those among the newly arrived *Gannenmono* who had no experience with manual labor, cutting sugar cane would come as a rude awakening. Over time, their dissatisfaction and disillusionment grew intense, and word of their plight reached Japan, where the Meiji government eventually interceded. As a result, 40 *Gannenmono* returned to their homeland while those who remained went on to complete their three-year labor contracts in Hawaii. Upon completion of their term, only 13 chose to return to Japan. The rest of the group remained in Hawaii, becoming the pioneers of the Japanese settlement there.[2]

While the *Gannenmono* slaved away on Hawaiian plantations, a pioneering group of Japanese overseas "colonists," led by a Dutchman, J.H. Schnell, was sailing to San Francisco by steamship. This second emigrant group following on the heels of the *Gannenmono* were 20 erstwhile samurai of the Aizu domain.[3] Because the Aizu had sided with the Shogunate and opposed the Imperial forces to the very end, it suffered a resounding defeat. Their domain lands were confiscated and many of its samurai retainers were forced to leave. Twenty of them went abroad, with San Francisco as their destination. The group ended up purchasing land on the outskirts of San Francisco, which they named the Wakamatsu Colony. They cultivated tea and planted mulberry trees (in order to raise silkworms). However, within a year, perhaps due to the inhospitable climate, the Wakamatsu Colony venture failed. Precious little is known about the subsequent fate of these individuals.

Workers on Break in a Cane Field in Pu'unene, Maui, Hawaii. The man on the left is holding a cane knife. The workers used the hook to pick up cane stalks from the ground. Circa 1912. Photographer: Baker, Ray Jerome. Courtesy of Bishop Museum.

Behind the Emigration Boom

The Japanese government agonized over what countermeasures to pursue in response to the plight of the *Gannenmono* and the failure of the Wakamatsu Colony. They suspended emigration authorization for nearly 20 years. In 1885, emigration finally resumed. The exchange of written agreements between the governments of Japan and Hawaii formalized the recognition of overseas migrant workers. This amounted to a government-sanctioned export of Japanese labor. Those workers were termed *Kanyakuimin*, or government-contract emigrants.

Japan was experiencing deflation and recession during this time and a growing surplus of unemployed laborers—from farming villages in particular—struggled under the weight of abject poverty. There were cases where whole municipalities encouraged emigration. The multitude of young people driven into desperate living conditions at home placed their hopes in the prospects that awaited them overseas. The first recruitment campaign for contract emigration yielded approximately 28,000 applicants, who thronged to fill the 600 available openings.[4] Of those, 994 applicants, selected on the basis of physical exams, set sail for Hawaii aboard the steamship, *City of Tokio*.

When these individuals arrived in Honolulu, they were put to work on sugarcane plantations located throughout the Hawaiian Islands. The three-year contract term with the Hawaiian government covered the travel expenses. Men were paid nine dollars (plus six dollars for meals) a month.[5] They had no voice in the kind of work they would do. While a day's labor in Japan consisted of long hours in the field, the work conditions were not much different in Hawaii. The field workers labored from sunrise to sunset. Truly wretched working conditions existed at this time for the masses of common folk everywhere.

When the Japan-Hawaii Travel Treaty concluded the following year, contracted emigration hit full stride. Remittance payments from Hawaii were high and so there was no end to the number of applicants. Until the Emigrant Protection Ordinance was passed in 1894, a total of 29,000 contract emigrants voyaged to Hawaii during the intervening nine years.[6]

Besides Hawaii, a host of applicants came forward for voyages to South America and other destinations. A veritable emigration boom was underway in Japan.

Torakichi Nambu, who emigrated from Kumamoto to Hawaii in 1907, said this about the new opportunity:

Being a peasant from rural Kumamoto, I was dirt poor. In the end, I just wanted to get out—to try and make it to a foreign country.[7]

Around that time, the laborers sang the well-known song "Hore Hore" in the sugarcane fields symbolizing the predicament those laborers were in. Nambu recalled the lyrics:

'Should I go to America? Should I return to Japan?' That's the problem with being in Hawaii.

Yet, Nambu reflected fondly upon how good it was to be able to eat white rice when he came to Hawaii.[8]

Early Immigration to America

Many of the early visitors to the American mainland were children of the samurai elite. They had come with the intention of gaining an education. As "schoolboys" they devoted themselves to study while living with Caucasian families and doing household chores. A considerable number went from being "schoolboys" to university graduates who would go on to make noteworthy contributions upon their return to Japan.

The Sons of Samurai Studying at Rutgers College in 1876. Courtesy of Nobuko Iinuma.

Chapter 1

Niijima, Jō. Source: © 2004 National Diet Library, Japan.

Nitobe, Inazō. Source: © 2004 National Diet Library, Japan.

Noguchi, Hideyo. Source: © 2004 National Diet Library, Japan.

Jō Niijima (1843-1890), for instance, had an enormous influence upon Japanese education after returning from his studies in the United States. Niijima was born in the Kanda ward of Edo (renamed Tokyo in 1868), in a residence owned by his feudal domain. When he was 19, he had an opportunity to sail the open sea, and for the first time he experienced life outside his small feudal domain. Seeing the world deeply impressed the young man, and he decided to try to wait for an opportunity to "sneak" out of the country. Niijima finally came to America in 1865, when he was 22, shortly after the Civil War ended. Eventually, he was baptized a Christian, graduated from Amherst College, and studied at the Andover Theological Seminary. Thereafter, he made a careful study of European educational methods.

After 10 years in the United States, Niijima returned to Japan and established the Doshisha English School in his house in Kyoto with eight students. In 1912, two years after his death, it was chartered as Doshisha University.

Niijima adopted the name "Joseph Hardy Neesima" while he was in the United States. Most of the libraries in the United States list him under Niijima.[9]

Inazō Nitobe (1862-1933) was another erstwhile samurai whose stay in America influenced him greatly. After graduating from Japan's Sapporo Agricultural College in 1884, Nitobe enrolled in a specialized curriculum at Tokyo University, but took a leave and went to study at the Johns Hopkins University in Baltimore, where he spent three years.

He then continued his university studies in Germany. He returned to Sapporo Agricultural College and taught on the faculty. He went on to hold a variety of positions including bureau chief to the Governor-General of Formosa and professorial posts at Kyoto and Tokyo University, among others. His well-known work, *Bushido — The Spirit of the Samurai*, was published in 1900. Nitobe wrote the book in English, in a deft and beautifully crafted style. In 1911, under the first Japanese-American professorship exchange, he lectured throughout the United States. Nitobe married an American woman, Mary Elkington.

Hideyo Noguchi (1876-1928) was another American university-educated immigrant whose world-class achievements in the medical field still stand today. He voyaged to America at the age of 24 and served as a fellow at both the University of Pennsylvania and the Carnegie Research Institute, then continued on to the Rockefeller Institute for medical research.

Noguchi also studied abroad in Europe and South America. While in Africa researching yellow fever, he unfortunately succumbed to the disease. His remains are buried in New York where he and his American wife, Mary Rouretta Dardis, once resided. The Noguchi Medical Research Institute in Philadelphia was established in his honor to promote Japan-America medical exchange.

Taichirō Morinaga, founder of the famous Morinaga Confectionery, returned to Japan after being trained in America and went on to become a great business success. A native of Hizen, Morinaga worked at a pottery store in Yokohama. In 1887, at age 24, he came to the United States in hopes of finding an American market for Kutani pottery, a traditional style of ornate porcelain ceramic-ware. Despite his pioneering efforts in this area of commerce, Morinaga's pottery venture failed. Then, hoping to reverse his ill fortune through a single stroke, Morinaga had his epiphany one fateful day when he suddenly realized how delicious was the taste of Western-style candy. Immediately, he decided to change careers and establish himself in the confectionery business. After receiving the requisite training, he opened a confectionery in Tokyo, which would eventually become the Morinaga Confectionery, one of Japan's leading companies to this day.

In the 1890s, the goal of U.S.-bound travelers changed from study abroad to work in the fishing and agricultural sectors. In the latter half of the decade, the number of such laborers increased dramatically. Though virtually all Japanese students had set their sights on the East Coast, most of the laborer immigrants found employment on the West Coast. According to Wattenberg's Statistical History of the United States (1976), 2,270 Japanese immigrated to the United States mainland from 1881 to 1890; 27,892 from 1891 to 1900; and 108,163 from 1901 to 1907. The peak of contract emigration to Hawaii and the increase of emigration to the United States mainland overlap, clearly indicating how strong the "work-abroad boom" had become in Japan.

In 1919, Henry Sugimoto, a painter whose portraits of life in wartime internment camps achieved widespread acclaim, traveled from Wakayama to California, spoke of the longing to go to America, which gripped the masses:

> Before leaving Japan, I had heard that this place called America had streets paved with gold! What's more, I heard about the lotteries, that if you had a lottery ticket and won, you'd become fabulously wealthy.[10]

Americans grew increasingly concerned about the dramatic increase in the number of Japanese workers. Their wariness turned into full-fledged anti-Japanese sentiment, and on the West Coast, an exclusionist movement became particularly virulent. In order to understand why Japanese were subjected to such treatment, we must look back on the history of California. Early American history centered on the East Coast, with the West remaining largely undeveloped until the 19th century. Things changed dramatically with the discovery of gold outside of San Francisco in 1848. The following year, people from around the world rushed to San Francisco, lured by the promise of instant wealth. The Gold Rush was on. Those who traveled cross-country in covered wagons were, for the most part, rough-and-tumble white men who risked their lives in the "Wild West" to strike it rich. They stood in stark contrast to the East Coast elite.

In 1850, in the midst of the Gold Rush, California was ceded to the United States by Mexico, whereupon speculators thronged en masse. California's political situation was not merely unstable; it was positively lawless. Small wonder, then, that in the eyes of these rugged forty-niners, the immigrants were not exactly welcomed. At the time, African-Americans were still regarded as slaves. Migrants from Asia and South America were also viewed as 'people of color' and were visible targets. Many Chinese were brought over to America to work in the coalmines, and were the largest Asian migrant group at that time. Of the roughly 67,000 immigrants to California in 1852, upwards of 20,000 were Chinese.[11]

Construction of the Transcontinental Railroad began in 1863. However, since the white workers took a generally dim view of railroad construction, a dangerous job that paid poor wages, Chinese were contracted instead. Then, with the 1870s, the winds of economic depression swept across the land. In California, toward the end of the Gold Rush, the white people who had made less of a fortune than they had hoped for grew increasingly anxious. After construction on the railroads ended, many Chinese settled in San Francisco and built a China Town. Anti-Chinese sentiment among unemployed whites reached a boiling point and violent attacks against Chinese increased in frequency. This led the U.S. government to prohibit Chinese immigration. Later, when the anti-Chinese backlash showed signs of abating, the Japanese became the low-wage work force that filled the vacuum.

Issei Railroad Workers. Circa 1915. Photographer: Kinsey. Courtesy of University Archives Division, Manuscripts Special Collections. (Negative #11549) University of Washington Libraries.

Issei: The First Settlers in the United States

If we consider the fact that Hideyo Noguchi sailed to America in 1900 and Inazō Nitobe embarked on his American lecture tour in 1911, we can understand that those who faced anti-Japanese sentiment were not of the educated elite, but rather belonged to the working class—specifically, those who eked out a living as migrant workers on the West Coast. Compared to the relatively privileged foreign students who became proficient in English and easily assimilated into American society, most migrant workers did not speak English and tried to hold on to their Japanese customs and way of life. As a rule, first-generation immigrants, regardless of country of origin, retain their mother tongue as well as the customs of their native land.

However, compared to the cultural roots of European immigrants, Japanese customs were markedly different and undoubtedly appeared strange to the white majority.

First-generation Japanese immigrants are called *Issei*. Many were migrant workers who traveled from farm to farm during the busy season. Because they were always on the move, carrying their worldly possessions rolled into blankets, they were called *buranke katsugi*, or "blanket bearers." Sam Wada, who came to the United States from Kagoshima in 1917, reflects upon his migrant experience:

> In the spring, when the strawberries were finished, we went into town and stayed in the cheap hotels. In July and August, we went to Fresno to pick grapes. When the grapes were done, we'd move on to Sacramento and Stockton to work on peaches, pears, and other fruits.(12)

Camps to house the migrant workers were set up on the farms and orchards, and one can easily imagine how large the encampments must have been. The living quarters looked much like army barracks, with crudely constructed buildings containing row upon row of beds, partitioned by boards. Spare as such accommodations surely were, it was better than sleeping out in the fields on an unfurled blanket, or in a stable next to the horses—which many indeed had to resort to.

Wada had this to say about life as a "blanket bearer":

> All of us were seasonal workers, so we were used to bundling our things up and moving from place to place. Whether it was Stockton, Fresno, or wherever it happened to be, we didn't worry about having a place to stay. Still, these weren't always places fit for people, if you know what I mean. Take Fresno, where we'd often have to sleep in barns or stables—with or without the horses. And we'd even have to sleep under the stars.(13)

Blanket Stiffs (Blanket Bearers). Courtesy of The Bancroft Library. University of California, Berkeley.

Money was generally in short supply, so when work was available—even on Sundays—people would work from dawn to dusk. However, in the context of a God-fearing white society imbued with Christian values and centered on attending Sunday church services, working on the Sabbath Day provoked much ill will toward the Japanese. Many of the *Issei* immigrants understood the basis for this hostility. Mitsuyori Kawashima, who came to the United States in 1915 from Mie prefecture and achieved considerable success in cultivating Japanese-type rice in California, had this to say:

> Why were we Japanese so reviled? For one thing, we were really hard workers. Not so with the white people. Sunday was their day off, and they'd basically just loaf around all day on Saturday. But we'd be out in the fields—men and women. The whites—they thought that making their wives work was cruel, inhumane. But all the farmers' wives in Japan work in the field side-by-side with their husbands. The white people couldn't quite grasp this. They had a pretty biased view of us as cruel and unfeeling.[14]

In the first place, Japanese immigrants came to America in order to work. Hardly any had the intention of settling down. Their common dream was to succeed and return home in triumph. Given the exchange rate and cost of living at the time, a migrant worker who could return home

with $1,000 or better yet, several thousand, could afford to build a substantial home and purchase enough land to live quite comfortably.[15] Sugimoto, had this to say about the *Issei*'s dream:

> Everyone figured that you'd get rich if you went to America. Then again, this is the way people thought the world over. In Japan back then, you'd receive next to nothing for working all day like a dog. And if you had a family to support, how could you make ends meet? So, it was simple—Go to America, strike it rich, and return home to live the easy life. This is how people thought.[16]

In fact, this thinking reflected the policy of the Japanese government. For example, passports of the time contained wording to the effect that those who had earned a certain amount of money were urged to send it back to Japan.[17] This was because the government hoped to get maximum benefit from the foreign currency earned by the migrant workers abroad. The *Issei* workers themselves were diligently setting aside their earnings, and they were most eager to send everything they saved back to Japan. This was despite the subsistence wages they were paid for work in the fields or the railroads. In this sense, while racism was no doubt at the root of anti-Japanese sentiment, another reason could have been that the Japanese laborers were sending all of their savings back home instead of investing in the local economy.

Japanese Immigration Regulations

The outbreak of the Russo-Japanese War in 1904 has been seen as yet another source of the expanding anti-Japanese movement. The Asiatic Exclusion League, formed in San Francisco in 1905, was the focus of this movement in California. On New Year's Day of 1905, Japanese forces took Lushen by storm. And just two weeks after the Asiatic Exclusion League was formed, Japanese naval forces defeated Russia's Baltic

Chapter 1

Fleet. Hence, Japan's victory in the war with Russia would seem to parallel increasing anti-Japanese sentiment.

Despite the fact that a peace treaty was signed through the offices of President Theodore Roosevelt and the war had ended, Russia refused to recognize its defeat and Japan failed to receive a single penny in war reparations. At the time, Russia had enjoyed a ten-fold superiority over Japan in terms of economic might. Yet this small Asian nation, which had relentlessly pursued its stated mission of *fukoku kyōhei*—becoming a wealthy nation with a strong military—had emerged as a serious threat to the Western powers. The peace treaty between Russia and Japan was duly signed in Portsmouth, New Hampshire. Japan's chief delegate, Jutarō Komura, contributed $10,000 to the city of Portsmouth during his stay there.[18] Komura was the first student sent by the Japanese Ministry of Education to study abroad. He had studied law at Harvard from 1875 until his graduation in 1878.[19]

Meanwhile, in March 1907 the anti-Japanese movement began to rear its ugly head, with the segregation of Japanese pupils and the designation of only certain schools they were allowed to attend. President Roosevelt signed a presidential order prohibiting the backdoor immigration of Japanese from Hawaii, Mexico, or Canada. Thereafter, laws regulating Japanese immigration would be enacted one after another.

Jutarō Komura. Circa pre-1911. Courtesy of The Ministry of Foreign Affairs of Japan.

The Japanese government was thrown into confusion by this presidential directive. Fearing that the anti-Japanese problem within the United States might blossom into an imbroglio on the world stage, Japan concluded the U.S.-Japan Gentlemen's Agreement the following year. This was an agreement by the Japanese government to limit its issuance of passports to Japanese nationals bound for the United States, except for students and businessmen. Over and above the ban on immigration from Hawaii, new immigrants from Japan were also restricted. Second-generation Japanese-Americans (*Nisei*), born and raised in the United States, saw the door slam shut on their hopes of expanding the Japanese-American community. The vast majority of those coming to America after 1908 were family members brought over by immigrants. There were a number who had to resort to smuggling themselves in illegally. Sam Wada, thinking to go abroad and making his mark in the world, took the roundabout route of obtaining an Argentine visa since he could not get one for the United States. From there, he managed to enter the United States illegally, via Mexico. He recalled the experience as follows:

> I found myself in a remote area near the border, far from any border patrol or immigration police. I could see the faint outline of mountains across what I took to be the border with the U.S., nothing but desert all around me.[20]

After three days of trekking across the wilderness, Wada finally crossed the border—and who should be there to greet him but a fellow Japanese:

> It was really weird—a Japanese coming to meet another Japanese person who'd just sneaked into the country from Mexico. In other words, arrangements must've been made by Japanese on both sides of the border for this to have been possible.[21]

Wada's experience suggests the magnitude of the illegal immigration at that time.

Tragic Tale of the Picture Brides

Single men suffered the most because of the U.S.-Japan Gentleman's Agreement. At the time, the ratio of men to women was a hundred to one. However, some have suggested that it was actually as high as five hundred to one. Most of these men were in dire need of marriage partners. Fortunately, there was a loophole in the Agreement. Passports could be issued as long as one's family resided in the United States. On that basis, men would temporarily return to Japan in search of a bride and, once married on Japanese soil, would return to the United States with their new bride. Thus, as a member of her new husband's family, the bride would be eligible to obtain a passport.

Few, however, had the money to return to Japan for an extended stay. Only a handful could afford this luxury, especially in view of the cost of two return trip tickets to the United States. Thus, the marriage-minded men resorted to writing letters to their families back home with their photos attached, relying upon them to find suitable brides. This was essentially a variant of the traditional *miai*, or arranged marriage, in which the parents of the potential bride and groom would negotiate until an agreement was reached. In those days, it was not unusual for the bride and the groom to first lay eyes upon each other on their wedding day. With a mere photo in hand and filled with anticipation, a steady stream of young Japanese women began showing up at West Coast destinations. These were the "picture brides."

As a potential bride would not likely consent to marry someone whose photo revealed a man dressed in overalls and posing in front of a barnyard, most men borrowed proper attire, gussied themselves up, and had photos taken in a more impressive setting, such as in front of a mansion. There were those who entirely falsified their background and situation. Thus, the handsome young man posing in high style beside a luxury automobile would turn out to be twice as old as the fellow in the photo, bearing no resemblance to him whatsoever. Such episodes inevitably surfaced in the accounts of the picture brides.

When one thinks of the overseas migrants' success stories, which were circulating in Japan at the time, one can easily imagine how young brides would cling to their dreams as they endured the long and difficult journey to American shores. Though it appears that a considerable number of these women were quite well educated and exceptionally bright, once they stepped foot on American soil their illusions would be shattered. Newly inducted into the local labor force, most could do little but trail obediently behind their husbands. Shinobu Matsuura, who came to the United States in 1918 as a Buddhist missionary's wife, spoke of her experiences with the picture brides this way:

Arrival of Picture Brides. Circa 1910. Angel Island, California. Courtesy of California State Parks.

Some girls made a scene and wanted to leave their husbands right away, to return home as soon as possible. As picture brides, the gap between their dreams and reality were just too much to bear. If they'd have come with the understanding that they'd be working alongside their husbands, then things might've been different. But they all shared the belief that, America being such a wealthy nation, they'd be free to do as they pleased. The disillusionment came as a bitter blow, I can tell you. Some of them had actually received higher education—very unusual for Japanese women back then. Yes, their lives in America were pretty miserable from the outset.[22]

Chapter 1

The sad tale of the picture brides was not restricted to the narrow sphere of husbands and wives. It also cast a dark shadow over the entire Japanese-American community. Shichinosuke Asano, who arrived from Iwate prefecture in 1918 and became a writer for the San Francisco *Nichibei Shinbun* (Japanese-American newspaper), saw it this way:

> Look, there were a lot of men, but very few women. So, there were many 'love triangles'—housewives taking up with unmarried men. Many young wives who ventured to the United States had a new way of thinking, but the reality was far different from ideas of life in America. Some of them ended up in divorce, but once divorced, what was a woman to do? Well, some resorted to prostitution. There were four or five houses of ill-repute in San Francisco where these desperate women would take refuge, as it were. There were men who would act as their intermediaries, so to speak. Male-female relations were a complete mess, I can tell you.(23)

In February 1920, the Japanese government banned the issuance of passports to picture brides. It is very difficult to obtain exact figures regarding their number. In the first place, calculations based on the number of passports issued to Japanese women at that time, are not a reliable indication whether a woman was a picture bride or whether she was sent for by relatives. Though their precise number remains unknown, it has been estimated as being anywhere from 20,000 to 70,000.

Incidentally, the year 1920 witnessed a landmark in American history—the passage of the 19th Amendment to the Constitution, which finally granted women's suffrage.

Anti-Immigration Act and Alien Land Act

Prior to its prohibition by the Japanese government, arguments for the abolition of picture brides had already arisen within the Japanese-American community. It was within this context that the State of California enacted the revised Alien Land Act in 1920. The law, which prohibited foreigners who lacked citizenship from

Women of Protest. Photograph of 14 suffragists in overcoats on a picket line, holding suffrage banners in front of the White House. One banner reads, "Mr. President How Long Must Women Wait For Liberty". The White House is visible in the background. Circa 1917. Washington, D.C. Photographer: Harris & Ewing. Source: Records of the National Woman's Party, Manuscript Division. Library of Congress.

owning land, was essentially aimed at immigrants of Asian descent. Following the Civil War, during which President Abraham Lincoln issued his Emancipation Proclamation, the revised Naturalization Law of 1870 recognized citizenship only for whites and freed slaves—immigrants of Asian descent were not included. At the time, Japanese *Issei* could not become American citizens even though they resided in the United States.

California's Alien Land Act was first enacted in 1913. At that point, despite the fact that land ownership was prohibited for those who were not U.S. citizens, land leases of up to three years were recognized. The revised law of 1920, however, prohibited this lease provision as well.

Among those striving to accumulate capital, there emerged the first generation to enter the field of agricultural management, establishing themselves near San Francisco, in Central California, and on the outskirts of Los Angeles. In the 10-year period from 1910 to 1920, Japanese immigrants were in the process of becoming major owners of agricultural land, and they were instrumental in bolstering California agriculture. It was clear, though, that if the amended land law were to pass through Congress, the blow to the Japanese-American community would be severe. Accordingly, Japanese men refrained from "ordering" picture brides in an effort to mollify anti-Japanese sentiment. However, their efforts were in vain, and the amended law passed. This was not simply a legislative formality. The new

Immigrant Farmer of Japanese Ancestry. An early pioneer posing proudly with his family prior to delivering his harvest to the marketplace. Los Angeles, California. Courtesy of Toyo Miyatake Studio.

law would have serious repercussions in Washington, Oregon, and other western states.

Yet even during this time of adversity when Japanese immigrants could not own land, many came up with creative methods that ultimately enabled them to emerge at the forefront of agricultural management. For instance, many ended up using the names of their American-born children, who were U.S. citizens, to purchase land as their legal guardians.

There are also cases in which Japanese immigrants founded stock corporations, installing a Caucasian as a proxy president. Until the bubble burst in 1929, Americans reveled in the business boom and the abundant wealth. There was money galore, and so the banks, expecting a strong return, eagerly invested in these Japanese-American enterprises. Mitsuyori Kawashima remarks as follows:

> Back in 1927, there was a big real estate agency near Fresno. The owner says to me, 'Look, why don't you people take up rice cultivation? I'll put up the land. How about it?' Well, the anti-Japanese land laws were on the books. But there are two sides to a coin, you know. Some folks were for us, some were against us. So I took the man up on his offer.[24]

Nearby towns enjoyed a degree of prosperity due to the Japanese labor force on large-scale farms and plantations, so there was no sign of the prevailing anti-Japanese sentiment. With the unparalleled productivity of the Japanese farms, it reached the point where the wealthy owners could build palatial homes in exclusive residential neighborhoods, and some could even be seen riding around town in big Cadillacs, flaunting their success.

The Japanese *Issei* used their ingenuity to work around the Alien Land Act. However, they were dealt another serious blow when President Calvin Coolidge signed the Immigration Act of May 26, 1924. This legislation limited the amount of newly arriving immigrants to the prescribed 2% limit for resident aliens originally established

Chapter 1

White Star Soda Works. Business owners pose in front of their shop in Little Tokyo. Shop co-owner, Yuzo Maeda, is grandfather to renowned Japanese-American photographer, Toyo Miyatake. Courtesy of Toyo Miyatake Studio.

in 1890—a mere 164,667 people, until June 30, 1927. From July 1, 1927 (later postponed to July 1, 1929), the government used the ratio of people of national origin based on the total number of inhabitants in the continental United States in 1920. It limited the number to the same ratio as 150,000. This law set the permanent limitation on immigration for the first time. Furthermore, it introduced the provision that, as a rule, no alien that is ineligible to become a citizen shall be admitted to the United States as an immigrant. This was aimed primarily at Japanese aliens.[25] In essence, it would no longer be possible to send for families or wives, owing to the severe restriction. With picture brides outlawed and the Anti-Immigration Act enacted, the road to matrimony was effectively closed, and many *Issei* had no recourse but to remain lifelong bachelors.

Emergence of "Japan Towns"

Many *Issei* continued to work tirelessly, intent on pinching pennies, sending money back to Japan, and becoming local heroes. However, those who would eventually return home basking in glory were indeed rare. A three-year stay turned into five years. In the meantime, what with marriage and family, people had their hands full just eking out a living day to day. Before long,

flophouses, eateries, and general stores run by fellow Japanese began to crop up near the farms. These formed the roots of the "Japan Towns" that would eventually emerge. In port cities such as Seattle and San Francisco, they would develop in the latter half of the 19th century. In the process, Japanese communal organizations were formed, and churches and Buddhist temples were established. In the face of the powerful exclusionary sentiment, fellow Japanese came to one another's aid. Living as part of a Japanese community was indeed a means of survival.

Those in need could expect support from *Kenjinkai*—associations of Japanese who hailed from the same prefecture. People from Fukushima, Wakayama, Hiroshima, and Yamaguchi prefectures were especially numerous during the first period of immigration, and the corresponding *Kenjinkai* were established in rapid succession in the early 1900s. Actually, a forerunner of the Wakayama prefectural association got its start in Oakland in 1897.[26] Hiroshima, too, sent many migrants, and it bears noting that its prefectural association in Seattle changed its name slightly to make it more accommodating to Japanese natives of other prefectures. Among other things, the *Kenjinkai* saw to the care of those who were ill and infirm.

According to Yoshito Fujii, who arrived in Seattle from Hiroshima in 1915, there were various social groups aside from these prefectural associations, which centered upon recreational activities, cultural pursuits—traditional poetry, for instance—and other pastimes.[27] These groups served as warm and welcoming venues for socialization—be it a picnic or a New Year's party.

Buddhist temples and church organizations supported the Japanese immigrants by furnishing lodging and meals free or at minimal expense, thereby playing the role of community center. Kawashima, who made his mark in rice cultivation, and Sugimoto, the noted painter, both shared the experience of being taken in and cared for by Buddhist temples or church groups during their hard-pressed student days. The aforementioned Matsuura, a wife of a Buddhist missionary, spoke of having started the Children's Home, a care center for children of working parents where youngsters would spend the night and commute to school in the morning.[28]

Toward the end of the 1910s, Japanese-Americans began to emerge in administrative posts within the Salvation Army. Masahide Imai, for instance, graduated from the Salvation Army College for Officer training and took a position in Fresno. Imai remarked as follows:

> There were many Japanese immigrants who led sad, lonely lives and died alone. During my stint in Fresno, I presided over funerals for 500 such people. The number of the infirm who came to the Salvation Army shelter must have numbered upwards of 1,500. And those with no family and not a penny to their name—there were never less than 15 such people in my shelter at any given time.[29]

The Salvation Army also took on a role traditionally played by Buddhist temples—providing refuge for aggrieved picture brides and other women in need. Imai continued:

> For the most part, the women who came seeking sanctuary were generally those whose husbands had left, or who'd run away from them for various reasons and had no place to go and no one to turn to. These women came to our women's division. There were always around 70 children there as well.[30]

Perhaps the most widely known Salvation Army effort was the "Eradication of Chinese Gambling" campaign that developed in Stockton, California. As the name implies, there was a problem with the many gambling houses that were run by the Chinese. Given the paucity of other amusements available to Japanese immigrants at the time, many of them—for the most part, single men—fell prey to the seductive allure of gambling. Asano, who worked for the *Japan-America Newspaper*, had this to say:

The Salvation Army. Founded in 1865 by one-time Methodist minister William Booth, The Salvation Army is a non-military evangelical Christian organization. The Salvation Army's presence in Southern California dates back to May 8, 1887, when an open-air meeting was held on the corner of Temple and Broadway in downtown Los Angeles. In 1892, The Salvation Army moved to First Street where it occupied almost the entire block with a men's transient hotel as well as a men's industrial complex—the forerunner of today's Adult Rehabilitation Centers. In 1899, The Salvation Army opened a rescue home for "fallen women" known as Booth Memorial Center. Los Angeles, California. Source: The Salvation Army website.

From July through September, thousands of migrant workers from all over, carrying their blankets, flocked into Fresno. They came to pick grapes, peaches, and apricots—all in season—in the nearby farms and orchards. Well, gambling dens targeting these laborers sprang up all over the place. The State of California had outlawed gambling, but it was widely tolerated. There were camps set up on the farms, I recall. The men would work from the crack of dawn 'til it was pitch dark and make a couple of bucks for their day's work. They'd eat right there in the camps, and on their one day off, they'd all go into town and hit the gambling houses. Of course, they'd also pay a visit to the local cat house while they were at it. Well, these fellows would get so caught up in the gambling frenzy that they'd totally lose control. Buck naked and stripped clean, they'd return to the camps, to their meager "blanket bearing" existence.[31]

Chapter 1

It was the Great San Francisco Earthquake of 1906 that spurred an exodus of Japanese who headed to Los Angeles. By then, Japanese-American farms were thriving in the area, and the city's "little Tokyo," which catered to the rising consumer class, began to take hold. Centering on the intersection of First and San Pedro, the area featured, as one might expect, Japanese restaurants and bakeries. However, it gradually came to include doctors' offices, public baths, and even movie houses featuring Japanese films.

This area of Los Angeles took on the name "Little Tokyo" at some point in the 1800s. Tōyō Miyatake (who came to the U.S. in 1909 and went on to photograph the Japanese Internment camps during the War), reflects upon the origin of the name "Little Tokyo":

> Actually, it wasn't the Japanese who came up with the name "Little Tokyo." It was the city of Los Angeles. As it turns out, there were 35 Japanese men working on the rails over on Weller Street, right in

that area. So the district was referred to as "Tokyo." When the trolley cars stopped there, the conductors would call out "Tokyo" to announce the stop. By and by, this became known as Little Tokyo.[32]

The worldwide financial panic of 1929 produced legions of the unemployed, but business owners in Little Tokyo pooled their resources and gradually put together financial collectives known as *tanomoshi*—communal funds that would be tapped, in turn, to help individuals in need make it through the depression as a community. At the same time, the United Church of Christ and the Japanese Methodist Church took hold, together with sects established by American missionaries who had proselytized in Japan and then returned home to continue their ministry. As for Buddhism in America, according to Miyatake—at first, it was a confederation of the major sects, and only later did it split off into separate sub-sects—for instance, the Higashi- and Nishi-Hongwanji branches of Salvationist Buddhism.[33]

Keizaburo Okamoto Family. Ca 1915. Courtesy of California State University, Sacramento, The Library.

Issei Farmers in California

According to the 1900 U.S. census, Caucasians owned or managed more than 70,000 of the 72,000 farms in California. Chinese immigrants managed approximately 1,000 of the remaining farms, Japanese immigrants managed fewer than 100, and individuals of other races managed the rest. Tenant farmers owned most of these farms and Japanese-Americans owned only four out of 100 farms. [1]

During the first two decades of the 20th century, the number of Japanese immigrant farms expanded dramatically. By 1910, farms increased by a factor of almost 20 to 1,816. This number rose to 5,152 farms by 1920. This was equivalent to the number of farms among foreign-born Caucasians and all other ethnic groups. Japanese farms were collectively worth $137,347,110 in land and buildings and held the highest value. [2]

Despite the implementation of the Alien Land Act, the number of farms run by Japanese-Americans continued to increase until the outbreak of World War II. On April 17, 1942, the *San Francisco Chronicle*

A Family Labors in a Strawberry Field at the Opening of the 1942 Season. The workers in the field were members of or related to the family who operated the farm. During harvest season, they worked approximately 10 to 12 hours every day except Saturday. Their home was beyond the strawberry rows. For many years, the Japanese produced approximately 95% of California's strawberry crops ranking California third in the nation in the production of this crop. Evacuation of the Japanese left 50 unoccupied strawberry farms in Santa Clara County. In California, Japanese harvested approximately 11,000 acres, with crop value around $100,000 annually. April 26, 1942. Mission San Jose, California. Courtesy of The Bancroft Library. University of California, Berkeley.

reported that California farms run by Japanese immigrants totaled some 11,000 acres. They also reported that approximately 95% of California's strawberry crop had been produced by Japanese farms, and that California ranked as the nation's third-largest strawberry crop producer. [3] Despite adversity, a number of these farms experienced remarkable growth before the War. Among the ranks of Japanese farm owners, two men rose to special prominence—Kenji Ushijima (aka George Shima,) who was known as "The Potato King," and Keisaburō Kōda, crowned "The Rice King."

The Potato King

Kenji Ushijima was born in Kurume City, Fukuoka, and came to the U.S. in 1889. Employed as a "school boy" in San Francisco, Ushijima recognized that potatoes were a staple of the American diet. With that knowledge in mind, he found a job on a potato farm in order to learn cultivation techniques. In 1891, he leased 30 acres in New Hope, California, on a crop share basis. He later purchased some land in the fertile "California Delta" and embarked on his own farming operation. He developed an irrigation system that resulted in years of successful crops. His potato farm was severely damaged in an 1894 flood, and it forced him to near bankruptcy. Seeking to recoup his losses, he resumed farming the next year on the outskirts of Stockton with a variety of potato he branded, "Shima Fancy."

Issei Farmers in California *continued*

George Shima's Ranch House near Stockton. Courtesy of The Bancroft Library. University of California, Berkeley.

Ushijima made his fortune during the Spanish American War in 1898, when potato prices soared nationwide. His business success and ultimate wealth established his reputation as the "Potato King." A "Shima Tract" farm can still be found on the outskirts of Stockton, although Shima no longer owns it. The San Joaquin Delta College's, "Shima Center," named in his honor, is located in Stockton and maintains a gallery exhibition to commemorate his achievements.

The Rice King

Keisaburō Kōda, the founder of present day Kōda Farms, was born in 1882. His father was a samurai of the Taira Clan. The family lived in the town of Ogawa in the Fukushima prefecture of Japan. The Clan supported the Shogun in the Boshin War (1868-69), in which the Shogun was defeated by Imperial loyalist forces that brought about the Meiji Restoration. Keisaburō's father later became a successful miller and broker of rice and rice flour.

The young Kōda yearned to travel to the United States, but instead attained a university degree and became a school principal at the age of 20. He persisted in his youthful ambition to travel and eventually came to the United States in 1908. The American government had already begun restricting immigration by that time, so Kōda came to San Francisco for the ostensible purpose of studying the educational system.

Keisaburō Kōda. Courtesy of the Koda family.

After embarking on a number of business ventures that included a dry cleaning business and a canning factory, Kōda bought a tract of land in the names of his two American-born sons, and started rice farming. Other Japanese immigrants in the United States had already achieved a certain success in rice farming but it was Kōda who became an early pioneer, beginning the mass production of Japanese-style rice. Among other innovative farming techniques, he was also a leading pioneer of sowing rice seed by air.

With a series of good harvests, the Kōda farms grew to several thousand acres, but with the outbreak of World War II, this period of abundance was to change dramatically for Kōda. When he was interned with others of Japanese ancestry during the war, Kōda was forced to leave his business in the hands of an absentee manager. By the time he was released, all of his property, including the land, the mill, equipment and airplanes, had been sold.

Issei Farmers in California *continued*

It was left to Kōda's sons, Edward and William, to restore the family's business. They started buying land, and continued Keisaburō's dream to produce rice that would resemble, as closely as possible, native Japanese rice. In 1963, they began marketing their rice under the brand name "Kokuho Rose." It had become enormously popular and remains so to this day. The Kōda farm is currently managed by the third generation of the Kōda family. Although Ushijima and Kōda cultivated soil in central California, Japanese-Americans took up many types of agriculture throughout California.

Keisaburo with Tatsuma Kujiraoke. Circa 1963. Courtesy of the Koda family.

Orange County Agricultural and Nikkei Heritage Museum

In March 2006, the Orange County Agricultural and Nikkei Heritage Museum at the Fullerton Arboretum, California State University, Fullerton, was opened to the public. The building interior is divided into four sections: *Nikkei* (Japanese-American) Pioneer, Educational, Transportation, and Geography. The museum highlights the history, development, and impact of agriculture, as well as the contributions of the Japanese-American community and the local pioneer families to Orange County.

The Nikkei Community Volunteer Committee, which was founded by the late Clarence Nishizu, has helped the university to organize fundraisers for the museum building project. Nishizu passed away January 25, 2006, before realizing the goal amount of $750,000, which was reached by the end of the year. The first exhibit, *Sowing Dreams, Cultivating Lives: Nikkei Farmers in Per-World War II Orange County* opened on February 10, 2007.

Orange County Agricultural and Nikkei Heritage Museum. The museum highlights the history, development, and impact of agriculture, as well as the contributions of the Japanese American community and the local pioneer families, to the growth of Orange County. Courtesy of the Fullerton Arboretum.

Chapter 2

from the 1930s~

Traumatic Consequences of the Pearl Harbor Attack

Santa Anita Assembly Center. Arcadia, California. Evacuees of Japanese ancestry from San Pedro, California, arrive by special train to Santa Anita Park assembly center. Evacuees are transferred later to War Relocation Authority centers for the duration. April 5, 1942. Arcadia, California. Photographer: Albers, Clem. Courtesy of The Bancroft Library. University of California, Berkeley.

CONTENTS

The American populace was reduced to a state of national hysteria following the attack on Pearl Harbor—a response brought on not by notions of justice, but rather by fear and panic. Japanese-Americans, regardless of their citizenship status, were collectively branded as "enemy aliens," despite having been the ones most traumatized by the outbreak of the war. Many *Nisei* resolved to dedicate their lives to the service of their country, in the belief that fighting on the frontlines would be the sole means for them to prove their loyalty and devotion as Americans.

Chapter 2

Japanese Community in Hawaii

Beginning with the "Manchurian Incident" of 1931, fascist rule came to the forefront in Japan in the 1930s. It was 1933 that witnessed the publication of the Japanese government-sponsored textbook, *Japanese Reader*, with its famous exhortation: "Forward, soldiers, ever forward!" Schools engaged in the vigorous indoctrination of patriotism and loyalty to the Emperor. Japanese citizens were referred to as "the Emperor's people," and in 1938, the National Mobilization Law, which authorized the government to mobilize resources and manpower for wartime use, was promulgated. When the military ran short of metal for the production of war materiel, even the bells of Buddhist temples were commandeered.

News dispatches issued by the Imperial Army were the only source of war-related information for *Issei* residing in the United States—the reason being was that since most did not speak English, they had to resort to shortwave radio broadcasts. Some *Issei* used what little money they had to buy Japanese war bonds, donate money, and produce care packages to support the Japanese Army. According to Shichinosuke Asano, a reporter who worked for the Japanese-American newspaper, *Nichibei Shinbun*, a group of *Issei* founded the *Hyōmusha-kai* (Soldiers' Association), to which members were to pay a dollar per month to aid bereaved families in Japan through the Red Cross. He recalled as follows:

> When Japan dispatched troops to Manchuria, men of all ages in our homeland were engaged in military combat. But our young people here in America could not take part. While others were giving their all for our country, we deeply regretted our inability to be involved. And so we created the *Hyōmusha-kai* in order to come to the assistance of bereaved families of Japanese soldiers.[1]

The association boasted approximately 10,000 members. As might be expected, this sort of activity on the part of the *Issei* was very worrisome to the American authorities. Above all, the situation with Japanese-Americans in Hawaii was a cause for concern.

As a territory of the United States, Hawaii had great strategic importance because of its many military facilities, including the naval base at Pearl Harbor. Owing to its geographical location, Hawaii would most likely be Japan's primary target were it to launch an attack upon the United States. When Hawaiian statehood had been proposed in 1937, some of the critical issues were the Japanese language schools and dual citizenship of *Nisei* (second-generation Japanese-Americans, the children of *Issei* parents).[2]

In fact, Japanese language schools had been established not only in Hawaii but in most of the "Japan towns" on the mainland as well. Teaching Japanese to the English-speaking *Nisei* children was crucial to improving communication in Japanese-American families. This system of schools for learning the mother tongue, which was well established within the European immigrant communities, had been the target of criticism. However, the Supreme Court had upheld the right to create such schools.[3]

Moreover, these schools had gained widespread public approval, insofar as the mother tongue was understood to serve the immigrants' children as nothing more than a second language.

Gakuen Hall. This is the only known example of a Japanese culture and language school designed and built by Japanese as a reaction to the California public school segregation laws of 1921. When the Japanese were forced into relocation camps during World War II, the local landowner held the building in trust until the Japanese could return. Today the building serves as a community center for the Japanese residents of Walnut Grove. Courtesy of National Park Service. U.S. Dept. of Interior.

However, Japanese language schools were not regarded in the same light, mainly due to the strong perception of cultural differences. While European cultures shared with the United States a common Judeo-Christian origin, Japanese culture was rooted in Buddhism and *Shinto*. The Japanese worshiped the Emperor as a god, and Japanese schools were typically run by the Buddhist temples. Some schools even promoted a code of loyalty to the Emperor and a strong patriotic spirit as part of an "ethics" curriculum. The situation with the Japanese language schools was the subject of frequent deliberation in the Territorial Congress, and as a result, it was decided that Japanese-Americans would eliminate the suspect ethics classes. It was further decided that the schools would employ only *Nisei* who held American citizenship as teachers, rather than *Issei*. The aim was to ensure a strict language-only curriculum.

More so than the Japanese language schools, the matter of *Nisei* dual citizenship was a pressing concern in Hawaii. Under Japanese law, *Nisei* born before 1924 were automatically granted Japanese citizenship regardless of their birthplace[4] — which differentiated them from the children of European immigrants who held only American citizenship. Many *Issei*, however, being unfamiliar with American law failed to register their children's birth in the United States. Rather, these births would be recorded at a later date, when Japanese consular officials made their census inspection of the various plantations, conducted once every five years. Consequently, many *Nisei* had obtained dual nationality without their even knowing it.

After April 1, 1924, Japanese citizenship was granted only to those who were registered with the consulates. The government was concerned about the loyalty of *Nisei*, given that many who held dual citizenship had approached draft age. There was widespread concern about the possibility that *Nisei* might engage in espionage, were war to break out between Japan and the United States. Such suspicions only increased with the worsening relationship between the two nations.

In 1938, the Hawaiian-Japanese Civic Association started a campaign for holders of dual nationality to renounce their Japanese citizenship. This reflected the desire among Hawaiian *Nisei* who had been born, raised, and educated in the United States to tangibly demonstrate their loyalty. In 1940, the Association leaders drafted a formal letter to Secretary of State, Cordell Hull. They explained the complexities involved in renouncing Japanese citizenship, expressing their indignation over the fact that perfectly loyal Americans of Japanese ancestry had become the object of so much 'undeserved and unwarranted' suspicion.[5] By the spring of 1941, the Japanese Consulates were processing around 400 applications per month to renounce Japanese citizenship, a number that was steadily increasing.[6]

Also, there was the matter of the *"Kibei" Nisei* — American citizens by birth, but who were sent to Japan to be educated. More than 600 *"Kibei" Nisei* were said to live in Hawaii alone, a fact that served to deepen suspicions among certain government officials regarding Japanese-American loyalties. It was common practice for *Issei* immigrants to send their children to relatives in Japan in order to receive a Japanese education. This only made sense, since most of the *Issei* had planned eventually to return to Japan. Others wished to protect their children from racial discrimination in the United States. There were also those couples with many children who had come to work on the plantations and who, for financial reasons, had to send some or all of the children back home. For a variety of reasons most of the *"Kibei" Nisei* returned to the United States before being drafted into the Japanese army. Some had a hard time adjusting to their lives in Japan, suffering reverse discrimination and being referred to as "Americans." These *"Kibei" Nisei* said they had "escaped" Japan in order to live with their parents in the United States.

Chapter 2

FBI's Top Priority: "Japanese Problem"

In August 1939, the government opened the FBI office in Hawaii, giving top priority to the "Japanese problem." The agent-in-charge of the FBI Hawaii office, Director Robert Shivers, teamed up with Military Intelligence to investigate the issue of Japanese-American loyalty. Since it would take too long to survey each Japanese-American, the FBI and Military Intelligence officials set up a racially diverse committee to implement a citizenship ethics campaign. For example, the Oahu Citizens Committee for Home Defense, consisting of Japanese-Americans, was brought into the fold. The aim here was to provide psychological support for Japanese-Americans in preparation for an outbreak of war, and to positively reinforce their spirit of loyalty to the United States. In their meetings, Military Intelligence promised the Japanese-Americans fair and non-discriminatory treatment so long as they were loyal to the country. This was the first official announcement by the U.S. military anticipating war with Japan. Subsequently, similar declarations were made in all kinds of meetings.[7]

Because of the prolonged investigation, Director Shivers came to place his trust in the Japanese-Americans, and Military Intelligence concluded as follows:

> If war with Japan did come, and it was fought in the western reaches of the Pacific, with no large-scale attacks against Hawaii, then the great majority of the *Issei* could expected to be "passively loyal" to the United States. Most of the *Nisei* would act as loyal American citizens.[8]

Curtis Munson's report on Japanese-American loyalty, compiled under the order of President Franklin Roosevelt, also concluded that:

> The *Issei*—first generation Japanese—many would take out American citizenship if allowed to do so. They are still legally Japanese. Yet they do break and send their boys off to the Army with pride and tears. The *Nisei*—second generation who have received their entire education in the United States, in spite of discrimination against them and a certain amount of insults accumulated through the years from irresponsible elements—show a pathetic eagerness to be Americans. The *Kibei* should be divided into two classes—those who received their education in Japan from childhood to about 17 years of age, and those who received their early formative education in the United States and returned to Japan for four or five years of Japanese education. The *Kibei* are considered the most dangerous element and closer to the *Issei* with special reference to those who received their early education in Japan. It must be noted, however, that many of those who visited Japan subsequent to their early American education come back with added loyalty to the United States.[9]

Despite the investigation having produced this sort of evidence pointing to the likely loyalty of Japanese-Americans, it failed to allay the misgivings harbored by the officials. By December 1941, the U.S. government persisted in its efforts to "solve" the Japanese loyalty problem by increasing the Army's counterespionage group within the Military Intelligence Section (G-2). Initially staffed by four regular agents, the office expanded to 30—with 12 officers and 18 special investigators—whose duties centered on the "Japanese Problem."[10]

The Burke-Wadsworth Act, which was passed by the Senate in August 1940, enabled African-Americans to enlist in the military. The key provision of this legislation was to establish a national selective service system for military training. It would also require the selective service system to enroll any person within the prescribed age limits "regardless of race or color." It was strongly opposed by some congressmen from the eastern and southern states and the War Department, since it would open the military to Japanese-American servicemen. Before this bill was passed there were countless incidents of Japanese-Americans being rejected for enlistment. Lieutenant General Charles Herron, military commandant in Hawaii since 1937, managed to counter these voices of opposition, claiming that:

> It seems people who know least about Hawaii and live farthest away are most disturbed over this matter. People who know the Islands are not worried about possible sabotage. I say this sincerely after my years of service here. I am sold on the patriotism and Americanization of the Hawaiian people as a whole.[11]

The Selective Training and Service Act of 1940 was passed by Congress and signed into law by President Roosevelt on September 16. This law required that men between the ages of 21 and 30 register with a local draft board (the age range was later changed to the ages of 18 to 45). The following month this peacetime conscription began for the first time in American history.

The Outbreak of War

Two days following the German invasion of Poland in September 1939, the United Kingdom and France declared war on Nazi Germany. Thus began the Second World War. In 1940, the Tripartite Pact was signed by Japan, Germany, and Italy. The United States re-introduced military conscription for the first time when the nation was not officially at war. While the majority of Americans were against entering the war, the military was making preparations in the Pacific by exercising jurisdiction over its territorial defense forces in Hawaii. In January 1941, the ABCD Embargo was put into effect—a

Pearl Harbor, Oahu, Hawaii. Fine-screen halftone reproduction of a photograph taken circa 1940, showing battleships moored alongside Ford Island (center and left), with cruisers and other ships also present. The Navy Yard is at the left and the Supply Base and Submarine Base are at the center-right and right. This view looks toward the northwest. Source: U.S. Naval Historical Center Photograph.

coalition of American, British, Chinese, and Dutch forces that implemented an economic blockade of Japan. With this measure, all-out war in the Pacific was simply a matter of time.

The decisive moment came on the morning of December 7, 1941, when Japanese forces attacked Pearl Harbor. The first wave of the aerial attack lasted some 30 minutes—from 7:55 a.m. to 8:25 a.m., when residents of nearby Honolulu—including the Japanese-American community—could easily see the billowing black smoke and hear the din of battle. Few, however, immediately realized that the Japanese were staging an attack. It was not until the second wave came, when Japanese Zeros emblazoned with the Rising Sun flag roared over the city, that the sickening realization came.

U.S. Senator Daniel Inouye (D-HI) recalled the shock:

> I felt that my life had come to an end at that point, because obviously the pilot in that plane looked like me.[12]

Chapter 2

A great many Japanese-Americans were outraged. Conrad Tsukayama, who would later serve in the 100th Infantry Battalion, wrote in his journal:

> My very first impulse that morning was to pick up a stone and hurl it against the low-flying Zeros or communicate my anger with some other gesture. My anger was based on betrayal, the deepest hurt that can be inflicted. The deep-rooted respect and admiration for the Japanese instilled in us from childhood was shattered. They were mercilessly killing their own emigrant citizens.[13]

The invasion news was as big a blow to Japanese-Americans on the mainland as it was to those in Hawaii. Even those who had donated to the Japanese military had not imagined that their contribution might support a war effort; rather, they had largely been motivated by a powerful bond of identity with their homeland. Nonetheless, these individuals, together with their relatives, were equally and summarily branded as "dangerous enemy aliens" because of the Pearl Harbor attack.

Kikuyo Utsumi, a resident of Little Tokyo, Los Angeles, was away at a nearby hot spring at the time of the Pearl Harbor attack:

> I came back as soon as I learned of the news on the car radio. "Japan Town" was closed. The power supply was cut off that night, and alarm sirens went on every day. The nighttime blackout continued for about a week. Then they proclaimed martial law, and we were prohibited from going out more than five miles from our homes.*

By 6:30 a.m., 736 Japanese-Americans were arrested in the United States.[14]

Support among the American public for entering the war was galvanized suddenly and dramatically in the wake of President Roosevelt's stirring speech, which famously labeled December 7, 1941 as "a date which will live in infamy."

War with Japan was formally declared, whereupon Germany and Italy declared war on the United States. Now that the nation was fully engaged in both theaters of conflict, the FBI initiated restrictions upon Japanese-, German-, and Italian-Americans as "dangerous individuals." The pejorative term "Jap" adorned the front page of American newspapers day after day, and articles alleging acts of espionage by Japanese-Americans appeared in rapid succession. Storefronts displayed "No Japs Allowed" signs. A series of attacks upon Japanese-Americans ensued. To avoid being the target of the anti-Japanese hysteria, other Asian immigrants resorted to displaying badges identifying themselves as "Chinese-Americans," and the like. Ironically, the widespread fear among mainland Americans that they would be attacked next helped make their anti-Japanese movement more extreme than it was in Hawaii, the actual target of the Pearl Harbor attack.

Internment of the Japanese-Americans

Many anti-Japanese regulations were enacted at this time. The California State Personnel Board barred from the civil service all American citizens whose ancestry was tied to one of the nations at war with the United States. This ruling, though, was enforced only against Japanese-

Pledge of Allegiance at Raphael Weill Public School, Geary and Buchanan Streets. Children in families of Japanese ancestry continued their education at facilities provided to them by the WRA. Photographer: Lange, Dorothea. Courtesy of Library of Congress' Prints and Photographs Division.

*Interviewed by the writer at Keiro Senior HealthCare Intermediate Care Facility, July 13, 2005.

Young Evacuees of Japanese Ancestry Arrive by Train. This was prior to being transferred by bus to Manzanar, a War Relocation Authority center. April 1, 1942. Lone Pine, California. Photographer: Albers, Clem Courtesy of the The Bancroft Library. University of California, Berkeley.

Japanese Fishermen. A thriving Japanese fishing village on Terminal Island, just before those of Japanese ancestry are evacuated to relocation camps. San Pedro, California. Courtesy of San Pedro Bay Historical Society.

Americans. A Portland American Legion Post urged the forced evacuation of Japanese-Americans, including citizens from all coastal areas. A West Coast congressional delegation petitioned President Roosevelt to evacuate Japanese-Americans from the states of California, Oregon, and Washington. The California Joint Immigration Committee made a similar request. Responding to the mounting pressure, President

Roosevelt signed Executive Order 9066 on February 19, 1942. With this stroke of the pen, the military was empowered to forcibly remove Japanese-Americans from certain restricted areas, leaving them no legal recourse whatsoever.

Four days later, on February 23, a Japanese submarine torpedoed an oil refinery in Santa Barbara harbor. On February 26, due to the close proximity to the naval base, the Navy responded by ordering the immediate evacuation of all residents of Japanese ancestry on Terminal Island. Residents were given only 48 hours to make preparations to leave the island.[15] Most had no recourse but to relinquish their worldly possessions for a fraction of its value. Those with nowhere to go sought refuge in the temples and churches in Little Tokyo. By September 1942, the Japanese submarine fleet would launch four attacks on mainland targets. These, as it turns out, would be the only attacks on the United States mainland during the war. [16]

In the meantime, on March 2, 1942, the military authorities officially designated Washington, Oregon, western California, and southern Arizona as "Military Area No. 1." On March 24, the first evacuation order was issued for 220 residents of Bainbridge Island, near Seattle.[17] The order applied to all alien and non-alien persons of Japanese ancestry—"non-alien" referring to holders of American citizenship. These 220 men, women, and children would be the first group sent to the hastily constructed internment camp at Manzanar.

FBI Arrests Japanese Civilians on Terminal Island, California. December 7, 1941. Publisher: Daily News. Courtesy of the Department of Special Collections/UCLA Library. Charles E. Young Research Library.

Chapter 2

Evacuees of Japanese Ancestry Entraining for Manzanar, California. The War Relocation Authority center is 250 miles away from where they are now. April 1, 1942. Los Angeles, California. Photographer: Albers, Clem. Courtesy of The Bancroft Library. University of California, Berkeley.

The Japanese-American Citizens League (JACL), a *Nisei* association, had made valiant efforts to avoid mass internment before the enactment of the law. However, once the Army issued the evacuation order, they appealed to the Japanese-American community to be good citizens and comply with the order; most did in fact comply. Not everyone, however, supported JACL's role, which was viewed as complicit. Indeed, some JACL leaders were subject to physical attack and abuse in the internment camps.

Baggage Search Outside Car. "The right of the people to be secure in their persons, houses, papers, and effects, against unreasonable searches and seizures, shall not be violated, and no warrants shall issue, but upon probable cause, supported by oath or affirmation, and particularly describing the place to be searched, and the persons or things to be seized."—Fourth Amendment, established 1791. Courtesy of Library of Congress.

Internees were given a week to prepare for their departure, and a great many ended up abandoning most of their property. Some, though, were given a helping hand. Utsumi, for instance, remarked that:

> We had just bought a car at that time, but my husband's Mexican employee sold the car for us and delivered the money to the Santa Anita racetrack, which served as our assembly center. Moreover, he returned all the furniture we entrusted to him when we returned from the camp.*

Sam Wada noted that a Christian group had prepared sandwiches and coffee for them on the morning of the evacuation.[18] The Quakers and the American Civil Liberties Union (ACLU) were among the few groups that opposed the internment.

On March 12, the Treasury Department ordered that property belonging to Japanese-Americans that had been purchased prior to the Alien Land Law should be managed by the Federal Reserve Bank of San Francisco, while farmlands and agricultural equipment should be managed by the Farm Security Administration. It was further stipulated that:

> ...no Japanese need sacrifice any personal property of value. If he cannot dispose of it at a fair price, he will have opportunity to store it prior to the time he is forced to evacuate by Exclusion Order. Persons who attempt to take advantage of Japanese evacuees by trying to obtain property at sacrificed prices are un-American, unfair, and are deserving only of the severest censure.[19]

Nonetheless, the Federal Reserve Bank would assume no responsibility for managing these properties and hence encouraged their sale. The Farm Security Administration, too, pressed Japanese-Americans to cede their farm properties to white tenants or companies to ensure regular harvests. As a result, most of them ended up losing all of their properties. The evacuation

*Interviewed by the writer at Keiro Senior HealthCare Intermediate Care Facility, July 13, 2005.

Evacuation of Farmers of Japanese Descent Resulted in Agricultural Labor Shortage on Pacific Coast Acreage. High school boys are recruited to offset the shortage in the garlic fields in Santa Clara County. Farmers and other evacuees will be given opportunities to follow their callings at the WRA centers where they will spend the duration. May 5, 1942. San Lorenzo, California. Photographer: Lange, Dorothea. Courtesy of The Bancroft Library. University of California, Berkeley.

Mexican Migrant Workers Travel by Train to Los Angeles, California. Facing an extreme shortage of farm labor workers due to the war, Congress enacts the Emergency Labor Program and sponsors The Bracero Program. In 1942, approving the temporary immigration of thousands of Mexican workers to replace the American men who are in the armed services. A bracero (from brazo, the Spanish word for arm), is a Mexican worker allowed entry into the United States for a limited time, usually to work on a farm. It serves as the temporary importation of workers from Mexico to aid the American agricultural economy. This is an important historical event that many Americans are unaware of today. During the 22 years of the Bracero Program, more than 4 million Mexican workers would leave their families behind and come to work in the fields of California. This migration has an enormous and lasting impact on the economy and demographics of California. Publisher: Daily News. circa 1942. Courtesy of Department of Special Collections/ UCLA Library. Charles E. Young Research Library.

itself was essentially completed by early summer, 1942, with the evacuees numbering over 120,000.

The Japanese-American evacuees were first dispatched to one of 16 federal provisional assembly centers that had been set up. Using facilities such as racetracks, these were to serve as temporary accommodations pending completion of the actual internment camps. In the Los Angeles area, temporary barracks were built at the Santa Anita racetrack. Utsumi's family of six, though, was housed in a stable instead of a barrack, and the stench of horse dung remained with them no matter how much they tried to get rid of it. In due course, the evacuees would be sent to their designated internment camp—ten of which were built.

Each camp consisted of barracks to house the internees, a communal dining room, a laundry room, and toilet facilities. The barracks were divided into four living spaces, with one family assigned to each. There was next to no privacy, with sheets being used as room partitions. One could hear virtually every sound—even from the adjacent barracks. What is more, the camps had been built in great haste, which necessitated the use of freshly cut green timber. As the wood dried, sand would be blown in through the resulting crevices, and it would pile up on the blankets and get into everything. The barracks

were sparsely furnished with army cots and little else. As a result, people tried to improve upon their surroundings by putting in flowerbeds and ponds near the barracks; and with the construction of a community auditorium, they brought some cheer and diversion into their lives by organizing various entertainments and activities.

Sites in the Western U.S. Associated with the Relocation of Japanese-Americans during World War II. Source: National Park Service.

Newcomers Move into Manzanar. A War Relocation Authority center for evacuees of Japanese ancestry. April 2, 1942. Manzanar, California. Photographer: Albers, Clem. Courtesy of The Bancroft Library. University of California, Berkeley.

Army Military Police on Duty. Military Police guard the boundaries of this War Relocation Authority center for evacuees of Japanese ancestry. April 2, 1942. Manzanar, California. Photographer: Albers, Clem. Courtesy of The Bancroft Library. University of California, Berkeley.

Santa Anita Assembly Center, Arcadia, California. Military Police on duty in the watchtower at Santa Anita Park assembly center for evacuees of Japanese ancestry. Evacuees transfer later to War Relocation Authority centers for the duration. April 6, 1942. Photographer: Albers, Clem. Courtesy of the National Archives and Records Administration.

Children Arrive at Turlock Assembly Center. Evacuees of Japanese ancestry transfer from assembly points to War Relocation Authority centers where they will spend the duration. May 2, 1942. Turlock, California. Photographer: Lange, Dorothea. Courtesy of The Bancroft Library. University of California, Berkeley.

War Relocation Authority

On March 18, 1942, the War Relocation Authority (WRA) was established under Executive Order 9102, to manage the Japanese internment. Its first director was Milton Eisenhower, younger brother of General Dwight Eisenhower (later to become the 34th President). Unhappy with the internment policies, Director Eisenhower would resign from his WRA post after only 90 days.

On April 7, WRA Director Eisenhower had sent out feelers to the governors of Nevada, Idaho, Oregon, Utah, Montana, Colorado, New Mexico, Wyoming, Washington, and Arizona, requesting that they consider taking in Japanese-Americans. However, with the exception of Colorado Governor Ralph Carr, none responded positively. Governor Carr spoke out on the subject of Japanese-Americans and their loyalty, and he appealed over the radio for the citizens of Colorado to accept Japanese-Americans. When Colorado's internment camp was up and running, the governor saw to it that some of the young *Nisei* women would be employed as house-keepers and have access to college courses.[20]

Young Boys Looking Forlornly Beyond the Barbed-Wire Surrounding Camp at Manzanar. Courtesy of Toyo Miyatake Studio.

Taps at Memorial Day Services at Manzanar, a War Relocation Authority Center for Evacuees of Japanese Ancestry. Boy Scouts and American Legion members participate in the services. May 30, 1942. Photographer: Stewart, Francis. Courtesy of The Bancroft Library. University of California, Berkeley.

Unfortunately, Governor Carr, who strongly opposed the violation of human rights and civil liberties based on racial discrimination, was defeated by a narrow margin in his bid for re-election, losing to Edwin Johnson, who opposed relaxing internment rules.[21] After the war, a Japanese-American community in Denver would express their gratitude by erecting a bronze statue of Governor Carr in Sakura Square, in Denver's downtown.

Milton Eisenhower explained to his successor, Dillon Myer, why he had resigned, "I can't sleep and do this job. I had to get out of it."[22] Director Myer, too, had his doubts regarding the rationale for the Japanese internment. In a statement issued on the first anniversary of WRA's creation, Director Myer remarked:

> Life in a relocation center is an unnatural and un-American sort of life. Keep in mind that the evacuees were charged with nothing except having Japanese ancestors; yet the very fact of their confinement in relocation centers fosters suspicion of their loyalties and adds to their discouragement. It has added weight to the contention of the enemy that we are fighting a race war, that this nation preaches democracy and practices racial discrimination... It is not the American way to have children growing up behind barbed wire and under the scrutiny of armed guards.[23]

Eisenhower, who became an assistant to Director Elmer Davis at the Office of War Information, also sent a letter to President Roosevelt on April 22:

> Persons in this group [*Nisei*] find themselves living in an atmosphere for which their public schools and democratic teachings have not prepared them. It is hard for them to escape a conviction that their plight is due more to racial discrimination, economic motivations, and wartime prejudices than to any real necessity from the military point of view for evacuation from the West Coast. Life in a relocation center cannot possibly be pleasant. The evacuees are surrounded by barbed wire fences under the eyes of armed military police. They have suffered heavily in property losses; they have lost their businesses and their means of support. Under such circumstances, it would be amazing if extreme bitterness did not develop... The Director of the Authority is striving to avoid, if possible, creation of a racial minority problem after the war, which might result in something akin to Indian reservations. It is for these reasons primarily, I think, that he advocates the maximum individual relocation as against the maintenance of all 10 relocation centers...[24]

Chapter 2

Japanese-Americans Registering with the WRA.
Residents of Japanese ancestry file forms containing personal data two days before evacuation, at Wartime Civil Control Administration stations. Evacuees will be housed in War Relocation Authority centers for the duration. February 4, 1942. San Francisco, California. Photographer: Lange, Dorothea. Courtesy of The Bancroft Library. University of California, Berkeley.

Dillon Myer, Director of the War Relocation Authority, looks over the Heart Mountain Sentinel with Several Evacuees from Heart Mountain. Eiko Narita (left) works as a stenographer with the Office of Price Administration. She lives with a Caucasian family who, she claims, treats her like one of the family. Joan spends two nights a week doing Red Cross work. John Kitasaka (right) is in the Japanese Editorial section of the Federal Communications Commission. September 1944. Washington, D.C. Photographer: Van Tassel, Gretchen. Courtesy of The Bancroft Library. University of California, Berkeley.

Like Milton Eisenhower, Director Myer encouraged Japanese-Americans to forge new lives outside the internment camps and the restriction zones, and he fostered their relocation by establishing a WRA office in Chicago. In July 1942, *Nisei* who had passed an FBI background check were allowed to leave the internment camps; *Issei* who met the same criteria would be eligible to move on as of that October.[25]

According to Kenji Muraoka, a dental technician:

> The governmental relocation center looked for someone who would employ Japanese-Americans and found a white dentist in Cincinnati who wanted to employ Japanese. So I left the camp.[26]

Muraoka had been in the Rohwer, Arkansas internment camp for seven months.

Thanks to Director Myer's advocacy, some 3,000 internees would move out of the camps by March 1943.[27] Nevertheless, individuals such as Eisenhower, Governor Carr, and Director Myer, who strongly advocated the rights and liberties of Japanese-Americans, were very much in the minority. In January 1944, 22 out of 23 congressmen from the West Coast petitioned President Roosevelt to remove Director Myer from the WRA post,[28] but the President would not honor this request and Director Myer stayed on the job until 1946, when the WRA was disbanded. Throughout his tenure, he continued to appeal for the closure of the relocation centers.

Life in the Camp

The internment camps were built in harsh, desolate environments. The Tule Lake (California) and Poston (Arizona) camps, for instance, were located on Indian reservation lands. Typically, the camps were surrounded by barbed wire with armed guards manning the watchtowers. The Poston camp, though, had no need of such facilities. Its desert location where summertime temperatures routinely were well in excess of 115°F. This was one of the largest camps, housing some 20,000 internees. It comprised three separate areas at three mile intervals.[29] Poston was the only internment camp not under WRA jurisdiction; rather, it was managed by the Office of Indian Affairs (until 1943).

Living Quarters of Evacuees of Japanese Ancestry. This is at the War Relocation Authority center, as seen from the top water tower facing southwest. July 1, 1942. Poston, Arizona. Photographer: Clark, Fred. Courtesy of The Bancroft Library. University of California, Berkeley.

It was hoped by the Native Americans that some of the resident internees who had agricultural expertise might be induced to remain in the area to improve farming efforts. The plan, however, did not materialize because it conflicted with the WRA strategy of encouraging internees to resettle outside of the designated military areas.[30] Be that as it may, in the fall of 1942, about 10,000 people were dispatched from all the camps to help out with the beet harvest on neighboring farms.[31]

English Classes in the Camps. At the Heart Mountain Relocation Center, night school classes in advanced English are very popular. For the first time, many *Issei* are now able to take advantage of the opportunity to read and write the language of their chosen country. January 11, 1943. Heart Mountain, Wyoming. Photographer: Parker Tom. Courtesy of The Bancroft Library. University of California, Berkeley.

The strictness of surveillance differed according to the camp's location and the kind of policies enforced by camp directors. From time to time, violent incidents occurred in the internment camps, and some with deadly consequences. Internees at Manzanar and Tule Lake, for example, were closely guarded since these camps were in California, while surveillance at Minidoka in Idaho was comparatively lax.

The *Issei* and *Nisei* tended to react differently to their internment experience. A number of *Nisei* had received a democratic education in American schools and had never been outside of the United States. They were understandably shocked and dismayed at being labeled as "4C"—enemy aliens—and deprived of their rights as American citizens. By way of contrast, many *Issei* who had struggled to make a living in the United States had a better, more stable life in the camps. Its guarantee of three meals a day and a roof over one's head came as welcome relief from uncertainty. Koryū Kariya, a picture bride who had come from Wakayama in 1920, remarked on her experience:

> Before entering the camp, we couldn't have had such comfortable lives for those three years. They gave us so much food we couldn't have ever possibly gotten outside the camp. I thought I'd be punished by God if I complained about such luxuries. Well, people interpret the same situation differently, I suppose. In the camp, we could learn whatever we wanted; like calligraphy or art, etc. The government covered the fees for the instructors.[32]

This was a time when the rationing system was in effect in the United States, and resources were generally in short supply.

There were indeed a number of adult education classes offered in the camps, where one could learn sewing, English, and so forth. Kariya continued:

Chapter 2

We were allowed to study at night and learn English for free. We couldn't really afford to do this outside the camp, even if we wanted to.[33]

In fact, many *Issei* began their study of English in the internment camps. Internees were also encouraged to work in the camps. They were paid $16 per month for unskilled labor and $19 for skilled work ($12 for apprentices), in addition to a clothing allowance for the family.[34] The government had initially planned to provide the same salary as that received by soldiers, but this plan was abandoned due to negative public sentiment. It was instead decided to provide the internee workers with free meals, clothing, housing, and medical treatment. Wada remarked:

> We were really relieved to be in the camp. We didn't have to worry about what to eat, wear, or where to live anymore. I think we would have had trouble if we hadn't been in camp. Before the camp, they wouldn't give us jobs and discriminated against us just because we were Japanese. We had small kids. We were in a bind.[35]

It is evident that there were some *Issei* grateful for the internment camps, owing to the considerable difficulties they had been subjected to before the war.

Chemists, Nurserymen and Plant Propagators. The men assemble to witness a new experiment in an attempt to resolve the amount of rubber produced in a small quantity from the guayule rubber plant. Seated is Frank Hirosawa, research rubber chemist. June 28, 1942. Manzanar, California. Photographer: Lange, Dorothea. Courtesy of The Bancroft Library. University of California, Berkeley.

Amache High School Graduation. January 23, 1945. Amache, Colorado. Courtesy of The Bancroft Library. University of California, Berkeley.

Issei not only had a hard time earning a living, but as the anti-Japanese movement expanded, especially on the West Coast, they also feared being subject to threats and attacks. Kiyasu Kunisada, a physician who was detained immediately following the outbreak of war, recollected:

> While I was in the detention center, I was worried about my family members who were not detained and who were left behind at home. Were they victims of assault? Were they having a hard time? Could they earn a living? I was relieved when I heard that they were moved to the internment camp.[36]

Internees were actually allowed to shop outside the camp, with permission. Utsumi remarked:

> I went out to buy fabric to make my daughter a costume for her school play, but usually I ordered through the Sears Catalogue.* Mrs. Matsuura, the missionary's wife, who had been in the Gila River camp in Arizona, mentioned that the camp provided funds for her to travel to Chicago to visit her son, who was attending a university on the East Coast.[37]

*Interviewed by the writer at Keiro Senior HealthCare Intermediate Care Facility, July 13, 2005.

Girls' Reserve Victory Dolls. Each doll is dressed by a Girl Reserves group in the Granada Center. The dolls represent various women's war-work activities. Jane Nagai and Boots Sotomura display their dolls at the Arts and Crafts Festival. March 6, 1943. Amache, Colorado. Photographer: Coffey, Pat. Courtesy of The Bancroft Library. University of California, Berkeley.

Judo Class. Lessons are held every afternoon and evening at this relocation center. November 11, 1942. McGehee, Arkansas. Photographer: Parker, Tom. Courtesy of The Bancroft Library. University of California, Berkeley.

Varsity Victory Volunteers

The preponderance of Japanese-Americans in the Hawaiian Territorial Guard—around half of the 3,000-man force—was a source of concern for American authorities at the outbreak of war. According to the 1940 U.S. Census, Japanese-Americans comprised 37.3% of the Hawaiian population, considerably in excess of the 24.5% white population. With the passage of the Burke-Wadsworth Act, which eliminated racial discrimi-

nation in the draft, 60% of the inductees were *Nisei* boys.[38] The first military conscription in Hawaii was conducted in November of 1940. Moreover, 350 of the 600 new recruits training at the Schofield Barracks at the outbreak of the war were Japanese-Americans.[39] The authorities were clearly confused as to how to deal with their Japanese-American recruits. On the third day following the war's outbreak, an order was issued to confiscate the recruits' rifles, which were gathered in a tent on base. However, two days later, the rifles were returned and the recruits' regular training was resumed.

Less than two hours after the Pearl Harbor attack, students in the Reserve Officers' Training Corps (ROTC) program were assembled in Honolulu military headquarters and enlisted as officers in the Hawaii Territorial Guard. Lieutenant General Walter Short, commander of the Hawaiian force, had been cautioned that many of the ROTC cadres were Japanese-Americans. But he went ahead with the plan to commission the group, saying that it would give them the opportunity to prove their loyalty to the country.[40] On the day after the attack, the military confiscated items to be banned during wartime—shortwave radios, cameras, fireworks, and so forth—and authorized the closing of Japanese newspapers and schools. At the same time, though, Lieutenant General Short made it clear that so long as alien Japanese kept the peace, obeyed all laws and regulations, and avoided active hostility, they would be given the considerations due to peaceful and law-abiding citizens.[41]

Yet the American public had been stirred up by inflammatory news reports. All sorts of rumors circulated about Japanese-American espionage, especially in Hawaii and on the West Coast. On January 5, 1942, the Selective Service designated Japanese-Americans as 4C (enemy alien) and banned any further enlistment. Some already-enlisted *Nisei* soldiers remained in the military even after this ruling, but a number of them were either discharged or made to perform menial duties.

Chapter 2

On January 21, the 317 Hawaii *Nisei* who had enlisted from the ROTC were discharged without explanation when a new commander, Lieutenant General Delos Emmons succeeded Lieutenant General Short.[42] Most of these soldiers were students at the University of Hawaii. On campus, where classes had been cancelled, they got together to discuss their situation. Now that they had been labeled as "enemy aliens" and discharged from the military, how could they possibly demonstrate their loyalty? The young men were frustrated and dispirited. But they found an ally in Hung-Wai Ching, then-director of the campus YMCA. Director Ching, a Chinese-American who would go on to become a leading Honolulu real estate broker and financier, actively defended the group with Director Shivers. With their encouragement, the discharged Japanese-American students accepted the idea of petitioning to offer voluntary service. One hundred and sixty nine former members of the Hawaii Territorial Guard signed the petition given to Lieutenant General Emmons, which asserted that:

> Hawaii is our home, the United States, our country. We know but one loyalty and that is to the Stars and Stripes. We wish to do our part as loyal Americans in every way possible and we hereby offer ourselves for whatever services you may see fit to use us.[43]

Colonel Kendall Fielder was one of those who sided with the Japanese-Americans on the issue of their loyalty. Before the end of February, Lieutenant General Emmons, pressed by Colonel Fielder, granted permission for the Japanese-American students to form their own military unit. This unit was officially designated as the Corps of Engineers Auxiliary, attached to the 34th Combat Engineers Regiment of the U. S. Army Corps of Engineers, but their technical status was that of civilian laborers. There was actually a critical need for physical labor in Hawaii, driven by wartime procurement demand, so naming themselves the "VVV"—Varsity Victory Volunteers—

and armed with tools instead of textbooks, the Japanese-Americans set to work on the construction of barracks, warehouses, and roads. It was around this time that they started referring to themselves as "AJA"—Americans of Japanese Ancestry.

Despite this sort of discriminatory treatment, Japanese-Americans in Hawaii did not have to undergo mass internment. Ironically, it was the thorough investigation of Japanese loyalty carried out in Hawaii before the war that resulted in the decision not to implement Japanese relocation. There were many who called for internment, along the lines of the system enacted on the mainland, and they would continue to do so until the Battle of Midway in June 1942. But Hawaiian military intelligence had concluded that mass relocation was not necessary.[44] In the first place, the prior investigations had turned up no acts of espionage by Japanese-Americans. Furthermore, Japanese-Americans had gone out of their way to demonstrate their loyalty by purchasing U.S. war bonds, participating in local blood drives, and so forth. In their relatively small, insular society, *Nisei* were keenly aware, early on, that it was incumbent upon them to prove their loyalty to the United States. *Issei*, too, did what they could to be supportive, if only to help ensure a better future for their American-born children.

Hawaii experienced a wave of prosperity thanks to wartime economic demands, and this led to the labor shortage that made involvement of Japanese workers indispensable. One officer noted that if you wanted to build even a barrack, you'd have to get the Japanese to do it.[45] Internment plans were simply not practicable. In the first place, the internment of Japanese-Americans would have disastrous economic consequences. What is more, the military opposed this notion of sending such a large group to the mainland for internment. It would use ships more urgently needed for troop transport. For security reasons, Washington decided that mass evacuations were necessary. At the end of June, Lieutenant General Emmons requested that due to labor shortages and other logistical problems, there would be only 5,000 Japanese-Americans transported.[46] But with the stunning naval victory in the Battle of Midway, the possibility of a Japanese invasion became less likely. This created less of a demand for evacuation, as judged by political and military leaders.

It is true that certain logistical factors contributed to the Japanese-Americans having ultimately escaped internment in Hawaii. But even more important was the role played by the pre-war "loyalty investigations," and the fact that individuals such as Director Shivers and Colonel Fielder had come to place their trust in the Japanese-Americans. Between October 1942 and March 1943, 930 individuals were relocated to the mainland.[47] Most were relatives of people arrested, relocated, and confined in the mainland by the FBI in the wake of Pearl Harbor and the declaration of war.

"One-Puka-Puka"

In Hawaii, tensions were at their highest between the Pearl Harbor attack and the run-up to the Battle of Midway in June 1942. A great many bombers took off from Hawaii. Women and children residing near the Honolulu Harbor were given evacuation instructions, and the authorities made radio appeals for citizens to carry gas masks at all times.[48] The military was faced with the prospect that a defeat of Admiral Chester Nimitz's naval forces would likely mean a Japanese invasion of Hawaii. Were Japanese soldiers to disguise themselves in U.S. military uniforms and mix in with American forces, it would be impossible to distinguish friend from foe. Consequently, the military decided to send Japanese-American soldiers to the mainland as an emergency safeguard.

So on June 5, the second day of the Battle of Midway, the U.S.S. Maui set out from Honolulu in utmost secrecy, with 1,432 Japanese-American soldiers onboard.[49] Having received emergency orders, these men had little time to prepare for their departure for an unknown destination. Only a handful of families were present to see them off to war. Aboard the Maui, they were greatly relieved to hear news of the victory at Midway, having feared the worst for their families in the event of a Japanese invasion of Hawaii. That said, it must have been terribly unsettling to be sent to the mainland in the midst of such an emergency at home. Maintaining a zigzag course—changing direction every 20 minutes to avoid torpedo attack—the Maui reached San Francisco a week later, sailing under the Golden Gate Bridge. For most of the men, this was their first view of the American mainland.

It was around this time that the group was officially designated as the 100th Infantry Battalion (separate entity). This was an unconventional name, and it revealed something of the perplexity of the military authorities. Normally, three battalions would comprise a regiment, which in turn belonged to a division. However, the "100th Infantry Battalion" did not belong to any larger military unit, since it was a separate entity, and was not intended for combat duty. Moreover, a battalion would normally consist of four companies, from A to D. But since the 100th Infantry Battalion contained more soldiers than normal, it required two additional companies, E and F. For the Japanese-American soldiers of the 100th Infantry Battalion, the very name of their unit caused them to reflect upon how unique they were. Many persisted in the belief that they would eventually be interned. Before long, they started calling themselves "One-Puka-Puka"— One Zero Zero. In Hawaiian, the word *puka* means both "hole" and "zero."

Lieutenant Colonel Farrant Turner was appointed commander of the 100th Infantry Battalion. He became affectionately known as "The Old Man" and was a great favorite among his men. A 47-year-old native of Hilo, Hawaii, Lieutenant Colonel Turner had gotten to know Japanese-American soldiers through his service in the Hawaii Territorial Guard. He had volunteered for command of the 100th Infantry

Chapter 2

Battalion upon hearing news of the creation of this Japanese-American battalion. Once appointed, Lieutenant Colonel Turner chose Captain James Lovell as his second-in-command. Captain Lovell would earn the trust of his men, to whom he was simply "The Captain." Born in Nebraska, Captain Lovell had worked as a teacher in Honolulu middle and high schools and served as coach for athletic teams. He had many dealings with *Nisei*. For their part, the men of "*One-Puka-Puka*" were overjoyed to learn that Lieutenant Colonel Turner and Captain Lovell would serve as their commanders.

Lieutenant Colonel Turner was a strict leader, but he regarded the Japanese-Americans under his command as "My boys." He did his best to defend them from unfair treatment and discrimination. By the same token, when any of his soldiers got into trouble or misbehaved, Lieutenant Colonel Turner would exhort them to the effect that "every one of your actions makes this battalion's reputation; your families' futures rest on your shoulders."[50]

The soldiers were expected to earn high marks in training and distinguish themselves on the frontlines as soon as possible. The men went so far as to make "Remember Pearl Harbor" their motto, as a means of motivating themselves. As a case in point: The U.S. Army Manual notes that one can earn a "satisfactory" rating by assembling a heavy machine gun in 16 seconds. Even at Fort Benning, the Army's officer candidate school, assembling the weapon in 11 seconds was regarded as "fast." At Camp McCoy, where the Japanese-Americans trained, several soldiers set the record for speed of assembly—five seconds.[51] An officer who saw their training records remarked:

> I'd rather have a 100 of these men behind me than a 100 of any others I'd ever been with.[52]

Hawaiian soldiers spoke pidgin English, a unique mixture of English, Hawaiian, and Japanese (with some Hiroshima dialect mixed in). Theirs was a very difficult language for outsiders to understand. But its speakers were by no means lacking in intelligence. Indeed, the censorship officers who inspected their correspondence were surprised at how well these men wrote, despite their seemingly ungrammatical and crudely spoken language. 95% of the "*One-Puka-Puka*" outfit was *Nisei* sons of Japanese immigrants; 35% had dual citizenship; 2% were "*Kibei*" *Nisei*; and about 85% had studied at Japanese language schools in the United States. Still, they managed to graduate from public high schools in three years, on the average, and some 12% had gone on to college, with 5% having graduated. The men of the 100th Infantry Battalion scored an average of 103 on the Army intelligence test. This meant that "*One-Puka-Puka*" contained a number of cadet-level soldiers; given that their test average was a mere seven points shy of 110, the score required for admission to cadet training.[53]

Despite the level of achievement on the test and their superior training scores, these men had virtually no hope of fighting on the frontlines. After all, the U.S. military prohibited Japanese-Americans from volunteering for service, having concluded that it would be dangerous to send individuals to the frontlines who could not be trusted and whose loyalty was in question. But the impressive record of "*One-Puka-Puka*" and the activities of the VVV would set in motion a re-evaluation of this policy.

A Group of Hawaiian Volunteers of Japanese Ancestry Accepted by the United States Army. February 2, 1943. Aiea, Oahu, Hawaii. Courtesy of The Manoa Library. University of Hawaii.

A Gun Crew of the 3rd Battalion Anti-Tank Platoon Practices Setting Up a 37mm Field Piece. The 442nd RCT at Camp Shelby composed entirely of Americans of Japanese descent who volunteered for services in the armed forces. This unit of approximately 8,000 men underwent intensive training in all branches of combat duty. They looked forward with eagerness to actual services on the front. July 1943. Camp Shelby, Mississippi. Photographer: Mace, Charles E. Courtesy of The Bancroft Library. University of California, Berkeley.

The Right to Die for One's Country

Around the time of the 100th Infantry Battalion's transfer to Camp Shelby in Mississippi in January 1943, the government was planning the formation of a Japanese-American combat team. This decision had been a long time coming. The concept of a Japanese-American unit had clearly been a matter of controversy. Some held that Japanese-American troops should not be engaged in combat roles, and should instead be assigned to duties far removed from the battlefield. Others insisted that outstanding fighting men were needed, regardless of their background. If Japanese-American soldiers fit the bill, then by all means, use them. This position was supported by the WRA. In addition, Admiral Nimitz and Lieutenant General Emmons believed that Japanese-American troops would distinguish themselves in battle.

Lieutenant General Emmons had previously been an advocate of the internment plan, but his view changed once he became familiar with the accomplishments of the students in the VVV and the high marks achieved by the trainees at Camp McCoy. What is more, Colonel Fielder was instrumental in Lieutenant General Emmons'

change of heart. It bears noting that Colonel Fielder also "lobbied" on behalf of the Japanese-Americans with others as well. For instance, when Assistant Secretary of War John McCloy came to inspect Hawaiian defense installations, Colonel Fielder made sure to put the Kole Kole Pass on his itinerary, which enabled Assistant Secretary McCloy to witness the impressive labors of the VVV students, who were working hard at breaking up rocks and boulders.[54]

In October of 1942, Director Davis of the Office of War Information, sent a letter to President Roosevelt calling for the incorporation of Japanese-American enlistees into the military:

> Loyal American citizens of Japanese descent should be permitted, after individual test[ing], to enlist in the Army and Navy. It would hardly be fair to evacuate people and then impose normal draft procedures, but voluntary enlistment would help a lot.[55]

At the time, Japanese military propaganda in Southeast Asia had been accusing the United States of waging "war by racial discrimination." The Office of War Information intended to deny this.

President Roosevelt passed the letter on to Secretary of War Henry Stimson, and Secretary Stimson brought it to Assistant Secretary McCloy's attention. Having heard many positive reports about the Japanese-Americans from Colonel Fielder, Assistant Secretary McCloy noted as follows on the letter; "I am firmly convinced that large numbers of them are loyal."[56] Secretary Stimson then forwarded the letter to General George Marshal, Chief of the War Department General Staff:

> I am inclined strongly to agree with the view of McCloy and Davis. I don't think you can permanently proscribe a lot of American citizens because of their racial origin. We have gone to the full limit in evacuating them—that's enough.[57]

Chapter 2

Lieutenant Eugene Bogard, Commanding Officer of the Army Registration Team. He explains to young evacuees details of volunteering in the Army Combat team, made up entirely of Japanese-Americans. February 15, 1943. Manzanar, California. Photographer: Stewart, Francis. Courtesy of The Bancroft Library. University of California, Berkeley.

Much like Lieutenant General Emmons, Secretary Stimson had initially advocated the internment, but he, too, came to embrace the notion that Japanese-Americans should be regarded as trustworthy and loyal.

The JACL convened a meeting in Salt Lake City to discuss the formation of a unit consisting of mainland Japanese-Americans. Some took the perfectly reasonable position that the matter should be dealt with only after putting an end to the internment. However, Executive Director Mike Masaoka made a strong case for the importance of Japanese-Americans distinguishing themselves on the battlefield. Masaoka argued that they should call for the voluntary enlistment system, whereby Japanese-American fighting men would be in a position to contribute to an Allied victory and thereby help achieve due recognition for Japanese-Americans in the postwar era.[58] Following Masaoka's lead, the JACL unanimously decided to lobby the government for the authorization of American volunteer enlistment.

Won over by Director Davis's view that it was "not fair" for internees in the camps to be drafted, the government moved to accept Japanese-American volunteers, but to defer a conscription system. The next item on the agenda was whether the Japanese-American inductees should all serve together in the same unit or be assigned to different units. Colonel William Scobey, Assistant Secretary McCloy's second-in-command, explained to Masaoka and the JACL leadership the Army's contention that opting for an exclusive Japanese-American unit would have the advantage of making it easier to publicize the collective achievements of these fighting men. The JACL endorsed the proposed plan, concluding that this would be the ideal means of proving, finally, Japanese-American loyalty. What is more, Masaoka made sure to visit Assistant Secretary McCloy and obtain his consent to implement a regular conscription system for *Nisei*, once the Japanese-American military unit was successfully instituted.[59]

All parties—the WRA (which managed the Japanese-American internment), the commandant in Hawaii who had sent out the 100th Infantry Battalion, and the top brass in the Office of War Information and the War Department—signed off on the formation of a Japanese-American regimental unit. So it was that in February 1943, President Roosevelt formally announced the creation of the 442nd Regimental Combat Team (RCT), although the conscription system for Japanese-Americans would not be put in place until January 1944. In his speech, based on a draft prepared by the WRA, President Roosevelt proclaimed: [61]

> Americanism is a matter of the mind and heart; Americanism is not, and never was, a matter of race and ancestry.[60]

The *Nisei* had finally earned the right to die for their country—on the condition, however, that they serve under white officers.

The 442nd Regimental Combat Team

Just when the creation of the 442nd RCT was being announced, the authorities started distributing a "Loyalty Questionnaire" to internees in the camps. Two of its questions were particularly problematic:

#27: Are you willing to serve in the armed forces of the United States on combat duty wherever ordered?

#28: Will you swear unqualified allegiance to the United States of America and faithfully defend the United States from any or all attack by foreign or domestic forces, and forswear any form of allegiance or obedience to the Japanese Emperor, to any other foreign government, power or organization?[62]

For *Issei*, who were ineligible for American citizenship, answering "yes" to these questions meant forsaking their homeland and being relegated to an alien, stateless identity. After the long and painful history of racial discrimination and mass internment, they felt reluctant to entrust their children's future to a country that could treat them in such a manner. Meanwhile, the *Nisei*, for their part, felt deeply humiliated at being forced to prove their loyalty despite being American citizens.

Those who answered "no" to both of the "loyalty" questions were moved to the Tule Lake camp, whereupon many chose to return to Japan. Those who answered "yes" to both questions and volunteered for military service were regarded as traitors by many of the camp internees. What had been a smoldering conflict of opinion among the *Issei*, *Nisei*, and "*Kibei*" groupings flared up in the wake of the questionnaire. Family members were pitted against each other and a chaotic environment prevailed. As a consequence, in contrast with Hawaii where Japanese-American volunteers enlisted in numbers nearly 10 times the available openings, a mere 5% of interned *Nisei* who met the minimum age requirement actually volunteered.[63] After all, they had been placed in a difficult bind and wanted to avoid being branded as betrayers of their community.

Ken Akune, who had served in the MIS (Military Intelligence Service), recalled the conflicted situation facing the *Nisei* internees:

When I told other internees that my brother and I have volunteered, they started to say, "What's the matter with you people. Here you claimed that you are American citizens but you are no better than we are. You are in the same camp that we are. Now you are saying you volunteered. You have parents in Japan. What are they gonna say?" And my thought was, 'You know the reason we are here is we don't have any past records for *Nihonjin*, Japanese, (who) could prove their loyalty. Now is our chance, and if we don't take the chance and do something about it, it's gonna be our fault. And some of us are not gonna come back but...' I felt that if it would change things for the better for the Japanese, it would be worth it. [64]

In Hawaii, well over 10,000 young men had thronged to apply for the 1,500 recruit positions. Since the yield of mainland volunteers was considerably less than expected, the number of Hawaiian positions was expanded to 2,600. While the volunteers and their families suffered abuse and derisive name-calling in the mainland internment camps, the situation in Hawaii was quite the opposite. Those who failed their physical exams were the ones who had to bear the shame. On March 28, 1943, the Honolulu Chamber of Commerce hosted a lavish farewell ceremony at the Iolani Palace, and 2,686 volunteers—among them, students from the VVV—paraded through the city. Tens of thousands of Japanese-Americans crowded along the parade route, waving their American flags and raising shouts of *banzai*!

In short, the Japanese-American servicemen from Hawaii and the mainland were subject to radically different treatment as they prepared to enter the war—the one group praised as heroes, the other as turncoats. It was only natural that the two groups should harbor a certain antagonism toward one another. It has been noted that this mutual dislike originated when Hawaiian

Chapter 2

soldiers arrived at Camp Shelby, the training facility for the 442ⁿᵈ RCT, only to find that every noncommissioned officer (NCO) post had already been occupied by mainland soldiers. The fact of the groups' very different backgrounds and enlistment experiences also needed to be taken into account. What men from Hawaii did not understand was that the mainland soldiers who occupied the NCO posts were indeed conscripted before the outbreak of war. The Army did not really know what to do with these Japanese-Americans, and so, much like the situation with the 100ᵗʰ Infantry Battalion, they were essentially left in limbo. In their ignorance, the soldiers from Hawaii simply concluded that they were being treated unfairly.

Furthermore, the difference in their spoken language also contributed to their mutual hostility. Those from the mainland could not understand the pidgin English spoken by the Japanese-Americans from Hawaii, who in turn were put off by the mainland soldiers' English, which to them sounded just like the white plantation owners whom they disdained. There was also the matter of the "haves" versus the "have-nots." The soldiers from Hawaii were able to tap into the money their parents had earned thanks to the wartime economic boom back home—not to mention the several hundreds of dollars they would typically be given as *senbetsu* (farewell gifts.) On the other hand, the parents of the mainland soldiers were whiling away in the camps with little or no funds and many of them had to rely on their sons to send money drawn from their Army paychecks.

The authorities were quite concerned about the bad blood between the two Japanese-American groups. In order to reinforce mutual understanding and goodwill, the military took the Hawaiian soldiers to visit the Jerome Internment Camp in Arkansas, the closest to Camp Shelby, which was in Mississippi. Daniel Inouye, a volunteer enlistee from VVV, who later would achieve a distinguished career in the U. S. Senate, was among the first group to make the trip to Jerome, recalled the experience:

So here we are with our ukuleles and guitars, if you can picture that. We are singing all the way from Mississippi to Arkansas; but once we got closer, and we turned into [the camp], we began to realize what was happening... And I believe what was running through the minds of most, if not all, was the question, "Would I have volunteered from that camp?"(65)

The Hawaiian and mainland soldiers were thus finally united as a Japanese-American combat team.

"Go For Broke"

One year and three months after the 100ᵗʰ Infantry Battalion had sailed from Honolulu in utmost secrecy, the soldiers from Hawaii, having completed their lengthy training, finally arrived at the front in North Africa on September 2, 1943. The invasion of Italy, "Operation Avalanche," began on September 3, with British landings at Calabria, followed six days later by the U.S. Fifth Army landings at Salerno and British landings at Taranto. On September 9, 1943, Italy surrendered and the German forces took control of Italy.

On September 22, the 100ᵗʰ Infantry Battalion, assigned to the 133ʳᵈ RCT under the 34ᵗʰ Infantry Division, landed at Salerno. They excelled on the

Members of the 232ⁿᵈ Engineers Line the Banks of the Leaf River. The men are watching an amphibian jeep during field training. July, 1943. Camp Shelby, Mississippi. Photographer: Charles E. Mace. Courtesy of The Bancroft Library. University of California, Berkeley.

battlefield right from the beginning. The media was much taken with these out-of-the-ordinary servicemen and their achievements, and would report on them in very positive terms. The military's aim of widely publicizing the exploits of Japanese-American soldiers worked out better than expected.

It was at the Battle of Monte Cassino where the Japanese-Americans did indeed distinguish themselves. The Allies were reluctant to bomb Cassino from the air, wishing to safeguard its historic monastery, built by Saint Benedict in 529 AD on a nearby hilltop. Instead, they would stage an infantry assault on the entrenched German force. This would prove difficult, though, since their objective was a fortress that the Germans would defend at all costs to prevent the Allies from reaching Rome. General Mark Clark, Commander of the Fifth Army, remarked after the war that the Battle of Cassino was "the most gruesome, the most harrowing, and in one aspect the most tragic, of any phase of the war in Italy."[66] As it turns out, the Allies were indeed unable to break through the Cassino defenses with infantry alone, no matter how many divisions they deployed. On February 15, 1944, they resorted to launching a concentrated air strike using 255 bombers that dropped more than 2,500 tons of explosives. With several of these bombing missions and the destruction of the Abbey, three more months passed before the Allies captured Monte Cassino.

Monte Cassino: The Approach. Courtesy of the National Archives (111-SC-337120).

Members of the 442nd RCT at a Memorial Day Service. Fay's Area, France. Source: Hawaii War Records Depository.

Before the fall of the Cassino fortress, the 100th Infantry Battalion was redeployed to Anzio to take part in the Allied landing there. The fall of Rome was all but guaranteed once they broke through at Anzio. In the meantime, the Allies were planning a large-scale invasion force that would land on the northern French coast, thus establishing a western front that would divert German forces engaged in fierce combat along the eastern front. This was none other than Operation Overlord, the epochal D-Day Normandy invasion, which would be the largest naval assault in history, involving more than three million troops. Restoring France to Allied control would depend upon the success of both the Normandy landing in the north and the Anzio campaign, which would effectively provide a gateway to southern France. The men of the 100th Infantry Battalion distinguished themselves in this campaign.

Following the fall of Anzio in May 1944, the Allies entered Rome on June 5. By the time the men of the 100th Infantry Battalion reached the city, it was 9:00 p.m. The troops had actually been at the vanguard of the Rome-bound force, but were ordered to stop at a point some 10 kilometers from the city so that others could be the first to enter. Jesse Hirata commented on this episode:

> During training, the infantry followed the tanks under protection of their armor. But in combat that never happened; they followed us way in the back... We advanced right up to the outskirts of

Chapter 2

Rome. Only then did we see tanks advancing to an objective. They had cameramen and newsmen to show the world the liberation of Rome. By then, we were stopped and ordered aside so they could roar into Rome as the conquerors. What a farce. As they were passing us, an artillery shell exploded ahead of them. They all stopped and the general ordered our company to go ahead of the tanks. Then the shelling stopped, and they put us aside. A shell came in again. The third time the general ordered us, no one moved for him.[67]

Quite by coincidence, it was precisely two years after "One-Puka-Puka" had set out from Honolulu, destination unknown, that the men entered Rome—a fact that few took notice of. The Normandy Invasion was launched the very next day.

King George of England Inspects the Troops. Cecina Area, Italy. Source: Hawaii War Records Depository.

It was around this time that the 442nd RCT had completed training and was sent to Italy. The regimental motto was "Go for Broke." Norman Ikari, a veteran of the 442nd RCT, related an interesting anecdote:

> By the time we were at the end of the voyage to land in Naples, I recall one incident there as we were unloading from the ships. There were caravans of white troops going by on trucks. And these white guys saw us and leaned out from

the back of the truck (shouting) 'One-Puka-Puka!'—which really meant that our reputations had been made ahead of time by the 100th.[68]

In fact, the exploits of the 100th Infantry Battalion were already well-known among the U.S. military officials. Lieutenant Colonel Gordon Singles, who succeeded the retired Lieutenant Colonel Turner, made it clear how fortunate he was for having been assigned to the 100th Infantry Battalion.[69]

With the arrival of the 442nd RCT at the European front, the 100th Infantry Battalion was reassigned as the first battalion of the 442nd RCT. But in deference to their distinguished record, they were allowed to keep the "100th Infantry Battalion" name. Despite the original thrust of the name as a sign of the group's outcast status, it had now become a badge of honor and distinction. The 100th Infantry Battalion and the 442nd RCT joined forces in the Battle of Belvedere, in the north of Rome, and thereafter as well. It took only three hours for the 442nd RCT to break through enemy lines at Belvedere, despite pre-battle estimates of several days. The 442nd RCT enjoyed great success in this, their first battle. With the 100th Infantry Battalion, they made a surprise attack from the rear, which all but wiped out the German forces—178 dead, 65 taken prisoner, and 2 tanks captured. The 100th Infantry Battalion suffered few casualties—four fallen and seven injured.[70]

Japanese-American Infantrymen of the 442nd RCT. Soldiers hike up a muddy French road in the Chambois Sector, France, late 1944. Source: Army Center for Military History.

As an acknowledgment of its distinguished battle record, the 100th Infantry Battalion was awarded the highest battalion-level commendation—the first Distinguished Presidential Unit Citation. General Clark of the 5th Army made a speech on this occasion that deeply moved many of those in *One-Puka-Puka*:

> All of you Americans of Japanese descent have a right to be proud today. You have demonstrated true Americanism and true American citizenship on the field of battle. You have another right to be proud, for you have reached the high standards of American fighting men... And let me tell you again, the 34th Division is proud of you. The Fifth Army is proud of you. America is proud of you.[71]

Toward the end of September, the 442nd RCT and the 100th Infantry Battalion were dispatched from Italy, in the heat of battle, to the French frontlines at Bruyeres. The men were ordered to the French front by General Dwight Eisenhower. Thus, after only one year of active duty, the Japanese-American fighting force had become a much sought-after unit among the military command.

Rescuing the "Lost Battalion"

The 442nd RCT landed at Marseilles and moved north, joining forces with the 36th Division, the so-called Texas Division. They had

The 442nd RCT Receives a Presidential Unit Citation at a Ceremony in Leghorn, Italy. September 1945. Leghorn, Italy. Source: Hawaii War Records Depository.

The 442nd RCT Participate in a V-J Day Parade in Leghorn, Italy. Source: Hawaii War Records Depository.

fought together with the 34th Division in Italy. In fact, two of the 36th divisional regiments were all but wiped out in the Battle of Cassino. Therefore, it was fortuitous that these veterans of the Italian campaign were reunited in the middle of the Vosges Mountains, near the German border. The region is better known as the Black Forest because of the dense coniferous forests that blanket the hills.

Bruyeres was a small town with a population of 4,000. It served as a vital transportation hub for the Nazis and was under *Schutzstaffel* (SS) control. Additionally, German troops lay scattered within the Vosges Mountains. Hitler had ordered his military to defend this strategically located town at all costs. This was to be a fight to the finish. The Bruyeres townsfolk, who had endured four years of German occupation, relished the prospect of liberation by the Allied forces. However, the Allies had found it very difficult to make their advance in this area, despite their triumphant entry into Paris on August 25. They were stymied by the fierce resistance of the German forces in the Black Forest.

The Allied forces faced formidable obstacles. The Nazis had laid countless landmines in the Vosges forests, many of which remain to this day. The men had to endure a relentless cold rain, and many suffered trench foot from the constant damp and chill. Exploding artillery shells showered them with potentially deadly branches

Chapter 2

and tree limbs. Enemy fire came from all quarters—there was no escape from the incessant shelling.

On October 19, 1944, the 442nd RCT finally managed to reach Bruyeres.[72] News of the Americans' arrival spread rapidly among the local townspeople, who had taken refuge in their basements. Imagine their surprise when they came out to greet the troops who emerged from the surrounding forest. Instead of the expected contingent of tall, white GIs, they beheld soldiers of short stature who looked Japanese, all of them smiling and saying, "OK! OK!" The citizens of Bruyeres were delighted with the arrival of these Japanese-American soldiers in their U.S. military uniforms.

The 36th Infantry Division was under the command of Major General John Dahlquist, who had long served under General Eisenhower in the British headquarters. Major General Dahlquist had been at his new post for less than two months, with ambition to be in command of the first division to enter Germany. He arrived at the front, issued a number of directives, and ordered what turned out to be a very ill-advised troop movement. This order, following right on the heels of the liberation of Bruyeres, would result in many casualties among the 36th Infantry Division. In particular, a contingent of the 100th Infantry Battalion involved in this operation was isolated in the small town of Biffontaine. They took the town upon Major General Dahlquist's orders, and captured 23 Germans. Soon the Germans re-grouped and surrounded the town. Even after the supply line was cut and no backup able to approach, the 100th Infantry Battalion refused to surrender and the next day attempted to carry out their wounded and the prisoners they had captured. Along the way, more than 10 soldiers were captured by German patrols in the forest near Biffontaine.

Meanwhile, the 1st Battalion of the 141st Infantry, the Texas outfit, also found itself surrounded by the enemy in the forests around Biffontaine. The 442nd RCT, which had just arrived in the town of Belmont for some much-needed rest following their service in the liberation of Bruyeres, was issued orders for a search-and-rescue mission the next day. Lieutenant-Colonel Singles of the 100th Infantry Battalion could appreciate how the 141st Infantry had lost its way in enemy territory. However, he could not fathom why his battalion, which had not had a chance to recuperate, had been singled out for this mission, when other well-rested battalions were in fact available. Some put it down to racial discrimination; others saw this as a vote of confidence in the Japanese-American troops who could be counted on in such difficult situations. There is no way to know for sure.

The 2nd Battalion was ordered out first, and men of the 100th Infantry Battalion and 3rd Battalion moved out of Belmont on October 26 at 4:00 a.m.[73] The forest was pitch dark—not even one's own hands could be seen. John Tsukano recalled the scene in the forest:

> We start marching. It's so dark we have to keep in touch by holding on to the shoulders of whoever is in front of us. We march for a couple of hours, groping in the dark. We slip and fall on the slippery ground. We don't know where we are heading. We wonder who is leading us. How does he know where he is going? The full field pack, weapons, and ammunition on our backs and shoulders get heavier and heavier. We are so weary. We are tired. We are like walking zombies.[74]

News of the Texan Battalion spread throughout the United States, the media having dubbed it the "Lost Battalion." The fate of Major General Dahlquist's military career virtually hinged upon the success of the rescue mission. Having heretofore relied on passing along his directives to those at the front, Major General Dahlquist made his way personally to the frontlines, together with his second-in-command. There he exhorted the Japanese-American troops, who were manning the trenches with rifles at the ready, to make a charge. Many of them climbed out of the trenches, screaming wildly and rushing desperately forward. The Japanese-American troops' famous "Banzai Charge" was echoed forth in this battle. Robert Sato had this to say:

> All of a sudden, I heard something like "Okaasan [mother]" coming from the twisted, bloody mouth [of one of our men]. My partner said he heard it, too. But the soldier's voice was so soft that I couldn't make out what he was saying. I felt very uneasy. I had some experience in the past in which 'Okaasan' was usually the last word spoken by the seriously wounded *Nisei* soldiers in battle.[75]

The men fought on, rushing headlong through minefields and bursting shells for six whole days. On October 30, Company B of the 100th Infantry Battalion broke through to reach the Lost Battalion. Company I and K of the 3rd Battalion were among the first to arrive.[76] The Lost Battalion, which their fellow soldiers from Texas had been unable to rescue, was finally saved by the 442nd RCT.

For the Japanese-American regiment, the fighting was not yet over. Moving counter to the rescued Texas soldiers who were coming down from the forested hills, the Japanese-American soldiers had been ordered by Major General Dahlquist to continue their advance. They would fight on for 10 more days before being ordered, finally, to fall back.[77]

When the 3rd Platoon of Company A, 100th Infantry Battalion was dispatched on their mission to rescue the Lost Battalion, there were only two original members who remained from the trainee group at Camp McCoy. Neither of these men reached the Lost Battalion.[78]

In the entire 100th Infantry Battalion, there were fewer than 10 soldiers who could say that they had landed on the beach at Salerno, the first point-of-entry into the European theater for Japanese-American soldiers. The rest were soldiers subsequently assigned to the unit as replacements. Company I, one of the first

companies to reach the Lost Battalion, initially started with 185 men. There were only eight still standing by the time the men reached the Lost Battalion.[79]

A ceremony was held three days later to honor the distinguished service of Japanese-American troops. Major General Dahlquist, who was on hand for the event, angrily remarked to a 442nd RCT colonel:

> "You disobeyed my order. I told you to have the whole regiment." The colonel looked him in the eye and reportedly said, "General, this *is* the regiment. The rest are either dead or in the hospital."[80]

The Japanese-American soldiers of the 442nd RCT liberated Bruyeres and rescued 212 men of the Texan battalion in 34 days of almost non-stop combat, continuing to push forward for nine more days. In the end, they lost almost half their number—216 dead and 856 injured in battle.[81] There is a street in the town of Bruyeres—"Liberation Avenue"—named in commemoration of the historic event. And, branching off from Liberation Avenue, heading toward the forest is "Rue de 442nd RCT." A monument erected at the entrance to the forest is inscribed as follows:

> For the soldiers of the American 442nd RCT, who taught us that race does not alter loyalty to one's country.[82]

French Monument Honoring *Nisei* Soldiers. This monument in Biffontaine, France, built and donated by Jean Bianchetti in remembrance of the 44nd Regimental Combat Team. Courtesy of the Seattle *Nisei* Veterans Committee.

Chapter 2

Japanese-Americans in the Military Intelligence Service

Founding of the MIS Language School

In November 1941, shortly before the attack on Pearl Harbor, the Military Intelligence Service (MIS) Language School was established at the Presidio Army Base in San Francisco. At a time when relations between Japan and America were becoming increasingly strained, the mission of this secret facility was to train intelligence agents in the Japanese language. The school opened with 60 enlisted students (58 *Nisei*) who were selected primarily based on language ability.[1] One of the school's first students, John Aiso, became the chief instructor and later the first mainland Japanese-American to hold a judiciary post.[2]

In the wake of the Japanese-American internment, the MIS school moved to Camp Savage in Minnesota and then to Fort Snelling as

***Nisei* Interpreters Question Prisoners at Simini, New Guinea**. Major Hawkins, (with wristwatch), and Bob Uhiro, of G-2, question a Japanese prisoner taken at Buna Mission. Japanese interpreters of the 32nd Division are with Major Hawkins. January 2, 1943. Courtesy of the National Archives.

the student body increased. In June 1946, the name changed to the U.S. Army Language School. The facility ultimately returned to California, but not before graduating 6,000 language students, 85% of whom were *Nisei* soldiers.[3]

Nisei Soldiers in the Pacific Theater

Unlike the men of the 442nd RCT, whose achievements on the European front were widely reported, the many contributions of the language school graduates were shrouded in secrecy, on account of their highly classified missions. These men were deployed to hard-fought arenas of conflict in the Pacific Theater such as Attu (in the Aleutians), Guadalcanal, the Philippines, and Okinawa. Their duties involved interrogation of Japanese POWs, the translation of confiscated documents, and the interception of Japanese military communications. These men were always accompanied by other American soldiers to avoid being mistaken for the enemy and fired upon.

The Japanese-Americans in the MIS played a key role as liaison between the American military and the Japanese people during and after the War. They contributed to the restoration of Japan through service in the Occupation Force. George Fujimori, one of the MIS soldiers who fought in the Philippines, recalled:

Japanese-Americans in the Military Intelligence Service *continued*

I always gave captive soldiers a cigarette first and told them that while it was looked upon as a disgrace for a Japanese soldier to return home alive, in the States such a soldier would be regarded as a war hero. "So don't throw your lives away," I'd tell them, "you've got to return home and help rebuild Japan."*

It was not until 1972, when President Richard Nixon issued Executive Order 11652, which declassified all military intelligence documents from WWII, that the MIS and its achievements became known.[4] Finally, in April of 2000, a Presidential Unit Citation was awarded to MIS veterans of the war.[5]

Interviewed by the writer on June 20, 2005 at the Go for Broke National Education Center.

The Gothic Line and the Dachau Concentration Camp

On March 25, 1945, the main corps of the 442nd RCT left France, having been secretly called back to the front in Italy.[83] For the eight months that the 442nd RCT had fought in France, the Allied forces had been unable to break through the Gothic Line—the German defensive perimeter in Northern Italy. The German military had taken full advantage of the sheer 3,000 foot cliffs in the area, constructing what would be the last stronghold of their army.

The Allies had no safe approach since the German forces commanded an unobstructed view for many kilometers from their mountaintop fortress. The Allied command devised a plan, which involved having the men of the 442nd RCT scale the mountainside under cover of darkness and stage a surprise attack at dawn. On the night of April 5, a force of several thousand Japanese-American troops, with their dog tags sewn into their uniforms to prevent any telltale noise,* began their climb. They ascended the mountain from three sides, in order to surround the fortress. For such a large force to accomplish a difficult ascent of the precipitous mountainside, in total silence, was no easy feat. One of the men ended up losing his footing and falling some 300 feet—without uttering a sound.[84] The ascent from the rear was especially steep, requiring no less than eight hours of struggling to negotiate a vertical incline of 60 degrees.[85]

The rear unit initiated attack just before dawn, at which point the other units that had surrounded the fortress engaged the enemy. The surprise attack succeeded brilliantly, as the men of the 442nd RCT occupied the fortress in 32 minutes.[86] They went on to break through the Gothic Line that night. General Clark had hoped to break through the enemy line in a week, but now that the Japanese-American force had joined them,[87] their accomplishment of the mission in a single day came as a great—and most welcome—surprise. General Eisenhower awarded a Presidential Unit Citation to the men of the 442nd RCT and the 232nd Combat Engineers for their key role in the attack on the Gothic Line.[88]

When the main force of the 442nd RCT made its second landing on Italian soil, the 522nd Field Artillery Battalion separated from the 442nd RCT to join the Allied advance into Southern Germany, deploying its divisions as necessity dictated during its push into German territory.

On April 29, 1945, a detachment unit encountered a shocking scene while on patrol east of Munich.[89] Entering a compound surrounded by barbed wire, they came upon a large group—

*From an interview with Tetsuo Asato, veteran of 442nd RCT, by the writer on June 20, 2005 at the Go for Broke National Education Center.

mostly Jewish people in ragged prison uniforms— virtual living corpses, little more than skin and bones, with sunken eyes and shaven heads. This was a Nazi slave labor camp, part of the notorious Dachau Concentration Camp, which had housed over 200,000 prisoners. The soldiers rescued the camp survivors, and would go on to rescue a group of desperate and dying prisoners near the Austrian border, victims of a horrific Nazi SS "Death March."[90]

It remains a matter of controversy as to which military unit deserves credit for having liberated Dachau. In 1985, the United States Holocaust Memorial Museum gave this recognition to only a few units, among them, the 42nd Infantry (Rainbow) Division. This, however, generated a great deal of resentment among those veterans left unacknowledged, and two years later, the Holocaust Memorial Museum and the center for Military History established certain guidelines for officially recognized "liberating units." It was decided to award this distinction only to units at the level of division.[91] Since the 522nd Field Artillery Battalion did not qualify according to this standard, it was not recognized.[92]

On April 30, 1945, the day after the liberation of Dachau, Adolf Hitler committed suicide. A week later, on May 7, Germany unconditionally surrendered to the Allied forces. The May 8 observance of the Allied victory in Europe, known as "V-E Day," was celebrated with unbridled rejoicing throughout the United States.

The struggle by the men of the 442nd RCT to prove their loyalty had ended. However, a vital mission would remain for Japanese-Americans in the postwar period—to achieve their full rights as American citizens.

'Go For Broke' Banner Proclaims the Return of 442nd RCT to Hawaii. U.S. Army Signal Corps. August 9, 1946. Source: Hawaii War Records Depository.

(Above) **Go For Broke Monument**. (Below) **Inscription on the Go For Broke Monument**.
Courtesy of Go for Broke National Education Center. Near Little Tokyo, Los Angeles, California.

Chapter 3

from 1945~

'Americans All' Booth at the Pan-Pacific Industrial Exposition, Los Angeles. Sponsored by the anti-racial civic organizations in cooperation with the War Relocation Authority (WRA). (Continuous motion picture showing *Nisei in Action* and *World We Want to Live In*.) September 6, 1945. Los Angeles, California. Photographer: Iwasaki, Hikaru. Courtesy of The Bancroft Library. University of California, Berkeley.

CONTENTS

Following the war, in an effort to insure that the courage and sacrifice of the *Nisei* soldiers was not in vain, the Japanese-American community forged a campaign to win civil liberties and equal rights based upon the achievements of the Japanese-American military units. Many ordinary citizens, together with Japanese-American leaders, struggled behind the scenes to repeal the various discriminatory statutes, achieve eligibility for naturalization, and revise the immigration laws.

People Who Made a Difference

On July 15, 1946, President Harry Truman awarded the Seventh Presidential Citation to the 442nd Regimental Combat Team (RCT) in a ceremony held in the White House Rose Garden. In his speech, the President remarked:

> You fought not only the enemy, but you fought prejudice—and you have won.[1]

The 442nd RCT consisted of fewer than 4,500 soldiers, but it suffered a casualty rate of more than 300%. Members of the 442nd RCT, together with the 100th Infantry Battalion, received an amazing 18,143 individual decorations.[2] In fact, Japanese-American regiments, in terms of their size and duration of military service, recorded both the highest per capita casualty and decoration rates in American military history.[3] Of the great number of repatriated regiments, the Japanese-American regiments were the only ones personally honored in this manner by the President.[4]

Chapter 3

Beginning in 1944, the year before the war ended, an increasing number of media outlets, including *Time*, reported on the extraordinary contributions and sacrifices made by Japanese-American soldiers. This led to support that was more vocal for the members of the Japanese-American community. Furthermore, Congressmen Walter Judd (R-MN) and Thomas Lane (D-MA) introduced media excerpts relating to the distinguished service of Japanese-American troops into the Congressional Record.[5] In March 1944, Lieutenant Colonel James Hanley, of the 2nd Battalion of the 442nd RCT, wrote a letter of complaint to Charles Pierce, editor of his hometown newspaper, *The Mandan Daily Pioneer,* that had printed a satirical column about the Japanese-Americans, commenting:

> A squib in a paper makes the statement that there are some good Jap-Americans in this country but it didn't say where they are buried.

Colonel Hanley's letter was printed in the newspaper on March 31, 1944:

> Yes, Charlie, I know where there are some GOOD Japanese-Americans. There are around 5,000 of them in this unit. You, the Hood River American Legion Post, the Hearst paper, and others make one wonder just what we are fighting for. I certainly hope it isn't to endorse racial prejudice. Come on over here, Charlie, and I'll show you where 'some good Japanese-Americans' are buried.[6]

The American Legion Post mentioned that Colonel Hanley's letter had, in fact, posted a list of soldiers from Hood River in its honor roll of veterans, displaying it in the town center, but it chose to omit the names of the 16 local Japanese-American servicemen.[7] They also placed advertisements in local newspapers asking Japanese-Americans who still owned property in Hood River to sell out or to not return. A major controversy ensued. For example, *The Stars and Stripes*, the Army's official periodical, reported

on the Hood River incident and said those who were most outraged were none other than the American soldiers of the 36th and 45th Divisions who had fought alongside the 442nd RCT. Among them were soldiers of the "Lost Battalion," whose lives were saved by their Japanese-American comrades. These soldiers initiated a campaign to send letters of protest to President Franklin Roosevelt, to U.S. congressmen, to the media and to the headquarters of the American Legion.[8] As a result of the media coverage, American Legion Posts across the nation directed the Hood River Legion Post to include the names of the Japanese-American soldiers.

Although deep-rooted anti-Japanese sentiment was by no means entirely eradicated, the number of Americans who expressed support for Japanese-Americans steadily increased, as word of the Japanese-American regiments and their remarkable contribution to the war effort became more widespread. As subsequently reported in the media, some of the strongest support came from the soldiers, who risked their lives alongside the Japanese-American fighting men.

Staff Sergeant Henry H. Gosho. Gosho served 16 months in the Burma-India Theater attached to Army Combat Intelligence with General Frank Merrill's Marauders until April 1945. He volunteered for duty at Camp Savage in November 1942, while living at the Minidoka Relocation Camp. His was the first unit to be created from Camp Savage, which left the United States for duty in June 1943. Photographer: Iwasaki, Hikaru. Denver, Colorado. April 21, 1945. Courtesy of The Bancroft Library. University of California, Berkeley.

For example, *The Stars and Stripes* reported the following incident: When a returnee from the 442nd RCT entered a bar in a Texas town wearing his uniform, the bartender shouted, "Get that Jap out of here," and attempted to throw him out. As it turns out some veterans from a Texas unit happened to be in the bar at the time. They ended up dragging the bartender from behind the counter, gave him a good beating, and served the Japanese-American soldier themselves.[9]

Senator Daniel Inouye, who fought in the European theater as a member of the 442nd RCT and lost his right arm in combat, stopped by a barbershop in San Francisco on the way back to Hawaii. He was still in uniform, but the owner of the shop refused to cut his hair.[10] Similar incidents involving other returning *Nisei* soldiers were happening all over the United States. The media coverage of these incidents brought to light the need for support for Japanese-American soldiers. Therefore, various support groups emerged. A front-page article in the *San Francisco Chronicle* (dated July 20, 1954) detailed the actions of 28 Pacific theater returnees attending a college in Stockton, California, who condemned anti-Japanese racism by restoring a vandalized Japanese graveyard and swearing to maintain it until the Japanese-American soldiers returned home.[11]

The meritorious record of Japanese-Americans in the European theater first came to be known by word of mouth — that is to say, accounts related by Americans who fought alongside the Japanese-American units ended up gaining broad media coverage. Thanks to this, and to the politicians who made these accounts part of the public record, their many contributions came to be acknowledged.

Riley Allen, Editor-in-Chief of the *Honolulu Star-Bulletin*, never allowed the use of the term "Jap" to appear in his paper during the war, even in reports on the Pearl Harbor attacks. Two Japanese-American editors working for the paper at the time of the attacks kept their jobs even after the war was declared. At that time, 12 *Honolulu Star-Bulletin* editors, including the two Japanese-American editors, petitioned to use the word "Jap," on the front page since all the other newspapers were doing so. Allen refused to allow this. For the duration of the war, he insisted on using the term "Japanese."[12]

Supreme Court Challenges

In December 1944, Lieutenant General John Dewitt, Western Defense Commander, a man known for making disparaging remarks against the Japanese-Americans[13] was relieved of his post and Major General Henry Pratt assumed it. On December 17, Public Proclamation No. 21 rescinded the evacuation orders which was set to go into effect on January 2, 1945.[14] On October 18, the War Relocation Authority (WRA) announced that it would close the internment camps by the end of 1945 and would conclude its mission by June 1946.[15] On this same day, decisions in two important cases concerning internment were handed down by the Supreme Court.

United States Supreme Court Building. Source: National Park Service.

In the case of *Korematsu v. United States* (323 U.S. 214, 1944), Fred Korematsu, who had been arrested for refusing to abide by the evacuation order, sued the United States, alleging that his imprisonment was unconstitutional. The Supreme Court rejected Korematsu's claim, declaring that in time of war, the needs of the nation superseded the rights of the individual. However, the Supreme Court found the government's actions unconstitutional in the other case, *Ex Parte Mitsuye Endo* (323 U.S. 283, 1944). Here, the plaintiff, Endo, did not refuse to surrender for the evacuation, but instead sued the United States after her internment, claiming it to be unconstitutional. The Supreme Court ruled:

Chapter 3

Whatever power the WRA may have to obtain other classes of citizens, the WRA had no authority to subject citizens who are concededly loyal to its leave procedure.[16]

The difference between *Korematsu* and *Endo* hinges upon the difference between criminal and civil cases. In addition to Korematsu, plaintiffs Gordon Hirabayashi and Minoru Yasui also protested the unconstitutionality of Executive Order 9066 and similar orders by violating evacuation and curfew regulations, resulting in criminal charges in all three of their cases. The Endo case, however, did not concern criminal conduct. This case had its origins in questionnaires sent by the California State Personnel Board to its Japanese-American staff.

According to the law, State civil servants had to be American citizens. With the onset of war, though, the Board attempted to manufacture grounds to dismiss Japanese-American employees by inquiring about their loyalty to the emperor, knowledge of the Japanese language, past visits to Japan, and other potentially incriminating matters. California Attorney General Earl Warren (who later became the Governor of California and the Chief Justice of the United States) warned that such dismissals were unconstitutional, and so the attempt failed. Nonetheless, some state senators began calling for the dismissal of Japanese-American staff, which engendered a level of anxiety and insecurity among the *Nisei* employees.

When the evacuation was initiated, the State Personnel Board suspended all of the Japanese-Americans employed in Sacramento, charging them with offenses such as neglect of duty, fraudulent employment application, and ineligibility for civil service. In response, the Japanese-American Citizens League (JACL) brought the matter to the attention of James Purcell, a San Francisco attorney favorably disposed toward Japanese-Americans, seeking to restore the rights of the suspended employees. However, the evacuation and internment orders were carried out before they could act. Consequently, Purcell

Earl Warren, 14ᵗʰ United States Chief Justice. In office October 5, 1953-June 23, 1969. Photographer: Harris & Ewing Photography Firm. Courtesy of the Harvard Law School Library Legal Portrait Project.

set out to find an internee who had not been charged with any crime, on whose behalf he could file a *habeas corpus* petition in federal court.

In 1944, Mitsuye Endo was a 22-year old woman living in Sacramento, an employee of the California Department of Motor Vehicles. Raised as a Christian, she could neither read nor speak Japanese, had never been to Japan, and had a brother who was serving in the U.S. Army. Though Purcell would not actually meet Endo until after the case was heard, he managed, through correspondence, to obtain her consent to file suit on her behalf. When the suit was filed, the WRA offered Endo permission to move outside the restricted area as an amicable settlement. Endo, however, chose to remain in the internment camp in order to challenge the constitutionality of the internment order in the Supreme Court. Though this would prove to be the most significant and successful challenge to the constitutionality of the evacuation and internment, Endo never actually appeared in court during the proceedings, and she made no public appearances even after her legal victory.[17]

The JACL played a significant role in the struggle for equality for Japanese-Americans after the war. When war broke out, the JACL was a small organization with a handful of members—

the young *Nisei* in their twenties, for the most part. The JACL leadership included Saburo Kido, who served as Chair, and Mike Masaoka, National Secretary and Field Executive. Since the *Issei* leadership group had all been rounded up by the FBI at the beginning of the war, the effort was left to the young *Nisei* to chart their course as Japanese-Americans in a time of great turmoil. Their decision to appeal to the Japanese-American community for compliance with the internment order did not receive unanimous support from the ranks. However, they remained steadfast in their resolve, and following the war, they became leaders of the Japanese-American community. The JACL played an active role in repealing several anti-Japanese laws and gaining civil rights for Japanese-Americans.

In addition to having the talented leadership of Kido, a successful lawyer, and Masaoka, a distinguished lobbyist, the JACL engaged the services of numerous other lawyers such as James Purcell and Dean Acheson, who would later be appointed Secretary of State by President Truman.

Repealing the Alien Land Act

The JACL supported Fred Ōyama in challenging the Alien Land Act, in *Ōyama v. State of California* (332 U.S. 633, 1948) and won the case. The suit stemmed from Ōyama's ownership of a farm in California that his father, an *Issei*, had purchased on his behalf when the son was still a minor. However, since Ōyama was a minor at the time, the land became a target for forfeiture by the state government. As mentioned in Chapter 1, there was a California law prohibiting first-generation immigrants from owning land in the state. For this reason, many people purchased land on behalf of second-generation relatives, who were U.S. citizens. However, during the internment of Japanese-Americans, in cases where the *Nisei* owners were minors, their lands were subject to forfeiture because the de facto owners were *Issei*.

Deciding to back the Ōyamas, the JACL appealed to the Supreme Court, entrusting the case to Dean Acheson (previous Undersecretary of State), who became Secretary of State the following year. Since Japanese-Americans had just been released from the internment camps, both Ōyama and the JACL were short of funds. Acheson agreed to serve without a fee as Chief Counsel in oral arguments on the case.[18] On January 19, 1948, the court decided in Ōyama's favor. However, the victory would only be a personal one for Ōyama. While the plaintiff did indeed prevail based on the facts of this particular case, the Alien Land Act itself was not declared unconstitutional and continued to be enforced.

Sometime thereafter, Sei Fujii, owner and publisher of the *Kashū Mainichi* newspaper, purchased a parcel of land in the eastern section of Los Angeles and intentionally subjected it to government forfeiture for the express purpose of challenging the constitutionality of the Alien Land Act. Fujii, who was *Issei*, hence an "Alien Ineligible to Citizenship," claimed that the

Returnees Arrive in Los Angeles by Bus from Manzanar Relocation Center. Some to resume residence in that city and others to board the train for other parts of the country. Two busloads came in, with 41 people (men, women and children; both Issei and Nisei). Six are staying to relocate in Los Angeles. All the others are going East, mostly to Philadelphia, New Jersey, Minnesota and Chicago. They took the first train out the same afternoon. May 22, 1945. Los Angeles, California. Photographer: Mace, Charles E. Courtesy of The Bancroft Library. University of California, Berkeley.

Chapter 3

forfeiture of his real estate was unconstitutional. In 1952, he won his case in the California Supreme Court.[19] At the time, the JACL considered Fujii's suit too risky, and attempted instead to secure a citizens' repeal of the Alien Land Act through initiative. Since such legislation had come through the initiative process, then moves for revision or repeal had to undergo the same process. JACL Leader Masaoka decided to challenge the ruling by purchasing land, building a house on it with government benefits from his brother Ben's death while rescuing the "Lost Batallion," and transferring the land to his widowed *Issei* mother. He instituted proceedings after completing the transfer contract, claiming it to be entirely unjust that "giving land to one's mother becomes illegal just because one is Japanese."[20] As a result, the Los Angeles Superior Court ruled in 1950 that the law was unconstitutional.

The state government then appealed to the California Supreme Court, and the lower court's decision was upheld. Then in 1956, the JACL appealed to the state legislature to put the repeal of the Alien Land Act to an initiative and in November of that year, California Proposition 13 passed and the law was indeed repealed by a large majority of the electorate.[21] It took 43 years (initially legislated in 1913) for the Alien Land Act to be repealed. However, the fact that the repeal was made possible through the active participation of the citizenry who cast their votes in favor of the initiative holds great significance.

At the close of World War II, the aggressive and virulent anti-Japanese movement that had lasted 43 years finally began to subside. Japanese-Americans were treated as second-class citizens before the war and as hostile aliens during the war. However, the decade following the war witnessed a dramatic change, with Japanese-Americans receiving a strong endorsement through the electoral process by a majority of the American public. This change in sentiment was due largely to the courage and sacrifice of the Japanese-American military units. However, one must also acknowledge the role of the WRA, which strived to educate the public about these units by dispatching returnees from the 442nd RCT and Military Intelligence Service (MIS) throughout the country and by holding press conferences.

As mentioned in Chapter 2, successive directors of the WRA had supported the reintegration of Japanese-Americans into society, even during the war. The organization also promoted social acceptance of the returnees by making the achievements of Japanese-American soldiers known, and provided material support with a sum of $25 to each released internee when the camps were closed. In addition, the WRA placed welfare department staff in the internment camps to provide support to internees who had lost their homes. Funds were provided for the purchase of household necessities and as a subsidy to cover the first month's rent.[22]

West Coast field offices encouraged church groups and other organizations interested in assisting Japanese-Americans to establish hostels as temporary accommodations for re-settlers. Approximately a dozen hostels were setup in principal West Coast cities. They also provided these sponsors with surplus equipment such as bedding, cooking utensils, and other necessary items for the relocation centers.[23]

Exterior of a Pasadena Hostel. This is where returnees, chiefly from Gila River, Colorado River, and Manzanar, were temporarily housed. Seen in the garden are Miss Katherine Fanning (left), chairwoman of the returnee committee of the Friends of the American Way, and Miss Marjorie Noble, executive secretary. The Pasadena Hostel is known as friendly, cozy and conveniently located. Returnees stay there while seeking permanent housing. Men, women, and children are accommodated in home-like surroundings. May 25,1945. Pasadena, California. Photographer: Mace, Charles E. Courtesy of The Bancroft Library. University of California, Berkeley.

With the end of the Pacific War in August 1945, the WRA's Dillon Myer sent the following message to the Japanese-American soldiers:

> I want you to know that we are going to see that your families in the centers get every kind of help they need so that they can resettle successfully, even without your help, and so that you can come back to find them out of the barracks and in the kinds of places which you can call home.[24]

Despite being in charge of the organization that oversaw the internment, Director Myer remained opposed to the internment policy. His message aptly reflects his empathy for, and understanding of, the internees' situation.

Miss Mae Tanaka of Topaz is shown in the Property Section of the Public Housing Authority. Miss Tanaka is employed as a secretary of the FPHA and is residing in San Francisco. Her brother Yosh Tanaka is stationed in Texas in the U.S. Army. July 23, 1945. San Francisco, California. Photographer: Iwasaki, Hikaru. Courtesy of The Bancroft Library. University of California, Berkeley.

Returning to Normalcy

The government's support could not change public sentiment overnight. This would require a slow, incremental shift in public attitude and opinion. While there were indeed communities that warmly welcomed the returning Japanese-American internees, many remained staunchly opposed to their resettlement.

For instance, the bereaved family of Sergeant Kazuo Masuda, a casualty of the Northern Italian campaign, met stern resistance when they tried to move back into their home in Santa Ana, near Los Angeles. When Sergeant Masuda's older sister, Mary, came to inspect the house, some local residents threatened her, claiming that if the family were to move in, they would be killed. When they made burial plans for their fallen kin, the city refused to give them permission to bury the ashes.[25] These events took place after the war in Europe had ended, at a point when Sergeant Masuda's two brothers were still in the army.

A few days before Sergeant Masuda was killed in action, he told Masaoka, who was in charge of public relations, that he was convinced if the men of the 442nd RCT could prove their worthiness in the battlefield, it would create a better place for his family in the United States.[26] Sergeant Masuda's words stood for the feelings of all Japanese-American soldiers. The government, in other words, regarded Sergeant Masuda as an ideal vehicle to alleviate hostile public opinion against Japanese-Americans.

In this connection, the military authorities used the threat against Sergeant Masuda's family to their favor. After General Joseph Stilwell pinned the Distinguished Service Cross on Mary Masuda in a simple ceremony on the porch of her small farmhouse in Orange County, a ceremony was held at the Santa Ana Bowl. General Stilwell said this at the ceremony:

> The amount of money, the color of one's skin does not make a measure of Americanism.

After that, an officer who was also a young movie actor delivered a speech. This was none other than Captain Ronald Reagan. He spoke of the *Nisei* soldiers' sacrifice by saying, "The blood that has soaked the sands is of one color."[27] This turned out to be his very first political speech.

In direct opposition to its original policy of mass internment, the Army now took the initiative to aggressively promote a postwar return

Chapter 3

George Tanaka and Father A. Sterns at the San Francisco General Hospital. Mr. Tanaka and Father Sterns, philosophers and friends for the past 20 years, are happy to be working together again. Father Sterns states, "Our work is parallel, my work is with souls and George's with flowers, both for the welfare and comfort of the patients." Mr. Tanaka, of Topaz and a native San Franciscan, began to work for the hospital in 1926 and prior to evacuation held the position of head nurseryman. At the outbreak of war, he was given an indefinite leave of absence and was reinstated to his position of head nurseryman upon his return to San Francisco. Mr. Tanaka says that his family was too large to remember the names of all the members in the Army. August 3, 1945. San Francisco, California. Photographer: Iwasaki, Hikaru. Courtesy of The Bancroft Library. University of California, Berkeley.

and reintegration of Japanese-Americans to their respective communities. Truman, President and Commander-in-Chief, took an active role in dealing with civil rights problems and issues, such as equal employment opportunities. In addition, he is said to have been critical of the Civilian Exclusion Orders against Japanese-Americans. In April 1946, President Truman submitted to Congress proposed legislation to establish an Evacuation Claims Commission, which would adjudicate claims for losses incurred by the internees in the process of relocation. In addition, in June 1946, he signed Executive Order 9742, which dissolved the WRA.[28]

California Attorney General Warren was among the hard-liners supporting the wartime relocation of Japanese-Americans. However, once he became Governor, he voiced criticism of the anti-Japanese movements. On January 21, 1945, *The San Francisco Examiner* reported attacks upon Japanese-American returnees from the internment camps—a farmhouse dynamited, a case of arson, and individuals shot at. On the same page, there was an article on Governor Warren's press conference, where he openly criticized the anti-Japanese movements, observing:

> I can't conceive of people who claim to be good Americans trying to further the war efforts doing of the kind.[29]

Governor Warren appealed to the public to show tolerance and goodwill in accepting the Japanese-American returnees back to the community.

In 1949, a noteworthy event occurred at the U.S. national swimming competition in Los Angeles. Despite the fact that Japan was under allied occupation, special permission was granted

Rohwer Special Roaring into Sacramento Monday Morning. A special train of seven cars brought some 450 Japanese-American residents of California back to their homes after over three years at the Rohwer Center of the War Relocation Authority, McGehee, Arkansas. Several officers of the WRA at Sacramento, as well as, Robert Allison, Assistant Relocation Officer at the Rohwer Center, accompanied the returnees. All passengers reported a satisfactory and uneventful trip during the 2,000 miles. They traversed over four lines of railways with equipment varying from a modern cafe car to antiquated wooden coaches of the gaslight era. However, there were no complaints from the returnees, numbering young, old, and babes in arms, with a tourist sleeper reserved for the aged and the few who were ill. Enroute, several crowded troop trains-in some cases bearing GI's newly returned from the South Pacific—met with the Rohwer Special on sidings. All report that hearty and cordial greetings were exchanged. Disembarking at various stations between Sacramento and Los Angeles, the returnees found many friends to greet them, both Caucasian and Japanese-Americans. July 30, 1945. Los Angeles, California. Photographer: Iwasaki, Hikaru. Courtesy of The Bancroft Library. University of California, Berkeley.

for Japanese swimmers to compete in the games. It was authorized by General Douglas MacArthur himself.[30] Incredibly enough, two Japanese athletes ended up setting new world records, one after the other. On this occasion, Governor Warren paid special tribute to these Japanese swimmers who monopolized the gold, silver, and bronze medals in the 1500-meter freestyle event. It was Hironoshin Furuhashi, the "Flying Fish of Fujiyama," who truly distinguished himself, setting the world record in the preliminaries and winning the finals.

In the area of discriminatory legislation, there was Section 990 of the California Department of Fish and Game Code, enacted by the State Fish and Game Commission, which regulated the issuance of commercial fishing licenses. In its ruling, enacted during the war, "alien Japanese" would be ineligible to receive commercial fishing licenses. This law shared much with the Alien Land Act. After the war, the term "aliens ineligible for citizenship" replaced "alien Japanese." This prohibited *Issei* from resuming their commercial fishing, and one such individual, Torao Takahashi, challenged the law in the Superior Court of Los Angeles County and won the case.

However, the State government appealed to the California Supreme Court where the lower court ruling was reversed. Undaunted, Takahashi appealed to the U.S. Supreme Court, where the 1948 decision, rendered in *Takahashi v. Fish and Game Commission* (334 U.S. 410, 1948), went in his favor.[31] In this manner, the Supreme Court made a number of decisions in the immediate postwar period that declared racial discrimination to be unconstitutional.

Although the American ethos proudly extolled equality and freedom, the gap between the cherished ideal and harsh reality was great. The Americans experienced chronic and deep-rooted problems in the area of civil rights since the nation's founding; one must keep in mind that nearly a century elapsed from its founding before President Abraham Lincoln issued the Emancipation Proclamation, and another hundred

Returning Home From Heart Mountain Relocation Center. Reversing the scenes of nearly three years ago, more than 11,000 evacuees are bidding goodbye to newly made friends and neighbors. They begin their return to their homes, or depart for new homes to work throughout the nation. April 1945. Heart Mountain, Wyoming. Photographer: Kubo, Yone. Courtesy of The Bancroft Library. University of California, Berkeley.

years passed before Martin Luther King, Jr. spearheaded the modern civil rights movement.

The South maintained its many forms of racial discrimination well into the 20th century. It was the Supreme Court decision in *Brown v. Board of Education* (347 U.S. 483, 1954) that legally mandated the end of discrimination. In its landmark decision, the Court declared that racial segregation in schools was inherently unequal and therefore unconstitutional. One could argue that the legal precedents, which years earlier had gone in favor of Japanese-Americans, built the groundwork for Brown.

Racial discrimination is a problem by no means limited to African-Americans or Asian-Americans. Its roots lie much deeper. In a nation with a Caucasian majority, it is not easy to alter attitudes without a committed and concerted expression of support from this majority. In this regard, it needs to be acknowledged that many Americans did indeed reach out, often behind the scenes, to help Japanese-Americans gain their rights shortly after the war ended.

Naturalization Rights for Parents

Following the war, the JACL gave its highest priority to amending immigration laws in order to give their aging *Issei* parents naturalization rights. The Anti-Discrimination Committee, which was

Chapter 3

established to oppose Proposition 15 in California (the measure to validate various amendments to the Alien Land Law), was the vehicle to raise funds for this effort. Mike Masaoka, the director of the committee, embarked upon a lobbying campaign.[32] This resulted in JACL gaining the cooperation of Congressmen Judd and Francis Walter (D-PA). In 1948, Congressman Judd submitted an anti-discriminatory Bill for the Equality in Naturalization and Immigration (#1030). At the hearings for this bill, General Mark Clark, Commander of the Army's 5th Division, and Assistant Secretary John McCloy who had helped override Army opposition to the creation of a Japanese-American combat team (442nd RCT), praised the achievements and sacrifices of the *Nisei* soldiers, and urged that their parents, through this legislation, be granted naturalization rights.[33] However, the Judd bill did not pass through Congress at this point.

Congressman Judd submitted another bill (HR 199) in 1949. Dillon Myer, former director of the WRA, wrote in support of this bill, stating that:

> ...many of those young Americans of Japanese ancestry volunteered for service in the American Army, either for intelligence work in the Pacific or as members of the 442nd RCT, with the knowledge that their parents could not fall heir to any lands they might own, in case they were killed in battle. Japanese aliens in relocation centers, many of whom had lived in this country for 30 or 40 years or more, dared not swear allegiance to the United States during the period of war for fear of losing their Japanese citizenship, with full knowledge that they could not attain American citizenship under our laws.[34]

The bill passed through the House, but it failed to gain Senate approval.

In 1950, it was Congressman Walter's turn to submit a bill (H.J. Res. 238). This time, the bill gained the approval of both houses, after much

seesawing over the matter of racial discrimination. However, President Truman vetoed the Walter bill.[35] What concerned President Truman was its Internal Security clause, inserted during the congressional debate on the bill. This clause, with its implications for immigration, was a delicate problem in the context of the time, when the United States had just entered the Cold War and Senator Joseph McCarthy (R-WI) was pushing through his "Red Purge." President Truman, however, was adamantly opposed to any form of discrimination.

In 1951, Senator Pat McCarran (D-NV) submitted a bill in the Senate, and Congressmen Walter, Judd, Sydney Yates (D-IL), and George Miller (D-CA) co-submitted a bill in the House. The Walter bill passed in the House on April 25, and the McCarran bill was passed in the Senate on May 21. The two bills were debated jointly and passed as HR 5678 on June 9.[36] It later became known as the McCarran-Walter Act.

While HR 5678 did in fact eliminate racial discrimination in immigration and naturalization, it also gave the Department of Justice the power to deport naturalized immigrants if they engaged in destructive activities.[37] With an unequal immigration quota and only 185 Japanese immigrants allowed per year,[38] this was far from the sort of bill the Japanese-American community had hoped for. However, this bill did resolve the urgent issue of granting naturalization rights to the aging *Issei*. Consequently, the JACL decided to support the bill, and it engaged in active lobbying. Congress passed the bill, but President Truman, again, vetoed it.[39] His rationale was twofold: The bill stipulated unequal immigration quotas, and the details of the Internal Security clause were too complicated.

Congress was about to recess, and time was running out for the *Issei*. It was clear that waiting for the perfect bill to pass the next congressional session made little sense, so Masaoka headed up a JACL campaign to override President Truman's veto. This would require a two-thirds majority vote in each house. Those in the House who supported the bill, including Congressman Walter, touted the Japanese soldiers' achievements in their attempt to garner support. Their efforts paid off, as they succeeded in gaining the needed two-thirds majority. The Senate, however, was another story, and success appeared doubtful. Here Masaoka's lobbying efforts moved into high gear, as he called on senators positively disposed toward Japanese-Americans but who supported the veto because of the Internal Security clause. Masaoka prevailed upon them to abstain.[40] In the end, the Senate vote was 57 in favor, 26 against—a two-thirds majority. Hence, the veto was overridden.[41] Thirteen senators were absent and did not cast a vote.

Thus, *Issei* received the right to be naturalized under the law, and immigration from Japan prohibited since 1924 was finally permitted, albeit in rather small numbers. It took some 80 years, culminating in a civil war, for African-Americans to gain naturalization and, it took another 82 years for Japanese-Americans to gain naturalization rights. The McCarran-Walter Act was put into effect on December 24, 1952, whereupon thousands of *Issei* immediately applied to be naturalized. Naturalizations of *Issei* jumped from 40 in 1952 to 6,750 in 1954 and 7,593 in 1955. The average number of years in which the *Issei* lived in the United States prior to naturalization was 38.6 years (1955).[42]

In 1952, the U.S.-Japan relationship entered a new phase. Though a peace treaty with Japan was signed in 1951, it was on April 28 of 1952 that the Allied occupation formally ended, the peace treaty was put into effect, and the U.S.-Japan Security Treaty was officially enacted.

JACL Leader Mike Masaoka
A Proud American of Japanese Ancestry

"Although some individuals may discriminate against me, I shall never become bitter or lose faith, for I know that such persons are not representative of the majority of the American people."

"The Japanese American Creed" read by Mike Masaoka before the United States Senate and printed in the Congressional Record, May 9, 1941

The most important item on the agenda at the JACL National Convention in November 1942, was whether or not the members should submit a formal request to the government to reinstate the Selective Service Act for Japanese-Americans.[1] When Japanese-Americans were forced into the detention camps and treated as "enemy aliens," their resentment toward the government grew. However, willfully ignoring these racist policies was Mike Masaoka. Acting as National Secretary and Field Executive of the JACL, Masaoka appealed for Japanese-Americans to be granted the right to die for their country.

Masaoka was born in 1915 in Fresno, California, and grew up in Salt Lake City, Utah. He graduated from the University of Utah in 1937 and a few years later took the position of National Secretary of JACL.[2]

Mike Masaoka. Courtesy of California State University, Sacramento. Library. Department of Special Collections and University Archives.

Chapter 3

When Masaoka heard about the formation of a military unit that was to be composed of Japanese-Americans, he volunteered on the spot and became the first to enlist. Because of his skills, Masaoka was assigned to Japanese-American soldiers to be under his guidance, he assigned duties to these soldiers as follows: Asking them to draft commendations to be given to soldiers fighting on the frontlines, sending notices of the commendations to the American press, and recording the history of the Japanese-American regiment.

> "If we can leave behind excellent records, this will be
> useful politically after the war."[3]

At this time, Masaoka was already convinced that this was a way in which the postwar freedom of Japanese-Americans could be secured. For this purpose, Masaoka believed that it was vital to have an organized plan.

The number of military decorations received by Japanese-American soldiers exceeded 18,000, also signifying the number of sacrifices made by the soldiers. However, Masaoka did not let their deaths go unnoticed. Masaoka's careful foresight and political savvy allowed the soldiers' feats of valor to be used as tactics after the war. In the year 2000, the government admitted that the selections for the highest military decorations were tainted by racism.[4] Regardless of the depth of sacrifices made by Japanese-American soldiers, without Masaoka's planning and leadership, it is doubtful that their distinguished military service would have been recorded.

Masaoka played a key role as the JACL lobbyist in Washington, D.C., in the various legislative actions such as the McCarran-Walter Act, which benefited Japanese-Americans in the post-war era. In 1963, Masaoka participated in Reverend Martin Luther King, Jr.'s March on Washington, representing JACL.[5] However, due to Masaoka's agreement with the government's program of interning Japanese-Americans, and his support for reopening the draft, there remained those who could not cast aside their ill feelings for Masaoka.

In order to prove his loyalty to the country, he claimed to be 200% American.[6] In 1991, Mike Masaoka passed away in Washington, D.C., where he was working as a lobbyist.

Hawaii's Admittance as a State

The inclusion of the Territory of Hawaii in 1959 as the fiftieth U.S. state had profound implications for the Japanese-American community. It bears noting that there were quite a few congressmen opposed to Hawaiian statehood. For one, it would be the only state with an Asian-American — specifically, a Japanese-American majority. However, *Nisei* congressmen who distinguished themselves in Hawaii after the war cooperated with Congressman Judd and others who favored the statehood initiative.

The number of *Nisei* congressmen increased rapidly after the war for two chief reasons: the GI Bill and the "Democratic Revolution" of 1954. The GI Bill provided veterans with educational expenses, and many Japanese-American veterans took advantage of its benefits to get a college education. A number of them held important posts in Hawaii after graduation. An individual named John Anthony Burns (a.k.a. Jack Burns) carried out a "Democratic Revolution" to leverage this phenomenon.[43] Up until that point, Hawaiian politics had been dominated by a group of Republicans who were supported by the

Hawaiian Politicians. After the "Democratic Revolution" of 1954, 13 out of 33 members of congress elected into the Territorial House of Representatives in Hawaii were *Nisei* Japanese-Americans. Source: Hawaii House of Representatives.

The Pursuit of Freedom and Equality

Raise your right hand and repeat after me," intoned Speaker Rayburn. The hush deepened as the young congressman raised not his right hand but his left and he repeated the oath of office. There was no right hand, Mr. Speaker. It had been lost in combat by that young American soldier in World War II. Who can deny that, at that moment, a ton of prejudice slipped quietly to the floor of the House of Representatives.[46]

In the 1962 election, Spark Matsunaga was elected to Congress and Daniel Inouye to the Senate. A second generation Chinese-American, Hiram Fong, also won a senatorial post. The JACL then appealed to these three congressmen to rectify the immigration quotas of the McCarran-Walter Act.[47] The reform legislation was enacted in 1965, when President Lyndon Johnson signed a bill establishing a new Immigration Act, which abolished the national origins quota system, eliminating national origin, race, and ancestry as a basis for immigration to the United States.[48] Thus, the inequities built into the McCarran-Walter Act, which had gone unamended for nearly a decade, were resolved in short order thanks largely to the efforts of these Japanese-American congressmen. The fact of Japanese-American politicians emerging so quickly and so effectively as voices for change stands in dramatic contrast to the pre-war situation, with all of its difficulties and pitfalls.

large plantation owners. Burns, a Honolulu police officer who was chairing the Democratic Party of territorial Hawaii, set in motion a major reformist program by persuading a number of Japanese-Americans to run in the 1954 elections. The Democratic Party swept the elections, claiming 22 of the 30 seats in the Territorial House of Representatives, and even defeating the incumbent Chair.[44] Among those who took office in this election were Daniel Inouye and Spark Matsunaga, prominent U.S. Senators to-be, and George Ariyoshi, who would later become the first Japanese-American governor. It is noteworthy that in the election of 1974, Burns, who went on to become the governor of Hawaii, was succeeded by Lieutenant Governor Ariyoshi.[45] Together with Burns, these Japanese-American political figures played a crucial role in the Hawaiian statehood campaign.

In 1959, Daniel Inouye was elected as the first Japanese-American congressman once Hawaii gained its statehood. When Senator Inouye arrived at the Capitol, the entire House looked on as the first Japanese-American representative from the newly admitted state of Hawaii took the oath of office. Congressman Leo O'Brien (D-NY) included the following account in the Congressional Record:

In Hawaii, Japanese-Americans were rapidly and impressively emerging on the political scene. It was Patsy Mink who in 1965 became the first Asian-American woman to be elected to the House.[49] This meant that Hawaii had fostered three Japanese-American congressmen within a 20 year span since the war's end. Moreover, a large number of Japanese-Americans in Hawaii, California, and elsewhere were appointed to judgeships at various levels, became prosecutors and public defenders, and held important posts in government and the private sector.

Keiro Senior HealthCare

The Original Founders. From Left: George Aratani, Gongoro Nakamura, Fred Wada; From Right: Edwin Hirota, Consul General Henry Shimanouchi, Frank Omatsu, Kiyo Maruyama, James Mitsumori, (Joseph Shinoda, not pictured). Photo courtesy of Keiro Senior HealthCare.

Just east of Little Tokyo, Los Angeles, is a place where Japanese seniors are able to live secure and carefree lives. The pond is stocked with *koi* and Japanese food is served in the dining hall. This impressive facility was established by the *Nisei* and ranks high among their many contributions to the Japanese-American community. It is managed by Keiro Senior HealthCare.

It all began in 1959 when Fred and Masako Wada took a self-financed trip to South America on behalf of the Japanese Olympic Committee. Their goal was to secure the votes held by the South American nations to enable Tokyo to host the 1964 Olympic Games. While in the suburbs of Sao Paulo, Brazil, they saw a big white building that looked like a hospital but turned out to be a home for elderly Jewish people.

With no such facility for the aging Japanese-Americans, Wada recognized the need and a few days later, he and his wife asked the Japanese consulate to make arrangements for them to tour the facility.[1]

Once back in the United States Wada met with *Nisei* leaders such as George Aratani to establish a non-profit Japanese-American welfare fund with the aim of creating a home for the aging *Issei*. What emerged from this planning was Keiro Nursing Home, which opened in 1969, made possible by the use of the Wada and Aratani homes as collateral.[2]

Some years later, Wada and his associates were discussing the establishment of a home for the elderly. The former Jewish Home for the Aged, in Boyle Heights, near Little Tokyo, came on the marketplace. Located on a three-acre parcel and comprised of 13 buildings, the property was offered at $6 million. Given that the buildings were dilapidated, Wada and the others hoped to negotiate a figure of $1 million, no easy sum in 1974. The group set about their fundraising and made substantial donations themselves. With the help of 600 volunteer fundraisers, they achieved their goal in five months.[3]

Keiro Senior HealthCare *continued*

On the day of the final negotiations for purchasing the Boyle Heights property, Wada was accompanied by a Japanese-American television reporter. He explained to the director of the now-defunct Jewish home that if negotiations were to break down, the reporter would go on TV with this news. The reporter would mention that all contributions would be duly refunded. It was implied that the director would appear in an unfavorable light. Having managed 17 grocery stores, Wada was a successful businessman and his skills as a negotiator had been proven through his role in helping to bring the Olympic Games to Tokyo. The matter at hand was Wada's final gamble, and his strategy paid off.

Keiro Building. Historic buildings, such as the one shown here, are among several structures on this land sold to Keiro by the Jewish Home for the Aging in 1974. Photo courtesy of Keiro Senior HealthCare.

The director not only agreed to sell the property for $1 million. He also agreed to provide an interest-free loan of $150,000 to cover initial operating expenses.[4] This was a great contribution from one minority group to another, and the Japanese Retirement Home opened in 1975.

Two years later, in 1977, Keiro Intermediate Care Facility opened, and in 1982, South Bay Keiro Nursing Home opened in Gardena. Today, Keiro Senior HealthCare consists of four care facilities, a Special Care Unit for Alzheimer's Disease and Dementia in Keiro Nursing Home, and the institute for Healthy Aging at Keiro, which help to meet the ever-changing healthcare needs of the Japanese American community. [5] In 1983, at the first meeting with the newly-appointed Consulate General of Japan, Yoshifumi Matsuda, Wada summarized the true mission of the care facility stating:

> Although we have been driven to provide user-friendly housing for elders, who had worked hard for years, this is a gift for their sons and daughters as well. That is another reason why the Retirement Home was necessary... I would like to say to people of the younger generation to work hard and not to be afraid of failing, because we will take care of all of your aging parents.[6]

His statement was a sincere expression of the passion *Nisei* leaders hold for the Japanese-American community.

Text excerpts from "Passion for the Motherland: The Man Who Brought the Olympic Games to Tokyo" by Ryo Takasugi. Published by Shincho-Bunko, October 1, 2000.

Chapter 3

At the same time, great changes were taking place in Japan. Benefited by opportunities created by the Korean War and the world market upswing of the fifties, Japan had substantially recovered from its wartime debacle by the sixties, when it was recording extraordinary rates of economic growth and productivity. The city of Tokyo had thoroughly revamped its urban infrastructure in preparation for the 1964 Tokyo Olympics.

Ryutaro Azuma, who would later head the Tokyo Municipal government, asked Fred Wada, a Nisei from Los Angeles, to lobby on behalf of Japan's selection for the 1964 Olympics. Wada, a major figure in the local food and produce trade had been responsible for taking care of the Japanese swimmers when they participated in the 1949 swimming competition mentioned earlier. Wada employed a large number of Hispanics and was himself fluent in Spanish. Armed with his language fluency, Wada and his wife embarked on a tour of Latin America, at their own expense. They succeeded in garnering support for Japan's Olympic bid.[50]

As a tangible symbol of the nation's economic and technological resurgence, the famous Bullet Train was put into service, cutting the travel time from Tokyo to Osaka to a little over three hours and spurring further economic growth.

With the impressive rise of Japan's economic power in the 1960s, Japanese trading companies, banks, and industries—especially in the electronics and automotive sector—made significant inroads in the American market. These companies were only able to send their managerial staff or other employees to the United States as a result of the new Immigration Act. In addition, it would not have been possible for them to build warehouses and factories were it not for the repeal of the Alien Land Act. Few recognize the efforts of the Japanese-Americans who spent years fighting against discriminatory laws and who were instrumental in promoting the prosperity of the Japanese companies when they arrived in the United States after the WWII. In a very important sense, the McCarran-Walter Act and the repeal of the Alien Land Act enabled Japanese companies to enter the American marketplace and made it possible for them to achieve their American dreams.

George Aratani
In Celebration of a Big Man

By Naomi Hirahara

A writer on the East Coast first introduced me to the concept of "big men" when I was working on the biography, *An American Son: The Story of George Aratani, Founder of Mikasa and Kenwood*. In order for the Japanese American community to have survived the 20th century, it needed to have big men, the writer told me.

I admit that I was at first skeptical. Japanese culture and Japanese American history are built upon the collective—how tenant farmers, gardeners, domestics, and small merchants worked together to create the foundation of our pre-World War II community. What role does a multi-national businessman fit into that formula?

Plenty, I learned, after completing research and writing a biography of this *Nisei* entrepreneur and philanthropist, George Aratani.

George Aratani: In Celebration of a Big Man *continued*

Probably the most poignant evidence of this is how during World War II the American government was going after the assets of Aratani's late father's business, Guadalupe Produce Company, a Santa Barbara County agricultural operation consisting of more than 5,000 acres. In the short run, the government won. It forced Aratani, a twenty-something man without blood parents or siblings, to sell his family business at a cut-rate price and start over. He had to do this while recovering from valley fever in the Gila River detention camp in Arizona.

This experience, of course, was not unique among Japanese Americans. Most who lived on the West Coast had to start over. But in Aratani's case, he was a business leader. Other people's livelihood, literally hundreds, depended on how he made his way back on top.

What Aratani decided to do was to use the skills and experience of the men around him. That included *Issei* and *Nisei* who had worked for Guadalupe Produce and teachers and students connected with the Military Intelligence School in Minnesota. Aratani, who spent three years studying at Keiō University in the 1930s, had a unique vantage point. He understood the importance of working with both the *Issei* and *Nisei*, Japanese nationals and Japanese Americans.

George and Sakaye Aratani Japan America Theatre. Adjacent to Japanese American Cultural and Community Center (JACCC) located in the heart of the Little Tokyo district in Los Angeles. Founded in 1971, the JACCC is one of the largest ethnic arts and cultural centers of its kind in the U.S. Its mission is to present, perpetuate, transmit, and promote Japanese and Japanese-American arts and culture to diverse audiences, and to provide a center for enhanced community programs. It is a preeminent presenter of Japanese, Japanese-American, and Asian-American performing and visual arts nationally. Courtesy of JACCC.

Aratani thought big. He thought beyond the confines of his Hollywood home and Southern California-based business and established an office in New York City. He introduced a new concept that is widely practiced today—instead of investing millions of dollars to create factories throughout the world, he would make deals with existing overseas factories to produce his products.

Even when his chinaware business was doing well, Aratani looked into other enterprises, specifically the distribution of stereo equipment. During that time, the 1960s, a time when made-in-Japan products were not valued, Aratani decided again to go against the mainstream and take a chance. Now, in addition to Mikasa, Kenwood Electronics has become a household name brand.

Aratani's devotion to his business did not keep him from getting involved in philanthropy. In the 1960s, he and his friend Fred Wada, a successful produce man, raised the seed money for Keiro Services to create a retirement home for Japanese American seniors. Aratani became involved in dozens of nonprofits, including the Japanese American National Museum, Japanese American Cultural and Community Center, Union Center for the Arts, and the Japanese American memorial commemorating *Nisei* patriotism in Washington, D.C.

Just imagine, if we did not have big men like George Aratani, we would not have Keiro Services, at least not on the same scale. We would not have a Japanese American Cultural and Community Center or a Japanese American National Museum.

George Aratani: In Celebration of a Big Man *continued*

Hundreds of Japanese Americans who have benefited from employment by either Mikasa or Kenwood would have had more struggles in securing good work. Japanese nationals and Japanese Americans would have not worked together so closely on projects that proved to be mutually beneficial.

And finally, we would not have strong business and philanthropic role models for future generations. Our collective job is now to tell others about our big men and women—to tell them about leaders like George Aratani.

Key Dates in the Life of George Aratani (taken from the book, *An American Son: The Story of George Aratani, Founder of Mikasa and Kenwood*, published by the Japanese American National Museum)

The George and Sakaye Aratani Japanese Garden at Cal Poly Pomona. This provides a living example of the respected landscaping method that will be integrated into future academic programs. Courtesy of Cal Poly Pomona, California.

※ **May 22, 1917** George Tetsuo Aratani born to Setsuo and Yoshiko Aratani in South Park, California—a community near the strawberry-growing center of Gardena.

※ **1919** Aratani family moves from South Park to Pacoima in the San Fernando Valley.

※ **1921** Setsuo Aratani family moves to Guadalupe, a town along California's Central Coast

※ **May 1923** Guadalupe Produce Company founded by Setsuo Aratani in partnership with *Issei* Naoichi Ikeda and Reiji "Ben" Kodama.

※ **June 1935** George Aratani graduates from Santa Maria Union High School.

※ **July 16, 1935** George Aratani and three *Nisei* friends set sail from San Francisco for Japan.

※ **December 20, 1935** Yoshiko Aratani dies at age 46 of asthma and heart failure.

※ **April 1936** George begins studies at Keiō University in Tokyo.

※ **May 31, 1936** Setsuo Aratani marries Masuko Matsui.

※ **April 16, 1940** Setsuo Aratani dies of meningitis at the age of 54 after contracting tuberculosis and recovering at the Maryknoll Sanatorium in Monrovia, California.

※ **Spring 1940** George Aratani attends Stanford University for two months before taking over leadership of Setsuo Aratani's businesses.

※ **December 7, 1941** Bombing of Pearl Harbor and U.S. entry into World War II.

George Aratani: In Celebration of a Big Man *continued*

※ **December 14, 1941** George Aratani officially becomes general manager of the Guadalupe Produce Company.

※ **February 19, 1942** Executive Order 9066 signed by President Franklin D. Roosevelt ordering all persons of Japanese ancestry in the Western region—citizens and aliens—into internment camps.

※ **August 1942** George and Masuko Aratani incarcerated at the Gila River concentration camp in Rivers, Arizona.

※ **February 1943** George Aratani suffers from valley fever, which recurs in 1944.

※ **June 30, 1943** Guadalupe Produce officially liquidated.

※ **May 1, 1944** George Aratani leaves Gila River for the Military Intelligence Service Language School at Camp Savage, Minnesota (later moved to Fort Snelling, Minnesota).

※ **November 23, 1944** George Aratani weds Sakaye Inouye in Minneapolis, Minnesota.

※ **January 22, 1946** First child, Donna Naomi Aratani, born to George and Sakaye Aratani in Minnesota.

※ **1946** George Aratani leaves the language school in Monterey to start his own business. He rents his first office in Little Tokyo.

※ **November 6, 1947** Second child, Linda Yoshiko Aratani, born.

※ **1949** George Aratani decides to open an East Coast office in New York City.

※ **November 1958** *Aratani v. Robert F. Kennedy* formally filed with the U.S. Court of Appeals, District of Columbia circuit, a class-action suit to recover yen deposits confiscated by the Alien Property Custodian.

※ **May 12, 1959** One of George Aratani's businesses, AMCO, holds the first postwar demonstration of a nuclear reactor in Japan at the International Science Exhibition in Tokyo.

※ **1961** Kenwood registered as the new name of Aratani's stereo company.

※ **1967** George Aratani and Fred Wada travel to Japan to raise money for Keiro Services. He later becomes involved in other philanthropic efforts for numerous organizations.

※ **1977** George Aratani inducted into the Audio Hall of Fame.

※ **1983** Sakaye Aratani receives *Kunsho* (Order of the Sacred Treasure, Fourth Order) from the Japanese government for her service on behalf of U.S.-Japan relations.

※ **1986** Trio Corporation in Japan acquires Kenwood's U.S. operation and changes its name to Kenwood.

※ **1988** George Aratani receives *Kunsho* (Order of the Sacred Treasure, Gold Rays with Rosette) from the Japanese government.

※ **1994** Mikasa, Inc. traded publicly on the New York Stock Exchange.

※ **1994** George and Sakaye Aratani establish the Aratani Foundation, an endowment that funds various nonprofit organizations serving the Japanese American and larger Asian American community.

※ **September 2000** Mikasa acquired by France-based J.G. Durand Industries, the parent company of the world's largest glass and crystal maker. George Aratani remains a major stockholder.

Chapter 3

Sansei Efforts for Redress Movement

In 1969, Senator Matsunaga played a key role in submitting a bill to repeal Title II of the Emergency Detention Act of 1950.[51] This act provided the attorney general with the power to detain individuals deemed likely to engage in acts of espionage or sabotage. The aim here was not only to prevent another internment of Japanese-Americans but also internment of any Americans in the future. The bill was overwhelmingly approved by Congress and was immediately signed by President Richard Nixon on September 25, 1971.

On February 19, 1976, the American Bicentennial, President Gerald Ford delivered "An American Promise," a presidential proclamation terminating Executive Order 9066. This day marked the 34th year since President Roosevelt issued this Executive Order, which provided the military with the power to incarcerate Japanese-Americans. President Ford began his proclamation with the following words:

> In this Bicentennial Year, we are commemorating the anniversary dates of many of the great events in American history. An honest reckoning, however, must include recognition of our national mistakes as well as our national achievements. Learning from our mistakes is not pleasant, but as a great philosopher once admonished, we must do so if we want to avoid repeating them.[52]

While it could be said that the bitter wartime memories would fade away with the demise of this potent symbol of anti-Japanese discrimination and mistreatment, a major issue remained unresolved — namely, the matter of formal governmental apology and indemnification. This issue was first raised within the Japanese-American community in 1970, and by the time of the 1978 national convention, the JACL resolved to demand a formal governmental apology for the internment, together with reparations amounting to

$25,000 for each person forcibly removed.[53] The reparations question had remained in limbo for nearly 30 years since the end of the war, owing to the fact that most *Issei* and *Nisei* regarded their internment experience with a sense of shame, and were hence reluctant to bring it up. In fact, many *Sansei* had never heard their parents say anything about the internment camps or their personal experiences there.

Beginning in the sixties, American society witnessed the rise of the Civil Rights Movement, Women's Lib, and anti-war activism. Under the sway of the prevailing "anti-establishment" mood and a prominent and assertive youth subculture, the young *Sansei* started blaming their parents' generation for having meekly acquiesced to the internment. Given this social milieu, it was only natural for the Japanese-American community to bring the reparations issue forward. The *Sansei* time had come, and young Japanese-American politicians were already making a name for themselves in the nation's capital.

Norman Mineta, who formally served as the U.S. Secretary of Transportation until his resignation in July 2006 (his was the longest tenure in this post in the history of the Department of Transportation), became a congressman in 1975, after having served as mayor of San Jose. He was the first Japanese-American to serve as mayor of a major U.S. city and the first from the mainland

The Pin Worn for Support of Japanese-American Redress/Reparation. Courtesy of California State University, Sacramento The Library.

to be elected to Congress. He was also the first Asian-American to hold a cabinet position, Secretary of Commerce, appointed by President Bill Clinton in 2000. As a boy of 10, Mineta was sent to the Heart Mountain internment camp, and he recalls how his baseball bat was taken away at the gate.[54]

Spark Matsunaga became the junior senator from Hawaii in 1976, which meant that Japanese-Americans occupied both of Hawaii's senatorial seats. Also, Patsy Mink was still representing Hawaii in the House of Representatives. Robert Matsui was elected to the House from California in 1978. Incidentally, Matsui was a six-month old infant when he and his family were interned.

By the end of the 1970s, Japanese-Americans occupied five seats in Congress. Of the five, two were veterans of the 442nd RCT and two had experienced the internment.[55] It bears noting that Senator Matsunaga was a highly decorated original member of the 100th Infantry Battalion (later attached to the 442nd RCT), wounded twice in battle, and awarded the Bronze Star.[56]

As for the redress issue, opinion within the Japanese-American community was divided. This reflects the fact that the living standard for Japanese-Americans had immeasurably improved in the postwar period. People took one of three positions on the issue. Some would just as soon forget the entire matter, being perfectly happy to get on with their lives. Some were calling for a formal apology but would not insist on reparations. Others wanted an apology and reparations. Those in the second category felt that it was impossible to place a price tag on what they had lost.

Moreover, there was the question of whether reparations, if granted, should go to individuals or to the Japanese-American community as a whole. The JACL ultimately decided to demand reparations of $25,000 for each surviving internee, since direct monetary compensation for damages is a broadly accepted tenet of American society, and the award of damages carries the force of chastisement.

Letter Sent to President Ronald Reagan

Senator Inouye presented a bill to Congress that would establish a Commission on Wartime Relocation and Internment of Civilians. The bill passed, was signed by President Jimmy Carter, and the Commission was established.[57] Its members consisted of former public servants such as Supreme Court Justice Arthur Goldberg and Senator Edward Brooke (R-MA). Judge William Marutani was its sole Japanese-American member. At this point, the JACL launched an extensive fund-raising campaign and recruited witnesses to testify at the hearings. A number of *Sansei* served as volunteers in this campaign. Just as the *Nisei* had fought on the battlefield and in the courts to win rights for their parents, now the *Sansei* fought to win redress for the wrongs inflicted upon their parents and grandparents.

Many people testified before the Commission. The wide-ranging testimony, which included the airing of wartime FBI documents, proved conclusively that Japanese-Americans had never been engaged in acts of espionage or sabotage. The Commission thus concluded that the relocation and internment had no justification based on military necessity or national security, but instead it amounted to race discrimination, war hysteria, and a failure of political leadership.[58] It recommended that there be a formal governmental apology and reparations of $20,000, among other things, to be paid to each surviving internee.

The mandated reparations figure, however, would mean a budgetary allocation of 1.5 billion dollars. Since such an outlay required Congressional approval, a Redress Legislation bill was introduced in the House—HR 442, the number chosen in memory of the 442nd RCT.[59] And by coincidence, this happened to be the 100th session of Congress. An identical bill was introduced in the Senate as well, and both passed.

However, problems still remained. In spite of (or perhaps due to) the administration's signature fiscal policy of "Reaganomics," the nation was burdened with serious and worsening deficits in trade and in the federal budget.

Chapter 3

Mamoru Eto, a Minister, Age 107. The Oldest Surviving Internee. Eto is one of the oldest recipients of the reparation check and the letter of apology from the U.S. Government at the great hall of Justice Department on October 9, 1990. Source: Department of Justice, Office of Redress Administration.[64]

Moreover, President Ronald Reagan, a dyed-in-the-wool conservative, expressed little support for this campaign from the beginning. It was feared that he might veto the bill. In order to persuade him otherwise, the Japanese-American community decided to make strategic use of the ceremony where Sergeant Masuda was awarded the Distinguished Service Cross—a ceremony that President Reagan had attended as a young officer, and where he had spoken out against racial discrimination. Sergeant Masuda's younger sister, June, sent a letter to President Reagan in which she made a point of reminding him of the speech he had made, and its noble sentiment.[60]

Despite the fact that HR 442 had passed the House in September 1987, it took a year for President Reagan to sign the bill. It was on August 10, 1988 that the President made the formal apology and signed HR 442 into law.[61] It has come to be known as the Civil Liberties Act of 1988.

Even after the 1988 Act went into effect, it was still no easy matter for the government to budget 1.5 billion dollars. Thus, the Japanese-American congressmen joined in passing a law to pay the amount over a three-year period, allocating 500 million dollars per year starting in October 1990. President George H.W. Bush signed the Appropriations bill in 1989.[62] The oldest surviving internees received their first payments and a letter of apology on October 9, 1990 in a ceremony held in the Great Hall of the Justice Department.[63]

"Righting the Wrongs" for the Future

Three wartime Supreme Court cases lost by Japanese-Americans, *Korematsu*, *Yasui*, and *Hirabayashi*, were re-examined in 1983 because petitions for writ of error *coram nobis* were filed in the respective U.S. district courts. Korematsu's case was first to be heard. The presiding Judge Marilyn Hall Patel reminded listeners that she could not reverse opinions of the Supreme Court, nor could she correct any errors of law made by the justices 40 years earlier; but, she granted the writ of error *coram nobis*, vacating Korematsu's 1944 conviction.[65] In 1998, President Clinton awarded Korematsu the Presidential Medal of Freedom, the government's highest award to a civilian. President Clinton praised Korematsu at the ceremony, stating as follows:

> In the long history of our country's constant search for justice, some names of ordinary citizens stand for millions of souls—Plessy, Brown, Parks. To that distinguished list, today we add the name of Fred Korematsu.[66]

Yasui's case was the second of the three to be heard. Unfortunately, Yasui passed away before his case was concluded, and so it died with him. As for Hirabayashi's case, in 1988, after four years of hearings and appeals, all of his wartime convictions were vacated.[67]

In 1987, as part of a commemoration of the Bicentennial of the U.S. Constitution, the Smithsonian Museum of American History presented an exhibition on Japanese-American history entitled "A More Perfect Union," which focused on the importance of civil rights protected under the law.[68] In 1999, the "Go for Broke Monument," upon which were engraved the names of more than 16,000 Japanese-American soldiers, was erected in Los Angeles' Little Tokyo.[69] Also, there is a highway interchange located near Los Angeles International Airport which was officially named the "Sadao S. Munemori Memorial Interchange." Sadao Munemori had been the only Japanese-American to receive the Congressional Medal of Honor as a soldier during World War II. Then, in recognition of the fact that the selection process for this most distinguished military honor had been racially biased, the federal government moved to rectify the situation. So, in the millennial year of 2000, 55 years after the war had ended, President Clinton awarded 22 Asian-American veterans, including Senator Inouye, the Medal of Honor. Twenty of these men were veterans of either the 442nd RCT or the 100th Infantry Battalion.[70]

In 1992, The National Japanese American Memorial Fund was established by federal statute, and plans were set in motion to construct a "Memorial to Patriotism" monument in Washington, near the Capitol. The monument honors the courage and patriotism of Japanese-American soldiers and at the same time pays respect to the nation for officially acknowledging the wrongs done to the Japanese-American community. Its impressive memorial plaques contain the names of more than 800 individuals who gave their lives for the nation, together with the names of the 10 internment camps.[71] The monument was opened to the public in June 2001,[72] and in April 2004, the Manzanar National Historic Site was opened at the former site of the Manzanar internment camp, under National Park Service management.[73] The camp's guard tower was restored in September 2005.[74] On December 5, 2006, Congress passed legislation establishing a $38 million program of National Park Service grants to restore and pay for research at all 10 camps.[75]

Throughout the 60 years since the war, the Japanese-American community has pursued civil rights and struggled against racial discrimination. In 1992 it opened the Japanese American National Museum, seeking to promote and protect the rights of not only Japanese-Americans, but of all human beings.[76] Immediately

following the attacks of September 11, 2001, the Museum issued a statement strongly cautioning against discrimination aimed at Arab-American citizens. In the words of Museum President and CEO Irene Hirano:

> It is important for the Arab-American community to know that there are those outside their own community who support them.*

The "Ansel Adams at Manzanar" exhibition was opened from November 11, 2006 to February 18, 2007, at the Japanese American National Museum in Los Angeles. Prominent photographer Ansel Adams made a number of trips to Manzanar, voluntarily and at his own expense, to capture the lives of thousands of Japanese-Americans incarcerated in the camp. His photographs were exhibited in the Museum of Modern Art in New York and also appear in his 1945 publication entitled *Born Free and Equal.* Japanese-American photographer Toyo Miyatake also preserved camp life through his numerous photographs. The Toyo Miyatake Studio, with the third generation now in charge, continues to archive images from those internment days.

The history of Japanese-Americans is not the exclusive property of this one community. It is rather an integral component of a larger American history shared by all the citizens of this great nation, which has been built upon the contribution of its many immigrant groups. The struggle for freedom and equality that has marked the 230 years of this rather brief history stands perhaps as one of the necessary growing pains of a young nation. The aftermath of "9/11" served to highlight the fragility of civil rights. Therefore, in order to ensure that we do not repeat our mistakes, it is vitally important to know our history, and to reflect upon it. To its credit, this nation has had the courage to admit its mistakes and to learn from them. May this continue to be the case, and may American history evermore continue to be told and carefully pondered.

Manzanar National Historic Site

Cemetery Shrine, Manzanar, Japanese Internment Camp. March 24, 2002
Photographer: Mayer, Daniel © 2002 GNU FDL.

Manzanar National Historic Site was established to preserve the stories of the internment of nearly 120,000 Japanese Americans during World War II and to serve as a reminder to this and future generations of the fragility of American civil liberties.

Relocations recur throughout the history of Manzanar and the Owens Valley. The Paiute and early settlers as well as Japanese Americans all were uprooted from their homes.

American Indians began utilizing the valley almost 10,000 years ago. About 1,500 years ago the Owens Valley Paiute established settlements here. They hunted, fished, collected pine nuts, and practiced a form of irrigated agriculture.

The town of Manzanar – the Spanish word for "apple orchard" – developed as an agricultural settlement beginning in 1910. Farmers grew apples, pears, peaches, potatoes, and alfalfa on several thousand acres surrounding the town.

The Los Angeles Department of Water and Power began acquiring water rights in the valley in 1905 and completed the Los Angeles Aqueduct in 1913. Land buyouts continued in the 1920s, and by 1929 Los Angeles owned all of Manzanar's land and water rights. Within five years, the town was abandoned. In the 1930s local residents pinned their economic hopes on tourism. With the onset of World War II tourism diminished.

In 1942 the U.S. Army leased 6,200 acres at Manzanar from Los Angeles to establish a center to hold Japanese Americans during World War II. Though some valley residents opposed the construction of the internment camp, others helped build it and worked here. Among these were a few Owens Valley Paiute whose own families had been exiled earlier from these lands.

National Park Service

Chapter 4

from the 1960s

Pioneers of a New Era

Aerial View of the Container Terminal at Long Beach Harbor, Long Beach, CA. Courtesy of the Port of Long Beach, California.

CONTENTS

In the midst of constant change, American society entered an era in which minorities transcended the boundaries of race. They achieved success and recognition in many fields. Minority groups experienced newfound respect. Young people within the Japanese-American community discovered their roots and laid claim to their culture and history.

Chief of Staff Eric Shinseki: The United States Army's Top Leader

Thanks to new social movements spearheaded by Reverend Martin Luther King, Jr. and others, the 1960s saw public awareness of civil rights increase dramatically. New opportunities began to open to people of all ethnicities. In the political realm, many elections resulted in victory by those previously unrepresented in government. The current Bush administration (2000-2008) is noteworthy for a Cabinet whose ethnic and racial diversity (including those of African, Asian, and Latin American descent) underscores this great societal transformation.

Former Secretary of Transportation Norman Mineta originally became a member of the Cabinet under President Bill Clinton in 2000 serving as Secretary of Commerce. However, the year before Mineta joined the Cabinet, Eric Shinseki became the first Japanese-American appointed to an elite post, when President Clinton chose him as the 34th Chief of Staff of the U.S. Army.

Chapter 4

Final Inspection at the 34th Chief of Staff of the U.S. Army Eric K. Shinseki's Retirement Ceremony. Courtesy of the National Archives.

Shinseki's grandfather immigrated to the U.S. from Hiroshima. Eric Shinseki, a *Sansei*, was born in Kauai, Hawaii, in November 1942, a year following the attack on Pearl Harbor.

He graduated from Kauai High School and entered the U.S. Military Academy at West Point. Upon his graduation in 1965, he attended Duke University and earned an M.A. in English literature. Shinseki pursued advanced military studies at the U.S. Army Command and General Staff College and the National War College. He completed two combat tours of duty in Vietnam, where he was injured twice. One of these injuries, caused by a landmine, resulted in the loss of several toes.

During the 1990s, after having been stationed in Europe for over a decade, Shinseki swiftly rose through the ranks. In 1996, he was promoted to Lieutenant General and became Army Deputy Chief of Staff for Operations. The following year, President Clinton appointed Lieutenant General Shinseki to the rank of General. He assumed the post of Commandant of American forces in Europe. General Shinseki became Vice Chief of Staff in 1998, and was appointed as the 34th Army Chief of Staff in June 1999. He became the first Japanese-American to attain this elite post.

The day after General Shinseki was sworn in, a ceremony was held in his honor. In a speech given by Defense Secretary William Cohen, he remarked:

> On the day he was born, Rick Shinseki was considered an enemy of the state. Today, we are honored to celebrate his appointment as the 34th Army Chief of Staff.[1]

In addition to his own military service, two of General Shinseki's uncles fought in World War II as part of the 100th Infantry Battalion, and one served with the 442nd Regimental Combat Team (RCT). At the ceremony in his honor, General Shinseki recalled many war stories told to him by these uncles when the family gathered around the dinner table. He expressed his deep admiration for all who served the United States in that great time of conflict:

> Because of their selfless contributions, I have lived my life without suspicion, without limitation, with the full rights and privileges of citizenship.[2]

Portrait of General Eric K. Shinseki Chief of Staff of the U.S. Army. He is the first Asian-American four-star General and the first to lead one of the four U.S. Military Services. February 3 1999. Photographer: Davis, Scott. Courtesy of Department of Defense Media.

Senior United States Senator Daniel Inouye from Hawaii. Senator Inouye is the first Japanese-American to serve in the U.S. House of Representatives, as well as the Senate. He has held his seat in the U.S. Senate since 1963. Senator Inouye is also the very first representative from the Statehood of Hawaii. Source: The U.S. Senate Historical Office.

Senator Daniel Inouye, who served in the 442nd RCT, keenly understood the significance of General Shinseki's appointment. When he introduced General Shinseki to the U.S. Armed Services Committee, Senator Inouye touched upon the fact of General Shinseki's having been an enemy alien at birth. He went on to state, that General Shinseki's nomination "could only happen in the United States."[3] Perhaps even more than his dedication, General Shinseki's achievement reflected the American spirit of tolerance and broadmindedness. After General Shinseki's Senate confirmation, Senator Inouye voiced the deep pride and satisfaction of the Japanese-American community:

> On this day, the shame that has been on our shoulders all these years has been completely washed away.[4]

NASA Astronaut Ellison Onizuka: The Tragic Fate of the Challenger

Ellison Onizuka began his career as an officer in the U.S. Air Force and became the first Asian-American astronaut. Onizuka was born in Kona, Hawaii, in 1946. His grandparents emigrated from Fukuoka prefecture to Hawaii in the 1890s.

They worked in coffee cultivation on the island of Hawaii.[5]

Onizuka grew up hearing the heroic exploits of the Japanese-American soldiers who served in World War II. After graduating from Konawaena High School, he entered the University of Colorado, where he participated in the Air Force ROTC program for four years. After completing graduate school, also at the University of Colorado, Onizuka went on active duty with the U.S. Air Force. In 1974, he began a year of special training at the Air Force Test Pilot School. Upon completion, he became a flight test engineer at Edwards Air Force Base in California.

In 1978, NASA chose Onizuka as an astronaut candidate. After a year of training and assessment, he began serving as a support crewmember at the Kennedy Space Center. In January 1985, Onizuka served as mission specialist aboard *Discovery I*, on the first Space Shuttle mission under the auspices of the Defense Department. Spending some 74 hours in orbit, Ellison Onizuka became the first Asian-American to journey into space.

NASA scheduled Onizuka's second shuttle mission for January the following year. He would again serve as mission specialist aboard the *Challenger*. Millions worldwide watched the shuttle's launch, broadcast live from the Kennedy Space Center. The *Challenger* lifted off at 11:38 a.m. but after 73 seconds in flight, it was engulfed in flames and disintegrated 16 miles above the earth.

Ellison Onizuka Mission Specialist aboard the Challenger. Courtesy of NASA.

Chapter 4

As the world watched in horror and disbelief, the lives of the seven astronauts, including two civilians, were extinguished in the conflagration. The next morning, the *New York Times* reported that burning fragments of the ill-fated space shuttle continued to rain down over the Atlantic, miles off the Florida coast, even an hour after the explosion. It was the worst disaster in the history of the space program.

In addition to Onizuka, two other mission specialists were aboard the *Challenger*—Ronald McNair and Judith Resnik. McNair's career was highlighted by a 1984 space voyage, where he became the second African-American in space. Resnik, who was Jewish, also had a distinguished career. She was aboard *Discovery*'s maiden voyage in 1984, becoming the second woman to orbit the Earth. Christa McAuliffe, one of two civilians aboard *Challenger*, was the high school teacher who had been selected from 11,000 applicants for NASA's "Teacher in Space" project. McAuliffe was to be the first teacher-astronaut, and she received a tremendous amount of media attention from the outset.

Following the *Challenger* disaster, the bereaved families came together and resolved to commemorate the astronauts in a fitting manner. This resulted in their establishing the Challenger Center. Not satisfied with just erecting a monument, of some sort, instead they chose to create

Ellison S. Onizaki Street in Little Tokyo, Los Angeles, California. Photographer: Ha'Eri, Bobak. Source: Creative Common Site.

an interactive educational center where young people could learn about planetary and space science. Thus, in 1988 the inaugural Challenger Learning Center opened at the Houston Museum of Natural Science. Currently, the Center is headquartered in Virginia, with 50 branch centers in 31 states, Great Britain, and Canada. New centers are being opened regularly, and they continue to further the mission of space-related education.

Ellison Onizuka's grave is in the National Memorial Cemetery of the Pacific, on the island of Oahu. The cemetery itself is located on a hill overlooking the ocean. Onizuka rests alongside many of the Japanese-American soldiers, the heroes of his childhood, who had fought in WWII.

As a way of commemorating this exemplary individual, the Astronaut Ellison Onizuka Space Center was founded in 1991, at the Kona Airport on the island of Hawaii. In addition, there is Astronaut Ellison Onizuka Street in Los Angeles' Little Tokyo, and a bridge bearing his name near the Onizuka's ancestral town in Fukuoka prefecture.

The Challenger Crew Members. Courtesy of NASA.

Interview with Dr. John Kashiwabara

John Kashiwabara, MD. Courtesy of Dr. John Kashiwabara.

One day, a young college student, John Kashiwabara, with a passion for sports like any other American youth, was forced to abandon his studies and was sent off to an internment camp—for the sole reason that his parents were Japanese. Rather than allow himself to be embittered by the experience, the young man maintained a belief in the goodness of his country of birth. He has lived his life as a model citizen, entirely devoted to bettering his community. For over half a century, this young man, who became a medical doctor, has made noteworthy contributions in the areas of medicine, education, and sports. In a predominantly white community, he has been widely acclaimed for his many accomplishments and is recognized as a valued civic leader. Dr. Kashiwabara has received over 20 awards for meritorious service and is a truly sterling example of Japanese-American citizenship.

In the academic arena, Dr. Kashiwabara was appointed to the Board of Trustees of the California State University system by the Governor of California. As the sole Japanese-American member of the Board, he participated in revenue management, budget decisions, appointment and evaluation of presidents and chancellors, and the formation of management policy for all 23 campuses in the system. Moreover, he has demonstrated his commitment to quality education for the next generation by establishing the John E. Kashiwabara scholarship at the Long Beach branch of the Japanese-American Citizens League (JACL).

Dr. Kashiwabara's achievements also loom large in the economic sphere. As a member of the Long Beach Harbor Commissioners, he worked tirelessly to develop the city's port. Furthermore, Dr. Kashiwabara actively promoted sports and served as physician to the local college teams where he became affectionately known as "Dr. John." He has also served for many years on the board of the Long Beach branch of the Red Cross.

Dr. John Kashiwabara was born in Florin, California, on November 30, 1921. His father, Matsuo Kashiwabara, came to America in 1905 and was a railroad worker. He was the third of six children in the family. While a student at Placer Junior College, the Japanese military attacked Pearl Harbor and the Pacific War began. In May of 1942, Dr. Kashiwabara, his parents and his siblings were relocated to the Tule Lake Internment Camp. He shared subsequent experiences with us:

> After I left the internment camp, I went to Chicago with my older brother, Kei, who had been wounded in Europe while serving with the 442nd Infantry Regiment. With his money from the GI Bill, we entered the University of Illinois together and after graduation, Kei moved on to dental school and I went to medical school. In 1950 I became a doctor and served as a medical officer in the United States Air Force, stationed in Japan for a time. Upon retirement, I moved back to California and ran a family practice clinic in Long Beach from 1954-1990.

Chapter 4

When our conversation shifted to daily life in the internment camps, Dr. Kashiwabara didn't bring up any negative experiences. Instead, he focused on the warmth and goodwill shown to him by people who were able to surmount the barriers of race. In the following, Dr. Kashiwabara recounts one such episode:

> In the wake of Pearl Harbor, when anti-Japanese sentiment was dramatically rising, I was a member of the Placer Junior College basketball team. Since I'm Japanese-American, I thought that my presence on the team would be a burden to my team-mates, so I decided to quit. But I wasn't sure when I should let the coach know. Then one day, the president of the college called me into his office. There I found myself in the company not only of the president, but the college trustees and my basketball coach as well. The president said, "John, we want you to continue playing just as before. You have nothing to worry about." My coach had realized that I'd been struggling with the situation. In the end, I stayed on the team and took part in our games.

However, he and the other Japanese-American students were eventually sent to the internment camps, and they had to withdraw from college. Then, one day in February of 1943, the president of Placer Junior College paid an unexpected visit to Dr. Kashiwabara's camp. He presented every one of the Japanese-American students with their graduation diplomas. Subsequently, Dr. Kashiwabara was transferred to the Amache Internment Camp in Colorado, where he taught basketball and formed a team for the children in the camp. Eventually, he was able to take them out of the camp to compete in games against area teams. He relates a memory of that time:

A Basketball Game at the Amache Relocation Center. December 24, 1943. Photographer: Parker, Tom. Amache, Colorado. Courtesy of The Bancroft Library; University of California, Berkeley.

> Once, while returning from a game in Denver, we decided to stop at a small café since the young players were hungry. When I finished placing our order and took a seat together with my team members, a white guy at the counter yelled several times at the owner of the café, "Hey, get those Jap kids outta here!" The owner wouldn't stand for this behavior, and he told the guy: "Say that one more time and I'll kick you out!" Well, the fellow wouldn't stop, so the owner opened the door, pointed outside, and yelled, 'Get out!' True to his word, he kicked the fellow out of the café. The frightened youngsters were finally able to relax and finish their meal. Even during those trying times, there were many courageous and kind Americans.

When Dr. Kashiwabara spoke, his voice swells with the deep feeling of a proud American.

Interviewed and written by Mami Mizuguchi

Shinta Asami:
A Man who Dreamed of Becoming a Sailor

Shinta Asami, a Japanese businessman whose career has been predominantly U.S.-based, has made notable contributions to the American distribution network by making the Long Beach Port the largest container shipping terminal in the United States. Asami, who spearheaded a number of key innovations in the containerized shipping business, linking the market internationally, was born in landlocked Saitama prefecture in 1925.

In this interview, he speaks of his life-long attraction to the sea, a love affair that helped mold his remarkable business career:

> In pursuit of my dream of becoming a sailor, I entered Tokyo Nautical College in 1942. Because of the war, I graduated early from the college and began working for the newly established Shipping Management Organization. While there were few cargo ships left available after the war and very few opportunities to get onboard, I received a cable request from General Douglas MacArthur with orders to serve in the repatriation campaign, a very challenging assignment. I went to Manchuria, Korea, the USSR, and China to help repatriate millions of Japanese stranded all over Asia.
>
> After finishing my repatriation duty, I was employed at Kawasaki Kisen as a navigation officer to work in domestic shipping. The stress led to the development of a stomach ulcer, which required surgery. My convalescence at home made me reconsider my future, and when I returned to work, I was determined to make a life for myself as a seaman.
>
> In 1951, I began working the overseas shipping routes to Thailand, Cambodia, and the Philippines, where we shipped steel for construction and returned with cargos of lumber and rice. Following my marriage in 1952, my routes expanded to more distant destinations such as the U.S. and Africa, with periods at sea for four to seven months. I was gone so long that when I'd return, my child hardly recognized me and would ask if "Uncle" would be staying overnight!

Establishing Shipping Service to Alaska

> In January 1960, I received orders to go to Anchorage, Alaska, to investigate the establishment of shipping services there. The governor expressed great skepticism, but after I suggested that establishing a shipping service between Japan and Alaska would substantially improve the living standard of Alaska's citizens, he agreed. The following day, the local newspapers ran headline stories about the possibility of opening up trade between Alaska and Japan. Soon our company was swamped with inquiries regarding freight shipments.

Chapter 4

Shinta Asami: A Man who Dreamed of Becoming a Sailor *continued*

The governor then put me in touch with Coast Guard officials, who provided information for us to navigate into Alaskan ports. As a result of my involvement, I was later appointed captain. Upon my second return trip to Japan, though, I was reassigned to New York to serve as Marine Superintendent and moved there in May 1961.

Seeing the light: Container Shipping in New York

I first learned about containerized shipping when I was invited by Malcolm McLean of SeaLand Industries to attend their inauguration party previewing a container ship. Prior to the advent of container shipping, prevailing practice was first to unload the trucks then put the cargo in storage before loading it onto the ship. But this new container system enabled the offloading of containers directly from trucks onto the ship. Thus, container shipping introduced far greater efficiency and safety, especially in inclement weather conditions. At the time, nobody imagined that containers would be the future of maritime industry, but I was quite sure that this would be the case.

Container Ship Being Loaded. Port of Long Beach, California. Courtesy of Port of Long Beach.

After returning to Japan, I began researching ways to improve transportation efficiency in my company's Maritime Affairs Division. In 1968, when greater interest in containerized shipping began to grow, I was appointed chief of our Container Division and soon became its strongest proponent. Though most of my colleagues feared that since the container system required not only the container ships, but also large cranes and wide handling space, the costs would be exorbitant. In one of our meetings, I was even accused of trying to ruin the company financially.

At that time, the entire marine shipping business was experiencing serious financial difficulties. To help facilitate the adoption of containerized shipping, the Japanese government organized the six major shipping companies into sub-groups of two and four companies. So, it was that Kawasaki Kisen was partnered with Mitsui O.S.K., Yamashita Shin-Nihon, and Japan Line. My chief responsibility concerned shipping terminals, and in 1971, I was assigned to head up the Port and Harbor Project Division.

Shinta Asami: A Man who Dreamed of Becoming a Sailor *continued*

Establishing a Container Terminal in Long Beach

Long Beach Terminal with a View of the Queen Mary. Courtesy of Port of Long Beach, California.

When Kawasaki Kisen planned to open a terminal in Long Beach, I began to design the layout for construction of the terminal, namely, the International Transportation Service (ITS), a locally based company that would manage the terminal operations. When I returned to the U.S. in 1972, I became the president of ITS, and later became its Chairman (1990) and Chairman Emeritus (1995-1999).

The existing container terminal at Long Beach was only five acres, while the new one was huge—100 acres. Critics attacked me for creating such a "monstrosity," but I was sure that we had to build big at the outset, or it would be very hard to expand later on. Once the terminal was complete and fully operational, the Japanese shipping companies adopted a wait-and-see attitude, choosing not to use the Long Beach facilities. Though frustrated after all our efforts in establishing the new shipping terminal, we set out in search of customers.

We went all over—the Middle East, Britain, Germany, France, Norway, Israel—visiting local shipping companies and trying to sell them on the Long Beach port facility. We stopped at company offices during the day, dined with management in hotel restaurants at night, and actively promoted our container terminal. This was a desperate business gamble at the outset, but we managed to sign contracts with several companies and the ships started arriving at Long Beach. Within a few years ITS became one of America's largest terminal companies.

The Challenge of Revolutionizing America's Transportation Economy

My next challenge was to overhaul the coast-to-coast transportation business. Back then, large freight shipments mainly went through the Panama Canal. But I felt we needed an alternative to the Canal, and my solution was a rail link between the East and West coasts through the so-called On-Dock Double-Stack Trains (DST). The DST system improves efficiency by bringing freight trains directly into the container terminal. By stacking containers on top of each other, we could double the amount of cargo on a train—hence the "double stack." It took several years to

Chapter 4

lobby the Port Authority and the city officials, but we were eventually able to construct a new rail spur. Although fully aware of the difficulties we encountered in creating the necessary infrastructure, other shipping companies didn't hesitate to emulate the On-Dock DST system. It never crossed my mind to patent the system, since this would have greatly impeded its growth.

A Double Stack Train in the USA. Source: FreePhoto.com

I also believed that it would be too risky to depend on our single port facility, so I had another container terminal constructed in Tacoma, Washington, to handle West coast shipping and one in Elizabeth, New Jersey, for the East coast. The small operation in Tacoma gradually developed into a major container port, and to show their gratitude, the Tacoma city fathers designated September 11th, the day of the port's official opening, as "Captain Asami Day."

The Importance of Thinking Big and Planning for the Long Term

I always tell young people to think big, to embrace their dreams, and to believe that anything is possible if they try hard enough. In my own case, it took years of negotiating to get permission to construct the railroad spur that made On-Dock DST possible. But I persisted because I believed that this would be in the best interest of the U.S. I'd always thought of my work as something that might benefit society at large rather than myself and our company, and I do believe it has. But above all, young people need to be steadfast and undaunted in striving for the goals they set for themselves.

In 1990, the City of Long Beach honored Shinta Asami as the "Father of On-Dock-Rail" which was recognized by the U.S. government and the Senate. He received the Japanese Foreign Minister's Award in 1993, the Order of Rising Sun in 1995, and the first Kasloff Foundation Japanese-American Pioneer Award in 2006. In 1998, at the request of the U.S. government, Shinta Asami became a naturalized U.S. citizen.

Text courtesy of Lighthouse, Los Angeles, California. September 1, 2006 issue.

Excerpt from Personal Interview of Shinta Asami

Minoru Yamasaki: The Designer of the World Trade Center in New York

Minoru Yamasaki was a *Nisei* whose parents immigrated from Toyama prefecture in Japan. Yamasaki was born in Seattle, Washington in 1912. He endured the virulent anti-Japanese climate as a boy growing up in the Northwest. He was educated at the University of Washington, paying his own way by working at a salmon cannery. After graduation, Yamasaki moved to New York City, where he attended night school at New York University. After completing a master's degree in architecture, he worked at a number of well-known architectural firms, including one that designed the Empire State Building and Rockefeller Center. Based on his impressive professional experience, Yamasaki became the chief designer for the firm of Smith Hinchman Grylls and Associates in 1945.

It bears noting that Yamasaki managed to train at these firms during the very height of wartime hostilities—a time when Japanese-Americans living on the West Coast, including Seattle, were being sent off to internment camps.

Minoru Yamasaki, Chief Architect of the World Trade Center. Yamasaki with his model of lower Manhattan. Courtesy of Minoru Yamasaki Associates. "I feel this way about it. World trade means world peace and consequently the World Trade Center buildings in New York ... had a bigger purpose than just to provide room for tenants. The World Trade Center is a living symbol of man's dedication to world peace ... beyond the compelling need to make this a monument to world peace, the World Trade Center should, because of its importance, become a representation of man's belief in humanity, his need for individual dignity, his beliefs in the cooperation of men, and through cooperation, his ability to find greatness." ~ Minoru Yamasaki. Cited in Robert Sullivan, ed., Life: One Nation: America Remembers September 11, 2001.

Although Anti-Japanese sentiment was prevalent, those in New York were spared the internment edict. Yamasaki remained employed at top architectural firms. There were those who recognized his talents and fostered his professional development, despite the "enemy alien" label assigned by the U.S. military. The role played by such fair and open-minded individuals must be acknowledged.

In 1949, Yamasaki and two of his fellow architects at Smith Hinchman Grylls formed a partnership and opened a new firm. This firm gained recognition for the design of the main terminal at Lambert-St. Louis Airport in 1955. That same year, Yamasaki received a major award from the Architectural Institute of Japan for his design of the U.S. Consulate in Kobe. In 1959, Yamasaki organized his own firm, Yamasaki & Associates. The firm went on to receive four awards from the American Institute of Architects.

Yamasaki's most famous project, which would gain worldwide acclaim, was the World Trade Center in New York. The World Trade Center was originally part of a larger project aimed at revitalizing Lower Manhattan. It was developed by the Port Authority of New York and New Jersey. The World Trade Center was a seven building complex providing office space for 50,000 and accommodating 200,000 visitors daily. The complex was sufficiently massive to warrant its own zip code.

The Twin Towers became the central landmark of the Manhattan skyline. Upon its completion in 1972, Tower One was the tallest building in the world, easily surpassing the Empire State Building. In 1973, Tower Two was completed. Construction of the Sears Tower in Chicago had already begun and in the end, the Twin Towers' "tallest building" claim lasted for only two years. However, with the influx of high-end corporate tenants in the 1980s and its proximity to Wall Street, the World Trade Center remained a dominant symbol of global finance.

In 1993, terrorists detonated a bomb in the World Trade Center's basement. Thanks to its

Chapter 4

September 11, 2001; Statue of Liberty and World Trade Center. Courtesy of National Park Service.

opinion were highlighted by the National Institute of Standards and Technology (NIST) report which concluded that:

> The towers likely would not have collapsed under the combined effects of aircraft impact damage and the extensive ,I; multi-floor fires if the thermal insulation had not been widely dislodged or had been only minimally dislodged by aircraft impact.[8]

Yamasaki, however, did not live to witness either the 1993 attack or the horrors of "9/11." He died of cancer in 1986.

advanced structural design, damage to the Trade Center's Twin Towers was relatively light. However, the hijacking of American Airlines and United Airlines passenger jets and subsequent impacts into the Towers during the terrorist attacks of September 11, 2001 had the experts reanalyzing the structural integrity of the Towers.

The North Tower was hit at 8:46 a.m. and South Tower at 9:03 a.m. It took 100 minutes for the building to crumble in to clouds of smoke and a great mountain of debris. Nearly 3,000 people lost their lives, including 343 firefighters and 23 police officers who had taken part in the rescue effort,[6] but the delay of the total collapse gave others time to escape.

In the initial design stage, the possibility of an airplane collision had been taken into account and factored in. Yet who could have imagined, back then, the large passenger jets would serve as terrorist weapons of destruction. In a report issued in 2002 by the Federal Emergency Management Agency (FEMA), the unique design of the Twin Towers was given credit for this delay.[7]

As a result of Yamasaki's structural design, it was concluded that 1,000's of lives were saved. In 2005, however, several years of divided

Ann Curry: The Face of the Morning News

Ann Curry is the anchor of "Dateline NBC," the news anchor of NBC News' "Today" and a co-anchor of the fourth hour of "Today." She was born in Guam in 1956. Her father was a career U.S. Naval man, and her mother was from a rice-farming family in Japan. In an interview, Curry explained that her mother came to America at a very trying time:

> It was very difficult to be Japanese here. People were still angry about the war. So she raised me to be American. She wouldn't even let me speak Japanese.[9]

Surprisingly, Curry's father taught her to take pride in her Japanese heritage.

> He told me, 'Never forsake either world. In fact, if you have to choose, choose your Japanese side.' He gave me permission to embrace the samurai side, the side of strong people he'd come to admire.

She also recalled her impressions of watching television when she was a child:

The women who were on television, and the men, were all Caucasians. Most of them were blond. I didn't even think there was a place for me.

In addition, Curry expressed a sentiment shared by other young Asian Americans:

When you're a child and you don't see people like you doing something, it doesn't enter your mind you could do it.

When her family finally settled in Ashland, Oregon, they had limited financial resources. For Curry, attending college seemed out of the question. However, with her parents' encouragement, she managed to attend the University of Oregon with the help of a few small scholarships and by taking on part-time jobs. She even worked as a housecleaner at Harrah's Casino in Lake Tahoe, where she scrubbed countless toilets. Curry explained:

I did everything I could to raise money for college, because it seemed well worth the effort.

In 1978, she received a degree in journalism, having gained more than just investigative skills. When presented with the 2003 University of Oregon Pioneer Award, Curry expressed her gratitude toward her mentors:

Professor Ken Metzler gave me what I needed. He made me feel as though I could do anything, that I was a good student, and that my dreams, if I worked hard, would come true. (10)

After embarking on her career at a local television station, Curry became a reporter for the Los Angeles station KCBS in 1984. While at KCBS, she received an Emmy Award for her coverage of the 1987 Los Angeles earthquake, and a second one for her coverage of the gas pipeline explosion in San Bernardino. In 1990,

Curry joined the staff of NBC News, and in 1997 she was named anchor of the popular *Today* show. She had become the "face of the morning news" in the highly competitive media market. In May 2005, she was selected to be co-anchor, alongside Stone Phillips, on the news program *Dateline NBC*.

Ann Curry was inducted into the University of Oregon School of Journalism and Communication Hall of Achievement in 2002. That year, she established the Ann Curry Scholarship for students aspiring to a career in broadcasting.

Curry has distinguished herself in global humanitarian reporting traveling three times to Sudan to report on the violence and ethnic cleansing taking place in Darfur and Chad. She traveled with First Lady Laura Bush throughout Africa reporting on issues that plague the continent such as the HIV/AIDS epidemic and women's rights and education. She was the first network news anchor to report from inside the tsunami zone in Southeast Asia, and she was also the first network news anchor to report on the humanitarian refugee crisis caused by the genocide in Kosovo.

In the first two weeks following the attacks of September 11, Curry reported live from ground zero every day. She reported from Baghdad in the weeks leading up to the war in Iraq, and then from the USS Constellation as the war began. She also filed reports from inside Iraq, from Qatar, and Kuwait during the first weeks of the war.

Curry has earned three Emmys, the most recent for her reporting in Darfur, four Golden Mikes, two Gracies, several Associated Press Certificates of Excellence, and an award for Excellence in Reporting from the NAACP. Curry was honored with the Simon Wiesenthal Medal of Valor for her extensive reporting in Darfur.

And in the wake of her sister's breast cancer diagnosis and the loss of her mother to gallbladder cancer, Curry has frequently reported about breast cancer and actively contributes to the campaign against the disease.

Chapter 4

Nobuko Iinuma:
Nonfiction Author

Nobuko Iinuma. Courtesy of the Iinuma Family.

Native-born Japanese author Nobuko Iinuma's nonfiction works have been lauded by the Los Angeles Japanese-American Women's Club, the City of Los Angeles, and many other associations and organizations. In the spring of 2006, her works were also awarded with the prestigious Order of the Rising Sun by the Japanese government.

Her 1992 publication, *Noguchi Hideyo to Sono Tsuma* (*Noguchi Hideyo and His Wife*), was the result of her research on the American wife of Hideyo Noguchi,* Mary Darges, who had earned a rather unsavory reputation. Iinuma's intent was "to resolve certain misunderstandings surrounding [her] and to learn what sort of person she really was." Her subsequent two-year research for the book on Noguchi and his wife brought many things to light, including the discovery of Noguchi's will.

In the following interview, Iinuma describes her marriage, immigration and life in the United States, and her writing career:

> When I was a sophomore living in the dorms at Jissen Women's University, a Japanese-American soldier came to see his friend's sister who happened to be my roommate. He said that he was drafted while attending the University of California and is currently stationed in Tokyo. Consequently, we came to know each other and were married and moved to the U.S.
>
> My first impression of the States was not a very positive one. After the ship arrived in Seattle, we decided to take a Greyhound bus to Los Angeles to see his relatives.
>
> En route, at a roadside restaurant, we were refused service. No one would even look at us. At first, I didn't quite understand what was going on but my husband quickly set me straight: "This is what racism is all about," he explained.
>
> My husband went to the Illinois Institute of Technology and worked part-time at an electronics company. But the division between the blue-collar and white-collar employees was such that they had separate elevators! This was 1954—a time when racial segregation was still rampant in the U.S. My husband firmly believed that the only way for Japanese people to counter racist treatment was to excel intellectually, and he did indeed compile an outstanding academic record. During the 1950s when engineers were in high demand and salaries were typically

---

* Hideyo Noguchi (1876-1928). A Japan-born medical researcher, who served as a fellow at the University of Pennsylvania and the Carnegie Research Institute, then continued his work at the Rockefeller Institute. (See Chapter 1, Page 18.)

determined by one's academic achievement, he landed a good job with Northrop Aviation in 1957. And how different our lives have become, compared to that day four years earlier when we couldn't even get someone to serve us lunch at a restaurant!

The opportunity to write professionally came about when my husband, who was raised in Kōchi prefecture, was asked by the head of the *Kōchi Newspaper* to write a review of a serialized drama, based on Toyoko Yamazaki's novel *Futatsu no Sokoku* (*Two Homelands*). It was being broadcasted on Japanese language television in Los Angeles at the time. He asked me if I'd do it instead. I sent off the requested review. After this assignment, they asked me to write a serial column for their paper. I agreed and the column, "*Notes from a Japanese-American Home in Los Angeles*," began its run in 1984.

A producer for Fukushima Television proposed that I write a biography of Hideyo Noguchi, who was a native of Fukushima known throughout Japan for his renowned major achievements in medical research.

The research on Noguchi's life in America was demanding. I came across Mary Darges' collected correspondence. Her letters revealed to me a person of deep sincerity—a far cry from the vulgar reputation that had come to be associated with this woman.

I am now working on a book about six American women who married Japanese men, including Mary Darges. I am interested in how these six women supported their husbands and helped them successfully integrate into American society.

After the war, Japanese-Americans strove to become fully Americanized. Yet despite their efforts to assimilate, they could not help but retain their Japanese identity. Their homeland may be the United States, but their roots are inevitably Japanese. For this reason, I believe it is important for Japanese-Americans to embrace the Japanese culture, to make it known, and to pass it along. History does not pass judgment on current events. It is only in the fullness of time that we will be able to evaluate the true meaning of what has gone before, and who has accomplished what. The esteem in which Japanese are held these days in this country is the result of something that has been built up over the years. The fabled "American dream" is something one must realize for oneself. It must be earned, and there is no substitute for sheer hard work and determination. That goes for everyone.

Text courtesy of Lighthouse, Los Angeles, California. August 1, 2006 issue.
Excerpt from Personal Interview of Nobuko Iinuma.

Chapter 4

Hiroshima: Fusing Jazz and Japanese Music

In the world of jazz-fusion music, the band *Hiroshima* has introduced traditional Japanese instruments into the American music scene. Formed around June and Dan Kuramoto, both Japanese-Americans, *Hiroshima* creates a unique sound by combining jazz styles and music played on instruments such as the *koto, taiko* drums, and *shakuhachi* (bamboo flute).

Hiroshima's self-titled debut album was released in 1979. The record company expressed concern with the group's name and its possible negative connotations. However, the band members had expressly chosen the controversial name in line with their aim of undoing stereotypes about Japanese-Americans, and they remained adamant on this score. Dan Kuramoto, leader of the group, remarked as follows:

> After suffering catastrophic devastation from the atomic bomb, the city of *Hiroshima* has recovered beautifully. And that positive image is contained in the group's name.*

In *Hiroshima*'s unique fusion of East and West, the sound of the *koto* is particularly striking. June Kuramoto, a virtuoso on the instrument, was born in Saitama prefecture and is the only member of the group born in Japan. Although her mother was born in Japan, June is Japanese-American based on her father's status, a *Nisei*. When June was six years old, her family moved to Los Angeles, and from the beginning, she was desperately homesick for Japan. During the mid-fifties, when the family came to the United States there were support groups for newly arrived Japanese immigrants, managed by the members of the *Nisei* community. It was at a meeting of *Sakurakai*, one such group that June had her first exposure to a *koto* performance. For the nostalgic six year-old, the sound of the *koto* was enchanting, and she immediately decided to take lessons.

Meanwhile, Dan Kuramoto was busy studying art and law at California State University in Long Beach. After graduation, Dan became the first Chair of the Asian-American Studies Department at his alma mater. At that time, artists such as Carlos Santana, *Earth, Wind and Fire*, and Jimi Hendrix were mixing Latin music, R&B, and jazz to create entirely new musical forms and styles. Dan happened to meet June just at the point where he understood that Japanese-Americans could make music in a similar fashion. June was already a well-known *koto* player who frequently performed at Japanese-American community events, such as *kenjinkai* picnics or at retirement homes.

In 1980, *Hiroshima*'s second release, *Odori*, was nominated for a Grammy award, and the band received its first Gold Record for *Another Place* in 1985. *Go*, released in 1987, topped Billboard's Contemporary Jazz charts for three months, and won a Soul Train Music Award for Best Jazz Album. Also, June played *koto* on "*Sukiyaki*" by Taste of Honey. "*Sukiyaki*," a remake of Kyu Sakamoto's song "*Ue o Muite Arukō*," went on to become a #1 hit in the United States. *Hiroshima* members have also performed on numerous soundtracks for movies such as *Black Rain, The Thin Red Line, Pirates of the Caribbean: The Curse of the Black Pearl*, and June was a featured musician on *The Last Samurai*. Furthermore, the group regularly supports and performs at charity concerts all over America and makes many contributions to the Japanese-American community. In 2006, June participated in *Nisei* Week as Parade Marshal.

Members of Hiroshima. Courtesy of Hiroshima.

*Interviewed by the writer at the home of June Kuramoto. August 8, 2005.

Madame Bando Mitsuhiro:
Japanese Classical Dance Master

Young Student of Madame Bando Performing on Stage. Courtesy of Madame Bando Mitsuhiro.

Madame Bando Mitsuhiro was born in the city of Yawatahama in Ehime prefecture in 1928. Her Japanese classical dance studies began at the age of four. She was granted her teaching credential or "*Shihan*" rank at the age of 26 by Grand Master Bando Mitsugoro VIII who later was designated as a Living National Treasure by the Japanese government.

On a sightseeing tour to Los Angeles in 1969, Madame Mitsuhiro visited relatives and was encouraged to teach Japanese dance to American children. Upon returning to Japan and giving it much thought, she decided to embark on a new adventure and returned to the Los Angeles area a year later intending to stay for only three years. However, since then, 39 years have quickly flown by.

For her dedicated efforts in enhancing the East-West cultural exchange over the years, Madame Mitshuhiro has received many commendations from local and state government officials including the current California Governor, Arnold Schwarzenegger, and the mayors and civic leaders who have served the various communities in which she has taught. Her tremendous accomplishments were recognized in Japan too, when Grand Master Bando Mitsugoro X awarded her the prestigious Kanbu Shihan rank in 2003.

Unlike her teaching experiences in Japan, Madame Mitshuhiro has encountered many difficult challenges teaching American students, one of which is to communicate in the English-speaking world. Imparting the nuances of Japanese classical dance, the gender, age, and personality of the character being portrayed have to be done using dance movements and facial expressions. Through the years, she has observed this mastery of skills in many of her students, and she often reflects upon their individual achievement with tears of joy.

Over the past 39 years, Madame Bando Mitsuhiro has taught more than 600 American students, and their performances have taken them throughout the United States and Canada. Today, there are about 80 students under her tutelage in six studios located in Los Angeles, Orange County, San Diego, Monterey, and Tacoma, Washington. Thirty-five students have attained the "*Natori*" rank (professional stage names), and while 10 have their "*Shihan*" rank (teaching credential).

Her boundless energy, dedication to Japanese classical dance, and her mission to share this traditional performing art throughout the Western world have kept her young and active at age 79.

Interviewed and written by Mami Mizuguchi, 2006.

Chapter 4

Cultural Exchange: The Liberalization of Overseas Travel

As mentioned in Chapter 1, *kenjinkai* and community centers provided for the social and recreational needs of first-generation Japanese-Americans who spoke little English, or none at all in many cases. Through traditional song and dance, Japanese immigrants nostalgically recalled their homeland and enabled their children to become familiar with Japanese culture. Even before World War II, martial arts such as *judo*, *kendo*, and *karate* were popular in the Japanese-American community. According to the *Encyclopedia of Japanese-American History*, published by the Japanese American National Museum, *judo* was first introduced into the United States in 1903. The following year, President Theodore Roosevelt took up *judo*, and it seemed as though the martial art might go on to achieve nationwide popularity.

Judo Competition at the Okinawa U.S. Air Base. Courtesy of the Okinawa U.S. Air Base.

However, after 1907, with a growing distrust toward the Japanese Empire, judo had lost its momentum in the United States. [11] Later, during the difficult days of wartime internment, traditional Japanese cultural activities, including judo, provided emotional support for many of the internees. Adults could take free courses in flower arrangement, and Japanese dance performed on makeshift stages provided welcome entertainment.

American Students of Urasenke attending Japanese Tea Ceremony. Courtesy of Urasenke Somi Numano.

With the war's end, Japanese culture moved beyond the confines of the Japanese-American community and spread to the larger American public. An important early catalyst was the Allied Occupation Force and their families stationed in Japan. As the Allies entered a bombed-out, devastated Tokyo, the soldiers came to appreciate firsthand how the Japanese had continued to fight, armed only with willpower and an undaunted spirit. For these soldiers, activities such as the tea ceremony, flower arrangement, and martial arts—traditional cultural practices that demanded spiritual attainment as well as technical virtuosity—were gateways into a fascinating new world.

The fine Japanese pottery, pearls and other items sold at the Post Exchange (i.e., Military Store) further acquainted the troops with traditional culture. Purchases of these items played a key role in helping to revitalize an economy that had been virtually decimated. The American soldiers and their families who were stationed in Japan experienced Japanese culture in many ways, perhaps most enduringly through food, such as *sukiyaki*. Upon their return to the United States, they brought with them a host of Japanese cultural souvenirs of all types.

The 1950 outbreak of the Korean War created a market for special procurements, a condition that strongly favored Japan's economic recovery. Japan enjoyed the benefits of the resulting economic boom, and in 1952 with the signing of the Peace Treaty and the Japan-America Security Pact, the Allied occupation ended. Spurred by the expansive global economy of the mid-fifties,

Japan entered a period of extraordinary productivity. In its *Economic White Paper*, the Japanese government declared that the nation had indeed emerged from the "postwar" period.

At the same time, Hollywood had entered its own golden era, and stars of the silver screen captivated audiences in Japan as elsewhere. Marilyn Monroe and Joe DiMaggio honeymooned in Japan where they received an enthusiastic welcome. Moreover, the hairstyle worn by Audrey Hepburn in *Roman Holiday* became wildly popular with women across Japan sporting the so-called "Hepburn" cut. Then when the late-fifties rock'n roll hit Japan with a vengeance, many well-heeled young people yearned to visit the United States and experience it for themselves. Among those who did, many would go on to promote Japanese culture in the United States.

With the arrival of the 1960s, television had become a fixed feature of the Japanese household. American programs appeared one after another— most notably, *77 Sunset Strip* (1960), *Combat!*, and *Route 66* (1962). As the seductive image of a prosperous and thriving America spread among the Japanese, a new era of foreign travel dawned. This was of course an impossibility during the war and even well into the postwar period, insofar as the government had placed restrictions on overseas travel in order to conserve foreign currency supplies. In 1963, however, the government eased this restriction and approved a single business trip abroad, per year, where up to $500 could be spent. The following year, this ruling was extended to include tourism. Individuals were now free to travel abroad, albeit with the $500 restriction.

In 1966, though, the restrictions were dropped, which meant that far more Japanese would be able to pursue their dream of traveling to the United States.[12] The cultural flow, which had previously gone in one direction, was now bilateral, and a rich Japanese and American cultural exchange emerged.

Together with the liberalization of foreign travel in the 1960s, and the engine of economic growth that undergirded it, U.S. sales of Japanese electronic goods and cameras increased dramatically. What a contrast with the 1950s, when the "Made in Japan" label was famously associated with cheap, shoddy goods. This image was put to rest thanks to the array of inexpensive, high-quality electronics goods that entered the U.S. marketplace. The high performance and low prices of these goods amazed American buyers.

Hollywood also moved to incorporate the new Japanese products, and before long many movie studios, television stations, and recording studios were using Japanese equipment. Companies of every description followed suit and Japanese goods became the acknowledged standard. It is interesting to note that America's first postwar "Japan boom" coincided with the Japanese government's liberalization of foreign travel in the 1960s.

The permeation of American culture in Japan, and the corresponding spread of Japanese culture in the United States, had much to do with the impact of certain iconic films. For instance, *Teahouse of the August Moon* (1956), starring Marlon Brando as the clever Japanese interpreter, Sakini, is set in Okinawa at the end of the Occupation. *Sayonara* (1957), which also starred Brando, tells of an American serviceman stationed in Japan during the Korean War who falls in love with a Japanese woman.

At the Academy Awards, Miyoshi Umeki won Best Supporting Actress for her role in the film, thus becoming the first person of Asian descent to win an Oscar. *Sayonara* was awarded four Oscars. During the 1960s, the James Bond thriller, *You Only Live Twice* (1967), which was set in Japan, enhanced Japan's visibility in the United States even further.

In the 1980s, the United States experienced a second Japanese boom, this time centering on television. NBC aired its very popular miniseries *Shogun* in 1980, which garnered high ratings. It turned the James Clavell novel, upon which the series was based, into a runaway bestseller. Americans were swept up in a samurai boom as well as a sushi boom. Ever since, the Japanese culture, in all of its rich variety, has become a familiar feature of the American lifestyle.

Noritoshi Kanai:
The Man Behind the "Sushi Boom"

Through a family connection, Noritoshi Kanai moved to the United States when he was 41. Today, Kanai manages a $100 million foodservice business and regards it as his mission to popularize Japanese cuisine. We asked Kanai to reflect upon his life and experiences:

Empathy for Neo-Liberalism at Hitotsubashi University

Noritoshi Kanai. Courtesy of Mutual Trading Co., Inc.

Since I was the third son in my family, I grew up relatively free and unconstrained. I was interested in foreign trade and decided to attend the Tokyo College of Commerce, but the nation soon went to war and we students were mobilized. As an officer, I was dispatched to Burma where I did accounting work and oversaw the procurement of food, clothing, building materials, and medical supplies. When our superior officer ordered us to defend with our lives the Burmese capital of Rangoon, I took this as a direct command from the Emperor and prepared myself accordingly. However, when I went to report to headquarters, I discovered that the orders were meaningless. The superior officers had reversed course and headed to Thailand–in other words, they had retreated. We followed their lead but were captured, and as prisoners of war, spent a year at hard labor on the railroads. With the end of the War, I did not feel the bitterness of defeat. Instead, I was simply happy to be alive, although I harbored a deep mistrust of people.

As a young person, I had my share of anxieties and misgivings. I read many books and found myself drawn to the words of Professor Teijirō Ueda, at one time the Chancellor of Hitotsubashi University: "To be free is the greatest fortune of humanity." and "Freedom is something that one can conceive of and choose for oneself." Resolving to put these words into practice, I decided to go into business for myself.

While my friends found positions in established companies, I launched two or three businesses on my own; each ended in failure. There I was, only a few years out of college and already burdened with 1,800,000 yen of debt. It would ordinarily take more than a lifetime to repay that much money and I must confess to having considered suicide, but I couldn't bear the thought of not repaying this debt, especially in view of all my big talk about freedom and free will. This was money lent to me out of goodwill, and I resolved to find some way to make repayment. Then I got the idea to salvage the boats [used by the *kamikaze* forces], which sank off the Miura Peninsula. I rebuilt the diesel engines, recycled them to make trucks, and with it, I repaid my entire debt in two years.

Noritoshi Kanai: The Man Behind the "Sushi Boom" *continued*

American Sushi-Eater

After this truck venture, I met Chūhei Ishii, an acquaintance of my mother's who immigrated to the U.S. before the War and had opened a successful grocery store in Santa Maria, California. Although Mr. Ishii had come back to Japan after having had all of his assets seized, he still wanted to return to the States and get back into the food business. In 1951, we formed a company, *Tokyo Kyōdō Bōeki,* in partnership with the Mutual Trading Company. The MTC was founded in 1926 in Los Angeles, but with the retirement of its first president, Sadagorō Hoshizaki, Mr. Ishii returned to the U.S. and purchased the business. I divided my time between the U.S. and Japan for the next 10 years. When Mr. Ishii suffered a stroke, without a designated business successor, I decided to take my wife and two children and moved to the U.S. for good. This was in 1964, and I was 41 at the time.

Back then, there were only four Japanese grocery stores and four or five Japanese restaurants in Los Angeles. Our company sold a broad line of goods including sea-weed, dried foods, canned fish, pickled vegetables, and soy sauce by the barrel. The market for Japanese foods was very limited and prospects were far from bright. To me, authentic Japanese food is very delicious, so I believed it would surely appeal to American consumers if made widely available. It seemed to me that the market potential was huge and it came down to a question of what to import from Japan. Everyone likes sweets, I thought, so we began selling Tohato Harvest Brand Cookies, which were light and crispy, and very popular, but Chinese and Korean companies began to sell imitations for lower prices so we soon lost our market.

I considered selling American-made appliances in Japan and went to Chicago to attend a big appliance show. There I met a Jewish-American businessman who said, "If you want to succeed in business in this country, it helps to have a Jewish friend." I hired this very savvy person as a consultant and we traveled to Asia together in search of marketing ideas.

During our stay in Tokyo, my friend went to Kanda and ate sushi at Shinnosuke. "I've got it!" he declared. "A sushi restaurant is just the thing—delicious and unique. You can't find it in the States. This is what you should be selling!" I couldn't quite fathom this. "Look, they eat raw fish in Europe," he added. "Americans will go for sushi, I assure you." And so, I decided to give it a try.

Dealing With the Second Japanese-Food Boom

Back in Los Angeles, the first step was to have a sushi counter installed at Kawafuku, a restaurant in Little Tokyo. When it was completed, non-Japanese customers began frequenting the place. Our second sushi venture was at the Eigiku,

Chapter 4

then Tokyo Kaikan. All were located in the Little Tokyo area. That's where sushi chef, Ichirō Mashita, came up with the now famous "California roll." In Century City, the Osho Restaurant served sushi to a predominantly white clientele including a lot of movie stars. It didn't take long for the sushi bar phenomenon to spread to New York, Chicago, and all across the States. Preparing sushi requires many supplies—fresh seafood, rice, vinegar, seaweed, sake, and various implements and utensils. My role in the spread of sushi bars was a logistical one: to enable the restaurants to procure all the necessary supplies.

When the movie, *Shogun,* was broadcasted in 1980, it helped spawn a Japan boom. Japanese cars and household appliances penetrated the American market, and Japan's image underwent a basic change. However, despite the subsequent trade friction and the expansion and bursting of Japan's bubble economy, sushi retained its popularity with American diners.

The U.S. is currently in the midst of a second Japanese food boom. *Izakaya*-style, casual dining bars, has become the new trend. The first Japanese food boom began in Los Angeles, but *izakaya*-style has its origins in New York. High-end *izakaya* such as Megu in New York have all their fish flown in. To meet the demand, our company had to install industrial-size freezers with sub-zero temperatures to -65°. Now, there are full-scale restaurants out there that feature 100 varieties of sake and employ a sake sommelier.

My goal is to expand the Japanese food culture by improving our distribution system whereby high quality, authentic Japanese food can be supplied throughout the U.S. Second, I want to create an open and congenial work environment for all our employees. Finally, I hope to give something back to the community. Working to achieve these goals keeps me very busy.

Text courtesy of JBA News. Excerpt from September 2004 issue. Entrepreneur Series-Yoshinori Kanai

Irene Y. Hirano:
Chief Executive Officer and President
Japanese American National Museum

Irene Hirano. Source: JEWL

Irene Hirano began her involvement in community service as a middle school student. Following graduate school, she started working for nonprofit organizations providing healthcare services to multicultural communities. She went on to spearhead a $13 million campaign to establish the Japanese American National Museum and a $45 million dollar campaign to expand the facilities of the Museum. She has also served in numerous advocacy groups and non-governmental organizations (NGO) committed to the development of Asian-American human resources and the protection of their rights. In addition, Hirano has remained active in the training of Japanese-American leaders and continues to play an important role in U.S.-Japan relations through her promotion of cultural exchange.

Irene Hirano was born in Los Angeles in 1948. She received her B.A. and M.A in public administration from the University of Southern California in 1970 and 1972, respectively. In 1988, after working for 13 years as Executive Director of the T.H.E Clinic, she became President and CEO of the Japanese American National Museum. In addition to her work at the Museum, Hirano serves on the Ford Foundation, the Smithsonian Institution's National Board, and chairs the American Association of Museums. Hirano has also served on the Board of the National Museum of American History (a division of the Smithsonian), the Los Angeles Convention and Visitors Bureau and on the President's Committee on the Arts and Humanities by Presidential appointment. She has received numerous awards for her distinguished service, including the Mayor's Award for her role in the 1996 Asian-Pacific American Heritage Month.

Interview with Irene Hirano

My paternal grandfather came to the United States in the early 1900s. I can remember him living with my family when I was a young child. My mother was born in Tokyo. This makes me a third-generation Japanese-American on my father's side and second generation on my mother's side. When I was three years old, I went with my mother for several months to Tokyo where I got to know my Japanese relatives.

Before the War began, my father was with the U.S. military, and he remained with the military after Pearl Harbor. As a result, my father was not sent to the internment camps during the war. However, my father's immediate family was taken to the

Chapter 4

Rohwer Camp in Arkansas. My grandmother, whose health was failing, passed away while her family was at the Santa Anita Assembly Center. This was where they were sent before being moved to Arkansas. Most Japanese-Americans are reluctant to discuss their internment experiences, and my family is no exception. I wasn't aware of the details until much later.

During college, I began to understand something about the conditions of life in the camps. For one of my classes I wrote a term paper about the internment experience, and for the first time, I heard stories told by my aunts and uncles. I would learn much more, though, only after the postwar reparation movement began when a great number of people started speaking out about their experiences.

In middle school and high school, I participated in many community service groups and developed an interest in pursuing a career in this area. I went to the University of Southern California and majored in public administration. Students in this field generally opt for jobs in government or nonprofit organizations. I've always been thankful that I chose to work in the nonprofit sector.

Following graduate school, my first position was with the Asian Women's Center, where I served as Associate Director. Then I moved to Washington, D.C. where I did research under the auspices of what was then the Department of Health, Education, and Welfare, with their advocacy project for the elderly. Subsequently, I returned to Los Angeles and worked at the nonprofit T.H.E. Clinic where I was involved with providing specialized healthcare services for a multicultural community. I served as the clinic's Executive Director for 13 years.

Thanks to the clinic's location at the center of the Crenshaw District, I was able to work with a number of public health agencies and organizations and had contact with families from diverse backgrounds. I had the privilege of providing health information in many languages and participated in the development of health services catering to specific ethnic and cultural backgrounds (e.g., the dietary treatment of an illness differs for African and Hispanic Americans). We developed programs that considered medical treatment based in part on the patient's cultural and ethnic background. I am fortunate as well, for having had the opportunity to launch a program providing health services for Asian Americans in addition to many other areas of service.

When compared to previous employment, my work with the Japanese American National Museum might appear to be quite a departure. In fact, there are a number of parallels relating to the management of a nonprofit organization and the mission of community education. In community education, for instance, a museum can

Irene Y. Hirano: Chief Executive Officer and President
Japanese American National Museum *continued*

serve a greater number of people over a longer period of time. Thanks to my extensive background with national public service organizations, I was confident that working for the Japanese American National Museum would be a wonderful application of this experience.

Funding is, of course, essential to establishing any type of organization. My work at the Museum involved funding as a top priority, together with the task of making people aware of the Museum's mission. I made trips to New York, Hawaii, Seattle, and Chicago, encouraging support for a Museum that would be established in Los Angeles.

Another challenge that we faced was the fact that we had no items to display in the Japanese American National Museum! Normally museums have their basis in a private collection that is to be made accessible to the public, but this was not the case with our museum. Furthermore, since we would be focusing on the collective story of Japanese-Americans, we needed to record and preserve the accounts of those who had experienced the internment camps. The Civil Liberties Act was signed into law the very same year I became Museum Director in 1988. As a result, many more people spoke out about their internment experiences than before the reparation movement was initiated. Even now, there are many who remain reluctant to discuss their experiences. I believe, though, that with the passage of time, however, more and more people will choose to share their stories.

We also faced the challenge of stimulating interest among non-Japanese-Americans. In order to attract people to the Museum, we had to get the point across that Japanese-American history is part of American history and not the property of a single minority group. I'm pleased to note that at present, the majority of our visitors are not Japanese-Americans, which is an achievement that I think points to our success.

The experience of Japanese-Americans really does transcend ethnicity. Almost every day we have young people who visit the Museum on school field trips and outings. What they learn they can compare with their own experiences. For example, the children of Hispanic immigrants can see how the lives of first-generation Japanese-Americans have a lot in common with their own parents' experiences.

After the terrorist attacks of September 11th, the Museum released a statement condemning discrimination against Arabs. I believe that this helped promote an awareness of how history has a way of repeating itself. Young Japanese-Americans all too easily fall prey to the notion that since World War II happened over 60 years

Chapter 4

ago, and the U.S. is a democratic nation, racism has become a thing of the past. Although very few people objected to the racist treatment of Japanese-Americans, many spoke out against discrimination in the wake of 9/11. It is of utmost importance for us to convey the message to both Arabs and non-Arabs alike that there is a community of people who strongly oppose racial discrimination.

Strengthening the bonds between Japanese and Japanese-Americans

One of my roles is to promote cooperative ties between cultural institutions and museums. As a part of this endeavor, I became associated with the Smithsonian Institution where we put on the 1998 exhibition "From Bento to Mixed Plate: Americans of Japanese Ancestry in Multicultural Hawaii." This exhibition traveled to Hiroshima, Okinawa, Osaka, and Niigata, where it was well received. Not only was it extremely popular at the Smithsonian, but it set a record for the highest number of visitors to a Smithsonian traveling exhibition.

"From Bento to Mixed Plate" originated in Hawaii, and when it was displayed at the Smithsonian, over a 100 people from the D.C. area with ties to Hawaii volunteered to staff the exhibition. Most of these volunteers were not of Japanese ancestry. But for those who had lived in Hawaii, regardless of ancestry, the stories on display that related to the ethnically blended culture of Hawaii ultimately told their own stories as well.

Japanese American National Museum. Courtesy of the Japanese American National Museum

One goal of mine has been to build a strong bond between the Japanese and Japanese-Americans. At the Museum, there are programs covering four areas; art, education, *Nisei* history, and international affairs. Over the next several years, we want to expand our efforts on an international program. I believe

It is essential for more Japanese-Americans, especially those in the third, fourth, and even fifth generations, to understand their Japanese roots. A key role of the Museum is to strengthen the ties between the Japanese and Japanese-Americans. Fortunately for me, because my mother was born in Japan, I have had a closer relationship with my Japanese relatives. But I know very little about my father's side of the family. Our museum aims at helping future Japanese-American leaders take pride in their heritage, and it supports the fostering of international understanding beyond the domain of U.S.-Japan relations. Finally, the Museum plays a key role in expanding the horizons of Japanese-Americans by providing a means to explore and understand their roots.

Courtesy of Lighthouse, Los Angeles, California. August 1, 2005 issue.

Excerpt from a personal interview with Irene Hirano.

Anonymous Heroes:
Courageous Acts to Remember

The path blazed by Japanese-Americans has by no means been smooth, but it is clearly an integral part of American history. The story of those early Japanese immigrants, who overcame hardships and squarely faced adversity, is a distinctly American story, which must be passed down as a legacy to the next generation. However, behind the scenes of the great societal shifts that marked this history were those many Americans who unstintingly lent their support to Japanese-Americans and their cause.

We must not forget the contributions of those who made many sacrifices, both political and personal, for the ultimate betterment of the Japanese-American community. It is therefore fitting, in conclusion, to acknowledge some of these exemplary individuals whose accounts we were unable to include in other chapters.

In addition to Ralph Carr, Governor of Colorado, and lawyers James Purcell and Dean Acheson, mentioned in Chapter 2, who held prominent positions, there were many more ordinary citizens who came to the support of Japanese-Americans during periods of racial hostility.

For instance, a Caucasian teacher at one of the internment camps chose to sleep in the same barracks as the Japanese-Americans, refusing to use the "whites only" facilities.

In addition, there was the young person who, after finding out that his Japanese-American friend was to be interned, decided to go and live with the friend in the camp. Such grassroots protests of the internment were obviously heartening to those in the Japanese-American community.

We have already called attention to the *Honolulu Star Bulletin* and its policy of using the term "Japanese" in lieu of the pejorative term

Chapter 4

"Jap." There is also the story of an early publisher of the *Orange County Register* and the founder of Freedom Communicatons, Inc., Reymond C. Hoiles. It was R.C. Hoiles who, despite the extreme anti-Japanese climate of Southern California, held forth against the internment of Japanese-Americans (and residents of Japanese descent living legally in the United States) during WWII. His near-singular voice in denouncing the policy became legend in the newspaper industry. In his newspaper, questioning the sorry state of civil liberties, he wrote as follows:

> It would seem that we should not become too skeptical of the loyalty of these people who were born in a foreign country and have lived in a country as good citizens for many years. It is very hard to believe that they are dangerous. [13]

When the forcible eviction of Japanese-Americans begun, it was Hoiles who published a column calling for an end to the evictions, and to the internment program overall. To use his newspaper as a forum for challenging a policy forged at the very epicenter of the anti-Japanese movement, when public sentiment approached a fever pitch of hysteria, was nothing less than a courageous act. In the face of what was sure to be a furious backlash among the paper's subscribers, Hoiles held fast to his beliefs and conducted himself with the utmost professional and moral integrity. His conduct was exemplary.

Reymond C. Hoiles. The Founder of the Freedom Communications, Inc. Courtesy of The Orange County Register/ Freedom Metro Information.

After the war, in the Congressional hearings on abolishing the discriminatory laws, a number of military officers who had fought on the front-lines together with soldiers from the Japanese-American regiments testified regarding the meritorious service of these men. But it is equally important to recall those many officers who could not testify before Congress, having either suffered injuries or died on the battlefield with their Japanese-American comrades. In other words, the record of illustrious military service on the part of Japanese-American soldiers was not theirs alone; it must be shared with their equally dedicated officers, who supported them in so many ways. Because of this support, Japanese-Americans were afforded the basis for their emergence, following the war, as fully vested members of American society.

Consider, for example, Young-Oak Kim, a Korean-American officer assigned to the 100th Infantry Battalion, who joined up with the Japanese-American soldiers at Camp Shelby. Kim displayed superior leadership and great prowess in the heat of battle, earning the respect and trust of the Japanese-Americans under his command. Kim's father, who had come to the United States as a refugee fleeing Japanese colonial rule, harbored a deep hatred of the Japanese. However, as a young person growing up in Los Angeles, his son likely had encountered racial discrimination no different from that directed against Japanese-Americans.

Following his graduation from the Infantry Officer Candidate School at Fort Benning, the only Asian-American in his class, 2nd Lieutenant Kim was the last member of his class to receive an assignment. Soon after he arrived at Camp Shelby, though, Kim was informed that he would be transferred. He asked for an explanation for this unexpected decision, whereupon Lieutenant Colonel Turner, battalion commander, explained:

> In case you don't know, your unit is Japanese and you are Korean. And coming from the islands, I know the Japanese and Koreans don't get along. I'll have you transferred immediately. [14]

116

The Japanese army had already overrun several countries in Southeast Asia, and in many American communities, there had been a rash of assaults on Japanese-Americans by people of Southeast Asian descent. Nevertheless, Kim made a strong and forthright reply to his commanding officer:

> No, that's wrong. They are Americans and I'm an American and we are going to fight for America.

Young-Oak Kim never wore a helmet on the battlefield. Instead, he would wear a knit cap. In addition, he would never dig a foxhole for himself. At their wits end, some of his Japanese-American troops dug one for him, but Kim would not use it. This was his way of combating fear and anxiety on the part of his men. Irving Akahoshi, a member of the 100th Infantry Battalion, reminisced:

> With Lieutenant Kim, we believed we'd survive a trip to hell and back. I would have followed him anywhere, without any hesitation. (15)

During the Korean War, Young-Oak Kim became the first Asian-American to command a regular U.S. combat battalion. (16)

Colonel Young-Oak Kim. Courtesy of Go for Broke National Education Center.

A Soaring Tribute. Barney Hajiro and Shizuya Hayashi, Medal of Honor recipients, and Ed Ichiyama pose in front of a C-17 Globemaster III named "The Spirit of 'Go for Broke'" during an arrival ceremony at Hickam Air Force Base in Hawaii. June 14, 2006. Photographer: Tech Sgt. Shane A. Cuomo. Source: The U.S. Air Force Official Website.

After retiring from the Army in 1972 with the rank of Colonel, Kim contributed not only to the Korean-American community, but to the Japanese-American community as well. He played an active role, for instance, in establishing the Go For Broke National Education Center and the Japanese-American National Museum. In 2005, he participated in the *Nisei* Week parade as Honorary Grand Marshal. Later that year, Kim died of cancer.

As a nation of immigrants, America is, in an important sense, a microcosm of societies throughout the world. It is never an easy matter for different ethnic and racial groups, each with its own values, practices, and beliefs, to coexist. Perhaps more than anything else, American history reveals this truth. However, in spite of many errors and miscalculations, this nation has inexorably pursued the path of coexistence, one step at a time. Prejudice and discrimination have yet to be eliminated. Immigration remains a fraught issue, and it defies simple solutions. Yet by coming to know one another's history, and learning to appreciate and share in different cultures, we can surely reduce the gap that separates us.

Perhaps the day will come when the people of the world will truly honor one another. Until then, it is our fervent hope that striving for mutual understanding and respect will serve the greater goal of peace.

CHRONOLOGY

JAPAN

YEAR	JAPAN
1837	Otokichi and six other castaways brought back to Japan on board the American Merchant ship *Morrison*. They are driven away by the Shogunate's cannons.
1846	Commander James Biddle is sent to Japan by the U.S. to open trade relations with the U. S.; Japan refuses.
1853	On July 8, Commodore Matthew Perry Arrives at Uraga, and July 14, Perry and the U.S. Navy men land at Kurihama, and deliver the U.S. President's letter to Japanese Government.
1854	Commodore Matthew Perry returns to Japan. The Treaty of Kanagawa (Treaty of Peace and Amity) is signed with Japan. Japan opens the Shimoda and Hakodate ports to U.S. vessels. Japan's self-imposed "Isolation Period" (Sakoku) comes to an end.
1856	Townsend Harris arrives in Shimoda as the first U.S. consulate to Japan.
1858	Ii Naosuke, the Edo Bakufu regent, signs the Treaty of Amity and Commerce with the U.S. opening free trade with six ports. Later, Japan signs similar treaties with England, Russia, Holland, and France.
1860	Seventy seven Bakufu officials travel to Washington, D.C. aboard the U.S. Navy ship "*Powhatan*" to ratify the Treaty of Amity and Commerce.
1861	Fukuzawa Yukichi founds a school based on western principles and subjects (precursor to Keio University).
1866	Oguri Kozukenosuke and French navy engineer Francois Verny build the Japan's first iron mill and shipyard in Yokosuka.
1867	Tokugawa Yoshinobu resigns as Shogun (end of Samurai era).
1868	Resumption of government with the Emperor as head of state. The five article Charter Oath is announced and taken by Emperor Meiji.
1869	Edo is renamed "Tokyo" and established as the capital city. The Department of Shinto religion is established. Tokyo Shokonsha, a shrine is built for those who died for the royalist cause during the Meiji Restoration (later renamed Yasukuni Jinja).
1871	A new currency system is adopted with the yen as the monetary unit. Japan's Population: 34,806,000.
1872	The government issues state-controlled education (primary school) to abolish illiteracy. Baseball is introduced to Japan, and the first railway constructed (from Tokyo to Yokohama).
1873	The Western calendar system is adopted.
1879	President Ulysses Grant and the First Lady visit Japan.
1881	Okuma Shigenobu founds a school (precursor to Waseda University).
1882	The Bank of Japan is created as the nation's central bank.
1885	A modern cabinet system is adopted. Ito Hakubun becomes the first Prime Minister.
1887	Electricity service starts in Tokyo.

AMERICA AND THE WORLD

YEAR	AMERICA AND THE WORLD
1837	Oberlin College enrolls its first female students.
1840	The U.S. population: 17,069,453.
1845	Immigration from Ireland begins. During the next 15 years, half of Ireland's population immigrates to the U.S. (1,500,000).
1846	The Mexican-American War (–48). The U.S. acquires California, Nevada, Utah, New Mexico, and parts of Arizona, Colorado, Kansas, and Wyoming for $15,000,000 with assumption of $3,250,000 in debt owed by Mexico to the U.S.
1848	The first Women's Rights Convention is held in New York (Elizabeth Stanton). Gold is discovered in California, and the gold rush begins.
1854	Commodore Matthew Perry opens Japan for trade, and the U.S. and Japan sign the Treaty of Peace and Amity.
1859	The uninhabited Midway Island is discovered by Captain Brooks; the U.S. claimed the island under the Guano Act of 1856.
1861	President Abraham Lincoln is inaugurated. The Civil War begins; conflict over slavery between Southern states (the Confederacy) and the Northern states (the Union).
1862	President Abraham Lincoln signs the Homestead Act. 200,000 freed slaves join the Union to fight for freedom.
1863	President Abraham Lincoln signs the Emancipation Proclamation freeing all slaves (4,000,000). The IRS established.
1865	The Confederacy defeated by the Union. 13th Amendment to the U.S. Constitution is ratified, abolishing slavery. President Lincoln is assassinated. The KKK founded by former confederate soldiers to suppress African-Americans.
1867	The U.S. purchases Alaska from Russia ($7,200,000), and the U.S. annexes the Midway Island in the Central Pacific.
1868	The Carnegie Steel Company is formed.
1869	Belle Babb Mansfield becomes the first female lawyer in the United States. The transcontinental railroad is completed at Promontory Point, Utah.
1870	The Standard Oil Company is formed.
1876	Alexander Graham Bell invents the telephone.
1877	Thomas Edison invents the phonograph and later, the electric light bulb.
1882	The Chinese Immigrant Exclusion Act is signed.
1886	President Grover Cleveland unveils the Statue of Liberty.

JAPANESE AMERICAN

YEAR	JAPANESE AMERICAN
1834	A merchant seaman Otokichi and his ship, *Hojunmaru*, are blown off course and drift ashore at Cape Flattery. Three Japanese castaways rescued by English seamen are taken to London via Hawaii.
1838	Otokichi returns to America and later sails to Makao.
1841	Manjiro, a 14-year-old fisherman, is rescued by the American whaler *John Howland* from the uninhabited island of Torishima.
1843	After a long whaling journey, Captain Whitfield brings Manjiro to Fairhaven, Massachusetts, and gives him a formal American education.
1851	Hikozo, a 13-year-old boy, is rescued by the American freighter *Auckland* with 16 other shipmates whose ship is wrecked by a severe storm. The Japanese men are taken to San Francisco (first Japanese to reach California).
1854	The U.S. and Japan sign the Treaty of Peace and Amity. Hikozo enters a Catholic school in Baltimore and is baptized as Josef Heko.
1858	The U.S. and Japan sign the Treaty of Amity and Commerce. Josef Heko becomes the first Japanese naturalized American citizen.
1860	Seventy seven Edo Bakufu officials arrive in San Francisco aboard the American Navy ship *Powhatan* to ratify a treaty in Washington, D.C. They also visit several east coast cities, including New York, and are received by a huge welcoming crowd.
1865	Niijima Jo, son of the Annaka clan's samurai, arrives in Boston. He graduates from Amherst College in 1870 as the first Japanese to receive an American degree, and from Andover Theological School in 1874. Later, he founds precursor to Doshisha University in Japan.
1866	Many feudal lords begin to send their clan's sons to study in the U.S. These men bring Western ideology, culture, and education systems back to Japan.
1867	Nagasawa kanae, a 15 year old son of the Satsuma clan's samurai, after studying in New York for seven years, moves to Fountain Grove, California, where he establishes a successful vineyard and winery business.
1868	153 Japanese laborers are transported to work on sugar plantations in Hawaii (Gannenmono).
1869	J.H. Schnell takes 40 Japanese to California to establish Wakamatsu Tea and Silk Colony.
1870	The Japanese government establishes the first legation in Washington, D.C. and the Consulate in San Francisco, and starts to send young elites to study in east coast colleges in the U.S.
1873	Junzo Matsumura is the first Japanese midshipman at the U.S. Naval Academy.
1880	The U.S. census: Japanese population 148
1884	Domoto, Einoshin and the Kentarou brothers arrive in San Francisco California. They form a large nursery business in California, the first Japanese to purchase farm land in California.
1885	The *City of Tokio* arrives in Honolulu carrying the first 944 official immigrants from Japan to work on a sugar plantation (three-year contract with the Hawaiian government). This was the beginning of Japanese labor immigration to Hawaii.

CHRONOLOGY

YEAR	JAPANESE AMERICAN
1890	The U.S. census: Japanese population 2,039. Most Japanese immigrants work in the railroad, oil fields, and agriculture as laborers
1894	The Japanese population in Hawaii reaches 29,000. The three-year Japanese contract labor to Hawaii is discontinued.
1895	The U.S. census: Japanese population (on the mainland) 6,000.
1898	In the Spanish-American War, seven Japanese Isseis are killed aboard the USS Maine. The Japanese newspaper Hokubei Nippo published in San Francisco. The U.S. annexes Hawaii.
1899	The first Nishi Honganji Buddhist priests arrive in California and set up the North American Buddhist Mission.
1900	The U.S. census: Japanese population 24,326 (only 410 women). Japanese begin to buy property and establish farms, vineyards, and orchards in Central California.
1901	Dr. Jokichi Takamine isolates adrenaline at John Hopkins University.
1902	The Seattle Japanese language school is formed.
1903	Seito Saibara, agriculturist, Doshisha University president, and the Japanese Parliament member, is invited by the Houston Chamber of Commerce to teach rice production to local farmers. He brings Japanese seed rice to Texas. He has been credited as establishing the gulf coast rice industry.
1905	The Japanese newspaper Rafu Shimpo published in Los Angeles. The Asiatic Exclusion League is formed in San Francisco.
1906	The Great Earthquake shakes San Francisco, and many Japanese move to Southern California. Abiko Kyutaro establishes the Yamato Colony.
1907	38,000 Japanese move to mainland U.S. from Hawaii. "Executive Order 589" bars Japanese from entering the continental U.S. from Hawaii, Canada, and Mexico.
1908	The Japanese government agrees not to issue passports to Japanese laborers wishing to work in the U.S. (Gentlemen's Agreement).
1909	The Southern California Japanese-American Society is established.
1910	Arthur K. Ozawa, graduate of the University of Michigan Law School, is the first Japanese American to become a lawyer. The U.S. census: Japanese population: 72,157
1913	The California Alien Land Law is signed, prohibiting "Aliens ineligible for citizenship" from owning the land.
1915	The Southern California Japanese Chamber of Commerce is established.
1917	During World War I, Japanese Isseis serve in the U.S. military.
1920	The Japanese government stops issuing passports to picture brides. The U.S. census: Japanese population 111,010
1922	Ozawa vs. U.S. Supreme Court upholds the Naturalization Law on the basis of race (this ban lasts until 1952).
1924	President Calvin Coolidge signs the Immigration Act of 1924, effectively ending Japanese immigration to the U.S. Cyrus Woods, the U.S. Ambassador to Japan, resigns in protest.
1927	The U.S. Supreme Court unanimously rules that the laws passed by Hawaii's legislature to control the Japanese Language School are unconstitutional.
1930	The Japanese American Citizens League (JACL) is founded. The U.S. census: Japanese population 138,834

YEAR	AMERICA AND THE WORLD
1890	The U.S. population: 62,947,714.
1891	James Naismith invents the game of basketball.
1892	Ellis Island opens to immigrants from European countries. 20,000,000 immigrants pass through by 1954.
1898	The Spanish-American War. As a result, the U.S. acquires Puerto Rico, Guam and the Philippines for $20,000,000. The U.S. annexes the Mariana Islands and Hawaii.
1903	The Wright brothers fly the first successful airplane. Ford Motors is formed.
1906	The Great Earthquake shakes San Francisco.
1909	The NAACP is founded, demanding equal civil, political and educational rights for African American people.
1910	The U.S. population: 91,972,266. Japan invades Korea and imposes military rule.
1912	The Titanic sinks south of Newfoundland and about 1,500 people drown.
1913	The Federal Reserve System is established.
1914	The Panama Canal opens. World War I begins.
1917	Revolution topples the Czarist government in Russia. The U.S. declares war against Germany (World War I – 1919).
1918	An influenza epidemic kills nearly 50C,000 Americans.
1920	The 19th Amendment gains women the right to vote. Radio broadcast starts.
1922	Italian dictator Benito Mussolini comes into power
1924	Wyoming and Texas elect the first female governors.
1927	Charles Lindbergh flies from New York to Paris.
1929	The stock market crashes, beginning of worldwide Depression.
1932	English scientist James Chadwick discovers neutron. Olympic Games are held in Los Angeles. Japanese troops invade Shanghai, China, and bomb the city.

YEAR	JAPAN
1890	The first Diet is elected and convened. Population: 40,000,000.
1894	Sino-Japanese War. Japan and China fight in Korea; Japan defeats China.
1895	The Treaty of Shimonoseki: China pays Japan an indemnity and cedes Formosa (Taiwan).
1897	Yahata Steel Company formed
1904	Japanese-Russian War(–05): Japan defeats Russia.
1905	The Portsmouth Treaty: Japan wins control of the Liaotung Peninsula, Korea and the southern half of Sakhalin Island.
1906	The Southern Manchuria Railroad Company is established.
1907	Japan and Brazil conclude an Immigration Treaty.
1908	The U.S. and Japan sign the Gentlemen's Agreement.
1910	Japan annexes Korea and imposes military rule.
1912	Emperor Meiji dies, followed by the enthronement of Emperor Taisho.
1914	World War I begins.
1915	Japan presents the list of Twenty-one Demands to China, and expands into Manchuria.
1917	Japan declares war on Germany.
1920	Depression hits Japan. Japan joins the League of Nations. Population: 56,666,000
1921	Japan joins the Washington, D.C., Naval Treaty with the U.S., England, and France (Four Power Pacific Treaty).
1923	A severe earthquake strikes Kanto area.
1925	All men over age 25 are granted the right to vote. Radio broadcasting starts.
1926	Emperor Taisho dies, followed by the enthronement of Emperor Showa.
1929	Japan's economy tumbles.
1931	The Japanese army takes over Mukden and moves into Southern Manchuria. The League of Nations calls for Japan to withdraw from Mukden and Manchuria.
1932	Japan sends troops to Shanghai and bombs the city. The army establishes the Manchukuo in Manchuria. Prime Minister Inukai is assassinated by right wing military officers, effectively ending party government.

CHRONOLOGY

YEAR	JAPANESE AMERICAN	AMERICA AND THE WORLD	JAPAN
1933		President Franklin Roosevelt launches the "New Deal" recovery program. Adolph Hitler, leader of Nazi Party, becomes chancellor of Germany.	The League of Nations calls for the withdrawal of Japanese troops from China and Manchuria; Japan withdraws from the League of Nations in protest.
1934	The *Nisei Week* starts.	Brazil signs the Japanese Immigrant Exclusion Law.	Brazil signs the Japanese Immigrant Exclusion Law. Japan abrogates the Washington Naval Treaty.
1935	President Franklin Roosevelt signs the "Nye Bill" into law, granting U.S. citizenship to 500 World War 1 veterans of Asian descent.	President Roosevelt signs the Social Security Act. Italy invades Ethiopia.	
1936		Japan invades northern China and Mongolia. Civil War erupts in Spain.	Japan abrogates the London Naval Treaty.
1937		Italy withdraws from the League of Nations.	Chinese-Japanese War: Japan mobilizes its military throughout the entire country and begins major military expansion throughout Northern and Central China.
1938		Hitler absorbs Austria and part of Czechoslovakia and invades Poland.	The Government enacts the National Mobilization Act. The Nomonhan Incident; Japan and Russia fight over the Manchurian borders, Japan defeated.
1939		Japan, Germany, and Italy sign a military alliance. World War II begins, following Germany's invasion of Poland and part of Czechoslovakia. Six million Jews killed by Adolph Hitler and the Nazis during the war.	Japan signs a military alliance with Germany and Italy.
1940	The leaders of the JACL meet with the Army and Navy Intelligence Service to pledge their loyalty.	Germany captures Norway, Denmark, Holland, Belgium, and Luxemburg. German planes bomb London. Italy invades Egypt and Greece. Japan attacks England, Holland and France's colonial holdings across Asia.	Japan completes its occupation of Northern French Indochina. All political parties are dissolved and Japan becomes a military-dominated country.
1941	On December 7, Japan attacks Pearl Harbor, Hawaii. The FBI and police arrest 1,291 Japanese *Issei* community leaders in Hawaii and on the West Coast. Between December 18th to 24th, the Japanese submarines attack eight American merchant ships along the U.S. West Coast (Seattle to San Diego). They sink two U.S. oil tankers. The entire West Coast becomes Military Area No.1.	President Franklin Roosevelt freezes German, Italian, and Japanese assets. Japanese planes and submarines attack Pearl Harbor, Hawaii, killing 2,403 soldiers and civilians. Japan attacks Philippines, Hong Kong, Malaysia, Thailand, Guam, and Wake Island. Beginning of the Pacific War.	Japan and Russia sign a Neutrality Treaty. General Hideki Tojo becomes the Prime Minister (military regime). A final Imperial Conference is held. Emperor Showa approves all military preparations and plans on December 8th as date for attacks on the U.S. Japan attacks Pearl Harbor in Hawaii, Guam, Wake Island, Philippines, Hong Kong, Thailand, and Malaysia. The war of the Pacific has begun.
1942	Executive Order 9066 authorizes the Secretary of War to relocate all Japanese-Americans on the West Coast. The Western Defense Command indicates that Japanese-Americans would be excluded from Military Area No.1, and encourages them to leave the area voluntarily. Fewer than 5,000 people leave the area. More than 110,000 forced to enter the ten War Relocation Centers. Japanese submarine bombs the Santa Barbara oil refinery in California and a floatplane, launched from a submarine, bombs Fort Stevens and Cape Blanco in Oregon.	President Roosevelt authorizes the internment of 112,000 Japanese-Americans. "Bataan Death March" occurs when 10,000 U.S. and 55,000 Philippine prisoners of war are forced to march 120 miles to Pampang by the Japanese army. More than 20,000 prisoners die. In the Battle of Midway, U.S. aircraft repel the Japanese assault in the Central Pacific.	Japan occupies Manila and Singapore and bombs Australia. The U.S. begins first air raids on Tokyo, Yokohama, Nagoya and Kobe. Japan loses the Battle of Midway.
1943	The 442nd Combat Team and the 100th Infantry Battalion (all *Nisei* units) fight in Europe, win numerous unit and individual citations.	Mussolini of Italy resigns and 250,000 German and Italian troops surrender in Tunisia.	Tokyo Rose (Iva Toguri) starts a propaganda radio program aimed at demoralizing U.S. soldiers in the Pacific. Japan loses the battle at Atts Island and Guadalcanal.
1944	*Nisei* eligibility for the draft is restored.	On D-Day, 156,000 allied troops storm the beaches of Normandy, France. In the Battle of Leyte Gulf, Japan's Imperial Navy loses almost all its ships and planes.	Saipan Island falls to the U.S. Tojo resigns as Prime Minister. Suicidal bombing starts on U.S. ships by Japanese Kamikaze pilots. Japan is defeated in the Battle of Leyte. The U.S. air raids begin over Tokyo on a major scale.
1945	Japan surrenders, World War II ends.	Hitler of Germany commits suicide and Germany surrenders to the Allies. The United Nations forms with 50 countries. The U.S. tests the atomic bomb in New Mexico, and then drops them on Hiroshima and Nagasaki. Japan surrenders.	Japan loses the Iwo Jima battle. Okinawa falls to the U.S. Large scale air raids are held over Tokyo and major cities by the U.S.. England, the U.S. and China issue the Potsdam Declaration to demand immediate surrender by Japan, or suffer prompt and utter destruction; Japan ignores the request. The U.S. drops atomic bombs on Hiroshima and Nagasaki; Russia declares war on Japan. Japan finally accepts the Potsdam Declaration and unconditional surrender; U.S. General MacArthur arrives in Tokyo. The Land Reform Act by Diet is passed.
1946	4,724 people of Japanese ancestry repatriated to Japan (supposedly many of them later returned to the U.S.)	Indonesia and the Philippines become independent countries.	The Shinto state is disestablished and the Emperor denounces his divinity. A new constitution is formed and women gain the right to vote. The first Diet election is held and the Diet passes the Fundamental Law of Education.
1947		The Cold War with the USSR (Russia) begins(–1990).	
1948	President Harry Truman signs the Japanese American Evacuation Claims Act.	The U.S. formally recognizes the State of Israel.	
1949	Iva Toguri (Tokyo Rose) is convicted for treason.	The U.S. joins the North Atlantic Treaty (NATO). The USSR tests the atomic bomb at Semepalalinsk. Mao Tse Tung proclaims the People's Republic of China and the National Chinese Government flees to Taiwan.	Hideki Yukawa, the first Japanese to receive Nobel Prize in physics.
1950		The Korean War begins(–53). The U.S. population: 150,693,361.	Population : 83,200,000
1951			The San Francisco Peace Treaty is signed by 48 nations. Japan regains status as an independent country. The U.S. and Japan sign a mutual Security Treaty.
1952	McCarran-Walter Act grants Japan an immigration quota and allows *Issei* naturalization.	England tests the atomic bomb near Monte Bello Island, west of Australia.	
1953	Lt. Col. John Aiso, the highest ranking *Nisei* World War II veteran, becomes the first Japanese-American to serve in the California State Judiciary and the Federal Appellate Courts.	Sir Edmund Hillary of England conquers Mt. Everest.	
1954		The French Garrison falls at Dien Bien Phu in Vietnam.	
1955	1,600 Japanese *Issei* become U.S. citizens.	Rosa Parks refuses to give up her seat to a white man on a Montgomery, Alabama city bus, leading to a year-long African-American bus boycott. Her act of defiance begins the modern civil rights movement that ends legal segregation in the U.S.	

CHRONOLOGY

YEAR	JAPANESE AMERICAN	YEAR	AMERICA AND THE WORLD	YEAR	JAPAN
				1952	U.S. occupation of Japan officially ends.
				1953	TV broadcasting starts in Japan.
				1954	Japanese Self-Defense Force is created.
1956	California repeals its Alien Land Law.	1956	Israeli forces invade the Sinai Peninsula. England and France bomb Egypt.	1956	Japan is admitted into the United Nations. Population: 93,419,000
1960	442nd Battalion veterans Daniel K. Inouye and Spark Matsunaga become the U.S. Senator and Congressman, respectively, from Hawaii. The U.S. census: Japanese-Amercian population 260,877	1959	Fidel Castro defeats the Batista regime in Havana, Cuba.	1960	Japan and the U.S. sign a revised Treaty of Mutual Security and Cooperation.
		1960	France tests the atomic bomb in the Sahara desert. The Food and Drug Administration approves the birth control pill.		
		1961	President John F. Kennedy is inaugurated. Russian Cosmonaut Yuri Gagarin becomes the first human to orbit the earth. U.S. Astronaut Alan Shepard launches into space. East Germany installs the Berlin Wall.		
		1963	President Kennedy is assassinated. U.S. steps up its military intervention in Vietnam.		
1964	Patsy Takemoto-Mink becomes the first Asian-American woman to serve in Congress as a representative from Hawaii	1964	President Lyndon Johnson signs the Civil Rights Act. China tests the atomic bomb in the South Pacific.	1964	The summer Olympic Games are held in Tokyo. Japan restores diplomatic relations with South Korea.
1965	Immigration Law abolishes "national origin" as a basis for allocating immigration quotas to various countries.	1967	Thurgood Marshall sworn in as the first African-American Supreme Court Justice.		
		1968	African-American civil rights leader Dr. Martin Luther King Jr. assassinated.		
		1969	U.S. Astronaut Neil Armstrong becomes the first human to walk on the moon		
1971	Norman Mineta becomes the Mayor of San Jose.	1971	The 26th Amendment gives 18-year-olds the right to vote. The U.S population: 203,211,926.	1972	Okinawa returns to Japan. Japan restores diplomatic relations with China.
1975	The Los Angeles "Keiro Retirement Home" is founded.	1974	President Richard Nixon resigns in the wake of the Watergate scandal, the first president in U.S. history to resign during office.	1973	Floating exchange rate system for the yen begins (free trade).
1978	The JACL adapts a resolution calling for redress and reparations for the internment of Japanese-American.	1975	The Vietnam War ends. India tests the atomic bomb.	1980	Population: 117,063,000
1980	The Japanese-American Culture Center opens. Eunice Sato, the first woman and the first Asian-American ever elected as a Mayor of Long Beach, California.	1979	Margaret Thatcher becomes the first female Prime Minister of England.		
1985	The Space shuttle Challenger explodes and the first Japanese-American astronaut, Ellison Onizuka, is killed.	1981	Sandra Day O'Connor is sworn in as the first female Supreme Court Justice. IBM releases the first personal computer. Doctors diagnose the first case of AIDS.	1989	Emperor Showa dies followed by the enthronement of Emperor Heisei. A 3% sales tax is instituted.
1986	Dr. John Kashiwabara becomes the first Asian-American to serve on the California State University Board of Trustees (1986–1994).	1988	Al Qaeda founded by Osama Bin Laden.		
1988	President Ronald Reagan makes formal apology for war-time relocation and internment of Japanese-Americans. He signs HR442 into law and grants reparation of $20,000 for each surviving internee and a $125,000,000 educational fund for the Japanese community.	1989	A pro-democracy demonstration is held in Tiananmen Square in Beijing, China. Chinese army kills several thousand demonstrators. The Communist regime collapses in Eastern Europe and the Berlin Wall is torn down.	1991	The downfall of the Japanese economy begins.
1990	The older surviving internees receive their reparation payment with a letter of apology at the Greater Hall of Justice.	1990	Germany is reunited. Iraqi troops invade and occupy Kuwait by force.	1995	An earthquake of magnitude 7.2 strikes the Kobe area, killing 6,000 people. The Aum Shinrikyo religious cult releases deadly Sarin gas In the Tokyo subway system, killing and injuring many people.
1992	The Japanese-American National Museum founded. Fifth-generation Japanese-American Kristi Yamaguchi wins gold medal in Olympic figure skating.	1991	The U.S., Western and Arab troops eject Iraq from Kuwait by force. The USSR dissolved and the Cold War ends.	1996	The U.S. President William Clinton visits Japan.
2000	The Japanese-American Memorial founded in Washington, D.C.	1993	President William Clinton inaugurated. Congress passes the North American Free Trade Agreement (NAFTA).	2000	Population: 126,284,805
		1996	Dolly the sheep is the first mammal to be successfully cloned.	2002	Toyota and Honda Motors start selling electric hybrid vehicles.
		1997	Pakistan tests the atomic bomb.	2004	A large earthquake shakes Niigata.
		1998	Europe starts a new currency system, the Euro.		
		2000	Researchers decode the human genome.		
		2001	Terrorists attack the World Trade Center in New York, the Pentagon and the Defense Department building in Washington D.C.; thousands of civilians are killed.		
		2002	The space shuttle Columbia flight ends in tragedy.		
		2003	The U.S.-led Iraq war starts.		

Castaway Joseph Heco (Hikozo) and his shipmates. First photograph of Japanese people ever taken.
Hikozo seated second from left in the top photograph.
January 22, 1853, *Frank Leslie Illustrated Newspaper*.
(Property of Nihon Camera Museum, Chiyoda-ku, Tokyo)

漂流民、彦蔵（ジョーゼフ・ヒコ）と船員仲間の銀板写真。日本人で始めて写真に写された人達。
彦蔵は上の写真の左から二番目、サンフランシスコにて。
1853年1月22日 *Frank Leslie Illustrated Newspaper*.
（東京都千代田区　日本カメラ博物館所蔵）

Sengokusen

Sengokusen (ship). The Edo government prohibited the construction of ocean-going ships during the Seclusion Period 1635-1854. The size of the ships was restricted by law, and their design specifications limited their sea-worthiness. Sengokusen were unrivaled in their suitability as commercial vessels for coastline sailing only, but could not withstand large storms at sea. Many of them were shipwrecked by storms. Wood block print by a Japanese artist.

千石船。幕府の鎖国政策（1635－1854）は大型船の建造を禁止した。日本沿岸で食料や日用品などを運ぶのみに適した小型の千石船は、外洋航海に適していなかった。構造的にもしけに弱く、嵐のためにおこる海難事故によって漂流者が多発した原因の一つとなった。日本人画家による木版画。

一八四一年六月、アメリカ捕鯨船
ジョン・ハウランド号のウィットフィールド
船長が、鳥島に漂流していた
土佐出身の万次郎他四人の
日本人漁師、救出の絵。

In 1841, a 14 year old castaway, Manjiro, was rescued by the American whaler , "John Howland" from the unhabited island of Torishima. The captain of the ship, William Whitfield, brought Manjiro to his hometown of Fairhaven, Massachusetts. Under the sponsorship of Captain Whitfield, Manjiro received a formal American education at Oxford School in Fairhaven.
Drawing of rescue by Fairhaven, Massachusetts artist, Arthur Moniz.

1841年、14才の漁師、万次郎は遭難し無人島、鳥島に漂着した。アメリカの捕鯨船ジョン・ハウランド号に救出され、ウイリアム・ウィットフィールド船長の好意でアメリカ東部のマサチューセッツ州フェアヘーブンに連れてこられた。後にオックスフォード・スクールに入学し、アメリカの教育を受けた初めての日本人となった。

Black Ships

Portrait of Commodore Matthew Perry
Photographer: Matthew Brady.
(Courtesy of Nihon Camera Museum, Chiyoda-ku, Tokyo)

マシュウ・ペリー提督の写真
写真家マシュウ・ブラディ撮影
(東京都千代田区 日本カメラ博物館所蔵)

Commodore Perry's flagship, the *USS Powhatan*. The Treaty of Kanagawa was signed on her deck in 1854. In 1860, she carried the first Japanese Bakufu diplomats to the U.S. to ratify the treaty. (Yokosuka City Museum, Yokosuka-shi, Kanagawa-ken).

ペリーの黒船の1隻の油絵。ポーハタン号。1854年に船上で神奈川条約調印が行われ、1860年遣米使節団が日米修好通商条約批准のため米国まで乗船した船。(神奈川県横須賀市自然・人文博物館提供)

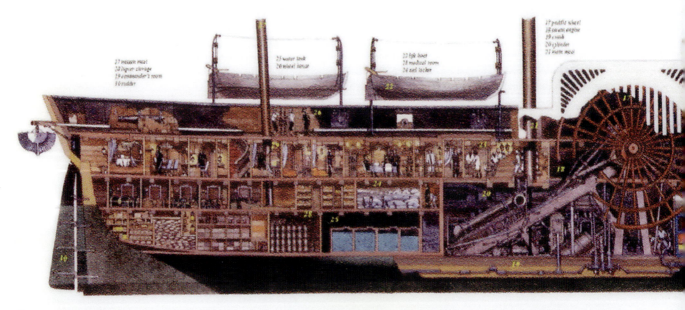

Cross-section of Commodore Perry's Black Ship, "*Susquehanna.*" Built in 1852, it boasted 4 levels, a coal-burning steam engine, and three large sails. It weighed 2,450 tons, and held a crew of 300. Livestock were carried on board for consumption by the crew.

Commodore Perry's "Black Ship" by a Japanese artist. Woodblock Print. 1854. (Nagasaki Prefecture Art Museum)
日本人の画家によるペリーの黒船、ポーハタン号の木版画。1854年。（長崎県立美術博物館）

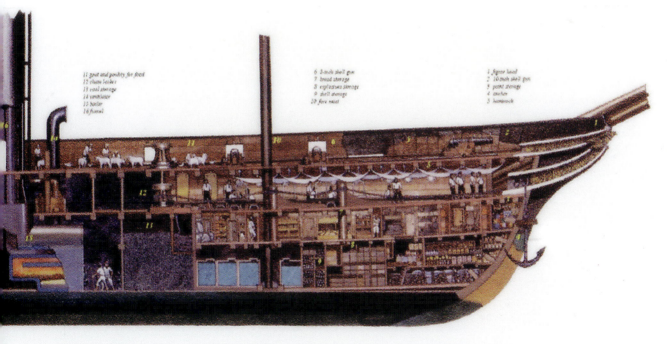

ペリー提督率いる黒船の一隻、サスケハナ号の断面図。1852年建造された3本マスト及び石炭使用の蒸気船。
2450トン乗組員約300人。四階建てで、食用の山羊や鶏まで飼っていた様子が伺える。

Landing of Commodore Perry at Kurihama

On July 8, 1853. four Black Ships led by Commodore Matthew Perry anchored in Uraga harbor at the mouth of Edo Bay. Perry was met by the Uraga Magistrate's officers who told him to go to Nagasaki, which was the only port open to foreigners. The Japanese Shogunate government had already been informed by Holland more than a year prior that the U.S. had planned to send the Black Ships to Japan. Perry firmly declined the order and demanded permission to present a letter from U.S. President Milford Fillmore to the Japanese Emperor. After a long discussion with the Uraga Magistrates and the Shogunate's advisors, the Shogunate government decided to accept the letter.

On July 14, 1853 the Black Ships offshore gave a thirteen gun salute. Commodore Perry and 400 seamen and marines from the U.S. Navy arrived at Kurihama in fifteen cutter boats. They were led by the Japanese Magistrate's official's boats. All of the Japanese officials were dressed formally for the occasion. The U.S. soldiers lined up along Kurihama Beach. From there, they marched to a temporary reception center which was built by the Shogunate government. U.S. Marine Major Zeilin led the procession with his saber drawn. He was followed by soldiers, a military band, and two boys bearing boxes containing President Fillmore's letter and Commodore Perry's credentials. At the rear were Commodore Perry, Commander Adams and Lieutenant Contee. The Japanese Magistrates and thousands of Shogunate soldiers watched the U.S. Marines and sailors rhythmical uniform procession, and they were deeply impressed. They found the march to be well trained and beautiful and a real display of their strength. This incident brought the end of over two centuries of Japan's self-imposed seclusion policy (Sakoku). Japan then began moving toward Westernization.

1853年7月8日、ペリー提督率いる'黒船'四隻は江戸湾の入口、浦賀に碇を下ろした。幕府はこのアメリカ船の来航を、一年以上前にオランダを通じて知らされていた。浦賀奉行は、ペリーに対し、直ちに長崎に行くように申し渡した。ペリーはそれを強硬に拒否し、来航の目的は、江戸においてアメリカのフィルモアー大統領の親書を日本の皇帝に手渡すことだと告げた。幕府側は長い協議の末、このままでは戦争になりかねないという幕府の役職や浦賀奉行の進言を容れ、7月14日に公式に大統領の親書を久里浜で受け取ることにした。そのため急挙、久里浜の海岸に土俵で造られた桟橋と仮設の応接所を設置した。7月14日の朝、沖の黒船から13発の祝砲が放たれ、陣羽織に袴で正装した浦賀奉行所の役人の船に先導され、カッター１５隻に分乗した400人のアメリカ海軍士官兵が久里浜海岸に上陸した。サーベルを抜いたゼーリン少佐を先頭に、正装した将校、水兵、軍楽隊と続き、そのあとに親書と全権委任状を収めた箱を持った二人の少年、そしてペリー提督がアダムス参謀とコンティー副官に守られて進んだ。軍楽隊の美しい音楽と共に軽快に一糸乱れず整然と行進するアメリカ海軍を始めて見た日本人たちは非常に驚き、役人や警備についていた各藩の数千人の侍までが強い軍隊の象徴と感じ'よく訓練されていて美しい、'と賞賛した。こうして二世紀以上にわたった長い鎖国制度は終焉をむかえ、日本は近代国家として出発することになる。

On July 14, 1853, the first landing of Americans in Japan under the command of Commodore Matthew Perry at Kurihama. Hand colored lithograph by Wilhelm Heine. (Courtesy of Yokosuka City Museum, Yokosuka-shi, Kanagawa-ken)

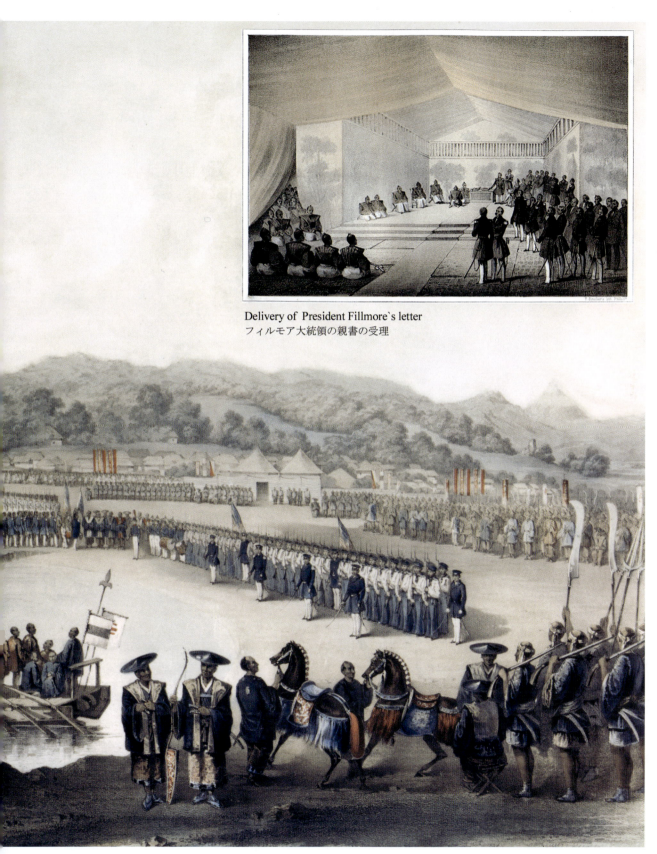

Delivery of President Fillmore's letter
フィルモア大統領の親書の受理

1853年7月14日ペリー提督久里浜（浦賀）上陸の図。アメリカ海軍専属画家、ウイルヘルム・ハイネの手書きリトグラフ
`Illustration of the Japan Expedition`より．（神奈川県横須賀市自然・人文博物館所蔵）

Commodore Perry Landing at Yokohama

1854, dinner party aboard *the USS Pow-hatan* with Commodore Perry and several Japanese government officials.
Drawn by American Navy artist, Wilhelm Heine.

1854年ペリーの黒船ポーハタン号船上でペリー提督が、幕府役人達を招き夕食会を催したときの絵。
アメリカ海軍専属の画家：
ウイルヘルム・ハイネ画

March 8, 1854, landing of Commodore Matthew Perry, meeting Edo Bakufu commissioners at Yokohama.
Hand colored lithograph by Wilhelm Heine. (Courtesy of Yokosuka City Museum, Yokosuka-shi, Kanagawa-ken)

1854年3月8日　ペリー提督横浜上陸の図。アメリカ海軍専属画家：ウルヘルム・ハイネの手書きリトグラフ
'Illustration of the Japan expedition' より。（神奈川県横須賀市自然・人文博物館所蔵）

The First Japanese Diplomatic mission to the U.S

Japanese diplomats and President Buchanan exchange the Treaty of U.S.- Japan Amity and Commerce at the White House, May 17, 1860. *Frank Leslie Illustrated Newspaper.* (Property of Tozenji, Takasaki-shi, Gunma-ken)

ホワイトハウスでブキャナン大統領と日米修好通商条約の批准書を交わす遣米使節団代表達。
1860年5月17日 *Frank Leslie Illustrated Newspaper* （群馬県高崎市 東善寺所蔵）

Portrait of Chief Ambassador Plenipotentiary Shinmi Yorioki Buzennokami, member of the first Japanese Edo Bakufu mission to the U.S. in 1860.
(Property of Yokosuka City Museum, Yokosuka-shi, Kanagawa-ken)

1860年、遣米使節正使、
新見頼興豊前守の肖像画
（神奈川県横須賀市自然・
人文博物館所蔵）

Portrait of the 15th U.S. President, James Buchanan.

ジエームス・ブキャナン
15代米国大領の肖像画

Welcoming Party & Parade in New York

A welcome party for Japanese diplomats at the Metropolitan Hotel in New York.
June 25, 1860. *Frank Leslie Illustrated Newspaper*. (Property of Tozenji, Takasaki-shi Gunma-ken)

ニューヨーク　メトロポリタンホテルでの遣米使節団歓迎パーティー。
1860年6月25日　*Frank Leslie Illustrated Newspaper*（群馬県高崎市　東善寺所蔵）

A welcome parade for Japanese diplomats on Broadway in New York.
June 25, 1860. *Frank Leslie Illustrated Newspaper*. (Property of Tozenji, Takasaki-shi Gunma-ken)

ニューヨーク　ブロードウェイの遣米使節団歓迎パレード。日の丸の旗でビルが飾られているのが見られる。
1860年6月25日　*Frank Leslie Illustrated Newspaper*（群馬県高崎市　東善寺所蔵）

The Washington U.S. Naval Iron Mill

The Japanese diplomats visit the Washington U.S. Naval Iron Mill and Shipyard in April 5, 1860.
Oguri Tadamasa seated second from right in first row.
(Property of Nihon Camera Museum, Chiyoda-ku, Tokyo)

1860年4月5日　ワシントン米海軍工廠、造船所見学の遣米使節一行の写真。
前列右から二人目が小栗忠順（小栗上野介）（東京都千代田区　日本カメラ博物館所蔵）

Portrait of Oguri Tadamasa Bungonokami
(Kozukenosuke).
(Property of Tozenji, Takasaki-shi, Gunma-ken)

小栗忠順豊後守（小栗上野介）の肖像画
（群馬県高崎市　東善寺所蔵）

In 1868, Oguri Tadamasa proposed the building of Tsukiji Hotel in Tokyo. It was the first western-style hotel in Japan. While he was in the U.S. as an envoy, he learned corporate investment strategies and implemented them into his hotel venture which was designed by Richard Bridges and contracted by Shimizu Kisuke.

1860年, 遣米使節の一人として渡米した小栗上野介がアメリカで見聞した株式会社の手法を使い民間資本を集め、清水喜助（現、清水建設の二代目）が建築を請負って完成した‘築地ホテル’。

The Yokosuka Iron Mill

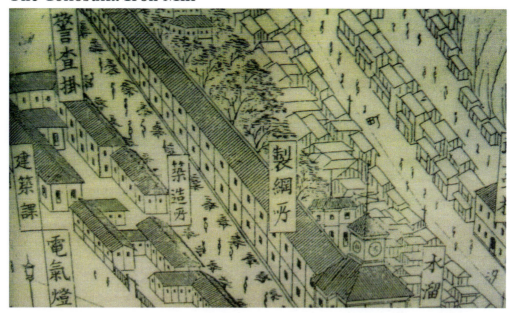

1865-1868. Oguri Tadamasa, inspired by the U.S. Iron Mill, builds the Yokosuka Iron Mill and Shipyard with the help of French shipbuilding engineer, Francos Verny.

横須賀製鉄、造船所。遺米使節として、アメリカで製鉄、造船技術を見た小栗上野介は日本にもその必要性を痛感し、勝海舟や幕閣の反対を押し切り，フランス人造船技師フランソワ・ヴェルニーの協力を得て横須賀に製鉄所と造船所を建造した。(1865〜68)(群馬県 高崎市 東善寺)

Tsukiji Hotel

World War II : Life in a Relocation Camp

1942 oil painting of Santa Anita temporary assembly center for Japanese-Americans.
Artist, James K. Furusawa. (Courtesy of Dr. Ray Oyakawa)

サンタ・アニータの競馬場内に設置された日系人仮集合所内の油絵。画家：ジェームス K. 古沢

"Being locked up behind barbed wire, with armed guards, made me feel sad like maybe I wasn't really a good American."
Poston Arizona Camp. Water color painting.
Artist, Chizuko Judy Sugita de Queiroz.

武装した兵隊に見張られて鉄条網の中にいる
わたしは、もしかして良いアメリカ人じゃ
ないのかなと悲しく思った。
画家：ジュディ・チズコ・スギタ

Traditional Japanese Culture Becomes Part of American Life

Madame Mitsuhiro Bando and Madame Sumi Hanayagi performing Japanese classical dance.

坂東三津拡師と花柳寿美師の共演

Karate is one of the popular martial arts in the U.S.

空手は、アメリカで人気の武術の一つとなった

A student of the Sogetsu School of Flower arrangement, Gloria Arnell.

草月流　グロリア・アーネル

James Keck and Barbara Hunter performing tea ceremony. Students of Urasenke, Madame Numano Somi.

裏千家　沼野宗美社中：ジェームス・ケック、バーバラ・ハンター

Beginning of New Chapter

President Ronald Reagan, signing HR442, the Civil Liberties Act, on August 10, 1988.

1988年8月10日に、1988年の公民法として知られるHR5442法案に署名するロナルド・レーガン大統領

The oldest surviving internee, Rev. Mamoru Eto, age 107. He was one of the oldest recipients to receive a reparation check and letter of apology from the U.S. Government at the Great Hall of the Justice Department, on October 9, 1990.

1990年10月9日、司法省のグレートホールで最初の謝罪文と補償金が渡された。受領者の一人、マモル・エトー牧師は107歳だった。

Children's Life in the Camps

Elementary school classroom at Poston Relocation Center, Arizona.
収容所内の小学校のクラス風景　（ポストン・アリゾナ）

Leaving for the Relocation Camps

Grandfather and grandchildren awaiting evacuation bus. The grandfather conducted a dyeing and cleaning business.
Photographer: Dorothea Lange
Hayward, California. 5/8/1942
収容所行きのバスを待つクリーニング店をやっていた祖父と孫たち。1942年5月カリフォルニア州ヘイワードにて。

写真家: ドロシア・ラング

Father and son evacuees of Japanese ancestry talk things over with military policeman prior to leaving for assembly center at Arcadia, California.
Photographer: Clem Albers
San Pedro, California. 4/5/1942
カリフォルニア州アーケディアの集合センターに旅立つ親子と子供をあやすアメリカ兵。
1942年4月 カリフォルニア州サンペドロにて。
写真家: クレム・アルバース

Orphans from San Francisco

Evacuee orphans from an institution in San Francisco who are now established for the duration in the Children's Village at this War Relocation Authority Center for evacuees of Japanese ancestry.

During World War II, the Manzanar camp's Children's Village was home to more than 100 foster children and orphans ranging in age from infants to teens. The children came primarily from Shonien Japanese-American Children's Home, Maryknoll Home of Japanese Children in Los Angeles, and the Salvation Army's Japanese Children's Home in San Francisco. Lillian Matsumoto, a social worker at Shonien who worked as the assistant superintendent at Children's Village, recalled when she and her staff traveled with the children on three buses from Los Angeles: "We tried to make like it was a picnic for the little ones. One four year old girl said, 'I will get up and sing,' and she sang 'God Bless America.' The young soldiers shed tears when they heard the little girl sing." When the war ended and the camp closed, the children either returned to their parents, were adopted, or were placed in foster homes.
Photographer: Dorothea Lange at Manzanar, California, July, 1942.
(Courtesy of *Rafu Shimpo*)

マンザナー　キャンプ内の孤児院チルドレンズ　ヴィレッジの子供達。　戦時中この孤児院にはロスアンジェルスの小児園とメリノール日系子供の家およびサンフランシスコの救世軍日系子供の家、各孤児院から送られた100人以上の子供達が生活していた。1942年6月、小児園の社会福祉員であり、後にチルドレンズ・ヴィレッジの副所長になったリリアン松本さんは、兵隊の護衛つきでロスアンジェルスからマンザナー収容所に職員や子供たちと三台のバスに乗せられて送られたときの事を語った。"小さな子供達はピクニックにでも行くのかと思ったのでしょう。四才の女の子が立ち上がって、歌をうたいたいと言いだし'God bless America'を歌ったのです。それを聞いて若いアメリカ兵が涙を流していました"。戦後、キャンプは閉鎖され、子供たちは親元に帰った子、養子になった子、里子として預けられた子と様々であった。

Life in Camp

Children are taught games in the nursery school at the Relocation Center. All desks, chairs, and other furnishings were made by evacuee workers in the furniture factory.
Photographer: Francis Stewart at Manzanar, California. 2/10/1943

マンザナーキャンプの保育園の工作時間。家具類はすべてキャンプ内で作られた。
写真家: フランシス・スチュアート　1943年2月

Sixth grade boys enjoy a game of baseball at recess time.
Photographer: Francis Stewart
Manzanar, California. 2/10/1943

1943年マンザナーキャンプにて小学六年生の
子供達が休み時間に野球をして遊ぶ風景。
写真家: フランシス・スチュアート

142

Dear Miss Breed (Clara Estelle Breed)

Clara Estelle Breed, also known as "Miss Breed," was the children's librarian at the San Diego Public Library from 1929 to 1945. Miss Breed was fond of all children, including the many Japanese-American children and teenagers who used to frequent the East San Diego branch library where she worked. Before World War II, Miss Breed was a mentor to many *Nisei* children who visited the library.

As the United States entered the war, these young *Nisei* were removed from their homes and placed in internment camps. Shocked and outraged, Miss Breed helped her young friends by becoming a lifeline to the outside world. She handed out stamped and addressed postcards at the railroad station on the day of their departure and encouraged them to write.

Upon receiving their letters, Miss Breed responded with books, care packages, and immeasurable emotional support. Yet, her commitment to her Japanese-American friends did not end with the letters and packages she regularly sent. Recognizing the injustice that the United States had committed against the Japanese-American community and seeing the need for others to speak out on their behalf, Miss Breed wrote various articles about the internment both during and after the war. Her actions, like those of the many people who reached out and helped Japanese Americans during this time, were all the more remarkable because of the widespread fear and hatred associated with anything Japanese.

After the war, Japanese Americans were allowed to return to their homes on the West Coast. Although Miss Breed no longer worked at the children's library, having been appointed to the position of Head Librarian in1945, she continued to exchange letters with many of her Japanese-American friends until her death at the age of 88 in 1994.She is remembered by all of her correspondents, now in their 60s and 70s, as a woman who restored their faith in themselves and in others during a time when this faith was sorely tested.

Miss Clara Breed はサンデイエゴ市立図書館のイースト子供図書館司書として、1929年から1945年まで働いていた。ミス ブリードと呼ばれていた彼女は子供好きで、図書館に出入りしていた日系の子供やティーンエイジャー達のよき相談相手として慕われていた。

日本との戦争が始まり日系人がキャンプに収容される事を聞き、彼女は非常に憤慨した。日系人がサンデイエゴを発つ日、これからキャンプ内で暮す幼い友人である子供たちの外界との架け橋になろうと自分の住所を書き、切手を貼ったはがきをたくさん携えて駅まで見送り、かならず手紙を書くようにと子供たちに渡した。子供たちから手紙がくると、ミス ブリードは返事のほか、定期的に本や小包を送り、子供たちへの計り知れない精神的支えとなっていた。彼女はそれだけに終わらず、この日系社会に対する国の不法な行為を日系人のために発言する必要性を感じた。戦時中は多くのアメリカ人が日本人に対し、恐れや憎しみを持っていた時代であったが、彼女はこの日系人強制収容の不法性を雑誌や新聞に書き、日系人の為に発言するように訴え、多くの協力者を得た。

戦後、図書館長の職にあったミス ブリードと西海岸に戻ってきた日系人たちとの交流は1994年, 彼女が88才で亡くなるまで続いた。ミス ブリードはこの信念を問われた時代に、自分の信念をしっかりと貫いたひとであった。

Relocation to Mid-West and Eastern States From Camps

In early 1944, the U.S. government began clearing individuals to return to the West Coast.
On January 2, 1945 the Exclusion Order was rescinded entirely.

Children have their own standards in their selection of friends and playmates. Color and ancestry simply don`t enter into it. Here, the sons of Japanese -American parents who have left the relocation centers and accepted employment in Chicago are welcomed into the neighborhood by Caucasian youngsters who share their toys with the new arrivals.
Photographer: Charles E. Mace
Libertyville, Illinois. 8/15/1943

1943年にイリノイ州シカゴに職を得てキャンプを出た一家の子供達が近所の白人の子供達と仲良く遊んでいる写真。彼等のように戦時中、アメリカ中西部や東部に職を得てキャンプを出た日系家族や、アメリカ人の宗教団体や教育者達の援助で大学に行った若者もたくさんいた。
写真家: チャールズ・メイス

Sachi Furuto and Sally Kusayanagi, formerly from Manzanar Relocation Center, at work in Des Moines, Iowa. Sachi operates the switchboard and Sally is employed as a stenographer. Both women are *Nisei.* Sally Kusayanagi says: "The people I am staying with are a minister and his wife, who are more than hospitable to me. As for the place I am working, it is just grand. The people here have accepted us as one of them, and they treat us well." Sachi Furuto states: "Our employer himself has more than willingly taken us in. The other employees have followed him and accepted us as one of them."
Des Moines, Iowa. January1944.

仕事をみつけてマンザナーキャンプを出、アメリカ中西部のアイオワ州デイモイン市の会社に電話交換手と速記者として就職した日系二世の女性達。"私は牧師夫妻の家で世話になっていますが、とても良くしていただいてます。職場も快適で、同僚も私たちを気持ちよく受け入れてくれました。"とサリー草柳は語った。1944年1月。

Everyone at the Hope Day Nursery in Philadelphia dearly loves Miss Chico. They should, for Chico Sakaguchi, a graduate of the University of California in Los Angeles, is a well trained and skilled social worker. She relocated to Philadelphia from Manzanar in April, 1944, and before that taught elementary classes at the center school.
Philadelphia, Pennsylvania. 7/24/1944

ホープ・デイ保育園の子供達に囲まれたチコ坂口先生。UCLAを卒業し、教師をしていた彼女は戦時中の1944年4月マンザナー・キャンプを出て、アメリカ東部のフィラデルフィア市に移転し、就職した。彼女達のように仕事を見つけてキャンプを出た人たちも少なくない。

Leaving the Relocation Camps

Closing of the Jerome Center, Denson, Arkansas. Children under 18 months, accompanied by their mothers, were provided pullman accommodations for travel to other centers. Here the mother of a small child is seen waving goodbye to her friends.
Photographer: Hikaru Iwasaki
Denson, Arkansas. 6/15/1944

1944年6月、アーカンサス州デンソンのジュロームキャンプが閉鎖され、18ヶ月以下の幼児と母親は汽車の個室を与えられ、旅立った。
写真家: ヒカル岩崎

Closing of the Jerome Center, Denson, Arkansas. A mother and very small infant, occupants of one of the pullman berths, waves goodbye from the car window.
Photographer: Hikaru Iwasaki
Denson, Arkansas. 6/19/1944

Closing of the Jerome Center, Denson, Arkansas. Travel is just another adventure to the children of the relocation centers.
Photographer: Hikaru Iwasaki
Denson, Arkansas. 6/15/1944

Bibliography

Books

• Hawaii Nikkei History Editorial Board. *Japanese Eyes, American Heart*. Tendai Educational Foundation, Honolulu.1998.

•「ブリエアの解放者たち」ドウス昌代著、文藝春秋、1983 年発行
Duus, Masayo. *The Liberators of Bruyeres*. (Title of American publication: *Unlikely Liberators*), Bungeishunju, Tokyo. 1983.

•「一世としてアメリカに生きて」北村崇郎著、草思社、1992 年発行
Iwata, Masakazu. *Planted in Good Soil*. Peter Lang Publishing, New York. 1992.

• Kitamura, Takao. *Living in America as Issei*, Tokyo, Soshisha, 1992.

• Masaoka, Mike and Hosokawa, Bill. *They Call Me Moses Masaoka: An American Saga*, William Morrow and Company, New York, 1987.

• Maki, Mitchell. T, Kitano, Harry. H. L., Berthold, S. Megan. *Achieving the Impossible Dream: How Japanese Americans Obtained Redress*, The Board of Trustees of the University of Illinois, Urbana, 1999.

• Murphy, Thomas. D. *Ambassadors in Arms – The Story of Hawaii's 100th Battalion*, Club 100 under special arrangement with University of Hawaii Press, Honolulu, 1954.

• Myer, Dillon, S. *Uprooted Americans*, The University of Arizona Press, Arizona, 1971.

• Niiya, Brian. (Ed.). Japanese American National Museum. *Encyclopedia of Japanese American History, Updated Edition*, Facts On File, New York, 2001.

•『真珠湾と日系人』西山千著、サイマル出版会、1991 年発行
Nishiyama, Sen. *Pearl Harbor and the Japanese Americans*, The Simul Press, Tokyo, 1991.

• Odo, Franklin. *No Sword to Bury: Japanese Americans in Hawaii during World War II*, Temple University Press, Philadelphia, 2004.

• Steidl, Franz. *Lost Battalions: Going for Broke in the Vosges, Autumn 1944*, Presidio Press, Novato, California. 1997.

• Takasugi, Ryo. *Passion for the Motherland: The Man Who Brought the Olympic Games to Tokyo*, Shincho-Bunko, Tokyo, 1990.

• tenBroek, Jacobus; Barnhart, Edward N; Watson, Floyd W. *Prejudice, War, and the Constitution*, Berkeley, University of California Press, Berkeley, 1954.

• Thomas, Dorothy S. and Nishimoto, Richard S. *The Spoilage*, University of California Press, Berkeley and Los Angeles, 1946.

• Weglyn, Michi. *Years of Infamy*, William Morrow and Company, New York, 1976.

Periodicals

• Greenhut, Steven. "Against the Tide," *The Orange County Register*. Santa Ana,California, November 20, 2005.

• Kakesako, Greg. "Native Son Joining Ranks of Eminent Army Leaders," The *Honolulu Star-Bulletin*. June 21, 1999. Retrieved on October 26, 2006, from starbulletin.com/1999/06/21/news/story2.html

• Mack, Ann and Ann Curry, "Living the Dream," *Newsletter of the School of Journalism and Communications, Flash*, Volume 18 No. 1, University of Oregon, Fall 2003. Retrieved on August 13, 2006, from flash.uoregon.edu/F03/curry.html

• Pichaske, Pete. "Shinseki is No.1 in Army," *The Honolulu Star-Bulletin*, June 22, 1999. Retrieved on October 26, 2006, from starbulletin.com/1999/06/22/news

• Stewart, Jocelyn Y. "Manzanar Icon Now More Than A Memory," *Los Angeles Times*, September 18, 2005.

• Werner, Erica. 'Internment Camps To Be Preserved," *Ventura Country Star, Camarillo Edition*, December 6, 2006.

• Zaslow, Jeffrey. "Straight Talk," *USA Weekend*. December 18-20, 1998. Retrieved on August 13, 2006. from http://www.usaweekend.com/98_issues/981220/981220talk.html

United States Federal Government Documents And Abstracts

• Burton, J.; Farrell, M.; Lord, F.; Lord, R "A Brief History Of Japanese American Relocation During World War II," *Confinement and Ethnicity: An Overview of World War II, Japanese American Relocation Sites*, Publications in Anthropology 74, Western Archeological and Conservation Center, Tucson, 1999, rev. July 2000. Retrieved on July 18, 2006, from National Park Service, U.S.; www.cr.nps.gov/history/online_books/anthropology74/ce3c.htm

• Census Bulletin No.164. "Table 5: Number and Per Cent of Farms of Specified Tenures, June 1, 1900, Classified by Race of Farmer, Agriculture California," *Twelfth Census of the United States*, p. 6. April 29, 1902. Retrieved on November 1, 2006, from U.S. Census Bureau; www2.census.gov/prod2/decennial/documents/03322287no164-208ch1.pdf

• Stewart, Walter J.and Harness, Gregory. 1990 H.J. Res 238, Presidential Vetoes, 1789-1988, Office of the Secretary of the Senate. Washington D.C., February 1992. Retrieved on August 14, 2006, from U.S. Government Printing Office; www.senate.gov/reference/resources/pdf/presvetoes17891988.pdf

• Department of Commerce. "State Compendium, California," *Fourteenth Census of the United States*, Washington, Bureau of the Census Library, Washington, 1924.

• Department of Commerce, Technology Administration, National Institute of Standard Technology. "National Construction Safety Team for the Federal Building and Fire Safety Investigation of the World Trade Center Disaster," *Final Report on the Collapse of the World Trade Center Towers*, September 2005. Retrieved on October 26, 2006, from wtc.nist.gov/NISTNCSTAR1CollapseofTowers.pdf

• Hamberger, Ronald; Baker, William; Barnett, Jonathan; Marrion, Christopher; Milke, James; Nelson, Harold "Bud". "Chapter 2 WTC1 and WTC2," *World Trade Center Building Performance and Study: Data Collection, Preliminary Observations, and Recommendations*, Federal Emergency Management Agency, May 2002. Retrieved on October 26, 2006, from www.fema.gov/pdf/library/fema403_ch2.pdf

• Heco, Joseph. James Murdoch (Ed.). *The Narrative Of A Japanese; What He Has Seen And The People He Has Met In The Course Of The Last Forty Years*, Maruzen, Tokyo, 1895. Retrieved on June 24, 2006, from Library of Congress, http://lcweb2.loc.gov/cgi-bin/query/r?ammem/calbk:@field

• "Immigration and Nationality Act Amendments of October 3, 1965, (79 Statutes-at-Large 911)." (n.d.). *Immigration and Naturalization Legislation from the Statistical Yearbook*, last modified on August 9, 2003. Retrieved on August 15, 2006, from U.S. Citizenship and Immigration Services; www.uscis.gov/graphics/shared/aboutus/statistics/legishist/526.htm

• Library of Congress. (n.d.). Timeline, "Chinese in California, 1850-1925." Retrieved on December 3, 2006, from American Memory; memory.loc.gov/ammem/award99/cubhtml/chron.html

• NASA. (n.d.). "Ellison S. Onizuka (Lieutenant Colonel USAF), NASA astronaut, Biographical Data." Retrieved on August 16, 2006, from Lyndon B. Johnson Space Center; www.jsc.nasa.gov/Bios/htmlbios/onizuka.html

• National Commission on Terrorist Attacks upon the United States, *The 9/11 Commission Report*, June 2004, p. 311.

• "Public Proclamation No. 21," Douglas County School District Re-1, Colorado. Retrieved on August 9, 2006, from www1.dcsdk12.org/secondary/chs/amache/WW46.html

• "Remarks On Signing The Bill Providing Restitution For The Wartime

Internment Of Japanese-American Civilians." (August 10, 1998). Retrieved on August 11, 2006 from Ronald Reagan Presidential Library; www.reagan.utexas.edu/archives/speeches/1988/081088d.htm

• Truman Presidential Museum and Library. (n.d.). "The War Relocation Authority & The Incarceration Of Japanese-Americans During WWII, 1942 Chronology." *Papers of Dillon S. Myer, Papers of Philleo Nash*. Retrieved on July 18, 2006, from www.trumanlibrary.org/whistlestop/study_collections/japanese_internment/background.htm,

• United States Army. (n.d.). General Eric K. Shinseki (Ret.). "Asian/Pacific Americans in the U.S. Army." Retrieved on August 16, 2006, from www.army.mil/asianpacificsoldiers/ShinsekiProfile.html

• U.S. Citizenship and Naturalization Services. "Naturalization since 1907," *INS Reporter*, Vol. 26, No. 3. (Winter 1977-1978), last modified on January 20, 2006. Retrieved on August 14, 2006, from U.S. Citizenship and Naturalization Services; www.uscis.gov/graphics/aboutus/history/since07.htm

• United States Holocaust Memorial Museum. (n.d.). "Honoring American Liberators." Retrieved on August 25, 2006, from www.ushmm.org/wlc/en/

• United States Senate. (n.d.). "Biography of Senator Daniel K. Inouye." Retrieved on August 15, 2006, from www.senate.gov/~inouye/bio.html

• U.S. Department of Homeland Security. (n.d.). "Repeal of the Chinese Exclusion Act." Retrieved on July 12, 2006, from U.S. Citizenship and Immigration Services, www.uscis.gov/graphics/aboutus/History/dec43.htm

• U.S. Department of the Interior. (n.d.). "Grand Opening, Manzanar National Historic Site." Retrieved on August 17, 2006, from National Park Service; www.nps.gov/manz/grandopening.htm

United States Local Government, University, and Organizational Web Sources

....

• *Haymond, Creed, McCoppin, Frank, Et. Al.* (Committee of the Senate of California), "The Social, Moral, and Political Effect of Chinese Immigration, Policy and Means of Exclusion," Chinese Immigration, State Printing Office, Sacramento, 1877. Original monograph. Retrieved on December 3, 2006, from The Bancroft Library, University of California, Berkeley. sunsite.berkeley.edu/cgi-bin/flipomatic/cic/brk4952

• Brockman, Jason. (n.d.). *Biography of Ralph L. Carr*. Retrieved on July 19. 2006, from The Governor Ralph L. Carr Collection at the Colorado State Archives: www.colorado.gov/dpa/doit/archives/govs/carr.html#bio

• Campi, Alicia. J., *The McCarran-Walter Act: A Contradictory Legacy on Race, Quotas, and Ideology*, The American Immigration Law Foundation. June 2004. Retrieved on August 15, 2006, from www.ailf.org/ipc/policy_reports_2004_mccarranwalter.asp

• California Historical Society. *California History Timeline Online*. Retrieved on July 18, 2006, from California History Online; www.californiahistory.net

• California State Road Museum. (n.d.). "River City Depot," *A Brief History Of Depots In The River City*, 1856-1910. Retrieved on July 12, 2006, from www.csrmf.org/doc.asp?id=145

• Challenger Center. (n.d.). "The History of the Challenger Center for Space Science Education," *Organization History*. Retrieved on August 16, 2006, from http://www.challenger.org/about/history.cfm

• Chronology of 1942 San Francisco War Events. Retrieved on July 18, 2006, from The Virtual Museum of the City of San Francisco; www.sfmuseum.net/war/42.html#top

• City of Bainbridge Island. (n.d.). *Island History*. Retrieved on July 18, 2006, from the official website of the City of Bainbridge Island; www.ci.bainbridge-isl.wa.us/default.asp?ID=490

• Go For Broke National Education Center. (n.d.). *Historical Information, News Release: Colonel Young Oak Kim*. Retrieved on August 1, 2006, from www.

goforbroke.org/history/history_historical_campaigns_cassino.asp

• Japanese American Citizen League. (n.d.). *Leadership Development, Mike M. Masaoka Congressional Fellowship*. Retrieved on August 18, 2006, from www.jacl.org/leadership_development_4.php

• Japanese American Historical Society. (n.d.). "Hood River Japanese-American Incident Stirs Infantrymen," *14 January 1945, 36th Division T-Patch* Volume 2., No. 10. Retrieved on August 8, 2006, from www.kwanah.com/36division/442rct/goforbroke.htm

• Kihara, Shigeya. "1997 Meeting," *The Role of the National Japanese American Historical Society; In the Movement for Redress*, Organization of American Historians, April 18 1997. Retrieved on August 11, 2006, from www.oah.org/meetings/1997/kihara.htm

• Keiro HealthCare. (n.d.). *History of Keiro Senior HealthCare*. Retrieved on September 6, 2006, from www.keiro.org/KSP/history.htm

• Kubota, Gaylord, C. and Dye, Bob. (Ed.). (1996). "The Lynching of Katsu Goto," *Hawaii Chronicles: Island History from Pages of Honolulu Magazine*, Honolulu, University of Hawaii Press, Honolulu, 1996. Retrieved on June 29, 2006, from Center for Education and Research, University of Hawaii - West Oahu: homepages.uhwo.hawaii.edu/~clear/KatsuGoto.html

• Mineta Transportation Institute. (n.d.). *Norman Y. Mineta*. Retrieved on November 30, 2006, from transweb.sjsu.edu/mtiportal/about/mineta.html

• National Japanese American Historical Society. (n.d.). *Japanese American History Timeline*, Military Intelligence Service Association of Northern California. 1970s. Retrieved on August 25, 2006, from Military Intelligence Service Research Center; www.njahs.org/misnorcal/timeline/timeline.htm#eight

• National Japanese American Memorial Foundation. (n.d.). *The Honor Roll*. Retrieved on August 16, 2006, from www.njamf.com/honor.htm

• Nisei Week Foundation. (n.d.). *Honorees*. Retrieve on August 16, 2006 & November 26, 2006, from www.niseiweek.org

• "President Gerald R. Ford's remarks upon signing a proclamation concerning Japanese-American internment during World War II." February 19, 1976. Retrieved on August 15, 2006, from Gerald R. Ford Presidential Library and Museum; www.fordlibrarymuseum.gov/library/speeches/760111.htm

• Randall, Peter and Doleac, Charles. "The Treaty Process, An Uncommon Commitment To Peace, Part Four - September 5, Tuesday: Treaty signed; Christ Church service," *Portsmouth Peace Treaty, 1905-2005*. 2005. Retrieved on July 23, 2006, from Japan America Society of New Hampshire http://process.portsmouthpeacetreaty.org/process/peace/peace4.html

• "Remarks By The President At Medals Of Freedom Presentation," *Speech by President at Medals of Freedom Event. January 15, 1998*. The White House, Office of Press Secretary. Retrieved on December 5, 2006, from William J. Clinton Foundation; www.clintonfoundation.org/legacy/011598-speech-by-president-at-medals-of-freedom-event.htm

• Robinson, Greg and Robinson, Toni. "The Supreme Court Appeal and the Brief, III Oyama Case, Japanese Americans and the Origins of Strict Scrutiny, 68 Law & Contemp. Probs. 29," *Law and Contemporary Problems*, Duke Journals, Duke Law. 2005. Retrieved on August 18, 2006, from www.law.duke.edu/shell/cite.pl?68+Law+&+Contemp.+Probs.+29+(spring+2005)

• Smithsonian Institution. (n.d.). "Justice, Service," *A More Perfect Union: Japanese Americans and the U.S. Constitution*, National Museum of American History. Retrieved on August 7, 2006, from americanhistory.si.edu/perfectunion/experience/index.html

• University of Hawaii. "*Biographical Chronology*," *Senator Spark Matsunaga Papers, Finding Aide*, January 2005. Retrieved on August 15, 2006, from Hawaii Congressional Papers Collection Archives and Manuscripts Department, • University of Hawaii at Manoa Library; libweb.hawaii.edu/libdept/congressional/matsunaga/SMMFindingAid_web.pdf

University of Hawaii at Manoa. (n.d.). "About Spark Matsunaga (1916-1990)," *The Sen. Spark M. Matsunaga Papers*. Retrieved on August 22, 2006, from University Archives; libweb.hawaii.edu/libdept/congressional/matsunaga/bio.

htm

・University of Utah. (n.d.). "Biography of Mike M. Masaoka," *The Mike Masaoka Papers (Ms 656)*. Retrieved on August 25, 2006, from J. Willard Marriott Library; www.lib.utah.edu/spc/mss/ms656/ms656.html#bio

Japanese Government Documents And Reports

....

・在ニューヨーク日本国総領事館、日米交流 150 周年記念、日米 150 年史、遣米使節団

Consulate General of Japan in New York. (n.d.). "150th Anniversary Of U.S.-Japan Relations," *150 Years of Shared History, The 1860 Japanese Embassy to America*. Retrieved on June 20, 2006, from ny.cgj.org/150th/html/home.htm, http://ny.cgj.org/150th/html/homeE.htm

・昭和 43 年運輸白書、第 4 章：国民の観光旅行の状況、第 3 節：国民の海外渡航の状況、国土交通省

Ministry of Land Infrastructure and Transport. (n.d.). "Chapter 4: Japanese citizens' overseas tourism, Section 3: Japanese citizens travelling overseas," *1968 White Paper on Transportation*. Retrieved on August 13, 2006. www.mlit.go.jp/hakusyo/transport/shouwa43/ind120403/000.html

・『遣米使日記』村垣淡叟著、P34, 1898 年、近代デジタルライブラリー国立国会図書館

Muragaki, Tanso. *The Embassy to America Diary*, Toyodo-shiten, Tokyo, 1898. Retrieved on August 24, 2006, from NDL Digital Archive Portal, Kindai Digital Library, National Diet Library: http://kindai.ndl.go.jp/BIImgFrame.php?JP_NUM=40010754&VOL_NUM=00000&KOMA=34&ITYPE=0

・外務省、万延元年遣米使節団のパナマ通過（1860 年）、「新見豊前守等米國渡航本條約書交換一件 六」（『続通信全覧』類輯之部 修好門）

The Japanese Ministry of Foreign Affairs(n.d.). *The 1860 Japanese Embassy to America: Panama Crossing*. Retrieved on June 20, 2006, from The Diplomatic Record Office of the Ministry of Foreign Affairs of Japan: www.mofa.go.jp/mofaj/annai/honsho/shiryo/j_latin_2005/2-1.html

Japanese Local Government, University, and Organizational Web Sources

....

・City of Tosashimizu. (n.d.). History of John Majiro, "Life in America, Achievement of Manjiro," *Home of John Man: Tosashimizu*, Retrieved on June 23, 2006, from www.city.tosashimizu.kochi.jp/john/default.htm
・City of Yokohama. *The 150th Anniversary of the Opening of Japan, Perry's Arrival in Japan and Yokohama. 2004*. Retrieved on August 30. 2006, from Yokohama City Board of Education; www.city.yokohama.jp/me/kyoiku/topics/160423.html
・Doshisha University. (n.d.). "*History of Doshisha*," The Doshisha. Retrieved on July 12, 2006, from www.doshisha.ed.jp/english/history/index.html
同志社大学新島遺品庫資料の公開【部分公開】新見襄ものがたり
・Doshisha University. (n.d.). *Story of Neesima*. Retrieved on July 12, 2006, from Neesima Room: joseph.doshisha.ac.jp/ihinko/bubun2/story/index2.html
・野口英世記念館、ロックフェラー医学研究所での英世
Hideyo Noguchi Memorial Hall. (n.d.). *Hideyo at the Rockefeller Institute for Medical Research*. Retrieved on July 12, 2006, from www.noguchihideyo.or.jp
・兵庫県播磨町 HP、 歴史上の人物、新聞の父「ジョセフ彦」
Hyogo prefecture, Harima-cho, (n.d.). "Historical Figures," *The Father of the Newspaper: Joseph Heco*. Retrieved on June 23, 2006, from www.town.harima.hyogo.jp/miru/prof/jinbutu/rekisi.htm
・Kawasumi, Tetsuo. *Introducing John Manjiro*. Updated November 5, 2003. Retrieved on August 29, 2006, from The Manjiro Society: www.manjiro.org/manjiro.html

宮崎県立図書館、宮崎が生んだ偉大な人物、小村寿太郎
Miyazaki Prefecture Library. (n.d.). Komura Jutaro, *The Great Native Figure*. Retrieved on July 23, 2006, from www.lib.pref.miyazaki.jp/hyuuga/komura.html
・新渡戸稲造の世界、新渡戸博士の業績
Nitobe Foundation. (n.d.). *The Achievements of Dr. Nitobe*. Retrieved on July 12, 2006, from www.nitobe.com
・社団法人日本船主協会、海運雑学ゼミナール、「201　漂流者たちが持ち帰った鎖国時代の海外知識」
The Japanese Shipowners' Association. (n.d.). "Marine Transportation Seminar," *The Knowledge of Overseas that Drifters Brought Back Home during the Japanese Periods of Isolation, 201*, Retrieved on June 22, 2006, from www.jsanet.or.jp/seminar/index.html
・咸臨丸子孫の会、ブルック家訪問
The Society of the Kanrin-maru Crew Descendants. (n.d.). *The Visit to the Brookes*. Retrieved on June 20, 2006, from: kanrin-maru.org/activity/2005activity/05x10_sfo/frameusa2005.html
・愛知県美浜町、にっぽん音吉漂流の記
・Town of Mihama, Aichi prefecture. (n.d.). *Nippon Otokichi Drifter's Diary*. Retrieved on June 22, 2006, from www.town.mihama.aichi.jp/main/index.html
Town of Mihama, Aichi prefecture. (n.d.). *The Real-Life Story of Otokichi*, Retrieved on August 29, from www.town.mihama.aichi.jp/main/english/6/1/index.html
・横浜市自然・人文博物館 HP 「近代日本外交の始まり」 ―ペリー来航から万延元年遣米使節への歩み― 【第 2 部】 万延元年遣米使節と浦賀の人々
Yokosuka City Museum. (n.d.). "From Perry's Arrival to the 1860 Japanese Embassy to America," *The Beginning of Modern Japanese Diplomacy*. Retrieved on June 23. 2006, from www.museum.yokosuka.kanagawa.jp/event/event2_1_2.html
・和歌山市民図書館移民資料室、和歌山県移民史年表
Wakayama Prefecture. (n.d.). Emigration History Timeline. Retrieved on July 14, 2006, from Wakayama City Library Emigrants Data Room: www.lib.city.wakayama.wakayama.jp/wkclib_doc/sub5.htm

Other Web Sources

....

・Abe, Frank and ITVS. (n.d.). "The Draft," *Compliance, Conscience, and the Constitution*, Public Broadcasting Service (PBS). Retrieved on August 25, 2006, from www.pbs.org/itvs/conscience/compliance/the_draft/index.html
・Gordon, Tei A. "The Voyage Home, True Life Adventures of Otokichi (1817-1867)," *Bright Lights Of Manhattan & The Opium War, Forcing Japan's Ports Open, 2004*. Retrieved on June 21, 2006, from Official Otokichi Homepage www.jmottoson.com/Otokichi-Story.htm
・井上篤夫の眼、ビジネストリビア、製菓王・森永太一郎の刻苦勉励
Inoue, Atsuo. (n.d.). "Business Trivia, The King Of Confectionery Production," *The World According To Atsuo Inoue*. Retrieved on July 12, 2006, from www.ainoue.com/trivia/tri-36.html
・"June Masuda Goto's letter to President Reagan on November 19, 1987." September 1999. *Shusterman's Immigration Update*. Retrieved on August 16, 2006, from http://www.shusterman.com/sep99.html#10
・そうてつグループ、WEB 相鉄瓦版、平成 15 年 4 月号、ニュースメディアの父、ジョセフ・ヒコ、特集横浜はじめて物語、くさまとしろう著
Kusama, Toshiro. (April, 2003). "*Joseph Heco: Father of News Media.*" Retrieved on August 31, 2006, from WEB Sotetsu Kawaraban: www.sotetsu-group.co.jp/kawaraban/116/hiko.htm
・Medeiros, Sara. (n.d.). *Carrying the Torch*, Hawaiian Electric Industries, Inc. Retrieved on October 26, 2006, from www.hei.com/hoahana/2001.Q4/6.html
・Schodt, Frederik L. *Native American in the Land of the Shogun: Ranald Macdonald and the Opening of Japan*. 2003. Retrieved on August 24, 2006, from www.jai2.com/RM.htm

• 戦後昭和史 www.shouwashi.com. *Showa History Timeline, after WWII*. (n.d.). (Japanese text), 1961, 1962. Retrieved on August 16, 2006, from shouwashi. s151.xrea.com

• Sterner, C. Douglas, (n.d.). "The Champagne Campaign," *HomeOfHeros. com*, retrieved on August 7, 2006, from www.homeofheroes.com/moh/nisei/ index8_cc.html

• *Teahouse of the August Moon*, (1956). Internet Movie Database. Retrieved on August 16, 2006, from us.imdb.com/title/tt0049830/;

• Ibid., *Sayonara*. (1957). Retrieved on August 16, 2006, from us.imdb.com/title/ tt0050933/;

Ibid., *You Only Live Twice*. (1967). Retrieved on August 16, 2006, from us.imdb. com/title/tt0062512/

• キネマ旬報、Goo 映画、『八月十五夜の茶屋』、『サヨナラ』、『007 は 2 度死ぬ』 Veerkamp, Phil. (n.d.). "*Epilogue*," Wakamatsu. Retrieved on June 26, 2006, from www.directcon.net/pharmer/Wakamatsu/Wakamatsu.html

• Widran, Johasan. (n.d.). "*Hiroshima, About The Band*." Retrieved on August 16, 2006, from Hiroshima Official Website; www.hiroshimamusic.com

DVD

Yahata, Craig and Yoneshige, David. *A Tradition of Honor*, Go For Broke National Education Center, Torrance, CA. 2003. (Available from Go For Broke National Education Center, 370 Amapola Ave., Suite 110, Torrance, CA 90501)

Chronology Reference - 年表参考文献

• 世界史年表－歴史研究会	岩波書店
• 日本史年表－歴史研究会	岩波書店
• 日本史年表	河出書房新社
• 日本史総合年表－児玉幸多	吉川弘文館
• 近代日本総合年表	岩波書店
•「昭和史」－半藤一利	平凡社
• 近代日本と東南アジア－後藤乾一	岩波書店
•「カリフォルニア移民物語」－佐渡拓平	岩波書店
• 日系アメリカ人の歴史	全米日系人博物館
•「アメリカ彦蔵」－吉村昭	新潮社
•「横須賀開国物語」－山本詔一	神奈川新聞社
•「亜米利加日系埼人伝」－野本一平	弥生書房
•「幕末遣米使節小栗忠順従者の記録－村上泰賢	上毛新聞社

• The United States Census Bureau

• The California State Military Museum － California State Military Department

• United States Department of the Navy － Naval Historical Center

• American History Timeline － Smithsonian Institution

• American History desk reference － The New York Public Library

• Syracuse University Library － Special Collection Research Center

• BBC News U K Edition Timeline － United States of America a Chronology of key events

• Japanese American National Museum, Encyclopedia of Japanese American History

• A Short Chronology of Japanese American History － Brian Niiya

Historical Gallery Archival Materials Sources
絵画・写真提供協力

横須賀自然・人文博物館	Yokosuka City Museum
神奈川県横須賀市深田台 95	95 Fukadadai, Yokosuka-shi,
	Kanagawa-ken
℡ 0468-24-3658	℡ 0468-24-3658
東善寺 - 村上泰賢住職	Tozenji Temple- Taiken Murakami
群馬県高崎市倉渕町権田 169	169 Gonda Kurabuchi-machi,
	Takasaki-shi, Gunma-ken
℡ 027-378-2230	℡ 027-378-2230
日本カメラ博物館	Japan Camera Museum
東京都千代田区一番町 25	25 Ichibancho, Chiyoda-ku, Tokyo
JII 一番町ビル	℡ 03-3263-7110
℡ 03-3263-7110	
高知県土佐清水市天神町	Tenjincho Public Relations Dept.
企画広報室	Tosashimizu-shi, Kochi-ken
℡ 0880-82-1111	℡ 0880-82-1111

Notes

日本語で表記している文献名は、日本語で書かれた文献を参考にしたことを意味し、英語のみで表記してある文献名は、英語で書かれた文献を参考にしたことを意味します。日本語の文献で著者による著書名などの英訳がないものに関しては、筆者が訳しました。注記の英訳も筆者によるものです。インターネットサイトで日英両語のサイトが用意してあるものに関しては、両方のウェブアドレスを記載しています。

The Japanese notations followed by English translations indicate that these references are based on Japanese textual sources. The English translations have been provided by author of the text. The Japanese Internet sources providing English translations of their texts are listed both in Japanese and English web addresses.

Prologue

1. 愛知県美浜町 HP、「にっぽん音吉漂流の記」、宝順丸の遭難
Town of Mihama, Aichi prefecture. (n.d.). Shipwrecked Hojunmaru, *Nippon Otokichi Drifter's Diary*. Retrieved on June 22, 2006, from www.town.mihama.aichi.jp/main/index.html

2. 愛知県美浜町 HP、「にっぽん音吉漂流の記」、生き残った３人
Ibid.

3. Gordon, Tei A. (2004). The Voyage home, *True Life Adventures of Otokichi (1817-1867)*, 4-5 Retrieved on June 21, 2006, from Official Otokichi Homepage: www.jmottoson.com/Otokichi-Story.htm

4. Town of Mihama, Aichi prefecture. (n.d.). Translating the Bible, *The Real-Life Story of Otokichi*, Retrieved on August 29, from www.town.mihama.aichi.jp/main/english/6/3/index.html

5. 社団法人日本船主協会、海運雑学ゼミナール、「201 漂流者たちが持ち帰った鎖国時代の海外知識」
The Japanese Shipowners' Association. (n.d.). Marine transportation seminar, *The Knowledge of Overseas that Drifters Brought Back Home during the Japanese Periods of Isolation, 201*, Retrieved on June 22, 2006, from http://www.jsanet.or.jp/seminar/index.html

6. Town of Mihama, Aichi prefecture. (n.d.). So Close to Home, *The Real-Life Story of Otokichi*, Retrieved on August 29, 2006, from www.town.mihama.aichi.jp/main/english/6/4/index.html

7. Gordon, Tei A. (2004). Bright Lights of Manhattan & the Opium War, *True Life Adventures of Otokichi (1817-1867)*, 2. Retrieved on June 21, 2006, from Official Otokichi Homepage: www.jmottoson.com/Otokichi-Story.htm

8. Ibid., Forcing Japan's ports open, 7.

9. Town of Mihama, Aichi prefecture. (n.d.). Assisting Other Japanese Sailors, *The Real-Life Story of Otokichi*, Retrieved on August 29, 2006, from www.town.mihama.aichi.jp/main/english/6/5/index.html

10. Schodt, Frederik L. (2003) *Native American in the Land of Shogun: Ranald Macdonald and the Opening of Japan*. Retrieved on August 24, 2006, from www.jai2.com/RM.htm

11. 愛知県美浜町 HP、「にっぽん音吉漂流の記」、山本音吉（乙吉）遺灰の帰郷について
Town of Mihama, Aichi prefecture. (n.d.). Concerning the homecoming of Otokichi's ashes, Retrieved on June 22, 2006, from www.town.mihama.aichi.jp/main/index.html

12. Town of Mihama, Aichi prefecture. (n.d.). Assisting Other Japanese Sailors, *The Real-Life Story of Otokichi*, Retrieved on August 29, 2006, from www.town.mihama.aichi.jp/main/english/6/5/index.html

13. 土佐清水市 HP、「ジョン万のふるさと土佐清水」ジョン万次郎の歴史
City of Tosashimizu. (n.d.). History of John Manjiro, Home of John Man: Tosashimizu, Retrieved on June 23, 2006, from http://www.city.tosashimizu.kochi.jp/john/john-04.htm

14. Kawasumi, Tetsuo. (Updated November 5, 2003). Introducing John Manjiro, copyright 1998-2002. Retrieved on August 29, 2006, from The Manjiro Society: www.manjiro.org/manjiro.html

15. 土佐清水市 HP 、「ジョン万のふるさと土佐清水」、アメリカの暮らし
City of Tosashimizu. (n.d.). Life in America, *Home of John Man: Tosashimizu*, Retrieved on June 23, 2006, from www.city.tosashimizu.kochi.jp/john/john-03.htm

16. 土佐清水市 HP、「ジョン万のふるさと土佐清水」、万次郎の功績
Ibid., The achievement of Manjiro.

17. 横浜開港資料館平成16年度第1回企画展示、横浜市教育委員会、「開国150周年　ペリー来航と横浜」
City of Yokohama. (2004). *The 150th Anniversary of the Opening of Japan, Perry's Arrival in Japan and Yokohama*. Retrieved on August 30, 2006, from Yokohama City Board of Education; www.city.yokohama.jp/me/kyoiku/topics/160423.html

18. Heco, Joseph. James Murdoch (Ed.). (1895). *The narrative of a Japanese: What he has seen and the people he has met in the course of the last forty years*, Tokyo, Maruzen, pp. 139-143, (Call number, CT1838.H4 A3 vol.2). Retrieved on June 24, 2006, from Library of Congress (Digital ID, calbk 113): cweb2.loc.gov/cgi-bin/query/r?ammem/calbk:@field(DOCID+@lit(calbk113div15)):

19. Ibid., p. 158.

20. Ibid., p. 240.

21. そうてつグループ、WEB相鉄瓦版、平成15年4月号、ニュースメディアの父、ジョセフ・ヒコ、特集横浜はじめて物語、くさまとしろう著
Kusama, Toshiro (April, 2003). Joseph Heco: Father of News Media. Retrieved on August 31, 2006, from WEB Sotetsu Kawaraban: www.sotetsu-group.co.jp/kawaraban/116/hiko.htm

22. 在ニューヨーク日本国総領事館、日米交流150周年記念、「遣米使節団」、アメリカの熱狂的な歓迎
Consulate General of Japan in New York. (n.d.). 150th anniversary of U.S.-Japan relations, Enthusiastic reception in America, *The 1860 Japanese Embassy to America*. Retrieved on June 20, 2006, from www.ny.us.emb-japan.go.jp/150th/html/kanrin2.htm

23. 外務省、万延元年遣米使節団のパナマ通過（1860年）、「新見豊前守等米國渡航本條約書交換一件 六」（『統通信全覧』類輯之部 修好門）
The Japanese Ministry of Foreign Affairs of Japan. (n.d.). *The 1860 Japanese Embassy to America: Panama Crossing*. Retrieved on June 20, 2006, from The Diplomatic Record Office of the Ministry of Foreign Affairs of Japan: www.mofa.go.jp/mofaj/annai/honsho/shiryo/j_latin_2005/2-1.html

24. 在ニューヨーク日本国総領事館、日米交流150周年記念、「遣米使節団」、遣米使節団が見たアメリカ人
Consulate General of Japan in New York. (n.d.). 150th anniversary of U.S.-Japan relations, Americans in the eyes of the embassy, *The 1860 Japanese Embassy to America*, n.d. Retrieved on June 20, 2006, from www.ny.us.emb-japan.go.jp/150th/html/kanrin5.htm

25. 在ニューヨーク日本国総領事館　日米交流150周年記念 「遣米使節団」、アメリカ人が見た日本の使節団
Ibid., The embassy in the eyes of Americans. Retrieved on June 20, 2006, from www.ny.us.emb-japan.go.jp/150th/html/kanrin4.htm

26. 『遣米使日記』村垣淡叟著、P34、1898年、近代デジタルライブラリー、国立国会図書館
Muragaki, Tanso. (1898). *The Embassy to America Diary*, Tokyo, Toyodo-shiten, p. 34, (Call number, YDM26894). Retrieved on August 24, 2006, from NDL Digital Archive Portal, Kindai Digital Library, National Diet Library: http://kindai.ndl.go.jp/BIImgFrame.php?JP_NUM=40010754&VOL_NUM=00000&KOMA=34&ITYPE=0

27. 外務省、万延元年遺米使節団のパナマ通過（1860 年）、「新見豊前守等米國渡航本條約書交換一件 六」（『続通信全覧』類輯之部 修好門）

The Japanese Ministry of Foreign Affairs (n.d.). *The 1860 Japanese Embassy to America: Panama Crossing*. Retrieved on June 20, 2006, from The Diplomatic Record Office of the Ministry of Foreign Affairs of Japan: www.mofa.go.jp/mofaj/annai/honsho/shiryo/j_latin_2005/2-1.html

28. 小栗上野介と会津、村上泰賢著、会津人群像、東善寺より、Murakami, Taiken, Oguri Kozuke-no-suke to Aizu, from Aizujin Gunzo, Tozen-ji

29. 在ニューヨーク日本国総領事館、日米交流 150 周年記念、「遣米使節団」、アメリカの本質を理解した日本人

Consulate General of Japan in New York. (n.d.). 150th Anniversary of U.S.-Japan Relations, Japanese who understood the essence of America, *The 1860 Japanese Embassy to America*. Retrieved on June 20, 2006, from www.ny.us.emb-japan.go.jp/150th/html/kanrin6.htm

30. 在ニューヨーク日本国総領事館、日米 150 年史、咸臨丸の太平洋横断の話、勝海舟の青い目の孫娘、http://ny.cgj.org/150th/html/history.htm

Consulate General of Japan in New York. (n.d.). 150th Anniversary of U.S.-Japan Relations, The Kanrin Maru crosses the Pacific, Katsu Kaishu and his blue-eyed granddaughter, *150 Years of Shared History*. Retrieved on June 20, 2006, from www.ny.us.emb-japan.go.jp/150th/html/history.htm#10

31. 在ニューヨーク日本国総領事館、日米 150 年史、ジョン万次郎物語、www.ny.us.emb-japan.go.jp/150th/html/history.htm

Ibid., The Story of John Manjiro.

32. 咸臨丸子孫の会、ブルック家訪問

The Society the Kanrin-maru Crew Descendants. (n.d.). *The Visit to the Brookes*. Retrieved on June 20, 2006, from: http://kanrin-maru.org/activity/2005activity/05x10_sfo/frameusa2005.html

Chapter One

1. Unite 71(40). Niiya, Brian. (Ed.). Japanese American National Museum. (2001). May 17, 1868, *Encyclopedia of Japanese American History, Updated Edition*, New York, Facts On File, p. 29.

2. Niiya, Brian. (Ed.). Japanese American National Museum. (2001). Gannen-mono, *Encyclopedia of Japanese American History, Updated Edition*, New York, Facts On File, p. 170.

3. 1870 年の国勢調査によると、カリフォルニア州在住の日本人は 33 人で、若松コロニーのあったエルドラドカウンティーには 22 人が記録されている。だがリサーチャーによって確認されている人物名の記録がないことなどから、正確な人数は不明。

According to the 1870 census, 33 Japanese people lived in California. Although 22 Japanese names were recorded in El Dorado County, the accuracy of the list may be doubtful because some Japanese immigrants, who were confirmed to have lived in the county, by the researchers, were not on the list. Ibid., p. 406. Veerkamp, Phil. (n.d.). Epilogue, *Wakamatsu*. Retrieved on June 26, 2006, from www.directcon.net/pharmer/Wakamatsu/Wakamatsu.html

4. 1884 年 12 月に実施された官約移民募集で選ばれたのは 945 人だが、ホノルルで上陸したのは 944 人となっている。

In December 1884 the first official contingency of 945 migrants, selected by the Japanese government, was sent to Honolulu, Hawaii. However, the official record at Honolulu lists 944 arrivals. Takaki 83(43)., United 71(90). Niiya, Brian. (Ed.). Japanese American National Museum. (2001). December 1884, *Encyclopedia of Japanese American History, Updated Edition*, New York, Facts On File, p. 30; Kotani 85(9-11)., Odo/Shinoto 85(39)., Takaki 83(43-44)., & United 71(94). Niiya, Brian. (Ed.). Japanese American National Museum. (2001). February 8, 1884, *Encyclopedia of Japanese American History Updated Edition*, New York, Facts On File, p. 30

5. Kubota, Gaylord, C., Dye, Bob. (Ed.). (1996). *The Lynching of Katsu Goto*, Hawaii Chronicles: Island History from Pages of Honolulu Magazine, Honolulu,

University of Hawai'i Press, pp. 197-214. Retrieved on June 29, 2006, from Center for Education and Research, University of Hawaii - West Oahu: homepages.uhwo.hawaii.edu/~clear/KatsuGoto.html

6. Niiya, Brian. (Ed.). Japanese American National Museum. (2001). Kanyaku imin, *Encyclopedia of Japanese American History, Updated Edition*, New York, Facts On File, p. 236.

7. 『一世としてアメリカに生きて』北村崇郎著、草思社、1992 年発行
Kitamura, Takao. (1992). *Living in America as Issei*, Tokyo, Soshisha, p. 26.

8. Ibid.

9. 同志社大学新島遺品庫資料の公開【部分公開】新島襄ショートストーリー
Doshisha University. (n.d.). *Story of Neesima*. Retrieved on July 12, 2006, from Neesima Room, joseph.doshisha.ac.jp/ihinko/bubun2/column/index.html

10. 『一世としてアメリカに生きて』北村崇郎著、草思社、1992 年発行
Kitamura, Takao. (1992). *Living in America as Issei*, Tokyo, Soshisha, p. 23.

11. 1850 年のカリフォルニア移民 5 万 7787 人中、中国人は約 500 人であったのが、1852 年には 2 万人にまで急増し、ほとんどが鉱山業に従事した。その後 20 年間、中国人移民は年間 8 千人以下に減少した。カリフォルニアの中国人移民に関する特別委員会の報告書によると、1877 年当時、カリフォルニア人口が 70 万人から 80 万人だったのに対して、中国人人口は 12 万 5000 人だった。Department of Homeland Security. (n.d.). Repeal of the Chinese Exclusion Act. Retrieved on July 12, 2006, from U.S. Citizenship and Immigration Services: www.uscis.gov/graphics/aboutus/History/dec43.htm; In 1850, Some 500 immigrants out of 57,787 arriving in California were Chinese. In 1852, Chinese immigration increased to 20,000, with most individuals proceeding to mining regions. This number decreased to under 8,000 annually during the next two decades. Library of Congress. (n.d.). Timeline, Chinese in California, 1850-1925. Retrieved on December 3, 2006, from American Memory; memory.loc.gov/ammem/award99/cubhtml/chron.html; The special committee concerning Chinese immigration estimated the Chinese population in California to be approximately 125,000. Total population of California was estimated at approximately 700,000 to 800,000. A committee of the California Senate. (1877). Sacramento, State Printing Office, p. 4. (Call number, e.g. xF870.C5.C51 v.1:10). Retrieved on December 3, 2006, from The Bancroft Library, University of California, Berkeley, (Digital ID, cubcic brk4952): sunsite.berkeley.edu/cgi-bin/flipomatic/cic/brk4952

12. 『一世としてアメリカに生きて』北村崇郎著、草思社、1992 年発行
Kitamura, Takao. (1992). *Living in America as Issei*, Tokyo, Soshisha, p. 58.

13. Ibid.

14. Ibid., pp. 70, 71.

15. Ibid., pp. 44, 192.

16. Ibid., p. 14.

17. Ibid., pp. 87, 119.

18. Randall, Peter and Doleac, Charles. (2005). The treaty process, An uncommon commitment to peace, part four - September 5, Tuesday: Treaty signed; Christ Church service, *Portsmouth Peace Treaty, 1905-2005*. Retrieved on July 23, 2006, from Japan America Society of New Hampshire from process.portsmouthpeacetreaty.org/process/peace/peace4.html

19. 宮崎県立図書館、宮崎が生んだ偉大な人物、小村寿太郎
Miyazaki Prefecture Library. (n.d.). Komura Jutaro, *The Great Native Figure*. Retrieved on July 23, 2006, from www.lib.pref.miyazaki.jp/hyuuga/komura.html

20. 『一世としてアメリカに生きて』北村崇郎著、草思社、1992 年発行
Kitamura, Takao. (1992). *Living in America as Issei*, Tokyo, Soshisha, p. 55.

21. Ibid., p. 56.

22. Ibid., p. 213.

23. Ibid., p. 90.

24. Ibid., p. 77.

25. Department of Homeland Security. (n.d.). Immigration Act of May 26, 1924 (43 Statutes-at-Large 153), Legislation from 1901-1940, pp. 3-4. Retrieved on December 3, 2006, from U.S. Citizenship and Immigration Service; www.uscis.gov/files/nativedocuments/Legislation%20from%201901-1940.pdf

26. 和歌山市民図書館移民資料室、和歌山県移民史年表
Wakayama Prefecture. (n.d.). *Emigration History Timeline*. Retrieved on July 14, 2006, from Wakayama City Library Emigrants Data Room: www.lib.city. wakayama.wakayama.jp/wkclib_doc/sub5.htm

27. 『一世としてアメリカに生きて』北村崇郎著、草思社、1992 年発行
Kitamura, Takao. (1992). *Living in America as Issei*, Tokyo, Soshisha, pp. 201-202.

28. Ibid., p. 214.

29. Ibid., p. 237.

30. Ibid., p. 239.

31. Ibid., pp. 91, 92.

32. Ibid., p. 153.

33. Ibid., p. 154.

Chapter Two

1. 『一世としてアメリカに生きて』北村崇郎著、草思社、1992 年発行
Kitamura, Takao. (1992). *Living in America as Issei*, Tokyo, Soshisha, p. 97.

2. Murphy, Thomas. D. (1954). *Ambassadors in Arms – The Story of Hawaii's 100th Battalion*, Honolulu, Club 100 under special arrangement with University of Hawaii Press, pp. 15-18.

3. Ibid., p. 8.

4. Ibid., p. 17.

5. Ibid., p. 21.

6. Ibid., pp. 23-4.

7. Ibid., p. 29.

8. Ibid., p. 30.

9. Weglyn, Michi. (1976). *Years of Infamy*, New York, William Morrow and Company, pp. 43-4.

10. Murphy, Thomas. D. (1954). *Ambassadors in Arms – The Story of Hawaii's 100th Battalion*, Honolulu, Club 100 under special arrangement with University of Hawaii Press, p. 30.

11. Ibid., p. 40.

12. Yahata, Craig. (Producer, Director). Yoneshige, David. (Producer). (2003). *A Tradition of Honor* (DVD), Go For Broke National Education Center. (Available from Go For Broke National Education Center, 370 Amapola Ave., Suite 110, Torrance, CA 90501).

13. Compiled by Hawaii Nikkei History Editorial Board. (1998). *Japanese Eyes, American Heart*, Honolulu, Tendai Educational Foundation, p. 16.

14. Kumamoto 79(69-70). Niiya, Brian. (Ed.). Japanese American National Museum. (2001). December 7, 1941, *Encyclopedia of Japanese American History, Updated Edition*, New York, Facts On File, p. 58.

15. 内務省管轄の国立公園サービスによると、海軍がターミナルアイランド在住の日系人立ち退きを発表したのは 1942 年 2 月 14 日で、当初は同年 3 月 14 日まで立ち退き期限が与えられていた。だがサンタバーバラ沖で日本軍による砲弾を受けた後、2 月 24 日に期限が繰り上げられ 2 月 27 日になった。2 月 24 日、ロサンゼルスで空襲警報が出され、心臓発作や交通事故で 5 人死亡したが、後にそれは日本軍ではなく気象風船だったと確認された。全米日系人博物館によると、ターミナルアイランドに立ち退き令が出たのは 2 月 25 日とされており、24 日の誤報による混乱で、住民に通達が行き届いたのが 25 日だった可能性もある。
According to the National Park Service under Department of Interior, the Navy announced an eviction order on February 14, 1942. Initially, the Navy gave a month notice to evacuate. After the Japanese military attacked off the coast of Santa Barbara, the deadline was moved up to February 27th from March 14th. On February 24th, the day the new deadline was announced, an air raid warning was issued in Los Angeles. One person died from a heart attack and four others from auto accidents due to the commotion. It was later determined to be a lost U.S. weather balloon. According to the Encyclopedia of Japanese American History, compiled by the Japanese American National Museum, the Navy ordered all Japanese-American residents of Terminal Island to leave within 48 hours starting February 25th, 1942. It may be possible that the order was issued on the 24th, but it did not reach the residents of Terminal Island until the 25th because of the commotion made by the false alarm.
Burton, J; Farrell; M; Lord, F; Lord, R. (1999). "Military Necessity", 17, Chapter 3: A brief history of Japanese American relocation during World War II, *Confinement and Ethnicity: An Overview of World War II, Japanese American Relocation Sites*, (rev. July 2000), Publications in Anthropology 74, Tucson, Western Archeological and Conservation Center. Retrieved on July 18, 2006, from National Park Service, U.S.; www.cr.nps.gov/history/online_books/anthropology74/ce3c.htm; Girdner/Loftis 69(109-10). February 24, 1942, Commission 82. February 25, 1942, Niiya, Brian. (Ed.). Japanese American National Museum. (2001). *Encyclopedia of Japanese American History, Updated Edition*, New York, Facts One File, p. 60.

16. Girdner/Loftis 69(109). Niiya, Brian. (Ed.). Japanese American National Museum. (2001). February 23, 1942, *Encyclopedia of Japanese American History, Updated Edition*, New York, Facts On File, p. 60; Port Orford Heritage Society. (2000). Port Orford lifeboat station, *Japanese Submarine Attacks on Curry County in WWII*. Retrieved on July 18, 2006, from www.portorfordlifeboatstation.org/article1.html; *Chronology of 1942 San Francisco War Events*. Retrieved on July 18, 2006, from The Virtual Museum of City of San Francisco; www.sfmuseum.net/war/42.html#top; Truman Presidential Museum and Library. (n.d.). The War Relocation Authority & the incarceration of Japanese-Americans during WWII, *1942 Chronology*. Retrieved on July 18, 2006, from www.trumanlibrary.org/whistlestop/study_collections/japanese_internment/1942.htm

17. ベインブリッジで立ち退き令第 1 号の対象になった日系人は、全米日系人博物館によると 45 家族で、ベインブリッジ市史によると 220 人。立ち退き令は計 108 号まで発効された。
According to the Encyclopedia of Japanese American History, forty-five Japanese-American families living on Bainbridge Island were ordered to evacuate by the first Civilian Exclusion Order. The City of Bainbridge Island reports 220 people were subject to this order. City of Bainbridge Island. (n.d.). *Island History*. Retrieved on July 18, 2006, from The official website of the City of Bainbridge Island; www.ci.bainbridge-isl.wa.us/default.asp?ID=490; Burton, J; Farrell, M; Lord, F; Lord, R. (1999). Evacuation, 9, Chapter 3: A brief history of Japanese Americans during World War II, *Confinement and Ethnicity: An Overview of World War II, Japanese American Relocation Sites*, (rev. July 2000), Publications in Anthropology 74, Tucson, Western Archeological and Conservation Center. Retrieved on July 18, 2006, from National Park Service; www.cr.nps.gov/history/online_books/anthropology74/ce3d.htm; Commission 82(109-112), U.S. Department of War 78(362-66). Niiya, Brian. (Ed.). March 24, 1943, Japanese American National Museum. (2001). *Encyclopedia of Japanese American History, Updated Edition*, New York, Facts On File, p. 61.

18. 『一世としてアメリカに生きて』北村崇郎著、草思社、1992 年発行
Kitamura, Takao. (1992). *Living in America as Issei*, Tokyo, Soshisha, p. 64.

19. Thomas, Dorothy. S.and Noshimoto, Richard. S. (1946). *The Spoilage*, Berkeley and Los Angeles, University of California Press, pp. 14-5.

20. 『真珠湾と日系人』西山千著、サイマル出版、1991 年発行
Nishiyama, Sen. (1991). *Pearl Harbor and the Japanese Americans*, Tokyo, The Simul Press, p. 39.

21. カー知事の信念に反して、コロラド州民の排日感情は高かった。コロラドに収容所ができると決定した時、ハイウェイ沿いには" Japs keep going" の看板が並んだ。知事はそれに対し、「彼らに危害を加えるのであれば、私にも加えなさい。私が育った小さな町では、人種偏見は恥だと教えられた。人種偏見は皆の幸せを脅かすのだ」と訴えた。
Regardless of Carr's firm belief in civil rights, there was a growing anti-Japanese sentiment in Colorado. When the government decided to build an internment camp in Colorado, the residents demonstrated their hostility toward Japanese-Americans by posting a series of highway billboards proclaiming "Japs keep going". Carr sacrificed his political career by bravely confronting the people of

Colorado. "If you harm them, you must harm me. I was brought up in a small town where I knew the shame and dishonor of race hatred. I grew to despise it because it threatened the happiness of you and you and you." Brockman, Jason. (n.d.). *Biography of Ralph L. Carr*. Retrieved on July 19. 2006, from The Governor Ralph L. Carr Collection at the Colorado State Archives: www.colorado.gov/dpa/doit/archives/govs/carr.html#bio

22．Weglyn, Michi. (1976). *Years of Infamy*, New York, William Morrow and Company, p. 299; When Myer asked Eisenhower if he should take the job, Eisenhower replied, "Yes, if you can do the job and sleep at night". Myer, Dillon, S. (1971). *Uprooted Americans*, Tucson, The University of Arizona Press, p. 3,

23．News release, Work of the War Relocation Authority, An anniversary statement by Dillon S. Myer, (March 1943), p. 4, Papers of Dillon S. Myer, The War Relocation Authority and the incarceration of Japanese-Americans during WWII. Retrieved on July 19, 2006, from Truman Presidential Museum & Library; www.trumanlibrary.org/whistlestop/study_collections/japanese_internment/documents/index.php?documentdate=1943-03-00&documentid=16&studycollectionid=JI&pagenumber=1

24．Weglyn, Michi. (1976). *Years of Infamy*, New York, William Morrow and Company, pp. 118-9.

25．News release, Work of the War Relocation Authority, An anniversary statement by Dillon S. Myer, (March 1943), p. 5, Papers of Dillon S. Myer, The War Relocation Authority and the incarceration of Japanese-Americans during WWII. Retrieved on July 19, 2006, from Truman Presidential Museum & Library; www.trumanlibrary.org/whistlestop/study_collections/japanese_internment/documents/index.php?pagenumber=5&documentid=16&documentdate=1943-03-00&collectionid=JI&nav=ok

26．『一世としてアメリカに生きて』北村崇郎著、草思社、1992 年発行 Kitamura, Takao. (1992). *Living in America as Issei*, Tokyo, Soshisha, p. 140.

27．News release, Work of the War Relocation Authority, an anniversary statement by Dillon S. Myer, (March 1943), p. 5, Papers of Dillon S. Myer, The War Relocation Authority and the incarceration of Japanese-Americans during WWII. Retrieved on July 19, 2006, from Truman Presidential Museum & Library; www.trumanlibrary.org/whistlestop/study_collections/japanese_internment/documents/index.php?pagenumber=5&documentid=16&documentdate=1943-03-00&collectionid=JI&nav=ok

28．Myer, Dillon. S. (1971). *Uprooted Americans*, Tucson, The University of Arizona Press, p. 84.

29．Burton, J; Farrell, M; Lord, F; Lord, R. (1999). Chapter 10: Poston Relocation Center, 4, *Confinement and Ethnicity: An Overview of World War II, Japanese American Relocation Sites*, (rev. July 2000). Publications in anthropology 74, Tucson, Western Archeological and Conservation Center. Retrieved on July 18, 2006, from National Park Service; www.cr.nps.gov/history/online_books/anthropology74/ce10.htm

30．Niiya, Brian. (Ed.). Japanese American National Museum. (2001). *Encyclopedia of Japanese American History, Updated Edition*, New York, Facts On File, p. 337.

31．News release, statement by Dillon S. Myer, (May 14, 1943), p. 5, Papers of Philleo Nash, The War Relocation Authority and the incarceration of Japanese-Americans during WWII. Retrieved on July 28, 2006, from Truman Presidential Museum & Library, www.trumanlibrary.org/whistlestop/study_collections/japanese_internment/documents/index.php?pagenumber=5&documentid=59&documentdate=1943-05-14&collectionid=JI&nav=ok

32．『一世としてアメリカに生きて』北村崇郎著、草思社、1992 年発行 Kitamura, Takao. (1992). Living in America as Issei, Tokyo, Soshisha, p. 172.

33．Ibid., p. 169.

34．Speech, "The Truth about Relocation," Dillon S. Myer to the Commonwealth Club in San Francisco (August 6, 1943). p. 7, Papers of Dillon S. Myer, The War Relocation Authority and the incarceration of Japanese-Americans during WWII. Retrieved on July 28, 2006, from Truman Presidential Museum & Library;

www.trumanlibrary.org/whistlestop/study_collections/japanese_internment/documents/index.php?pagenumber=7&documentid=24&documentdate=1943-08-06&collectionid=JI&nav=ok

35．『一世としてアメリカに生きて』北村崇郎著、草思社、1992 年発行 Kitamura, Takao. (1992). *Living in America as Issei*, Tokyo, Soshisha, p. 65.

36．Ibid., p. 125.

37．Ibid., p. 223.

38．Murphy, Thomas. D. (1954). *Ambassadors in Arms – The Story of Hawaii' s 100th Battalion*, Honolulu, Club 100 under special arrangement with University of Hawaii Press, p. 43.

39．Ibid., p. 45.

40．Ibid., p. 52.

41．Ibid., p. 48.

42．Ibid., p. 52.

43．Odo, Franklin. (2004). *No Sword to Bury: Japanese Americans in Hawaii During World War II*, Philadelphia, Temple University Press, p. 147.

44．Murphy, Thomas, D. (1954). *Ambassadors in Arms – The Story of Hawaii' s 100th Battalion*, Honolulu, Club 100 under special arrangement with University of Hawaii Press, p. 57.

45．Ibid., p. 57.

46．Ibid.

47．Ibid., p. 58.

48．Ibid., p. 69.

49．Ibid.

50．Ibid., p. 78.

51．Ibid., p. 79.

52．Ibid., p. 76.

53．Ibid., p. 68.

54．『ブリエアの解放者たち』ドウス昌代著、文藝春秋、1983 年発行 Duus, Masayo. (1983). *The Liberators of Bruyeres* (Title of American publication: *Unlikely Liberators*), Tokyo, Bungeishunju, retrieved from Japanese version, p. 86.

55．Murphy, Thomas. D. (1954). *Ambassadors in Arms – The Story of Hawaii' s 100th Battalion*, Honolulu, Club 100 under special arrangement with University of Hawaii Press, p. 106.

56．Ibid., p. 106.

57．Ibid., p. 107.

58．Masaoka, Mike and Hosokawa, Bill. (1987). *They Call Me Moses Masaoka: An American Saga*, New York, William Morrow and Company, p. 121.

59．Ibid., p. 125.

60．Myer, Dillon, S. (1971). *Uprooted Americans*, Tucson, The University of Arizona Press, pp. xx-xxi.

61．Masaoka, Mike., Hosokawa, Bill. (1987). *They Call Me Moses Masaoka: An American Saga*, New York, William Morrow and Company, p. 127.

62．Collins, Donald. E. and Niiya, Brian. (Ed.). Japanese American National Museum. (2001). *Encyclopedia of Japanese American History, Updated Edition*, New York, Facts On File, p. 261.

63．当初の計画では、ハワイから1500 人、本土から3000 人の志願兵で結成する予定だった。本土の兵役年齢にある2 万3606 人のうち、応募したのは1256 人に留まった。約1 万人が志願したハワイでは増員され、2686 人が訓練へと旅立った。1943 年3 月28 日、イオラニ宮殿で出発を祝う式典が開催された日には、ホノルルで1 万5 千人から1 万7 千人の日系人が集った。

The original plan called for a quota of 3,000 volunteers from the mainland and 1,500 from Hawaii. Only 1,256 mainland *Nisei* volunteered out of 23,606 *Nisei* of draft age. Nearly 10,000 Hawaii *Nisei* volunteered and 2,686 were sent off to basic training on the mainland. It was reported that 15,000 to 17,000 Japanese Americans gathered in Honolulu for a gala celebration in Iolani Palace. Niiya, Brian. (Ed.). Japanese American National Museum. (2001). *Encyclopedia of Japanese American History, Updated Edition*, New York, Facts On File, p. 163.

64．Yahata, Craig. (Producer, Director). Yoneshige, David. (Producer). (2003). A

Tradition of Honor (DVD), Go For Broke National Education Center. (Available from Go For Broke National Education Center, 370 Amapola Ave., Suite 110, Torrance, CA 90501).

65.　Ibid.

66.　Go For Broke National Education Center. (n.d.). Cassino, Historical information. Retrieved on August 1, 2006, from www.goforbroke.org/history/history_historical_campaigns_cassino.asp

67.　Compiled by Hawaii Nikkei History Editorial Board. (1998). Japanese Eyes ,American Heart, Honolulu, Tendai Educational Foundation, p. 61.

68.　Yahata, Craig. (Producer, Director). Yoneshige, David. (Producer). (2003). *A Tradition of Honor*. (DVD), Go For Broke National Education Center. (Available from Go For Broke National Education Center, 370 Amapola Ave., Suite 110, Torrance, CA 90501).

69.　『ブリエアの解放者たち』ドウス昌代著、文藝春秋、1983 年発行
Duus, Masayo. (1983). *The Liberators of Bruyeres* (Title of American publication: *Unlikely Liberators*), Tokyo, Bungeishunju, retrieved from Japanese version, p. 185.

70.　Go For Broke National Education Center. (n.d.). Belvedere, Historical information. Retrieved on August 1, 2006, from www.goforbroke.org/history/history_historical_campaigns_belvedere.asp

71.　Yahata, Craig.(Producer, Director). Yoneshige, David. (Producer). (2003). A *Tradition of Honor*, (DVD), Go For Broke National Education Center. (Available from Go For Broke National Education Center, 370 Amapola Ave., Suite 110, Torrance, CA 90501).

72.　Go For Broke National Education Center. (n.d.). Timeline of events, Historical information. Retrieved on August 1, 2006, from www.goforbroke.org/history/history_historical_timeline_1944.asp

73.　Murphy, Thomas. D. (1954). *Ambassadors in Arms – The Story of Hawaii's 100th Battalion*, Honolulu, Club 100 under special arrangement with University of Hawaii Press, p. 239.

74.　Compiled by Hawaii Nikkei History Editorial Board. (1998). *Japanese Eyes, American Heart*, Honolulu, Tendai Educational Foundation, p. 195.

75.　Ibid., p. 112.

76.　Murphy, Thomas. D. (1954). *Ambassadors in Arms – The Story of Hawaii's 100th Battalion*, Honolulu, Club 100 under special arrangement with University of Hawaii Press, p. 242.

77.　第百大隊は 11 月 7 日と 8 日に後退しており、第 2 大隊と第 3 大隊に「後退」命令が出たのが 11 月 9 日だった。
The 100th Battalion moved back to Bruyeres on November 7th and 8th. The 2nd and 3rd Battalion were ordered back on November 9th. Ibid., pp. 244-5.

78.　Ibid., p. 244.

79.　Go For Broke National Education Center. (n.d.). The rescue of the Lost Battalion, Historical information. Retrieved on August 1, 2006, from www.goforbroke.org/history/history_historical_campaigns_rescue.asp

80.　Ibid.

81.　Ibid.

82.　『ブリエアの解放者たち』ドウス昌代著、文藝春秋、1983 年発行
Duus, Masayo. (1983). *The Liberators of Bruyeres* (Title of American publication: *Unlikely Liberators*), Tokyo, Bungeishunju, retrieved from Japanese version, p. 17.

83.　Go For Broke National Education Center. (n.d.). Gothic Line and Po Valley Campaign, Historical information. Retrieved on August 1, 2006, from www.goforbroke.org/history/history_historical_campaigns_gothic.asp

84.　Ibid.

85.　Ibid.

86.　Ibid.

87.　Yahata, Craig. (Producer, Director). Yoneshige, David. (Producer). (2003). A *Tradition of Honor*, (DVD), Go For Broke National Education Center. (Available from Go For Broke National Education Center, 370 Amapola Ave., Suite 110, Torrance, CA 90501).

88.　Go For Broke National Education Center, Gothic Line and Po Valley Campaign, Historical information. Retrieved on August 1, 2006, from www.goforbroke.org/history/history_historical_campaigns_gothic.asp

89.　Ibid., Central Europe Campaign (522nd Field Artillery Battalion). Retrieved on August 1, 2006, from www.goforbroke.org/history/history_historical_campaigns_central.asp

90.　Ibid.

91.　United States Holocaust Memoriam Museum. (n.d.). Honoring American liberators. Retrieved on August 25, 2006, from www.ushmm.org/wlc/en/

92.　第 552 野砲部隊は 4 月 27 日から 30 日までの 4 日間、第 4 歩兵師団とともにミュンヘン南部の攻撃に参加していたが、第 4 歩兵師団はダッハウ付属キャンプの解放者として認定されている。
The 552nd joined the 4th Division's drive south, toward Munich, from April 27th to 30th. The United States Holocaust Memoriam Museum and the Center for Military History recognize the 4th Infantry Division as the liberating unit of the Dachau subcamp. Ibid; Go For Broke National Education Center. (n.d.). Central Europe Campaign (522nd Field Artillery Battalion), Historical information. Retrieved on August 1, 2006, from www.goforbroke.org/history/history_historical_campaigns_central.asp

Chapter Three

1.　Commission 82(260)., Murphy 54(282). Niiya, Brian. (Ed.). Japanese American National Museum. (2001). July 15, 1946, *Encyclopedia of Japanese American History, Updated Edition*, New York, Facts On File, p. 74.

2.　Smithsonian Institution. (n.d.). Honors and Awards, Service, *A More Perfect Union: Japanese Americans and the U.S. Constitution*, National Museum of American History. Retrieved on August 7, 2006, from americanhistory.si.edu/perfectunion/non-flash/service_honors.html

3.　Niiya, Brian. (Ed.). Japanese American National Museum. (2001). *Encyclopedia of Japanese American History, Updated Edition*, New York, Facts On File, p. 164.

4.　『ブリエアの解放者たち』ドウス昌代著、文藝春秋、1983 年発行
Duus, Masayo. (1983). *The Liberators of Bruyeres* (Title on American publication: *Unlikely Liberators*), Tokyo, Bungeishunju, retrieved from Japanese version, p. 32.

5.　『真珠湾と日系人』西山千著、サイマル出版、1991 年発行
Nishiyama, Sen. (1991). *Pearl Harbor and the Japanese Americans*, Tokyo, The Simul Press, pp. 189-90.

6.　Steidl, Franz. (1997). *Lost Battalions: Going for Broke in the Vosges, Autumn 1944*, Novato, Presidio Press, pp. 173-4.

7.　Niiya, Brian. (Ed.). Japanese American National Museum. (2001). *Encyclopedia of Japanese American History, Updated Edition*, New York, Facts On File, p. 199.

8.　フッドリバー支部の日系兵に対する行為に特に激怒したのは、第 442 連隊に救出された「失われた大隊」の第 36 師団第 141 連隊第 1 大隊だ。以下は同大隊 C 中隊の兵士たちが書いた抗議の手紙の一部。「日系人はゴメンだといってふんぞり返っている男たちよりも、日系兵のほうがオレゴンの町に住んでしかるべきだ。日系兵にこんなことをする人の権利と自由を守るために闘っているのかと思うとやりきれない」「第 1 大隊があるのは、すべて日系兵たちのおかげだ。我々を救出するために戦死していった大勢の日系兵を我々は見ている」
The "Lost Battalion" soldiers of C Company, 1st Battalion, 141st Infantry, 36th Division, who were rescued by the men of the 442nd, were outraged when they heard about the Hood River incident. Here are some excerpted quotes from the protest letters these soldiers wrote:
These boys deserve this Oregon town a helluva lot more than the men sitting around there who don't want them around, and we feel pretty lousy having to fight for rights and liberties of people who would do something like that to Japanese-Americans fighting over here.

"If it was not for the Japanese-Americans there wouldn't be no 1st Battalion. And we saw plenty of them who died to get through to rescue us." Japanese American Historical Society. (n.d.). "Hood-River Japanese-American Incident" stirs infantrymen, 14 January 1945,*36th Division T-Patch Volume 2.*, No. 10. Retrieved on August 8, 2006, from www.kwanah.com/36division/442rct/goforbroke.htm

9. 『真珠湾と日系人』西山千著。サイマル出版会、1991 年発行
Nishiyama, Sen. (1991). *Pearl Harbor and the Japanese Americans*, Tokyo, The Simul Press, p. 140.

10. Maki, Mitchell.; Kitano, Harry, Berthold, S. Megan. (1999). *Achieving the Impossible Dream: How Japanese Americans Obtained Redress*, Urbana, The Board of Trustees of the University of Illinois, p. 171.

11. 『真珠湾と日系人』西山千著、サイマル出版社、1991 年発行
Nishiyama, Sen. (1991). Pearl Harbor and the Japanese Americans, Tokyo, The Simul Press, pp. 143-4.

12. Odo, Franklin. (2004). *No Sword to Bury: Japanese Americans in Hawaii during World War II*, Philadelphia, Temple University Press, pp. 145-6.

13. Kitayama, Glen and Niiya, Brian. (Ed.). Japanese American National Museum. (2001). *Encyclopedia of Japanese American History, Updated Edition*, New York, Facts On File, p. 151.

14. Public Proclamation No. 21, Douglas County School District Re-1, Colorado. Retrieved on August 9, 2006, from www1.dcsdk12.org/secondary/chs/amache/WW46.html

15. Truman Presidential Museum & Library. (n.d.). Chronology 1944, The War Relocation Authority and the incarceration of Japanese-Americans during WWII. Retrieved on August 9, 2006, from www.trumanlibrary.org/whistlestop/study_collections/japanese_internment/1944.htm

16. tenBroek, Jacobus; Barnhart, Edward N; Watson, Floyd W. (1954). *Prejudice, War, and the Constitution*, Berkeley, University of California Press, p. 253.

17. Ibid. p. 252, Kitayama. Glen and Niiya, Brian (Ed.). Japanese American National Museum. (2001). *Encyclopedia of Japanese American History, Updated Edition*, New York, Facts On File, pp. 159-60.

18. Robinson, Greg and Robinson Toni. (2005). The Supreme Court Appeal and the Brief, III Oyama Case, Japanese Americans and the Oginins of Strict Scrutiny, 68 Law & Contemp. Probs. 29, *Law and Contemporary Problems*, Duke Journals, Duke Law. Retrieved on August 18, 2006, from www.law.duke.edu/shell/cite.pl?68+Law+&+Contemp.+Probs.+29+(spring+2005)

19. Yamamoto, Dennis and Niiya, Brian. (Ed.). Japanese American National Museum. (2001). *Encyclopedia of Japanese American History, Updated Edition*, New York, Facts On File, p. 165.

20. Masaoka, Mike., Hosokawa, Bill. (1987). *They Call Me Moses Masaoka: An American Saga*, New York, William Morrow and Company, pp. 214-5.

21. Rafu Shimpo, 7 Nov. 1956:1. Niiya, Brian. (Ed.). Japanese American National Museum. (2001). *Encyclopedia of Japanese American History, Updated Edition*, New York, Facts On File, pp. 79-80.

22. Speech, Relocation: The final chapter by Dillon S. Myer. (n.d, c. 1945). pp. 4-5, Papers of Dillon S. Myer, The War Relocation Authority and Incarceration of Japanese-Americans during WWII. Retrieved on July 19, 2006, from Truman Presidential Museum & Library; www.trumanlibrary.org/whistlestop/study_collections/japanese_internment/documents/index.php?pagenumber=1&documentdate=1945-00-00&documentid=55&studycollectionid=JI&nav=ok

23. Annual report of the Director of the War Relocation Authority, Myer to the Secretary of the Interior, for the fiscal year ended June 30, 1945. (July 1945). pp. 8-9, Papers of Dillon S. Myer, The War Relocation Authority and Incarceration of Japanese-Americans during WWII, Truman Presidential Museum & Library, retrieved on August 9, 2006. www.trumanlibrary.org/whistlestop/study_collections/japanese_internment/documents/index.php?pagenumber=8&documentdate=1945-07-14&documentid=50&studycollectionid=JI&nav=ok

24. Memorandum to American soldiers of Japanese ancestry, (August 1945). p. 1, Papers of Dillon S. Myer, The War Relocation Authority and incarceration of Japanese-Americans during WWII. Retrieved on August 9, 2006, from Truman Presidential Museum & Library; www.trumanlibrary.org/whistlestop/study_collections/japanese_internment/documents/index.php?documentdate=1945-08-00&documentid=52&studycollectionid=JI&pagenumber=1

25. Kihara, Shigeya. (April 18, 1997). 1997 meeting, *The Role of the National Japanese American Historical Society, In the Movement for Redress*, 11, Organization of American Historians. Retrieved on August 11, 2006, from www.oah.org/meetings/1997/kihara.htm

26. Maki, Mitchell; Kitano, Harry Berthold, S. Megan. (1999). *Achieving the Impossible Dream: How Japanese Americans Obtained Redress*, Urbana, The Board of Trustees of the University of Illinois, p. 43.

27. Remarks on signing the bill providing restitution for the wartime internment of Japanese-American civilians. (August 10, 1998). Retrieved on August 11, 2006 from Ronald Reagan Presidential Library; www.reagan.utexas.edu/archives/speeches/1988/081088d.htm

28. Truman Presidential Museum & Library. (n.d.). 1946 Chronology, The War Relocation Authority and Incarceration of Japanese-Americans during WWII, retrieved on August 11, 2006, from www.trumanlibrary.org/whistlestop/study_collections/japanese_internment/1946.htm

29. Smithsonian Institution. (n.d.). *A More Perfect Union: Japanese Americans and the U.S. Constitution*, Post-war, Justice, National Museum of American History. Retrieved on August 11, 2006, from americanhistory.si.edu/perfectunion/non-flash/justice_postwar.html

30. 『祖国へ、熱き心を：東京にオリンピックを呼んだ男』高杉良著、新潮文庫、2001 年 10 月 1 日出版
Takasugi, Ryo. (1990). *Passion for the Motherland: The Man Who Brought the Olympic Games to Tokyo*, Tokyo, Shincho-Bunko, pp. 13-4.

31. Yamamoto, Dennis and Niiya, Brian. (Ed.). Japanese American National Museum. (2001). *Encyclopedia of Japanese American History, Updated Edition*, New York, Facts On File, p. 381.

32. Japanese American Citizen League. (n.d.). Leadership Development, Mike M. Masaoka Congressional Fellowship. Retrieved on August 18, 2006, from www.jacl.org/leadership_development_4.php

33. Masaoka, Mike and Hosokawa, Bill. (1987). *They Call Me Moses Masaoka: An American Saga*, New York, William Morrow and Company, p. 221.

34. Statement of Dillon S. Myer in Support of H. R. 199 before a Special Committee of the Senate Judiciary Committee. (July 19, 1949). p. 2. Papers of Dillon S. Myer, The War Relocation Authority and the incarceration of Japanese-Americans during WWII. Retrieved on August 14, 2006, from Truman Presidential Museum & Library; www.trumanlibrary.org/whistlestop/study_collections/japanese_internment/documents/index.php?pagenumber=2&documentid=18&documentdate=1949-07-19&collectionid=JI&nav=ok

35. Compiled by the Senate Library under the direction of Stewart, Walter J. and Harness, Gregory. (February 1992). 1990 H.J. Res 238, *Presidential Vetoes, 1789-1988*, pp. 403-404. Washington D.C., Office of the Secretary of the Senate. Retrieved on August 14, 2006, from U.S. Government Printing Office; www.senate.gov/reference/resources/pdf/presvetoes17891988.pdf

36. Masaoka, Mike and Hosokawa, Bill. (1987). *They Call Me Moses Masaoka: An American Saga*, New York, William Morrow and Company, pp. 226-30.

37. マッカラン議員は反共産主義の旗手で、国家保障小委員会の委員長だった。1950 年には、共産党員に司法省登録の義務を課したマッカラン国家補償法を成立させていた。トルーマン大統領は拒否権を発動したが、両院はそれを覆した。ウォルター議員は 50 年代後半に反アメリカ的活動委員会の委員長になった。ウォルター議員がマッカラン議員と組んで発案したこの法案は、冷戦状態にある緊張の中で共産主義者を狙い撃ちしており、思想を理由に国外追求を可能にした一面を持つ。また日系人に帰化権を与えたものの、移民割り当てが不平等で、そ

の 70％がイギリス、アイルランド、ドイツに割り当てられていた。日米開戦の恩恵で、同盟国であった中国系は 1943 年、米政府支配下のフィリピン系と英政府支配下のインド系は 1946 年に帰化権を得ていた。Pat McCarran (D-Nevada), head of the Senate Judiciary Committee's Internal Security Subcommittee, was a leading figure in the anti-communist movement. He promoted the McCarran Internal Security Act of 1950, which required American Communist Party members to register with the Attorney General. President Truman vetoed the bill but Congress overrode the veto and it became law. Congressman Francis Walter (D-Pa), who became chairman of the Committee on Un-American Activities in the late 1950s, teamed up with McCarran to write this bill. It was directed against communists and made exclusion or deportation of aliens possible purely based on ideological grounds. Although this law granted the right for Japanese-Americans to be naturalized and permitted Japanese to immigrate, 70 percent of all immigrant slots were allotted to natives of the United Kingdom, Ireland, and Germany. As major allies against the Japanese during WWII, Chinese gained the right of naturalization in 1943, and U.S.-governed Filipinos and British-governed Indians gained the right in 1946. Campi, Alicia. J., (June 2004). *The McCarran-Walter Act: A Contradictory Legacy on Race, Quotas, and Ideology*, The American Immigration Law Foundation. Retrieved on August 15, 2006, from www.ailf.org/ipc/policy_reports_2004_mccarranwalter.asp

38. Yamamoto, Dennis and Niiya, Brian. (Ed.). Japanese American National Museum. (2001). *Encyclopedia of Japanese American History, Updated Edition*, New York, Facts On File, p. 206.

39. Compiled by the Senate Library under the direction of Stewart, Walter. J. and Harness, Gregory. (February 1992). *Presidential Vetoes, 1789-1988*, 2016 H.R. 5678, pp. 408-9, Washington D.C., Office of the Secretary of the Senate. Retrieved on August 14, 2006, from U.S. Government Printing Office; www.senate.gov/reference/resources/pdf/presvetoes17891988.pdf

40. Masaoka, Mike and Hosokawa, Bill. (1987). *They Call Me Moses Masaoka: An American Saga*, New York, William Morrow and Company, p. 236.

41. Compiled by the Senate Library under the direction of Stewart, Walter. J. and Harness, Gregory. (February 1992). *Presidential Vetoes, 1789-1988*, 2016 H.R. 5678, pp. 408-409, Washington D.C., Office of the Secretary of the Senate. Retrieved on August 14, 2006, from U.S. Government Printing Office; www.senate.gov/reference/resources/pdf/presvetoes17891988.pdf

42. Naturalization since 1907, *INS Reporter*, Vol. 26, No. 3 (Winter 1977-1978) pp. 41-6, last modified on January 20, 2006. Retrieved on August 14, 2006, from U.S. Citizenship and Naturalization Services; www.uscis.gov/graphics/aboutus/history/since07.htm

43. Endo, Traci and Niiya, Brian. (Ed.). Japanese American National Museum. (2001). *Encyclopedia of Japanese American History, Updated Edition*, New York, Facts On FIle, p. 132.

44. Compiled by the Hawaii Nikkei History Editorial Board. (1998). *Japanese Eyes, American Heart*, Honolulu, Tendai Educational Foundation, pp. 361-2.

45. 1973 年、バーンズ知事が病気を理由に退任したため、副知事だったアリヨシが知事代理を務めていたが、1974 年の知事選に当選し、日系初の州知事になった。
Jack Burns stepped down from the governatorial post because of illness. Lieutenant Governor Ariyoshi became acting governor. Ariyoshi became the first governor of Japanese ancestry by winning the 1974 election. Compiled by the Hawaii Nikkei History Editorial Board. (1998). *Japanese Eyes, American Heart*, Honolulu, Tendai Educational Foundation, pp. 365-7.

46. United States Senate. (n.d.). Biography of Senator Daniel K. Inouye. Retrieved on August 15, 2006, from www.senate.gov/~inouye/bio.html

47. Masaoka, Mike and Hosokawa, Bill. (1987). *They Call Me Moses Masaoka: An American Saga*, New York, William Morrow and Company, p. 300.

48. Immigration and Nationality Act Amendments of October 3, 1965 (79 Statutes-at-Large 911). (n.d.). *Immigration and Naturalization Legislation from the Statistical Yearbook*, last modified on August 9, 2003. Retrieved on August 15, 2006, from U.S. Citizenship and Immigration Services; www.uscis.gov/graphics/shared/aboutus/statistics/legishist/526.htm

49. Kanshiro, Edith and Niiya, Brian. (Ed.). Japanese American National Museum. (2001). *Encyclopedia of Japanese American History, Updated Edition*, New York, Facts On File, p. 277.

50. 『祖国へ、熱き心を：東京にオリンピックを呼んだ男』高杉良著、新潮文庫、2001 年 10 月 1 日出版
Takasugi, Ryo. (1990). *Passion for the Motherland: The Man Who Brought the Olympic Games to Tokyo*, Tokyo, Shincho-Bunko, pp. 325-31, 356-415.

51. University of Hawaii. (January 2005). *Biographical Chronology*, Senator Spark Matsunaga Papers, Finding Aide, p. 6. Retrieved on August 15, 2006, from Hawaii Congressional Papers Collection Archives and Manuscripts Department, University of Hawaii at Manoa Library; libweb.hawaii.edu/libdept/congressional/matsunaga/SMMFindingAid_web.pdf

52. President Gerald R. Ford's remarks upon signing a proclamation concerning Japanese-American internment during World War II. (February 19, 1976). Retrieved on August 15, 2006, from Gerald R. Ford Presidential Library and Museum; www.fordlibrarymuseum.gov/library/speeches/760111.htm

53. Kitayama, Glen and Niiya, Brian. (Ed.). Japanese American National Museum. (2001). *Encyclopedia of Japanese American History, Updated Edition*, New York, Facts On File, p. 342.

54. Maki, Mitchell; Kitano, Harry; H. L., Berthold, S. Megan. (1999). *Achieving the Impossible Dream: How Japanese Americans Obtained Redress*, Urbana, The Board of Trustees of the University of Illinois, p. 162.

55. University of Hawaii at Manoa. (n.d.). About Spark Matsunaga (1916-1990), *The Sen. Spark M. Matsunaga Papers*. Retrieved on August 22, 2006, from University Archives; libweb.hawaii.edu/libdept/congressional/matsunaga/bio.htm

56. ミネタ前運輸長官が陸軍に入隊したのは、大学卒業後の 1953 年。情報将校として日本と韓国に駐屯した。
Former Secretary of Transportation Norman Mineta joined the Army in 1953, after graduating from the University of California at Berkeley. He served as an intelligence officer in Japan and Korea. Mineta Transportation Institute. (n.d.). Norman Y. Mineta. Retrieved on November 30, 2006, from transweb.sjsu.edu/mtiportal/about/mineta.html

57. Masaoka, Mike and Hosokawa, Bill. (1987). *They Call Me Moses Masaoka: An American Saga*, New York, William Morrow and Company, p. 322.

58. 戦時下における市民の強制退去と収容委員会（CWRIC: Commission on Wartime Relocation and Internment of Civilians）は、1981 年 7 月から 12 月まで東海岸と西海岸を中心に全米 10 カ所で公聴会を開き、750 人以上が証言した。証言したのはおもに元収容者だったが、わずかながら強制収容の正当性を擁護する証人も証言台に立った。その 1 人が、日系部隊の設立に尽力したジョン・マックロイで、彼の証言は日系社会を落胆させた。
The Commission on Wartime Relocation and Internment of Civilians held public hearings from July to December of 1981, at ten locations, mainly on the East and West Coasts. More than 750 witnesses testified. Most of the witnesses were former internees and a few of them were apologists, who justified the mass incarceration. One of them was John McCloy, who supported the establishment of the 442nd Regiment. McCloy's testimony disappointed the Japanese community. Kitayama, Glen and Niiya, Brian. (Ed.). Japanese American National Museum. (2001). *Encyclopedia of Japanese American History, Updated Edition*, New York, Facts On File, p. 264.

59. Maki, Mitchell; Kitano, Harry; Berthold, S. Megan. (1999). *Achieving the Impossible Dream: How Japanese Americans Obtained Redress*, Urbana, The Board of Trustees of the University of Illinois, p. 153.

60. ジューン・マスダ・ゴトーはマスダ軍曹の妹で、スチルウェル将軍が勲章をつけたのは、もう 1 人の妹メアリー。南カリフォルニアのファウンテンバレーに、マスダ軍曹の栄誉を記念して名付けられたカズオ・マスダ中学があり、ジューンは何度も同校でマスダ軍曹の叙勲記念式典におけるレーガンのスピーチを紹介していた。ジューンだけでなく、レーガン大統領の下には 2 万通を超える署名を促す手紙や式典の模様を伝える新聞記事の切抜きが送られた。

June Masuda Goto was one of Sgt. Masuda's sisters. It was Mary, another Sgt. Masuda's sister, the whom General Stilwell pinned the medal on at the ceremony to award Sgt. Masuda Distinguished Service Cross. Kazuo Masuda Middle School in Fountain Valley, California was, named in Sgt. Masuda's honor. June was asked many times to speak at the school, where she quoted Reagan's remarks at the ceremony to the history classes. June was not the only one to send a letter to President Reagan. More than 20,000 letters and news clippings of the news article reporting the ceremony were sent to the President in support of the bill. Kitayama, Glen and Niiya, Brian. (Ed.). Japanese American National Museum. (2001). *Encyclopedia of Japanese American History, Updated Edition*, New York, Facts On File, p. 344; June Masuda Goto's letter to President Reagan on November 19, 1987. (September 1999). Shusterman's immigration update. Retrieved on August 16, 2006, from www.shusterman.com/sep99.html#10

61. Kitayama, Glen and Niiya, Brian. (Ed.). Japanese American National Museum. (2001). *Encyclopedia of Japanese American History, Updated Edition*, New York, Facts On File, p. 140.

62. Pacific Citizen, 1 Dec. 1989:1. Niiya, Brian. (Ed.). Japanese American National Museum. (2001). November 21, 1989, *Encyclopedia of Japanese American History, Updated Edition*, New York, Facts On File, pp. 95-6.

63. Pacific Citizen, 12 Oct. 1990:1. Niiya, Brian. (Ed.). Japanese American National Museum. (2001). October 9, 1990, *Encyclopedia of Japanese American History, Updated Edition*, New York, Facts On File, p. 96.

64. Ibid.

65. Kitayama, Glen. Ibid., p. 145.

66. Remarks by the President at Medals of Freedom presentation, Speech by President at Medals of Freedom event. (January 15, 1998). The White House, Office of Press Secretary. Retrieved on December 5, 2006, from William J. Clinton Foundation; www.clintonfoundation.org/legacy/011598-speech-by-president-at-medals-of-freedom-event.htm

67. Kitayama, Glen and Niiya, Brian. (Ed.). Japanese American National Museum. (2001). *Encyclopedia of Japanese American History, Updated Edition*, New York, Facts On File, pp. 145-6.

68. Tozai Times 4(Oct. 1987):1, 8-9. Niiya, Brian. (Ed.). Japanese American National Museum. (2001). *Encyclopedia of Japanese American History Updated Edition*, New York, Facts One File,, p. 95.

69. Go For Broke National Education Center. (n.d.). Monument name locator, The Monument. Retrieved on August 16, 2006, from www.goforbroke.org/history/history_historical_medal.asp

70. Ibid., Medal of Honor Recipients, Historical Information.

71. National Japanese American Memorial Foundation. (n.d.). The honor roll. Retrieved on August 16, 2006, from www.njamf.com/honor.htm

72. Smithsonian Institution. (n.d.). Japanese Americans Today, Justice, *A More Perfect Union: Japanese Americans and the U.S. Constitution*. Retrieved on August 16, 2006, from National Museum of American History; americanhistory.si.edu/perfectunion/non-flash/justice_today.html

73. U.S. Department of the Interior. (n.d.). Grand Opening, Manzanar National Historic Site. Retrieved on August 17, 2006, from National Park Service; www.nps.gov/manz/grandopening.htm

74. Stewart, Jocelyn Y. (September 18, 2005). Manzanar icon now more than a memory, *Los Angeles Times*.

75. Werner, Erica. (December 6, 2006). Internment camps to be preserved, *Ventura Country Star, Camarillo Edition*.

76. Niiya, Brian. (Ed.). Japanese American National Museum. (2001). April 30, 1992, *Encyclopedia of Japanese American History, Updated Edition*, New York, Facts On File, P96.

Chapter Four

••

1. Pichaske, Pete. (June 22, 1999). Shinseki is No.1 in Army, The Honolulu Star-Bulletin. Retrieved on October 26, 2006, from starbulletin.com/1999/06/22/news/

2. Ibid.

3. Kakesako, Greg. (June 21, 1999). Native Son Joining Ranks of Eminent Army Leaders, *The Honolulu Star-Bulletin*. Retrieved on October 26, 2006, from starbulletin.com/1999/06/21/news/story2.html

4. Ibid.

5. Medeiros, Sara. (n.d.). *Carrying the Torch*, Hawaiian Electric Industries, Inc. Retrieved on October 26, 2006, from www.hei.com/hoahana/2001.Q4/6.html

6. National Commission on Terrorist Attacks upon the United States, *The 9/11 Commission Report*, June 2004, p. 311.

7. Hamberger, Ronald; Baker, William; Barnett, Jonathan; Marrion, Christopher; Milke, James; Nelson, Harold "Bud". (May 2002). Chapter 2 WTC1 and WTC2 *World Trade Center Building Performance and Study: Data Collection, Preliminary Observations, and Recommendations*, Federal Emergency Management Agency, pp. 2-36, 2-37, 2-38. Retrieved on October 26, 2006, from www.fema.gov/pdf/library/fema403_ch2.pdf

8. Department of Commerce, Technology Administration, National Institute of Standards and Technology. (September 2005). National Construction Safety Team for the Federal Building and Fire Safety Investigation of the World Trade Center Disaster, *Final Report on the Collapse of the World Trade Center Towers*, p. 189. Retrieved on October 26, 2006, from wtc.nist.gov/NISTNCSTAR1Collapseof Towers.pdf

9. Zaslow, Jeffrey. (December 18-20, 1998). Straight Talk, *USA Weekend*. Retrieved on August 13, 2006, from www.usaweekend.com/98_issues/981220/981220talk.html

10. Mack, Ann. (Fall 2003). Ann Curry: Living the Dream, *Newsletter of the School of Journalism and Communications, Flash*, Volume 18 No. 1, University of Oregon. Retrieved on August 13, 2006, from flash.uoregon.edu/F03/curry.html

11. Ibid.

12. Ibid.

13. Smith, Joseph and Niiya, Brian. (Ed.). Japanese American National Museum. (2001). *Encyclopedia of Japanese American History, Updated Edition*, New York, Facts On File, p. 233.

14. 昭和43年運輸白書、第4章：国民の観光旅行の状況、第3節：国民の海外渡航の状況、国土交通省

Ministry of Land Infrastructure and Transport. (n.d.). Chapter 4: Japanese citizens' overseas tourism, Section 3: Japanese citizens travelling overseas, *1968 White Paper on Transportation*. Retrieved on August 13, 2006. /www.mlit.go.jp/hakusyo/transport/shouwa43/ind120403/000.html

15. Greenhut, Steven. (November 20, 2005). Against the Tide, *Orange Country Register*.

16. Yahata, Craig, (Producer, Director). Yoneshige, David. (Producer). (2003). *A Tradition of Honor*. (DVD). Go For Broke National Education Center. (Available from Go For Broke National Education Center, 370 Amapola Ave., Suite 110, Torrance, CA 90501).

17. 『ブリエアの解放者たち』ドウス昌代著、文藝春秋、1983年発行

Duus, Masayo. (1983). *The Liberators of Bruyeres* (Title of American publication: *Unlikely Liberators*), Tokyo, Bungeishunju, retrieved from Japanese version, p. 192.

18. News Release, Colonel Young Oak Kim (U.S. Army Ret.), 86: Decorated U.S. WWII and Korean War veteran. (December 29, 2005). Go For Broke National Education Center. Retrieved on August 16, 2006, from www.goforbroke.org/about_us/about_us_news_press010306.asp

Columns

••

MIS

1. Niiya, Brian. (Ed.). Japanese American National Museum. (2001). *Encyclopedia of Japanese American History, Updated Edition*, New York, Facts On File, p. 274.

2. Ibid., Rafu Shimpo. (July 5, 1985). A12-13, p. 77.

3. Ibid., p. 275.

4. National Japanese American Historical Society. (n.d.). 1970s. Japanese American History Timeline, Military Intelligence Service Association of Northern California. Retrieved on August 25, 2006, from Military Intelligence Service Research Center; www.njahs.org/misnorcal/timeline/timeline.htm#eight

5. Ibid., www.njahs.org/misnorcal/timeline/timeline.htm#eleven

Mike Masaoka

1. Abe, Frank and ITVS. (n.d.). The Draft, *Compliance, Conscience and the Constitution*, Public Broadcasting Service (PBS). Retrieved on August 25, 2006, from www.pbs.org/itvs/conscience/compliance/the_draft/index.html

2. University of Utah. (n.d.). Biography of Mike M. Masaoka, *The Mike Masaoka Papers* (Ms 656). Retrieved on August 25, 2006, from J. Willard Marriott Library; www.lib.utah.edu/spc/mss/ms656/ms656.html#bio

3. 『真珠湾と日系人』西山千著、サイマル出版、1991 年発行
Nishiyama, Sen. (1991). *Pearl Harbor and the Japanese Americans*, Tokyo, The Simul Press. p. 100.

4. 日系兵で唯一、最高勲章を受賞したサダオ・ムネモリも、最初は殊勲十字章の受勲に留まっていたが、ユタ州選出のアルバート・トーマス上院議員が強く後押しをし、終戦直後に最高勲章に格上げされたという経緯がある。マサオカは自伝『モーゼと呼ばれた男マイク・正岡』（マイク・正岡・ビル・細川共著、塩谷紘訳）で、誰かが申請書のランクを１つ下げていたのではないかとの疑惑を抱いており、恩師であるトーマス議員がイタリアを訪れた時に相談したと綴っている。同著によると、トーマス議員が調べた時にまだ採決が下っていなかったのがムネモリに対する推薦の章だけだった。1996 年、ダニエル・アカカ上院議員が日系人とその他のアジア系などの第 2 次大戦における評価を再検討する法案を提出し、それによって 2000 年のクリントン大統領による叙勲が実現した。
Masaoka wrote in his autobiography *"They Call Me Moses Masaoka,"* (co-author Bill Hosokawa) that he had talked to Senator Thomas, Masaoka's university professor, about his suspicion when Thomas visited soldiers in Italy. Masaoka had suspected that someone had been downgrading Japanese-Americans' commendation files. According to the autobiography, when Thomas made an inquiry about this matter, Munemori's commendation was the only one that had not been acted upon.. In 1996, Senator Daniel Akaka (D-Hawaii) sponsored legislation ordering the re-evaluation of WWII awards to Japanese-Americans and other Asian/Pacific Islanders who fought in both theaters. As a result of this action, President Clinton awarded 22 Medal of Honor in 2000.
Masaoka, Mike and Hosokawa, Bill. (1987). *They Call Me Moses Masaoka: An American Saga*, New York, William Morrow and Company, pp. 176-7; Sterner, C. Douglas. (n.d.). *The Medal of Honor*, HomeofHeroes.com. Retrieved on August 28, 2006, from www.homeofheroes.com/moh/nisei/index99_moh.html

5. Masaoka, Mike and Hosokawa, Bill. (1987). *They Call Me Moses Masaoka: An American Saga*, New York, William Morrow and Company, p. 290.

6. マサオカは 1982 年 4 月 10 日、ロサンゼルスで開催された JACL 全国大会で、戦時中の方針に対する批判に対し、反論のスピーチを行ったが、その中で「我々が親のため、子供のため、孫のために何らかの祖国を残すためには、忠誠心を証明しなければならなかった。今日、そのために我々は 200％アメリカ人だと批判されているが、まさにその通り。なぜなら我々はそのために努力していたのだから」と語っている。
Masaoka issued a rebuttal to his critics in a statement to the JACL national convention in Los Angeles on April 10, 1982. In his speech, he claimed to be 200% American. The following is an excerpt: "And we felt that if you are going to have any kind of country left for ourselves, our parents, our children, our children's children, we had to prove our loyalty. And so today we are accused by some who say, 'You were 200 per cent American.' That's right! We were! Because we were working for something."
Abe, Frank and ITVS. (n.d.). *Conscience and the Constitution*, Statement of Mike Masaru Masaoka, Rebuttal to Critics, Looking Back, Who Writes History? Public Broadcasting Service (PBS). Retrieved on August 28, 2006, from www.pbs.org/itvs/conscience/who_writes_history/looking_back/02_masaoka.html

Keiro HealthCare

1. 『祖国へ、熱き心を：東京にオリンピックを呼んだ男』高杉良著、新潮文庫、2001 年 10 月 1 日出版
Takasugi, Ryo. (1990). *Passion for the Motherland: The Man Who Brought the Olympic Games to Tokyo*, Tokyo, Shincho-Bunko, p. 521.

2. Ibid.

3. Ibid., p. 534.

4. Ibid., pp. 535-38.

5. Keiro HealthCare. (n.d.). History of Keiro Senior HealthCare. Retrieved on September 6, 2006, from www.keiro.org/KSP/history.htm

6. 『祖国へ、熱き心を：東京にオリンピックを呼んだ男』高杉良著、新潮文庫、2001 年 10 月 1 日出版
Takasugi, Ryo. (1990). *Passion for the Motherland: The Man Who Brought the Olympic Games to Tokyo*, Tokyo, Shincho-Bunko, pp. 576-7.

Agriculture

1. Census Bulletin No.164. (April 29, 1902). Table 5: Number and Per Cent of Farms of Specified Tenures, June 1, 1900, Classified by Race of Farmer, Agriculture California, *Twelfth Census of the United States*, p. 6. Retrieved on November 1, 2006, from U.S. Census Bureau; www2.census.gov/prod2/decennial/documents/03322287no164-208ch1.pdf

2. Department of Commerce. (1924). State Compendium, California, *Fourteenth Census of the United States*, Washington, Bureau of the Census Library, p. 65.

3. University of California, Berkeley. (April 26, 1942). The Bancroft Library. Retrieved on November 1, 2006, from Online Archive of California; ark.cdlib.org/ark:/13030/ft9q2nb5zf

Acknowledgement

We wish to express our heartfelt gratitude to all whose generosity has made this project possible. **Bridge of Hope** *has been over two years in the making, and our donors have been instrumental in its construction. They have helped to build a gift for future generations. A tangible expression of the spirit exemplified by our many forerunners, whose hopes and achievements we honor in this volume.*

Aratani Foundation
Kawaguchi-Kihara Memorial Foundation
Mami Mizuguchi
Kihei & Kimiko Otani/Bernie & Fumiko Lin
    (In Memory of Yoshiko & Hisako Tanaka/Haruye Otani)

Hiroko Asano
Duplo U.S.A. Corporation
Junko Horii
Akira & Hisako Imamura
    (In Memory of Koichi Tom & Toyo Nerio)
Jack H. & Kaya Naito
Yoshiko Nakahiro
    (In Memory of Toshi Nakahiro)
OESS Corporation
Reytec Industries, Inc.
Enki Seki
Sushi Boy, Inc.
Union Bank of California N.A.

Bando Mitsuhiro Kai
Kumi Inaoka Dinsmore
Fuji Natural Food, Inc.
Frank S. & Betty S. Hiji
    (In Memory of Saheiji & Emi Hiji/ Tanichiro & Kama Ige)
Takumi & Mirei Kagawa
Lee & Sakahara Architects A.I.A., Inc.
Amy A. Masuda
Plus A-One, Inc.
Projex Pacific, Inc.
Toshio J. Shimoda
Shogun Cruises & Tours
Yamaha Corporation of America-Music Education Division
Yamaha Music Centers-Irvine, Laguna & Torrance

Dr. Akiko Agishi
Ken & Donna Anami
    (In Memory of Our Parents)
Shinta & Toshiko Asami
Dr. Hisayo Grace Austin
Neil & Masako Boissonnault
Calsoft Systems
Ecore Corporation
Hitoshi & Keiko Fujiwara
Henken Gallery
Tamako Henken
Akira & Joann Hirose
Hochiki America Corp.
Yoko Hongo
Ito Farm
Louis K. & Shizue Ito
    (In Memory of Kenji Ito)
K Trucking Co.
K.I. Group, Inc.
Kamerycah, Inc.
Clinton S. & Teruko Kanase
Richard Y. & Mary Y. Karasawa
Yasuo & Junko Kasuya
Soyu Koizumi
Hideyuki & Setsuko Komuro
Gary & Teri Kuwahara
Lighthouse/Takuyo Corp.
Link International US Corp.
Tsutomu Maehara & Family
Ken & Sumi Maruyama
    (In Memory of Kojiro & Hana Maruyama)
Isao S. & Kathryn H. Matsuura
Mack & Sachiko Miyazaki
    (In Memory of Harry Genji Nagayama)
Wilson & Mayumi Morishita
    (In Memory of Masashi Kawaguchi)
Brian A. Nagata
Terry & Anne Nakahiro
    (In memory of Moriichi & Natsuyo Sasaki)
Yasu & Atsuko Nakahiro
    (In Memory of Genzo & Tamiyo Nakahiro)
Yutaka & Hisako Nakamura
Kenji & Cindy Oda
    (In Memory of Shinobu Oda)
Akiko G. Omi CPA
Ikue Onodera
Kihei & Kimiko Fujita Otani
    (In Memory of Natsuko Tanaka/
     Toshio & Sadako Yamasaki)
George M. & Janet K. Ouchi
    (In Memory of Masao Ouchi)
Chikako Oyama
Mia Ellen Powell
Michael F. & Janet L. Powell
Dr. Akihisa Saitoh
Ruben C. & Takako I. Sanchez
Howard, Mika & Akeko Sawada

Kuniaki & Naoko Seto
Dr. Hiroshi Sumiyama
Sushi Kappo Suzumaru
Masahiro & Kaoru Takahashi
Hiroko Tatebe
Satoshi & Seiko Tsukada
Tamiko Umezawa
Kyoko Watanabe

Atsuko Anthony
Takeshi Asada
Reiko Niwa Berg
Fujiko Carter
DB Commercial Investments, Inc.
Kazue T. Elliot
Joseph L. & Hisae Firoved
Munehiro & Chika Hirahuku
Roy & Takako Honda
Yoshiko O. Hug
Kumiko Ide
Kiyomi Inoue
Wako Iwamura
Hiromi Iwatsubo
Japonaise Bakery, Inc.
Junma Commercial Mortgage Corp.
K2 Automotive Service
Toshi & Carolyn Kanesaki
Yoshimi Koda
Hiroyuki Kodama
Jun Kurasako
Fumie & Aya Kuratani
Lavender I.P., Inc.
H. Michael Lew
M and M Fasteners Inc.
Kazuko Maekawa
Akiko Maruta
Gary Matsuura & Mary Palchak
Yoshihiro Mizuochi
Sam & Kimiko Moriyama
Noriko Nakanishi
Shiomi Nishio
John B. & Miyoko O'hara
Kiyoshi & Mayumi Oda
Satomi Otsubo
Takako & Raymond Palucki
Pearls by Emiko
Q & B Foods, Inc.
Eiichi & Yoshie Sonoyama
Katsumi & Taeko Sumiyama
Machiko Tanaka
Masashi Tanaka
Teritime, Inc.
Tokai Seigi Co. Ltd.
Mas & Hiroko Tokubo
Hiroto & Kyoko Uechi
Donald & Kazue Zennie

日系アメリカ人の辿った道

日系人として人の役に立ちたい

序文

JEWL（日本女性経営者の会／Japanese Executive Women's League）は、第二次世界大戦後しばらくして日本から渡米し、南カリフォルニアで事業を始めたり、企業の管理職に従事する七人の女性によって勉強会と交流を目的として一九八五年に発足しました。

会員たちは常に多くの問題に直面していました。英語、複雑な法律、商習慣、人間関係、そして女性であるというもう一つのハードルをのり越えなければなりませんでした。しかし、私たちがこれらの障害を抱えながら現在、経済的自立を果たし得ている背景には、多大な犠牲を払ってアメリカ市民としての権利を勝ち取ってくれた日系移民先駆者たちの百年以上にも及ぶ苦労と努力の歴史があったからでした。

日系先駆者たちが、この未知の国で多くの艱難辛苦に耐えながら日系社会を根付かせ、豊かな土壌を残してくれたからこそ、我々が夢と希望の種を蒔き、収穫が出来ているという現実を認識しました。

我々の先駆者が残した足跡は、アメリカの歴史の一ページを飾る注目すべき遺産です。JEWLは、その功績が次世代へと長く語りつがれていくことを願い、先駆者への深い尊敬と感謝の思いを込めて、この「Bridge of Hope／日系アメリカ人の辿った道」を編纂しました。

目次

三章

自由と平等の追求

1941 年ロングビーチでマーケットを経営していた東久保家の人たち。(Courtesy of Tokubo family 1941)

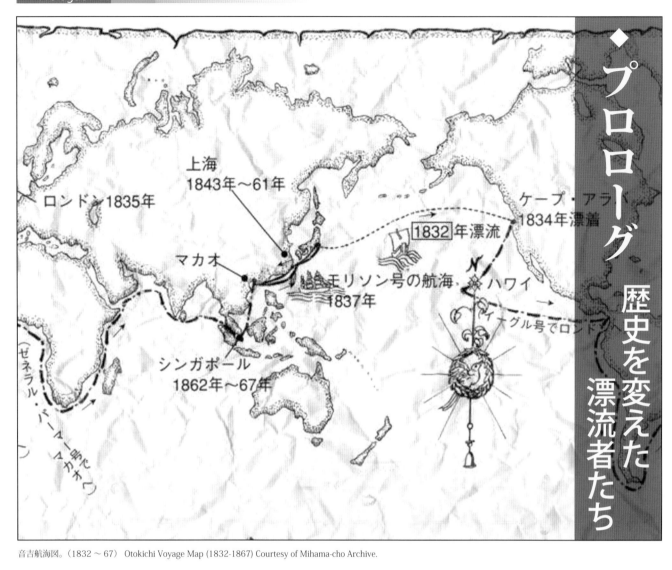

上海
1843年〜61年

ロンドン 1835年

マカオ

シンガポール
1862年〜67年

ケープ・アラゴ
1834年漂着

1832 年漂流

モリソン号の航海
1837年

ハワイ

イーグル号でロンドン

1832 年漂流

（ゼネラル・ハー〜マカオ）

音吉航海図。（1832 〜 67） Otokichi Voyage Map (1832-1867) Courtesy of Mihama-cho Archive.

◆プロローグ 歴史を変えた漂流者たち

西部開拓を謳いアメリカで幌馬車が初めてロッキー山脈を越えたころ、日本では海外との接触を断つべく鎖国令が相次いで発令されていた。遠洋航海用の大型船の製造も禁止になり孤島となった日本から、ふとした運命のいたずらでアメリカの土を踏んだ男たちがいる。日本沿岸で遭難し、潮流に乗って漂着したり、外国船に救助された漂流民たちだ。数奇な運命に翻弄された彼らは、与えられた環境の中で懸命に生きぬき、日本の近代化や日米関係の構築に貢献した。

太平洋を一四カ月漂流・異国に骨を埋めた音吉
（ジョン・マシュウ・オトソン）
一八一七―一八六七

アメリカ本土に始めて上陸した日本人の一人として知られているのが、愛知県美浜町出身の音吉（乙吉ともいう）だ。見習い船員で十四才だった音吉が、米や陶器を積んだ宝順丸に乗り組み、江戸に向け出航したのは一八三二年十一月のこと。二八才の船乗り岩吉、十五才の見習い久吉など十四人を乗せた宝順丸は、鳥羽に寄港した後、消息を絶つ。故郷の人々が冬の荒波で難破したものと思い、悲しみに暮れて墓を立てたころ、宝順丸は日本沿岸を離れ、海流に乗って太平洋を北西に漂っていた。海上をさまようこと十四ケ月、音吉たちが漂着したのは、ワシントン州ケープアラバ付近にあるフラッタリー岬だった。

1

宝順丸は千石船と呼ばれる極めて頑丈な造りの沿岸航海用の船で、一五〇トン程度の積荷が可能であった(1)。遭難しても難破することもなく十四ヵ月もの長期間生き延びることが出来たのは、積荷に米を積んでいたことと、海水を蒸留して真水をとる「ランビキ」という方法が知られていたからだ(2)。当時の遭難船が思いのほか多くの生存者を出したのもその遭難船が思いのほか多くの生存者を出したのもその遭難船が思いのほか多くの生存者を出したのもそのためだが、沿岸航海用に航海図はなく、遠洋の航海技術を持つ人間もいなかった。嵐に遭遇して一本しかない帆柱が折れてしまうと、あとは潮と風に運命をまかせるしかなかったのだ。

一年以上かけて太平洋を横断しているうちに乗組員たちは次々に倒れていき、フラッタリー岬に到着した時に生存していたのは、音吉、久吉、岩吉の三人だけだった。ワシントン州は当時、合衆国にも加盟していない原住民の住む未開の地で、三人はマカ族に助けられたところを、毛皮の交易に来たハドソン湾社のイギリス人社員に発見され、南方約二〇〇キロにある毛皮交易所フォートバンクーバーに連れて行かれた。そこでジョン・ボール寄宿学校に預けられ、シェパード牧師から英語教育を受けた。その後、ハドソン湾社は音吉たちを利用して日本との交易を開きたいと考え、ハワイ経由でわざわざロンドンまで連れて行ったが、イギリス政府は首を縦に振らず、結局三人はロンドンに十〇日間滞在しただけでマカオに送られることになる。ただロンドン滞在中に一日だけ上陸許可が出て、日本人として初のロンドン見物をした(3)。

モリソン号。米国商船、音吉ほか６人の日本人漂流者を乗せ江戸湾に来航。江戸幕府は大砲を撃ち、退去させた（モリソン号事件）。（国立公文書館）

マカオは当時、中国で唯一、外国人の住む地域で、鹿児島から八〇石の回船に乗って天草沖でしけに合い破船し、西南方向に吹き流されてフィリピンに漂着し、スペイン船でマカオに送られてきていた。この三人は帰国の機会を待つことになる。そこで三人はドイツ生まれの宣教師、チャールズ・ギュツラフの世話になっていた。ギュツラフは彼らの協力を得て、一年がかりで、「ヨハネ伝福音書」と「ヨハネの手紙」の初の日本語訳を完成させた(4)。

また、マカオで三人は自分たちと同じ境遇の漂流民、力松たち四人と出会った。彼らは、一八三五年、マカオに乗ってマカオだけでなく、記録に残っているだけで、北はカムチャカ半島やアリューシャン列島から、南は中米、太平洋諸島、台湾、ルソン島、ベトナムなど、さまざまな海流に乗って日本人の漂流民が流れ着いていた(5)。

一八三七年七月、七人にようやく帰国の機会が訪れた。広東にあったアメリカの貿易会社が日本との貿易を実現するために、モリソン号で日本に向かうことになったのだ。美浜町を出てから五年、悲願の帰国のはずだったが、現実はかくも残酷であった。

モリソン号は江戸湾の浦賀沖に入ると、突如大砲の砲撃を受けた。日本史にも登場するモリソン号事件だ。西欧諸国がアジアの植民地化を進める中で、江戸幕府は一八二五年、異国船打ち払い令を発令していた。音吉たちの帰国は、時期的に不運だった。異国船打ち払い令は、一八四〇年に起きたアヘン戦争で清国が敗北したことにより、外国船に対するむやみな攻撃は危険と考えて、二年後には薪水給与令に緩和された。

この事件で彼らは帰国を断念し、異国の地で生きていく決心をする。一八三八年、音吉はモリソン号に乗ってニューヨークまで行き、マンハッタンのイーストリバー地区にある船員用の宿舎に短期間滞在した(7)。その後、マカオに戻り、ここで音吉はキリスト教の洗礼を受け、ジョン・マシュー・オトソンと改名した。マカオではイギリスの貿易会社に勤めていたが、その後、上海に転勤になった。モリソン号の一件で二度と日本に帰らないと心に誓った音吉であったが、運命の糸は意外な経緯で音吉の帰国を実現させた。トルコとロシアの間で勃発したクリミア戦争が、音吉を帰国の途に着かせることになったのだ。イギリス軍はトルコを支援して参戦し音吉はイギリス海軍のスターリング艦隊とともに、ロシア船を探してアジアの海を航海していた。その時偶然にも行き着いたのが、長崎港であった。一八五四年のことで、その前年にはペリーの黒船が来航していた。

鎖国令にはキリシタンの取締りと海外貿易の禁止に異国渡航を禁止する条項もあり、異国に居住して日本に帰国すると、死罪という厳しい処罰が待ち受けていた。やむなく音吉は通訳を務めたが、音吉の機転を利かせた通訳が功を奏して、イギリスは後に日本と初の条約を成立させるに至った。条約交渉における功績が認められ、イギリス市民権の取得を許可されただけでなく、多大な報酬も受け取った(8)。

その後、音吉は上海のイギリス人居留地で優雅な暮らしをしていたことが分かっている。彼は自分と同じような漂流民が来ると、日本へ帰れるように尽力した。「自分の二の舞は踏ませたくない」という思いが強かったに違いない。

上海でイギリス人女性と結婚し、男児ジョン・ウィリアムを授かった。イギリス人の妻が死亡した後、マレー人と再婚し、一八六二年、妻の故郷であるシンガポールに移住した。遣欧使節団の一員であった福沢諭吉の記録によると、使節団がシンガポールに立ち寄った時、音吉はわざわざ使節団を訪問していた(9)。

音吉は一八六七年、明治維新の前年に、シンガポールで四九才の生涯を閉じた。一旦はキリスト教徒墓地に埋葬されたが、一九七〇年、墓地が都市計画によって公園に転用された後、遺骨の移転場所は不明になっていた。音吉の埋葬場所が明らかになったのは二十一世紀になってからだ。シンガポール日本人会とシンガポール国家土地管理局の協力で、二〇〇四年、シンガポール国立墓地に移されていたことが判

遣欧使節団には、通訳として森山栄之助が同行していた。森山は長崎で、イギリス人とアメリカ原住民を両親に持つラナルド・マクドナルドから英語を学んだ。そもそもマクドナルドが日本に行ったのは音吉の影響だった。

マクドナルドの出身はフォートバンクーバーで、父親のアーチボールド・マクドナルドは、音吉が連れて行かれた毛皮交易所のハドソン湾社の社員だった。当時、極東の未知の国から漂流してきた音吉たちの存在は、町で大きな評判を生んだものと思われる。マクドナルドは「漂着」した音吉たちに感銘を受け、日本への興味を募らせ、自分も漂着することを思いつく。一八四八年、捕鯨船に乗り、船長の反対を押し切って小船で漂流者を装い、北海道の利尻島にたどり着いた。当時の慣習に従い長崎に送還され投獄されるが、マクドナルドの人懐っこい人柄は好感を持たれ、囚われの身でありながら何時しか英語を教えるようになった。当時の通訳はオランダ語しか知らなかったので、何人もの通訳が格子越しに英語を学んだ。そんな通訳の中の一人が森山だった。マクドナルドは一年後にアメリカに強制送還された(10)。

明し、二〇〇五年二月、一七三年ぶりに音吉は遺牌となって帰国を果たした。⑾　また音吉の息子ジョン・ウィリアムは、父の遺志をついで一八七九年に来日している。山本音吉と名のって、兵庫県神戸市の民間企業に勤務していたところまでは確認されているが、その後の消息は分からない。⑿

漁師から最高学府の教授に 幸運に恵まれた万次郎（ジョン・万次郎） 一八二七―一八九八

音吉たちが攻撃されたモリソン号事件から四年後の一八四一年、土佐から出航した一隻の漁船が、足摺岬で冬の嵐に巻き込まれた。漁船に乗っていたのは、幡多郡中ノ浜の万次郎のほか四人だった。万次郎は最年少の十四歳で、幼いころに父親を亡くし、早くから母親を助けて働いていた。⒀

強風に吹かれること十日間、五人が命からがら流れ着いたのは、アホウドリが住む無人島の鳥島だった。アホウドリの肉などで飢えをしのぐこと五ヶ月、幸運にも島に立ち寄ったアメリカの捕鯨船ジョン・ハウランド号に救出された。

遭難して鳥島に漂着した船員たちは少なくない。なかには二〇年も無人島で生きぬいた人や手製の小船で決死の帰国を試みた記録もあり、社団法人日本船主協会によると、江戸時代に漂流して帰国した人の例は記録に残るものも百数十例にも上る。しかもこれらはあくまで無事

に帰還できた事例で、二度と故郷を見ることもなく現地に骨を埋めた人の数は、それよりもはるかに多かったはずだ。五ヶ月で救助された万次郎はむしろ幸運で、その後の彼の人生は、この日を境に多くの幸運に恵まれることになる。万次郎を一介の漁民から歴史に残る人物に押し上げたのは、彼の生まれ持った進取の気質と努力によるところも大きい。

五人を乗せたジョン・ハウランド号は鎖国の日本に向かうこともできず、ハワイのオワフ島に寄港した。四人はハワイに残ったが、万次郎は仲間と離れ、一人でアメリカへ向う決心をする。この前向きな積極性はジョン・ハウランド号の船員たちに好感を

持って受け入れられ、船の名をとって「ジョン・マン」と呼ばれて可愛がられた。二年後、ジョン・ハウランド号は全米最大の捕鯨基地として栄えたマサチューセッツ州ニューベッドフォードに寄港し、万次郎は東海岸から上陸した初の日本人となった。

ウィリアム・ホイットフィールド船長は万次郎を故郷のフェアヘブンに連れて帰ると、我が子のように世話をして自分の子供たちと同じ学校に通わせ、英語、数学、航海術、測量術、造船技術などの教育を受けさせた。日本では貧しくてろくに寺小屋にも通えなかった万次郎が、アメリカへ来て初めて教育を受ける機会に恵まれたのだ。万次郎は船長の期待

土佐清水市足摺岬に建立された万次郎の銅像　（高知県土佐清水市提供）
The Statue of John Manjiro at Ashizuri Misaki Tosashimizu-shi, Kouchi-ken.
Courtesy of Tosashimizu-shi.

を裏切ることなく次々と新しい知識を吸収した。ここで受けた教育が、彼の人生ばかりか日本の近代化を左右する日本の財産になるとは、万次郎も気付かなかったに違いない。

学校を卒業すると、捕鯨船フランクリン号の航海士として乗船し、後に一等航海士副船長となった[14]。

三年半で世界中を周って戻ると、町はカリフォルニアで見つかった金鉱の話で沸き立っていた。ゴールドラッシュの幕開けである。めぐってきた好機は逃さない類まれな行動力は、ここでその本領を発揮する。すぐカリフォルニアに向かったのは言うまでもないが、二ヶ月あまりで六〇〇ドルを稼ぎ、船を購入すると、ただちにハワイへと旅立った[15]。ハワイで難破仲間の伝蔵と五右衛門と合流した万次郎はついに念願の帰国の途についた。死罪が待っているかもしれない帰国は人生最大の賭けであったに違いない。だが時代は万次郎に味方した。

土佐を出てから十年後の一八五一年、万次郎たちは先ず琉球に上陸し、そこから薩摩に送還されて尋問を受けた。上陸すら叶わなかったモリソン号事件から十四年、日本はまさに幕末を迎えており、これ以上の好機はなかったといえる。送還された薩摩藩が倒幕派の旗手であったことも幸いした。このころになると薩摩沖には外国船が頻繁に出没しており、海外との架け橋として活躍した万次郎の功績は計り知れない。

万次郎は、今や貴重な土佐藩では、倒幕の推進者である万次郎の出身地土佐藩では、倒幕の推進者である万次郎は、今や貴重な存在であった。坂本竜馬が頭角を現しており、万次郎の噂を聞きつ

万次郎の漂流物語は、当時から「中浜万次郎異国物語」や「漂流奇談」など何冊も出版され、幕末の人々に夢を与えるベストセラーになった。アメリカ建国

後に、明治政府の命を受けて、開成学校（現東京大学）の教授として日本最高学府の教壇に立った。万次郎は岡山大学の教授であった長男の家で、七二才で他界するまで幕末から明治にかけて、日本の近代化及び、海外との架け橋として活躍した

沢諭吉と一緒にサンフランシスコでウエブスターの英語辞書を購入した話は有名だ。

尉と一等航海士の万次郎がいなければ難破していた可能性もあったほどの難航だった。この訪米で、福丸に航海士および通訳として乗り組んだ。咸臨嵐にあい、この航海は米海軍のジョン・ブルック大た幕府の遣米使節団に随行した幕府の蒸気船、咸臨約の批准書交換のために米船ポーハタン号で渡米し中浜万次郎と名を改めた時は、まだ二六歳だった。授を務めた万次郎は、一八六〇年、日米修好通商条

日本初の航海学書・年表「アメリカ合衆国航海学書」や英会話書を編集した。また、軍艦教授所の教

この年、浦賀にペリーの黒船が来航している。異例の出世を果たしたのだ。出身地の名前を取って万次郎は名字帯刀を許される名士となり、死罪を恐れていたはずの日本で、万次郎は名字帯刀を許される名士となり、死罪を恐れていたはず寄せられ幕府直参となった。「教授館」の教授になったが、翌年には江戸に呼び研究所が催した「海外からの米国訪問者展」では「ア究所が催した「海外からの米国訪問者展」では「ア

けた坂本竜馬は、早速彼を土佐に呼びつけて十分に取り立てている。ここで万次郎は、高知城下の藩校

二〇〇〇年を祝してワシントンDCのスミソニアン研究所が催した「海外からの米国訪問者展」では「アメリカ見聞録」を著したイギリスのチャールス・ディッケンズらと並んで、その二九人の中に万次郎も選ばれている[16]。

晩年の万次郎とその家族。（高知県土佐清水市提供）

5

ジェームス・ブキャナン 米国大統領
Portrait of President James Buchanan

フランクリン・ピアス 米国大統領
Portrait of President Franklin Pierce

エイブラハム・リンカーン 米国大統領
Portrait of President Abraham Lincoln

三人の大統領と謁見した日系アメリカ人

第一号彦蔵（ジョゼフ・ヒコ）
一八三七─一八九七

一八三五年より数回にわたって発令された鎖国令は外国船の来航、日本人漂流者の帰国をも禁じていたが、一八〇〇年代になると日本近海にも度々外国船が出没し難破船の救助、及び燃料や食糧補給のための開港をせまっていた。一八四六年、アメリカ政府の使節ジェームス・ビドル提督も二隻の軍艦を率い開港を求めて来航したが、幕府によって退去させられている。一八五三年、日本の鎖国制度に終止符を打つきっかけとなったペリー艦隊の一隻、サスケハナ号に乗せられて日本に連れて来られた仙太郎という漂流者は乗船してきた浦賀奉行の役人の説得にも応じず、幕府の刑罰を恐れて下船を拒否し、アメリカに戻っていった。

こうした江戸幕府の厳しい鎖国政策により日本に帰国できない多くの漂流者の一人に、後に三人のアメリカ大統領と謁見し、日系アメリカ人第一号となった彦蔵がいた。

船頭、万蔵ほか十六人の水夫たちの乗った栄力丸がしけに遭い、遭難したのは一八五一年、彦蔵十三歳の冬のことだった。五一日間漂流した後、アメリカ船オークランド号に救助された彼らはサンフランシスコに上陸する。その頃アメリカ政府はマシュウ・ペリー提督を日本に派遣する計画を立てていたところで、漂流民を外交に利用しようと考えた。彼らは

一年間サンフランシスコに滞在したのち、日本に帰されるべくアメリカ海軍のセントメリー号に乗せられて、太平洋を渡りマカオのサスケハナ号で香港に連れて行かれた。そこでペリー艦隊の到着を待った。しかし、香港で前述のモリソン号に音吉と共に乗っていた漂流者の一人、十八年も日本に帰れないでいるという力松に出会ってモリソン号の話を聞き、彦蔵たちは帰国に二の足を踏む[17]。

前年にはジョン・万次郎が帰国を果たしていたから、時代は大きな転換の時を迎えていたのだが、この時サンフランシスコに戻る決心をしたことで、彦蔵には思いがけない幸運の女神が微笑むことになる。サンフランシスコに戻った彦蔵は、漂流民の通訳を頼まれたのがきっかけで、税関長であり地元の有力者のビバリー・C・サンダースと知り合う。万次郎の運命を変えたのがホイットフィールド船長であったように、彦蔵もサンダースと出会ったことで人生が思わぬ方向に進んでゆく。彦蔵はサンダースに可愛がられ、ニューヨークやワシントンDCに同行した。ニューヨークでは初めてガス灯や汽車を見て驚き、ワシントンではフランクリン・ピアス大統

ジョセフ・ヒコ

領に紹介され、計らずもアメリカ大統領に謁見した初めての日本人となった。ホワイトハウスを訪れた彦蔵は、庶民と変わらぬ服装の大統領や物々しい城門のないホワイトハウスの造りが信じられなかったという(18)。

万次郎と同様に、彦蔵も帰国後は日本の近代化に貢献したが、二人には共通点がある。漂流したときの年齢が十三歳、十四歳と若かったこと、アメリカ人の恩人に出会えたこと、そして彼らの援助によりアメリカの学校教育を受けられたことだ。彦蔵もサンダースの援助でボルチモアのカトリック系学校の寮にはいり、英語、天文、地理、数学、聖書などを学ぶ機会に恵まれた。一八五四年、サンダース夫人の薦めでクリスチャンの洗礼をうけ、ジョゼフ・ヒコと名のった。その後ヒコは、サンダースの友人、ウイリアム・グイン上院議員のワシントン事務所で働き、彼の紹介でジェームス・ブキャナン大統領にも謁見した。一八五八年、ヒコはサンダースの薦めもあり、アメリカ市民権を取得し、日系アメリカ人第一号となっている(19)。

ヒコがアメリカに帰化した年に日米修好通商条約が調印され、日本は正式に開国した。翌年、日本のアメリカ総領事となったタウンゼント・ハリスと知り合ったヒコは、新任の神奈川領事となるE・M・ドールの通訳として九年ぶりに日本への帰国を果たした。遣米使節団が出発したとき、ヒコは領事館に勤めていたが、咸臨丸に乗船した友人のブルック海軍大尉を見送りに来た折にジョン・万次郎とも顔を合わせているのが興味深い(20)。

一八六一年、三度目の渡米を決心したのは外国人襲撃事件が多発していた為だった。そのころアメリカでは南北戦争が勃発していた。そんな最中、ヒコはエイブラハム・リンカーン大統領とも謁見し、三人もの大統領に謁見する快挙を成し遂げた。

二五歳の時に再び領事館通訳として横浜に戻ると、「国立銀行条例」の編纂に従事し、大阪造幣局の創設に尽力し、明治維新前後の日本に多大な貢献をした。また日本初の新聞「海外新聞」を発行して「新聞の父」とも呼ばれ、その六号ではリンカーン大統領暗殺を報道している(21)。一八九七年、六〇歳で他界するまで日本に滞在し東京青山霊園内に永眠している。

遣米使節団と咸臨丸の アメリカ体験とその後

一八六〇年一月、ハリス総領事のすすめもあって、幕府は日米条約の批准書交換のために外国奉行の新見正興を正使とし、副使に村垣範正、目付けの小栗忠順とその他、従者含む総勢七七人の使節団をアメリカに派遣した。彼らが公式にアメリカを訪問した最初の外交使節だ。使節団はアメリカ政府が提供した軍艦ポーハタン号で太平洋を渡ったが、このポーハタン号はペリー提督が日本に来航した際の旗艦であった。サンフランシスコまで護衛と遠洋実習のためにポーハタン号に随行したのが、ジョン・万次郎も乗船していた咸臨丸だ。

使節団はアメリカの国賓として迎えられ、そのためにアメリカ議会は五万ドルの予算を計上した(22)、使節団の一行はハワイとサンフランシスコに寄港し、太平洋から大西洋に抜けるためパナマを訪れた。パナマ運河はまだ完成しておらず、一行はパナマ鉄道

遣米使節団 （左から）副使村垣範正淡路守、正使新見頼興豊前守、観察小栗忠順豊後守。1860年フィラデルフィアの写真師、W.L.Germon撮影。（群馬県高崎市東善寺提供）
The Edo Bakufu Diplomats from left to right; Vice Ambassador Muragaki Norimasa awajinokami, Chife Ambassador Plenipotentiary Shinmi Yorioki Buzennokami, and Inspector Oguri Tadamasa Bungonokami. Photograph taken by Philadelphia photographer W.L.Germon in June, 1860.(Courtesy of Tozenji, Takasaki-shi Gunma-ken)

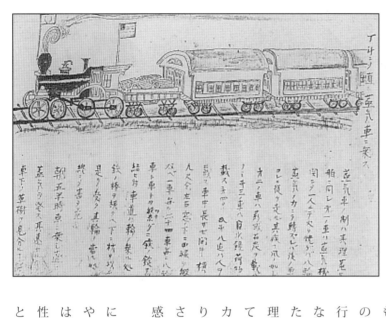

「蒸気車の絵」 1860年遣米使節団がパナマ横断したときに乗った世界初の大陸横断鉄道、パナマ鉄道の蒸気車のスケッチ。小栗上野介の従者、佐藤藤七の『渡海日記』より。パナマ鉄道は使節団を歓迎し、日米の国旗を掲げて大西洋に向かって走った。（群馬県高崎市　東善寺　村上康賢氏）
In 1860 Japanese diplomats traveled to Atlantic Ocean and onward to Washington D.C. by way of the Panama Railroad steam engine train (the world's first trans-continental railroad). The railroad welcomed them by displaying a Japanese flag and an American flag on train. Sketched by Sato Toshichi, subordinate of Oguri Tadamasa (courtesy of Tozenji)

の蒸気機関車で大西洋側の港に移動したが、村垣範正は初めて汽車にのった感想を「車の轟音雷の鳴はためく如く、左右を見れば三、四尺の間は、草木もしまのよふに見へて、見とまらず、更に咄しも聞へす・・・、殺風景のもの也(23)」と記している。汽車の速度と騒音は静かな城中の生活に慣れた武士の度肝を抜いたようだ。

一行がパナマから大西洋に出てワシントンDCに到着したのは、浦賀を出てから約半年後の五月一五日だった。ワシントンではウイラードホテルに三週間滞在したが、ちょん髷姿の侍の訪米はアメリカでも大きな話題となり、その姿を一目見ようとホテルの前には連日、黒山の人だかりが出来たという。一行がウイラードホテルに到着した時、群衆の熱狂的な歓迎を、村垣は「江戸の祭日のようだ。どうしてまったくの遠慮もなくあのように騒々しく振る舞うのか理解に苦しみ困惑した、さらに時々心から笑いが出てしまった(24)」と日記に残している。一方、アメリカの新聞は使節団一行のことを「物静かで威厳があり、驚きや賞賛といったものを言葉にも表情にも出さない(25)」と報じている。互いに文化の違いを肌で感じ取ったことは確かなようだ。

一行はその後、フィラデルフィアやニューヨークにも足を伸ばし、各地で大歓迎を受けた。パレードや晩餐会、舞踏会などが開催されたが、最大の驚きはダンスであったらしい。村垣範正の日記には、女性のドレス姿を「両肩を顕し、多くは白き薄物をまとい、腰には例の袴のひろかりたるものをまとい」

正は初めて汽車にのった感想を「男女組合で足をそばたて調子につれてめくるはこま鼠の廻るか如く、何の風情手品もなく幾組もまはり、女のすそには風いよいよひろかりてめくるさま、いとおかし」と感想を書き留めている。高官から若輩者まで数百人の男女が「終夜かく興するよし現か分からぬはかりあきれたる」と否定的な見方をしていることからも、武士の目にダンスは奇異に映ったことがうかがえる(26)。

使節はホワイトハウスでジェームス・ブキャナン大統領と謁見し、日米修好通商条約の批准書交換を行い、帰路はアフリカの喜望峰を回ってジャカルタ、香港を経由して十一月一〇日、江戸に帰港した(27)。

なお、咸臨丸は船体の損傷が激しかったため、サンフランシスコで補修した後、再度太平洋を渡って帰国している。

使節団の使命は純粋に批准書交換だけで、それ以上の政策的役割は与えられていなかったが、小栗忠順は、滞在中に見聞した鉄道や造船、鉄筋建築など、鉄を豊富に使う技術力と、それを民間の資金で運営している仕組みなどを日本に紹介した。帰国後に勘定奉行となった彼は、一八六七年に民間の商人同様に、民間資本による外国人向けの本格的なホテル「築地ホテル」を建設させた。また小栗は、日本の近代化のためには「木と紙の国」から「鉄あふれる国、アメリカ」に近づける必要があると考え、造船にも呼びかけて日本初の株式会社「兵庫商社」を設立。横須賀に製鉄所と造船所を建設し、造船所の建設を提案。

8

遣米使節団が乗船した米国海軍ポーハタン号の模型（群馬県高崎市　東善寺所属）
Model of the USS Powhatan.(courtesy of Tozenji, Takasaki-shi, Gunma-ken)

一八六九年からは、造船所として本格的に稼動させた(28)。

一方、サンフランシスコまで使節団に随伴した咸臨丸には、日本の封建主義とアメリカの民主主義の違いを見抜いた人物が乗船していた。福沢諭吉と倒幕の立役者である勝海舟だ。福沢諭吉は著書『学問のすすめ』で「天は人の上に人をつくらず人の下に人をつくらず」と説いた。勝は帰国後、日米の違いを老中に問われ、「わが国と違い、かの国は、重い職にある人は、その分だけ賢うございます」と平然と言ったと伝えられている(29)。ちなみに勝の長男小鹿は、アメリカのアナポリス海軍士官学校を卒業している。小鹿と異母兄弟の梶梅太郎は、一橋大学設立のために政府から招聘されたウィリアム・ホイットニーの娘クララと結婚し、六人の子供を授かっている(30)。

万次郎も、日系アメリカ人第一号となったヒコも結果的には帰国し、最期は日本でその生涯を閉じたが、彼らの経験や遣米使節団などの体験が、日本の近代化の基礎をつくり、明治の幕開けとともに始まった移民急増に影響を与えたことは疑いない。

藩士の子弟たちもこぞってアメリカ東部に留学し、文化、思想、教育制度などの専門知識を習得し、それらを日本に持ち帰って、閉鎖的な封建社会であった日本に民主主義を紹介した。それにより、一般庶民の中にもアメリカという近代国家への憧れが生まれた。

英語もわからない漂流者の万次郎やヒコを引き取り、学校に通わせて世話をしたアメリカ人たちの厚意は、巡りめぐって多くの日本人が恩恵を受けることになった。万次郎は帰国後も恩人ホイットフィールド船長の親切を終生忘れず、彼らの子孫は五代にわたって交流を続けており(31)、咸臨丸の乗組員の子孫たちは二〇〇五年、嵐の中で航海を助けたブルック大尉の子孫をバージニア州レキシントンに訪ね、感謝の意を表すとともに交流を深めている(32)。

ハワイの砂糖キビ畑では1880年代になると、牛馬に引かせていた耕作用鍬に代わって蒸気耕作機が使用され種まき用のサクを作った。（ビショップ博物館）

CONTENTS

ペリーの黒船来航で開国の幕が切って落とされると、多くの若者が柳行李に夢と希望を詰めて太平洋を渡った。だが豊かなアメリカで彼らを待ち受けていたのは、排斥と差別の渦巻く過酷な現実だった。若者たちは逆境にあっても相互扶助の精神で助け合い、懸命に働いて、いつしか異国の地に根を張り、日系社会の基盤を築いていった。

日本人移民の草分け

ハワイの「元年者」

一八五三年、フィルモア大統領の命を受けて神奈川県の浦賀にペリーの黒船がやってきた。それは、新しい時代の始まり、日本の近代化の夜明けを象徴する出来事だった。翌年には日米和親条約（神奈川条約ともいう）、一八五八年には日米修好通商条約が調印されて、日本はついに二二〇年もの長い鎖国に終止符を打つ。七〇〇年近く続いた封建制度の崩壊は、一般庶民にも国際化の機運をもたらすきっかけとなった。

一八六八年、明治の幕開けとともに海外渡航したつわものたちがいる。五月十七日、横浜からサイオト号に乗船してハ

ワイへ向かった一五三人だ(1)。同年、明治と改元されたため、彼らは「元年者」と呼ばれた。旧幕府から明治政府への変換期だったこともあり、新政府の許可なしに出発した彼らは、ハワイに着いて厳しい現実に直面する。彼らに与えられた仕事は、サトウキビ耕地での農作業だった。元年者の中には書生など肉体労働を知らない人もいたというから、炎天下での重労働は予想外の展開だったであろう。すぐに不満が噴出し、その声は日本にまで届いて、ついには明治政府が介入する事態となった。その結果四〇人が帰国したが、残りは残留し、無事三年の契約を終了している。契約終了後、日本に帰国したのは十三人だけで、残りはハワイの日本人移民の草分けとなった(2)。

　元年者がハワイのプランテーションで厳しい労働に耐えていたころ、一八六九年日本人初の植民開拓団が、オランダ人ヘンリー・シュネールに連れられてサンフランシスコに向けて出航している。海外集団移住の第二号ともいえるのが、会津出身の藩士たちだ(3)。幕末に旧幕府側に立った会津藩は、領地没収・旧藩士拘束と悲劇的な敗戦を迎えた。多くの会津人は故郷を離れ、そのうち数十人が海外を目指した。彼らはサンフランシスコ郊外の土地を購入し、「若松コロニー」と名付けて茶や桑の栽培に精を出した。だが気候が適さなかったのか、一年余りでコロニー経営は失敗している。その後の消息がわかっているものは、ごくわずかしかいない。

1893年頃、カリフォルニア州中部のパハロバレーに木村サクロー氏によって建てられた日本人独身季節農業労働者用の"親友クラブ"の建物の前に集まった当時の労働者たち。木村氏は宿泊と食事、仕事の斡旋、農場主と労働者間の通訳や仲介役として日本人季節労働者たちの世話をした。(サンタクルーズパブリック図書館)

海外移住ブームを作った「官約移民」

　元年者の対策に苦慮した明治政府は、若松コロニーの失敗もあり、この後二〇年近く、日本人の海外移住を許可しなかった。海外移民が再開されたのは、一八八五年。ハワイ政府と日本政府間で日本人移民ハワイ渡航約定書が交わされ、政府公認の海外出稼ぎが正式に始まった。日本政府による労働力の輸出といえるだろう。彼らを「官約移民」と呼ぶ。

　当時の日本は不況で労働者が余っていた状態にあり、特に農村は赤貧にあえいでいた。自治体が移民を奨励した例もあり、生活に絶望していた多くの若者たちが海外に夢を託した。第一回官約移民募集には、六〇〇人の枠に二万八千人もの応募が殺到し、そのうち身体検査などで選ばれた九四四人がシティ・オブ・トキオ号でハワイへと出航した(4)。ホノルル到着後は、各島のサトウキビ耕地に分かれて就労した。約定書の契約期間は三年で、渡航費用はハワイ政府が負担し、月給は男性九ドルと食費六ドル(5)。移民たちに労働の選択権は与えられなかった。炎天下におけるサトウキビ耕地での労働は過酷であったが、当時は日本国内でも、農家は日の出から日没まで農作業をするのが一般的で、労働条件は劣悪な時代だった。

　翌年、日布渡航条約が締結されて、官約移民は本格化する。ハワイ移民からの送金が高かったこともあり、希望者は後を絶たなかった。一八九四年に移民保護規則が公布されるまで官約移民は九年間続き、約二万九千人がハワイへと渡った(6)。またハワイ以外にも、南米などへの渡航希望者が続出。一種の海外移住ブームが起こっている。

　自由渡航になっていた一九〇七年、熊本からハワイに移住した南部虎喜さんは、渡米のきっかけをこう語っている。「熊本の田舎の百姓生まれで、赤貧洗うがごとくですたい。結局は、外国へでも飛び出してみるか、いうような心持ちで来たですよ(7)」。いつのころからかサトウキビ耕地で歌われるようになっ

た『ホレホレ節』は、プランテーション労働の過酷さの象徴として語られることが多いが、『行こかメリケン、帰ろかジャパン、ここが思案のハワイ島』と歌いながらも、南部さんは「ハワイに来てですな、白いご飯が食べられたというのは、よかったですよ⑻」と述懐している。

藩士の留学から労働者の時代へ

一方、初期の本土への渡米者には、藩士の子弟が多い。彼らは留学目的で渡米し、白人家庭で世話になりながら家の用事をする「スクールボーイ」をしながら勉学に励んだ。

スクールボーイから大学を卒業し、帰国後、多大な貢献をした人は少なくない。渡米がきっかけとなって、日本の教育界に大きな影響を与えたのは新島襄だ⑼。江戸神田の安中藩邸内で生まれた新島は十九歳の時、初めて長期間江戸を離れて航海に出て、狭い藩内での窮屈な生活に嫌気をさすようになった。それ以降、密出国の機会をうかがっていたが、彼がついに渡米を果たしたのは、アメリカで南北戦争が終結した一八六五年、二二歳の時だ。キリスト教の洗礼を受けて、アーモスト大学に進み学位を取得後、アンドヴァー神学校で学んでいる。その後ヨーロッパの教育を視察して、十年ぶりに帰国すると同志社英学校を京都に開校し、後の同志社大学の基盤を作っ

もう一人、日米に大きな影響を与えた人物に、新渡戸稲造がいる。札幌農業大学卒業後の一八八四年、東京大学専科を退校して渡米し、ジョン・ホプキンズ大学で三年間学んだ後、ドイツの大学でも勉強を続けた。のちにアメリカ人女性と結婚し、札幌農学校教授、台湾総督府局長、京都帝大教授、旧制第一高等学校長などを歴任している。一九〇〇年には、アメリカでかの有名な英文著『武士道』の初版を出版した。一九一一年には、初の日米交換教授としてアメリカ各地で講義も行っている。

医学の分野で世界的な功績を残した野口英世も、一九〇〇年二四歳で渡米し、ペンシルバニア大学助手、カーネギー学院研究所助手、ロックフェラー医学研究所へと進んでいる。野口は留学や研究のためにヨーロッパや南米へも出かけ、最期は黄熱病の研究のために滞在していたアフリカで、自らが黄熱病にかかって死亡した。ニューヨークでアメリカ人女性と結婚し、没後もニューヨークの墓地に葬られている。現在フィラデルフィアには、日米医学交流の進展を目的に、野口の功績を讃えて設立された野口医学研究所がある。

アメリカで修業し、帰国後ビジネスマンとして大成功を収めたのは、森永製菓の創設者、森永太一郎だ。肥前伊万里の出身で、横浜で陶器屋に勤めていたが、アメリカで九谷焼を広めようと一八八七年、二四歳で渡米した。企業進出の先駆けといえる。だがアメリカでの九谷焼事業は失敗。スクールボーイをしな

新渡戸稲造
（日本国会図書館）

野口英世
（日本国会図書館）

新島襄
（日本国会図書館）

1870年、ニュージャージー州、ラトガース大学の日本人藩士の留学生。
（ラトガース大学提供）

がら一発逆転のチャンスを狙っていたある日、キャンディーの美味しさに感激して洋菓子職人になるべく転職する。工場などで修業を積んだ後、帰国して東京で洋菓子屋を開店した。これがのちの森永製菓だ。

渡米の目的が、留学から漁業や農業に移り変わりを見せるのは一八九〇年ころだ。九〇年代も後半になると、労働者が激増する。ほとんどの留学生が東海岸を目指したのとは反対に、労働者の多くが西海岸に留まった。ワテンバーグの『合衆国の統計史』（一九七六年）によると、一八九〇年は二三七〇人だった在米日本人が、一九〇〇年に二万七九八二人、ピークだった一九〇七年には、なんと十万八一六三人までに跳ね上がっている。この数にハワイ官約移民の興隆と、アメリカ本土移住者の増加は軌を一にしており、いかに海外出稼ぎが日本でブームになっていたかを如実に示している。

一九一九年、和歌山からカリフォルニアに渡ったヘンリー杉本さんは「日本を出る前には、アメリカというところは、道路は金で舗装してあると聞いたこともあります。（中略）それから富くじというものがあって、当たれば、大した金満家になるんだちゅうようなことも、ずいぶん聞きましたね。富くじというのをよく聞いたねぇ。（中略）それから富くじというものがあって、当たれば、大した金満家になるんだちゅうようなことも、ずいぶん聞きましたね」と一般庶民の中に根付いていた偶像化されたアメリカへの憧れを語っている。

一八六三年に大陸横断鉄道の工事が始まったが、白人が嫌がった危険な鉄道工事を低賃金で請け負った移民六万七千人のうち、二万人以上が中国人だった。一八七〇年代は、折りしも不

会に排斥運動の芽が生まれ、西海岸では特に激化の況の風が全米に吹き荒れていた。ゴールドラッシュも一段落したカリフォルニアは、思ったほど大儲けできなかった白人たちに焦りが色濃く出た時期でもある。鉄道工事が終わり、多くの中国人がサンフランシスコに定住してチャイナタウンを築くと、仕事を奪われた白人たちの排中感情は大きく膨れ上がった。大規模な中国人襲撃事件が頻発し、政府は中国人移民の受け入れを禁止する。それによって排中運動がいくらか落ち着きを見せたころ、中国人の穴を埋めるようにしてやってきた低賃金労働者が、日本人の海外出稼ぎ者だった。

「ブランケ担ぎ」して
農園から農園へ

野口英世が渡米したのは一九〇〇年、新渡戸稲造が全米を講義して回ったのが一九一一年であることを考えると、排日の対象になったのは知識層ではなく労働者、特に西海岸に住む出稼ぎ移民であったことがわかる。留学生組が英語を習得し、比較的アメリカ社会に同化したのに比べて、海外出稼ぎ組はほとんど英語を話さずに、日本の習慣をそのまま継続して生活していた。どの国からの移民も一世は皆母国語を話し、母国の習慣を引きずるものだが、ヨーロッパからの移民に比べると日本人は文化や生活習慣の違いが大きく、白人の目には奇異に映ることも

を見せるのは一八九〇年ころだ。

アメリカの歴史は建国以来、東海岸を中心に発達しており、一九世紀半ばまで西部はほとんど未開の地だった。状況が一変したのは、一八四八年にサンフランシスコ郊外で金鉱が発見されたことによる。翌年には世界中から一攫千金を狙った人々が、サンフランシスコに押し寄せた。「ゴールドラッシュ」と呼ばれる現象だ。遠路幌馬車を連ねてやってきた白人たちは、一山当てようと西部の荒野を命がけで越えてきた荒くれ男たちで、東部のインテリ層とは一線を画していた。カリフォルニアがメキシコからアメリカに譲渡されたのは一八五〇年のこと。政情もまだ不安定な荒野に、海千山千の投機家が大挙して訪れた当時のカリフォルニアは無法地帯であった。

彼らにとって、移民が目障りな存在だったであろうことは、容易に察しがつく。当時はまだ黒人が奴隷として扱われていた時代で、肌の色が違う南米やアジアからの移民は特に目の敵にされた。この時に入植したアジア系は中国人だった。炭鉱で働くためにカリフォルニアに入植した人も多い。一八五二年にカリフォルニアに入植した移民六万七千人のうち、二万人以上が中国人だった。

多かったのだろう。

コラム　「キング」と称された日系農場経営者

「ポテト・キング」の牛島

牛島は福岡県久留米市の出身で、一八八九年に渡米した。サンフランシスコでスクールボーイなどをした後、ポテト農園で働きながらポテト栽培の方法を習得した。一八九一年、カリフォルニア州ニューホープの農場の一部を借りてポテト栽培に乗り出した。翌年にはカリフォルニア州カリフォルニア・デルタと呼ばれる肥沃な土地に目をつけ、兄や数人の協力者と共に、ポテト農場の経営に乗り出した。灌漑設備などを整え、当初は順調な船出にまで遭い、破産寸前にまで追い込まれた。一八九四、九五年と続けて水害に遭い、当初は順調な土地の経営に乗り出した。だが牛島は、この逆境を乗り越えてストックトン郊外で耕作を開始し、一八九八年五月に勃発した米西戦争（フィリピン領有を巡ったアメリカとスペインの戦争）により全米でポテトの需要が高まったことから価格が高騰。この波に乗って牛島は巨万の富を得、ポテト・キングの名を確立した。現在もストックトン郊外には、経営者は変わったものの「シマ・トラクト」農園がある。ストックトンの大学には「シマ・センター」と名付けられたビルがあり、彼の功績を称えるギャラリーが設置されている。

一九〇〇年の国勢調査によると、カリフォルニア州の農場七万二〇〇〇軒のうち、七万軒以上が白人以外の農場で、白人以外の農場は一五〇〇軒強に過ぎなかった。その一五〇〇軒の約半数を中国系が占めており、日系農場は八七軒しかない。しかも多くが小作人で、日系の所有農場はわずか四軒だった。[1]

日系農場数が急激な右肩上がりを示すのは、その後の二〇年間だ。一九一〇年には約二〇倍の一八一六軒、一九二〇年には五一五二軒にまで増え、外国生まれの農場経営主の中では農場軒数でも最大となり、建物を含めた農場経営主の地価（一億三二四万七千二一〇ドル）でも、群を抜いてトップに躍り出ている。[2] 日系人が経営する農場は、外国人土地法の施行にもかかわらず第二次大戦勃発まで増え続けており、サンフランシスコ・クロニクル紙（一九四二年四月十七日付）によると、開戦時、カリフォルニア州で日系が経営する農場は約一万一千エーカーに上ったという。全米三位を誇ったイチゴ生産では、その九五％が日系農場によるものだった。[3]

このように、戦前、逆境にありながら急激な増加を遂げた日系農場経営者の中で、「キング」と称えられた人物が二人いた。「ポテト・キング」の名で知られる牛島謹爾（別名：ジョージ・シマ）と「ライス・キング」の異名をとった国府田敬三郎だ。

「ライス・キング」の国府田

国府田敬三郎は磐城平藩士の息子で、戊辰戦争に敗れた後、実家は精米業を営んでいた。アメリカへのあこがれを抱いていたが、両親の反対にあったため、渡米を断念してものの、師範学校を卒業した。その後、教育の道に入ったものの、一九〇八年、夢を叶えようと渡米を決行する。移民規制が始まっていた時期で、仕方なく「教育視察」という名目でサンフランシスコに入港した。

洗濯屋や缶詰工場など数々の事業を手がけた後、アメリカ生まれの二人の息子名義で土地を購入し、彼らと共同で米作りに乗り出した。当時、すでにアメリカにも米作りで成功した日本人が現われていたが、国府田たちが着手したのは日本米の大量生産だった。飛行機による種まきは、米作りでは彼らが始めてであった。豊作に恵まれて、数千エーカーの大農場に発展したが、太平洋戦争勃発で事態は一変する。政府の命令で、余儀なく他人に任せて収容所に入ったが、終戦後まですべて売却されていた。

戦後の復興は息子であるエドワードとウィリアムが担い、土地から飛行機までですべて徐々に土地を買い戻し、今日に近い商品を作ろうと改良を重ね、二人はできる限り日本米に近い商品を作ろうと改良を重ね、一九六三年、発売になったのが、今日でも人気ブランドの一つである「国宝ローズ」だ。同農場は現在も三代目によって運営されている。

牛島や国府田が耕地として選んだのは中央カリフォルニアであったが、日系人はカリフォルニア州各地で、さまざまな分野の農業に貢献した。二〇〇六年三月、カリフォルニア州立大学フラトン校の管轄下にあるフラトン植物園の敷地内に、日系ヘリテージ博物館が建造された。同博物館では、カリフォルニア州オレンジカウンティーにおける農業の発展と共に、農業における日系人の歴史やその功績を広く紹介している。

日本からの移民一代目を一世と呼ぶ。彼らの多くは、農繁期の農園から農園を渡り歩く季節労働者だった。自分の全財産をブランケットに包んで移動したことから、彼らを「ブランケ担ぎ」と呼んだ。鹿児島県から一九一七年に渡米したサム・ワダさんは「春のイチゴがすんだら町に出て安ホテルに泊り、七月、八月になると、フレスノのほうに葡萄をとる作業に行くんです。葡萄がすんだら、次はサクラメントとかスタクトンのほうに行って、モモとかナシとか、ああいう果実をとるんですねぇ(12)」と述懐している。

大農園には寝泊りできるキャンプが用意されていたというから、いかに季節労働者が多かったかがうかがえる。キャンプは兵舎のようにベッドがずらりと並び、ベッドとベッドの間を板で仕切っただけの粗末な建物だった。キャンプがあればまだましで、

1915年、鉄道工事現場で働く一世たち。(ワシントン大学古文書博物館)

ブランケットにくるまって農園で野宿をしたり、馬小屋で寝泊りする者も少なくなかった。「みな、季節労働者だから、自分の財産を袋に入れて、あちこち移動するのが私たちの常でしたよ。スタクトンでもフレスノでも、どこへ行っても住むところは心配ないんです。もっとも人間の住むようなところじゃないんですが。たとえばフレスノなんか空の馬小屋に寝るか、馬と一緒に寝るか、それとも、まあ暑いから、だいたい外で寝るんですね(13)」とワダさんは証言している。

彼らは収入が不安定なため、仕事のある時は夜明け前から日没まで、日曜日も休まずにこつこつと働いた。日曜日には教会に行き、地域活動に貢献するという、キリスト教的教えが基盤の白人社会においては、それがいっそうの反感を買う結果となった。

なぜ反感を買ったのかを理解していた一世は少なくない。一九一五年に三重県から渡米した川島充因さんは、カリフォルニアで日本の米作りに取り組み大成功を収めたが、排斥の原因をこう語っている。

「たとえてみれば、農業ですね。白人なんか、サンデイは休みね。サタデイはぐずぐずしておる。(中略)日本人は、男だけじゃない、ワイフもみな野良で働く。ところが白人は、ワイフに仕事させるというのは、非常に残酷と思うとる。日本の農家だったら、奥さん、みな働くでしょ。(中略)それを白人は知らんのよ。だからちょっと見て、日本人は残酷なことやるなあ、というのは、私は偏見とわかってきたんだがね(14)」。

そもそも彼らは出稼ぎ目的で渡米したのであって、アメリカに定住する気のない人がほとんどであった。一旗揚げて故郷に錦を飾ることが、彼らの共通した夢だった。最低一千ドル、できれば二〜三千ドル持参で凱旋帰国すると、当時の日本では一生生活に困らないだけの田畑が買え、大きな家を建てることができたという(15)。

のちに日系人収容所を描いた絵が脚光を浴び、画家として成功した前述の杉本さんは、「要するにアメリカへ行って金持になる。その考えが、私は全世界に共通でしょうと思います。なぜっていったら、日本で一生懸命働いたって、僅かな金しか儲からないし、子供が出来れば、生活していくちゅうことも、なかなか難しい時代だから、アメリカへ行って、一攫千金をものにして帰れば、立派な金持として生活

ブランケットに巻いた全財産を担いで農園から農園に移動する日本人季節労働者。(カリフォルニア大学バークレー校バンクロフト図書館提供)

日米紳士協定で
日本人移民の規制

排日運動が激化した一因に、一九〇四年に勃発した日露戦争があったともいわれている。カリフォルニアにおける排日運動の要となった「アジア人排斥同盟」がサンフランシスコで結成されたのは一九〇五年だが、日本軍が中国の旅順を陥落したのはその年の元旦。アメリカ国内の排日感情の高まりと、日露戦争での日本軍の優勢は並行線を描いていると、日露戦争での日本軍の優勢は並行線を描いていると、日露戦争での「アジア人排斥同盟」が結成された二週間後に、連合艦隊がロシアのバルチック艦隊を破ったかに見える。「アジア人排斥同盟」が結成された二週間後に、連合艦隊がロシアのバルチック艦隊を破っている。

セオドア・ルーズベルト大統領の仲介により日露講和条約が調印され、日露戦争は終結したが、ロシ

アはあくまで敗戦を認めず、日本はロシアから賠償金を一銭も取れずに終わった。だが当時、日本とロシアの国力は経済力で十倍ほどの差があったため、日露講和条約の底力は、欧米諸国を脅かすのに十分だった。

日露講和条約が調印されたのは、アメリカのポーツマスだ。この時、日本の首席全権である小村寿太郎は、ポーツマスの街に一万ドルの寄付をした[18]。小村は一八七五年、文部省の留学生として、ハーバード大学で法律の勉強をした経歴を持つ[19]。

排日運動が形となって現れ始めていた一九〇七年三月、ルーズベルト大統領は、ハワイ、メキシコ、カナダからの日本人転航移民を禁止する大統領命令に署名した。これ以降、日本人移民を規制する法律が、次から次へと制定されていく。

大統領命令の発令で、慌てたのは日本政府だ。アメリカ国内での排日問題が、日米の国家問題にまで広がるのを恐れ、翌年には日米紳士協定を締結した。これは日本政府が、日本人のアメリカ行き旅券の発行を自主的に規制するという約束事だ。ハワイからの転航が禁止された上に、日本からの新規渡米者も規制され、アメリカ生まれの二世も現れて拡大を目指していた日系社会は、ここに来てその道を断たれたのだった。

一九〇八年以降に渡米した人たちの多くが、親による呼び寄せか結婚だったが、なかには密入国という強硬手段におよんだ人も少なくなかった。「外国

写真一枚で嫁いだ
写真花嫁の悲劇

日米紳士協定でもっとも被害を受けたのが、独身男性だった。当時、一世の男女比は一〇〇対一とも五〇〇対一ともいわれ、多くが結婚相手に事欠く深刻な事態となった。ただ、日米紳士協定には抜け道があった。家族がアメリカに在住していれば旅券が発行されたのだ。そこで男たちは花嫁探しのために一時帰国し、日本で結婚してから新妻とともに再渡米するという手段を取った。日本に一時帰国している間に結婚しているわけだから、再渡米時には、妻

はアメリカ在住者の家族として旅券を取得できた。

だが誰もがそうやすやすと一時帰国できたわけではない。長期間の休暇を取るような贅沢や、二人分の渡航費を負担する経済的な余裕のない男たちがほとんどであった。そこで彼らは日本の家族に手紙を書き、写真を添えて、花嫁探しを依頼した。いわゆる「見合い」だ。見合い結婚は日本古来からある風習で、親同士で話を進め、花嫁と花婿が初顔合わせをしたのは結婚式当日だった、というのは、当時の日本では珍しい話ではない。たった一枚の写真を手に、期待に胸膨らませて、若き花嫁たちが西海岸の港に続々と到着するようになると、彼女たちは「写真花嫁」と呼ばれた。

男たちは、馬小屋のような場所で農作業服を着て写っていたのでは「誰も嫁に来てくれない」と、借り物で身なりを整え、他人の車や農場主の邸宅の前で写真を撮った。経歴を偽った人もいたらしい。大きな自動車の横でさっそうとポーズを決めていたハンサムな若者は、会ってみると、炎天下の労働のた

労働局の用箋に貼られた写真花嫁とその夫の身分証明書。The I.D. letter of picture bride and her husband, issued by the Department of Labor. (Japanese-American Historical Society of San Diego)

め年は倍ほどにみえ、背格好もまるで別人だった、というエピソードは、写真花嫁を語る時に必ず登場することから、決して少なくなかったと思われる。

当時、海外移住者の成功談が日本で華々しく伝えられていたことを考えると、花嫁たちがどれほどの夢を持って船の長旅に耐えてきたかは想像に難くない。女学校を出た才女も少なくなかったらしいが、彼女たちは港に降り立ったが最後、新しい労働力として働かなければならない立場となり、多くがなすすべもなく夫の後をついて行った。

開教師の妻として一九一八年に渡米した松浦しのぶさんは、「すぐ別れる、帰る言うて騒ぎますやら

……、現実と理想が違いすぎてですね。共働きで苦労してでもやっていくんだ、という気持で来ればよいのですが、アメリカはお金持ちの国で、なんでも自由になるようなつもりで来ますから、失望もまた大きいわけですね。日本でも当時では珍しい女学校出も憧れて来ましたでしょ。ところが、来てみたら家もなければ、理想の一つもないところでしょ、そりゃ初めての生活はあわれなもんでした[22]」と話した。

写真花嫁の悲劇は夫婦間に留まらず、日系人社会にも大きな影を落としたようだ。「とにかく男が多く、女が少ない。それで、家庭の主婦と独身男の、いわゆる三角関係が多かったんですね。それから、日本からアメリカに来る人は、日本でも新しい考えを持った人が多かったんですが、こっちに来て思想と合わず離婚のケースもある。離婚しても行くところがない。それで、醜業婦に身を投じた人もありますしね。

めて、その当時はサンフランシスコにも、四、五軒の女郎屋があったんです。そういうところへ逃げ込むとか、また、橋渡しをする男なんかもいましてね。非常に男女関係というのは乱れておったんです[23]」と話したのは、一九一八年に岩手県から渡米し、サンフランシスコで発行されていた「日米新聞」の記者になった浅野七之助さんだ。

一九二〇年二月、日本政府は写真花嫁に対する旅券の交付を禁止した。写真花嫁の実数を正確に把握するのは難しい。なぜなら旅券の発行数だけでは、それが写真花嫁なのか、呼び寄せなのか、日本で見合いをしてから来たのか、判断ができないからだ。写真花嫁の数は二万人とも七万人ともいわれ、その実数すらわかっていない。同年、アメリカでは憲法

東洋からの正規移民の窓口、エンジェル・アイランドに1910年に集団で渡米した日本人写真花嫁たち。(カリフォルニア州エンジェル・アイランドの記録より)

修正条項第十九条の婦人参政権が可決されている。

排日移民法と外国人土地法

日本政府によって禁止される以前から、写真花嫁の廃止は日系社会ですでに議論に上っていた。その背景にあるのが、一九二〇年にカリフォルニア州で制定された改定外国人土地法だ。外国人土地法とは、市民権を持たない外国人の土地所有を禁じる法律で、市民権を持たない外国人とは、すなわちアジア系移民を指す。というのも、奴隷解放宣言が行われた南北戦争後の一八七〇年に改定された帰化法で、市民権の取得が認められたのは「白人と解放された黒人」でアジア系移民は含まれていない。当時、一世たちは何年アメリカに在住しても、市民にはなれない状況にあったのだ。

カリフォルニア州外国人土地法が最初に制定されたのは一九一三年。この段階では、市民権を持たない外国人の土地所有を禁じてはいたものの、三年までの借地権は認めていた。その借地権さえも禁止したのが、この改定法であった。

こつこつと働いて資金を作った人の中には、サンフランシスコ南部や中央カリフォルニア、ロサンゼルス近郊などで農場経営に乗り出す一世も出現し、一九一〇年から二〇年の十年間で、日本人移民はカリフォルニアの農業を支える重要な農場主になりつ

つあった。だがこの修正案が議会を通過すれば、日系社会に大打撃を与えるのは火を見るよりも明らかだった。そこで彼らは写真花嫁を自粛することで、排日感情を和らげようとしたのだ。だがその努力もむなしく、同法案は議会を通過し、正式に法制化されただけでなく、ワシントン州やオレゴン州などの西部諸州にまで波及した。

土地を所有できない時代にも、人々は逆境の中であらゆる知恵を出して農場経営に進出した。もっとも多かったのが、出生によるアメリカ市民である子供の名義で土地を購入し、自分が後見人になるケースだ。

また株式会社を設立し、白人を書類上の社長に据える人もいた。一九二九年に経済恐慌が始まるまで、アメリカは好景気を謳歌しており、金余り状態だった。そのため良い投資になると見込めば、銀行もすすんで日系人に投資した。

こうして日系人に（キャリフォルニア州中部）のフレスノの近くに、中加日土地法があっても裏と表があるからね。それで私は堂々とやった[24]」と語ったのは先述の川島さんだ。

大農園で働く日本人労働者によって繁栄した最寄りの町に、排日の風潮は見えなかったという。日本人農園の生産性の高さは群を抜いていたため、成功した農園主の中にはキャデラックを乗り回したり、白人の高級住宅地に豪邸を建てる人まで現れた。

一世たちはこうして知恵を絞り外国人土地法を切り抜けたが、それ以上の大打撃を与えたのが、一九二四年にクーリッジ大統領によって署名された排日移民法だった。これは新しく受け入れる移民の割合を、一九二七年六月三〇日まで（のちに一九二九年六月三〇日まで延長）は、一八九〇年に在住していた各国の移民の二％と規定して、年間一六万四六六七人だけを受け入れ、それ以降は一九二〇年の基準に合わせて一万五千人を受け入れるという法律で、移民の規制を恒久的に定めた初の法律といわれている。だが日系社会にとって決定的な打撃になったのは、帰化権を持たない民族に対して、移民として入国を禁止するという条項だった[25]。この条項は主に日本人を狙って盛り込まれたもので、これが排日移民法と呼ばれるゆえんだ。これで、事実上、家族や配偶者の呼び寄せが一切できなくなった。写真花嫁の禁止と排日移民法で結婚する道を断たれ、一生独身で終わった一世は少なくない。

相互扶助の精神で
日本人町が発展

爪に火をともすような思いで日本へ送金し、故郷に錦を飾ろうと休む間もなく働き続けた一世たちであったが、希望通り凱旋帰国できた人は多くない。三年の予定が五年になり、そのうち結婚して子供ができると、毎日を生活していくだけで精一杯になる。

戦前（1940年頃）のロスアンジェルスの日本町（リトルトーキョー）の風景。
Los Angeles, Calif. -- Street scene in Little Tokyo near the Los Angeles Civic Center, prior to evacuation residents of Japanese ancestry. Photographer: Albers, Clem -- Los Angeles, California. 04/11/1942 Courtesy of The Bancroft Library. University of California, Berkeley.

いつしか農園の近くには、日本人相手の木賃宿や雑貨屋などを始める一世も現れ、それが日本人町の原型となった。港があったシアトルやサンフランシスコでも、一八〇〇年代後半には日本人町が形成され、激しい排日の風が吹き荒れる中、日本人同士で助け合い、日系コミュニティーの中で生活するのは、彼らが生き抜くための方策だったのだろう。

同郷人同士で援助の手を差し伸べたのが県人会だ。初期の渡米者には、福島県、和歌山県、広島県、山口県などの出身者が多く、一九〇〇年代初期にこれらの県人会が次々と設立された。和歌山県人会の前

身である紀友会が、オークランドで結成されたのは一八九七年だ[26]。広島県も移民を多く出した県で、広島県人もシアトルに入会できるように、広島の字を少し変えて「広稜会」を結成し、病人などの世話にあたった。一九一五年に広島県からシアトルに移住した藤井良人さんによると、県人会以外にも娯楽の会や歌の会など趣味の会もかなりあったようだ[27]。これらの団体はピクニックや新年会などを通して慰安の場にもなった。

寺や教会は、宿泊所や食事などを無料あるいは安価で提供するなど、あらゆる形で移民を支援しており、コミュニティーセンターのような役割も果たしていた。先述の米作りで成功した川島さんも、画家として活躍した杉本さんも、苦学生の時は教会や仏教などの寄宿舎で世話になった経験を持つ。開教師の妻の松浦さんは、夫婦で働く農家のための託児所「チルドレンズ・ホーム」を作ったと証言している[28]。子供たちは「チルドレンズ・ホーム」で寝泊りし、そこから通学したらしい。

一九一〇年も後半になると、救世軍（キリスト教の慈善団体）にも日系人の幹部が登場した。救世軍の士官学校を卒業し、フレスノなどで日系人の世話にあたったのが今井正英さんだ。「どこの誰ともわからなくて、寂しく死んでいったという方はずいぶん多いですね。私はフレスノにおった期間に五〇〇名の人を葬式しておるですよ。そして、病気で来た方の数は、実際一五〇〇人ぐらいなんですよ。家族もない、お金も全然ない人たちで、私の家に泊まっ

ておるそういう人は、いつも一五名を下ることはなかったですね[29]。救世軍は写真花嫁など女性の駆け込み寺のような役割も果たしており、「そこあたりに来ている婦人はたいがいミスターがおらなくなったか、あるいは、おったんだけれども別れてしまって、行くところがないから、救世軍に来たという。そういう方々が婦人部に入っておられたですね。およそ七〇名の子供たちがいつもおったです[30]。

救世軍の活動としてもっとも知られているのが、ストックトンで展開された「シナ賭博撲滅運動」だ。「シナ賭博」あるいは「チャイナ賭博」と呼ばれる中国人経営の賭博場が各地にあり、他にこれといった娯楽もなかった当時、独身男性を中心に多くの移民

馬に引かせたソーダー水売り。1930年代のリトルトーキョー（東洋宮武スタジオ提供）One of early Little Tokyo business, The White Star Soda Works, and a family on a horse-drawn carriage. Courtesy of Toyo Miyatake Studio.

が賭博の誘惑に陥った。「日米新聞」の記者だった浅野さんは賭博について、「七月末から九月にかけて、フレスノあたりにはブランケットを担いだ何千人もの人々が各地から集まって来ます。移民もいれば留学生もいるという賑いです。葡萄の摘採、それにピーチとかエイプルカット（アンズ）の季節で、広いフルーツランチ（編集注〈果樹園〉へ入るわけです。その労働者をねらって、賭博場があちこちで開帳される。賭博場の経営というものは、本当はキャリフォルニアではできないんですが、非常に寛大に取り扱っておったんです。（中略）朝早く起きて、夜遅くまで働いてキャンプで食事をし、そして何百円というお金を稼ぐ。一週間に一回ぐらいの休みがありますから、その休みにタウンに出ると、シナ賭博へ行く。女のところへ行く。賭博は熱してくると、とことんまでやりますからね。そうして、真裸になって、またブランケ生活に戻るんですね(31)。

救世軍や寺、教会が、身寄りのない老人たちのために開いた葬式を出した身寄りのない老人たちの多くが、賭博で身を滅ぼした人たちだったという。

一九〇六年のサンフランシスコ地震を境に、ロサンゼルスにも多くの日本人が移ってきた。当時のロサンゼルス郊外は日系人の農業が盛んで、リトルトーキョーは彼らを相手にした商売で成り立っていた。当時はファーストとサンペドロストリートが街の中心で、日本食レストランや和菓子屋はもとより、銭湯もあり、日本人医師もいた。映画館では日本映画も上映されていた。

日本人は金を出し合って「たのもし」と呼ばれる共同資本源を作り、それを順に使い合って不況を乗り越えた。また合同教会、美似教会などのキリスト教会も数多く設立され、日本へ布教活動に行った牧師が、帰国して信者のために開いた宗派もある。仏教は当初、各派が集まって仏教連盟を結成し、宗派を越えて布教に当たっていたが、その後、東本願寺と西本願寺などに宗派分れしたと、宮武さんは語っている(33)。

日本人経営の苗卸売り会社、ロスアンジェルス1941年。（南加大学近郊歴史図書館）

ダウンタウンの日本人町が「リトルトーキョー」と呼ばれるようになったのは、一八〇〇年代だったという。一九〇九年に渡米し、日系人収容所内の様子を写真に撮って、貴重な記録を数多く遺した宮武東洋さんはこう述懐した。「このトーキョーというのは、日本人が付けたんじゃないんです。ロサンゼルス・シティが付けたんです。千八百何年だったか、ついそこのウエラ・ストリートに三五人の日本人が鉄道の仕事で来ていたんですね。そのとき、シティのほうがトーキョーと付けたんです。だから、電車がここへ着くと、『トーキョー』とコンダクター（車掌）がどなったもんです(32)。」

一九二九年の経済恐慌では多数の失業者が出たが、リトルトーキョーの店主たちは、資金を少しずつ出

1942年4月5日、カルフォルニア州サンペドロから集合所として使用されたサンタアニタ競馬場に特別列車で到着した日系人。後にそこから各収容所に送られた。
（カリフォルニア大学バークレー校バンクロフト図書館提供）

第二章 日米開戦の衝撃 一九四〇年以降

CONTENTS

日本語学校と
二重国籍問題

一九三〇年代の日本は、三一年の満州事変に始まり、ファ

日本軍によるパールハーバー奇襲攻撃で、全米はヒステリックな不安に陥った。彼らを支配したのは、正義ではなく恐怖心だった。日系人はアメリカ市民であるかどうかに関わらず「敵性外国人」の烙印を押された。日米開戦でもっとも衝撃を受けたのは日系人自身であったかもしれない。アメリカ人であることを証明するには、前線で戦う事が唯一残された道であると、多くの二世たちが若い命を国のために捧げる決意を固めていった。

当時アメリカの統治領だったハワイは、海軍基地であるパールハーバーを中心に多くの軍事施設を抱える軍事的要所であった。地理的に見ても、日本が侵略してくるとすればハワイの可能性が高い。また、日本語学校以上に大きな問題になったのが、二世たちの二重国籍問題だ。一九二四年以前に生まれた二世は、日本政府の方針により、出生地のいかんに関わらず自動的に日本国籍を有していた。これが基本的にアメリカ市民でしかあり得ないヨーロッパからの移民の子孫と日系二世が、大きく異なった点だった。アメリカの事情がわからず保険局に出生届を提出していない一世が多かった一方、日本領事館は五年ごとにプランテーションを回って綿密な国勢調査を実施していたため、出生による アメリカ市民である彼らは、自分たちでも気づかないうち二重国籍になっていたのだ。

一九二四年四月一日以降は、日本領事館に届け出た人にだけ日本国籍が与えられるようになったが、二重国籍である二世の多くが兵役年齢に近づくにつれ、政府の懸念は二世たちの忠誠心に注がれるようになった。日米開戦が現実になった時に、彼らはどちらの国のために戦うのか。スパイ工作をするのではないか。日米関係は日を追って悪化しており、疑惑の声は高まるばかりだった。

一九三八年、二世グループからなるハワイ・アメリカ市民協会が、二重国籍者に日本国籍の離脱を促すキャンペーンに乗り出した。ハワイを故郷として、アメリカへの教育を受けた二世たちの中に、自分たちはアメリカの立場にあるのだという自覚が生まれていたのだ。

するなど、純粋な言語学校としての方向性を示す努力を重ねていた。

一九三七年、政府は両院合同特別委員会を設置しハワイの州昇格を検討したが、その争点になったのが、日本語学校と二世の二重国籍問題だった。

ハワイに限らず、日本人町には必ずといっていいほど日本語学校が設立された。一世と二世親子のコミュニケーションを維持するには、英語で教育を受ける二世に日本語を教える事が不可欠であったためだ。母国語学校の設立はヨーロッパ移民がすでに確立していたシステムだったが、以前から批判の的に立っていた。だが連邦最高裁が母国語学校運営の権利を是認し[3]、世論も時間が経てば母国語はあくまでも第二外国語としての影響しか与えないことがわかってきたため容認する傾向にあった。

だが日本語学校は、ヨーロッパ移民の母国語学校と同じような寛大さでは受け入れられなかった。この原因になったのは、文化の違いの大きさだ。アメリカの文明はキリスト教に基づくヨーロッパの文明が基礎になってできたものだが、日本は天皇を神と敬う国で、日本語学校はたいてい寺などが運営し、なかには修身の授業で「忠君愛国」の精神を教えるリカ市民協会が、二重国籍者に日本国籍の離脱を促すキャンペーンに乗り出した。ハワイを故郷として、

シズムが台頭した時代だった。「ススメ、ススメ、へイタイ、ススメ」で知られる国定教科書『国語読本』が登場したのは一九三三年だ。修身の授業では天皇に対する忠誠心と愛国心が「忠君愛国」として叩き込まれた。日本国民は皇民と呼ばれ、一九三八年には国家総動員法が交付された。戦争の本格化にともない、飛行機や軍艦などの兵器に使う金属資源が不足し始めると、寺の梵鐘まで供出された時代だった。

アメリカに住む一世たちが入手した情報も、これら皇軍が発信するニュースだった。なぜなら彼らのほとんどが英語を話さなかったため、情報源を短波ラジオに頼っていたからだ。一世たちは、つつましい生活の中から日本の戦時国債を買い、献金をし、慰問袋を作って日本軍を支援した。「日米新聞」記者の浅野さんの話によると、毎月一ドルの会費で、赤十字を通じて日本での出征者の遺族の慰問にあてる「兵務者会」なる組織まであったという。「日本が満州に出兵して、祖国の青年・壮年はみんな兵士として戦っていた。ところが、アメリカに来ている若人は結果としてお国の役に立てません。おなじ日本の人々が一生懸命働いているのに、われわれは祖国のために何もできない。せめて、日本の出征者の家族・遺族を慰問しようじゃないかというので、生まれたのが兵務者会でした[1]。兵務者会の会員は一万人ほどいたという。このような一世たちの活動は、アメリカ政府内に不安をもたらした。なかでも特に政府の懸念の対象になったのが、ハワイに住む日系人だった。

リカ政府の教育を受けた二世たちの中に、自分たちはアメリカへの忠誠心を証明しなければならない立場にあるのだという自覚が生まれていたのだ。

教員も一世ではなくアメリカ市民である二世を採用する学校もあった。ハワイでは日本語学校のあり方をめぐって何度も統治領議会で審議されたため、日系人たちは学校存続のために修身の授業を撤廃し、日系人たちは学校存続のために修身の授業を撤廃し、リカ市民である二世を採用

一九四〇年、同協会は当時、国務長官だったコーデル・ハルに嘆願書まで送っている。その中で彼らは日本国籍離脱の手続きの複雑さ、待ち時間の長さなどを挙げ、「そのため日系人は他のアメリカ人と同じように忠誠心を持っているのに、不当な疑惑をもたれている⑸」と切々と訴えており、ハワイ在住の日系人が疑惑に対していかに危機感を覚えていたかがわかる。一九四一年の春、日本領事館は毎月四〇〇件の割合で国籍離脱の申請を受理しており、それは増える傾向にあると公表した⑹。

さらにハワイだけで約六〇〇人いたとされる帰米二世の存在も、政府の不信の種になった。帰米二世とは、出生によるアメリカ市民だが、日本で教育を受けて戻ってきた人たちを指す。たいていの場合、子供は日本の親戚に預けられ、親はアメリカに残った。一世たちはいずれ日本に帰るつもりでいたから、「子供たちの教育は日本で」と考えたり、人種差別のあるアメリカ社会での子供の将来を危惧した人が少なくなかった。プランテーション（大農園）で働く子沢山の夫婦の中には、経済的な理由から子供を日本の親戚に預けた例もあったようだ。

理由は何であれ、ほとんどの帰米二世は日本で徴兵される前にアメリカへ戻ってきた。中には日本で「アメリカ人」と逆差別を受けて、親恋しさから逃げるようにして戻った子供もいたという。

FBIの最優先課題
「ハワイの日本人問題」

一九三九年八月、政府はFBIハワイ支局を開設し、「日本人問題」を最優先課題として取り組んでいる。ロバート・シバーズ支局長はただちに軍情報部と連携して、日系人の忠誠に関する調査に乗り出した。だがすべての日系人を個別に調査すると時間がかかることから、FBIと軍情報部は多人種による委員会を設置し、アメリカ市民としての道徳キャンペーンを行うことにした。

その一環として設立されたのが、日系人からなるオアフ市民防衛委員会だ。日米開戦に備えて、日系コミュニティーを心理面から支え、本来あるアメリカへの忠誠心を高めようという目的で結成された。集会で軍情報部は、背信行為をしない限り、日系人も公平で差別のない扱いを受けると約束した。これが日米開戦をにらんで米軍が出した最初の公式な声明となり、それ以降、あらゆる集会で同様の声明が発せられている⑺。

シバーズ支局長は長い捜査の結果、ハワイの日系人へ信頼を寄せるに至り、軍情報部も「ハワイが直接攻撃されない限り、一世も二世もアメリカへ忠誠を示すだろう⑻」と結論付けている。国務長のカーティス・マンソンがフランクリン・D・ルーズベルト大統領の命令を受けて提出した「ハワイの日本人問題」の調査書でも、「一世は法律が許すなら、アメリカ市民権を取得するであろうと思われる。彼らは法律上日本人だが、誇りを持って二世を米軍に送るだろう」とし、二世に関しては「長年の偏見や無責任な中傷を受けているのにもかかわらず、彼らはアメリカ人として認めてもらうために痛ましいばかりの熱意を見せている。彼らの九〇％から九八％はアメリカに忠誠」、また帰米二世に関しては「彼らは幼少期から十七歳まで日本で教育を受けた者と、初期教育をアメリカで受けたあと日本に行き、四、五年目に日本の教育をアメリカで受けた者は一世の考え方に近く、もっとも危険因子であると思われるが、初期教育をアメリカで受けてから日本へ行った者は、多くの場合、アメリカにより忠誠を感じるようになって帰国していることを明記しておきたい⑼」と結んでいる。

実際にハワイで調査した関係者がこれだけ証言していたにもかかわらず、本土の中央政府は疑惑を払拭できず、四人で発足した陸軍情報部課報機関は、一九四一年十二月までに増員された十二人の調査官と、十八人の特別捜査官を抱えるまでの規模になり、そのほとんどの調査が「日本人問題」に絞られている⑽。

一九四〇年八月、平和時における徴兵を可能にするバーク＝ワッズワース法案が上院で議論された。この時、同時に取り上げられたのが、志願に関するこの条項に「人種のいかんに関わらず」という一節を加える案だった。これは、黒人にも平等に志願のチャンスを与えるための案であったが、一部の政治家の大反対にあった。反対理由の一つとして議論された

米開戦は時間の問題となっていった。

日本軍によってパールハーバーが攻撃されたのは、現地時間一九四一年十二月七日の朝だ。第一波攻撃は七時五五分から八時二五分。ホノルルに住む多くの日系人が、爆音とともにパールハーバーから黒煙が上がるのを目撃した。それが日本軍による攻撃だと認識した人は少ない。第二波が、ホノルル上空を低空飛行した時、その機体に日の丸を見つけて、人々は愕然とした。「人生が終わったと思いました。なぜならパイロットは私と同じような顔をしていたからです[12]」とダニエル・イノウエ上院議員（ハワイ州選出）はその衝撃を語っている。

日本に激怒した日系人も少なくない。「低空飛行するゼロ戦に石を投げるか何かして、怒りを伝えたい衝動に駆られた。（中略）裏切られた思いで、深く傷つけられたことによる怒りだ。子供のころから植えつけられてきた日本人への尊敬の念が音を立てて崩れた。彼らは同じ日本人である移民を無情に殺したのだ[13]」と日記に記したのは、のちに第一〇〇大隊として参戦したコンラッド・ツカヤマさんだ。

直後に急報が届いた本土でも、日系人の受けた衝撃の大きさに変わりはない。日本に献金していた人なども日米開戦を想定していたわけではなく、純粋な祖国への想いから生まれたものだ。だが日本軍がパールハーバーを攻撃したことにより、彼らは一瞬にして「アメリカの国益にとって危険とみなされる敵性外国人」という立場に陥った。

フランクリン・D・ルーズベルト大統領が「一九四一年十二月七日は、屈辱の日として残るであろう」と演説すると、世論は一変して参戦へと傾いていった。アメリカは正式に日本に対して宣戦布告をし、ドイツとイタリアがアメリカへ宣戦布告したのを受けて全面戦争に参入。FBIは日系人、ドイツ人、イタリア人などを「危険人物」として拘束した。「ジャップ」という蔑称が、連日新聞の一面を飾るようになり、日系人のスパイ行為を匂わせる記事が相次いで掲載され、町の商店には「ジャップお断り」などと書かれた紙が張り出された。日系人を狙った傷害事件も多発し、他のアジア系移民は「中国系アメリカ人」

サンペドロのロサンゼルス湾にあるターミナル・アイランドは、当時三千人余りの日系人が住む、いわゆる「日本人漁村」を形成していた。だが島の東半分が海軍基地だったため、開戦直後に米兵に包囲された。全米では日本語学校の関係者や宗教家、日系団体のリーダーたちが、FBIによって一斉に検挙された。

リトルトーキョーに住んでいた宇津見きくよさんは、パールハーバーが攻撃された時、家族で近場の温泉旅行に出かけていた。「車のラジオでニュースを聞いてすぐに家に戻りましたが、日本人町は通行止めになっていました。その夜から停電が始まり、毎日のように警報が鳴りました。夜間停電は一週間くらい続いたでしょうか。戒厳令が出て、自宅から五マイル以上は行けなくなりました*」と話した。翌朝六時半までに全米で七三六人の一世が検挙されている。[14]

のが、「日系人にも志願の道を開くことになる」ことであった。それまでは、日系人も入隊を拒否されることが少なくなかった。だが、一九三七年よりハワイで指揮を執ってきたチャールズ・ヘロン中将は、「遠距離にいてハワイのことを知らない人たちが不安がっているようだが、この島の住人による破壊工作などあり得ないことを知っている。長年この地に勤務して、私はハワイの人々の愛国心に全幅の信頼を寄せている[11]」と反対派を一蹴した。同法案は可決され、九月には同案を基盤にした徴兵訓練サービス法が成立した。これにより、二一歳から三六歳までの男子は徴兵のための登録を義務付けられ、翌月にはアメリカ史上で初めて、平和時における徴兵が開始された。

日米開戦で受けた 日系人たちの衝撃

一九三九年九月、ドイツ軍がポーランドに侵攻を開始し、その二日後、イギリスとフランスがドイツに宣戦布告した。第二次世界大戦の始まりである。翌日には日独伊三国同盟が締結された。アメリカ世論は参戦反対が多数を占めていたが、史上初めて平和時に徴兵制度が導入され、ハワイ統治領防衛軍も米陸軍の管轄下に置かれた。翌年一月、ABCD包囲（アメリカ、イギリス、中国、オランダの四国）によって日本に対する経済封鎖が実施されると、日

＊ 2005年7月13日、敬老シニアヘルスケア中間看護施設にて取材

た。

などと明記した大きなバッジを胸につけて外出した。全米に「ハワイの次は本土」という恐怖感が浸透し、皮肉にも直接攻撃を受けたハワイよりも、未知の不安に襲われた本土で日系人排斥運動が過熱していった。

日系立ち退きを第一面で報じる新聞、サンフランシスコ・エグザミナー（国立公文書）。The San Francisco Examiner reports `Japanese-American evacuation' on the front page of the newspaper. (The National Archive and Record Administration)

軍事指定地域と日系人強制収容

西海岸のカリフォルニア州人事委員会は、対戦国を祖先に持つアメリカ市民が公職に就くことを禁止し、その決定を日系人に対してだけ適用した。在郷軍人会ポートランド支部は、アメリカ市民も含めて日系人を海岸線から移動させるように促し、西海岸にある州代表の連邦議会議員団も、大統領に日系人をカリフォルニア州、オレゴン州、ワシントン州から移動させるように要請した。カリフォルニア州合同移民委員会も同様の要請を出し、一九四二年二月十九日、ルーズベルト大統領は世論に押されるように大統領令九〇六六号に署名した。これは裁判や公聴会なしに、特定地域から日系人を排除する権限を陸軍に与える法律である。

四日後、サンタバーバラ沖の製油所が日本軍の潜水艦から砲弾を受けると、その三日後にはターミナル・アイランドの日系人たちに、海軍が立ち退きを言い渡した。立ち退き準備に与えられた時間は四八時間[15]。多くの人が財産を二束三文で処分し、行く当てのない人はリトルトーキョーの寺や教会に身を寄せた。その後、西海岸では九月までに計四回、日本軍の潜水艦から砲弾攻撃を受けたが、アメリカ本土が直接攻撃されたのは結果的にその四回だけだった[16]。

三月二日、ワシントン州、オレゴン州、カリフォルニア州の西半分とアリゾナ州南部が陸軍により第一軍事地域に指定され、同二四日、シアトルのベインブリッジに住む日本人家族三〇人に対して、強制立ち退き令第一号が発令された[17]。対象は、「日本人の祖先を持つ外国人および非外国人」。「非外国人」とは、すなわちアメリカ市民（二世）を指す。彼らがマンザナー収容所の最初の入所者となった。

二世からなるJACL（Japanese American Citizens League: 日系市民協会）はそれまで数々の案を出して必死で強制収容を回避しようと試みたが、強制収容が実行に移されると、「市民として政府の命令に従おう」と日系社会に呼びかけた。結果的にほぼすべての日系人が従順に立ち退きに応じたが、必ずしも全員がJACLに賛同していたわけではない。収容所内では、後にJACLを狙った暴行事件も起きている。

立ち退きに与えられた期間は約一週間で、多大な財産を失った人がいた一方、心ある市民に助けられた人も少なくない。先述の宇津見さんもその一人だ。「車を買ったばかりだったのですが、主人の下で働いていたメキシコ系従業員が代わりに売ってくれ、そのお金を集合センターになっていたサンタアニタ競馬場まで持ってきてくれました。また収容所から出てきた後は、預けておいた家財道具もすべて返してくれました*」と話した。サム・ワダさんは立ち退きの朝、キリスト教団体がサンドイッチやコーヒーを用意してくれたと回顧している[18]。クエーカー教徒は、ACLU（American Civil Liberties Union: アメリカ人権保護連合）と同様に日系人の強制収容に反対の声を上げた数少ない団体の一つだった。

財務省は三月十二日、外国人土地法成立以前に購入された日系人所有の土地は連邦準備銀行サンフランシスコ支局が管理し、農地や農具などは農地保障管理局が管理するように任命し、「日系人が立ち退きで財産を失わないように、公正な取引が行われない場合は保管する機会を与え、立ち退きに便乗するような非アメリカ的な行動は取らないように[19]」と通達したが、連邦準備銀行は保管に関して「当局は一切

＊ 2005年7月13日、敬老シニアヘルスケア中間看護施設にて取材

シエラ山脈の麓、砂塵の嵐が吹きつけるマンザナー収容所。
Scene of barrack homes at this War Relocation Authority Center for evacuees of Japanese ancestry. A hot windstorm brings dust from the surrounding desert. -- Photographer: Lange, Dorothea -- Manzanar, California. 07/03/1942 Courtesy of the Bancroft Library. University of California, Berkeley.

'I am an American' (私はアメリカ人だ) と日本軍、真珠湾攻撃の翌日にオークランドの自分の店に張り紙を出した日系人。（カルフォルニア大学バンクロフト図書館）A Japanese-American store owner, posted the `I AM AN AMERICAN' sign on his storefront on December 8, 1941 the day after Pearl Harbor. Courtesy of the Bancroft Library.

の責任を持たない」として財産の処分を推進し、農地保障管理局も農作物が通常通り収穫されるために白人借地人や企業への譲渡を促したため、ほとんどの人が財産を失う結果になった。立ち退きがほぼ完了したのは夏ごろのことで、その総数は十二万人以上に上った。

立ち退きになった日系人が最初に集められたのは、全米十六ヵ所に仮設された集合センターだ。こうした集合センターは収容所が完成するまでの一時的な施設で、たいてい競馬場などが使用され、ロサンゼルス界隈ではサンタアニタ競馬場に仮設バラックが建てられた。前述の宇津見さん一家のような六人家族にはバラックではなく馬小屋があてがわれ、馬糞の匂いはどんなに拭いても取れなかったという。日系人たちは地区ごとに、そこから全米十ヵ所に建設された収容所へと送られていった。

収容所には住居用バラックと、共同の食堂、洗濯場、浴室、便所などがあった。住居用バラックは四部屋に仕切られ、たいてい一部屋に一家族が入居したが、シーツなどで仕切ってもプライバシーはなく、隣室の話し声さえ筒抜けだった。ほとんどの収容所は急ごしらえで建てられたものだったため生木を使用したところも多く、乾燥すると隙間ができ、朝起きると隙間から吹き込んだ砂が毛布の上に積もっていることも珍しくなかったという。部屋には軍用ベッド以外に家具もなかったが、人々はバラックの周りに花壇や池を作ったりして少しずつ環境を整え、公会堂が建つと演芸会などを催したりして、収容所内の生活向上に努めた。

日系人収容を統轄したのは、一九四二年三月十八日、大統領命令第九一〇二号によって創設されたWRA（War Relocation Authority：戦時転住局）で、初代長官はミルトン・アイゼンハワーだった。彼は戦後、第三十四代大統領となったドワイト・アイゼンハワーの弟である。

四月七日、アイゼンハワーは、ネバダ、アイダホ、オレゴン、ユタ、モンタナ、コロラド、ニューメキシコ、ワイオミング、ワシントンそしてアリゾナの各州に日系人の受け入れを打診している。だが、快く受け入れを承諾したのは、コロラドのラルフ・カー知事だけだった。カー知事は「日系アメリカ人は他のアメリカ人同様、忠実なアメリカ人だ」と日系人を歓迎する方針を取り、ラジオ放送を通じて州民に日系人の受け入れを訴えた。コロラド州に収容所ができた時も、知事は収容所から数人の二世子女を家事使用人として採用し、大学に進学させている。(20) 知事は日系人以外にも人種差別による人権侵害に反対したが、次期知事選で日系人受け入れに反対したエド・ジョンソンに僅差で敗れた。(21) 現在、デンバーの中心地にある日系センター「サクラスクエア」にある知事の銅像は、戦後日系人が感謝の意を表して建てたものだ。

アイゼンハワー長官は日系人の強制収容所政策に辞易して、九〇日で辞職した。辞職の理由を「この

28

仕事をしていると夜も眠れない(22)」と後任のディロン・マイヤーに語ったが、引き継いだマイヤーもまた、日系人収容の必然性に疑問を抱いていた。WRA設立一周年に出した声明でマイヤーは「転住センター（注：収容所）での生活は非道で、反アメリカ的なものだ。入居者は日本人を祖先に持っているというだけで、どんな罪も犯していないことを忘れてはならない。彼らは忠誠心を疑われ、それがかえって忠誠を妨げる原因になっている。また敵国に人種差別による戦争だと主張させる原因となり、アメリカは民主主義を謳いながら人種差別を行っていると非難を浴びている。子供が有刺鉄線の中で番兵に見張られて育つのが、アメリカ的といえるだろうか(23)」と訴えている。

　辞職翌日の二二日付の書簡で、WRA辞職後、戦時情報局にいたアイゼンハワー前長官もルーズベルト大統領あてに以下のように書き綴っている。「教育にも支障をきたしている若い二世たちは、自分たちの苦境は軍事上の理由からではなく、人種差別、経済的因子、戦争による偏見から来たものではないかという疑いを拭えずにいます。　有刺鉄線に囲まれ番兵に見張られている転住センターの生活が居心地良いはずはありません。日系人は立ち退きにより財産を失い、職を失い、生活の糧を失いました。（中略）このような状況で、彼らが反感を抱かないとしたら不思議なほどです。　局長はインディアン居住地に見るような人種差別が起こらないように努力しており、そのため十カ所の転住センターを保持するのではなく、個人の転居を推薦しているのだと思います(24)」。

WRAデイロン・マイヤー長官とワシントンD.C.で公務員として働く日系人。（カリフォルニア大学バークレー校バンクロフト図書館提供）

　マイヤーはシカゴにWRA事務局を設置して、日系人の移住を斡旋した。雇用先を見つけ、FBIによる身上調査に合格した日系二世が収容所外への移転を許されたのは、収容が始まった年の七月だが、三ヵ月後の十月には、同様の条件を満たした日系一世にも移転許可が下りている(25)。歯科技工士だった村岡献次さんの場合は、「政府のリロケーション・センターが、日本人を使う人がないかと探したのです。するとシンシナティのある白人のデンティスト（歯科医）が日本人を使いたいって言う、それに応じて私は出たのです(26)」と証言し、村岡さんがアーカンソー州のローワー収容所にいたのは七ヶ月だったと語っている。

　こうした支援を得て、一九四三年三月までに約三千人が収容所を出ている(27)。だがアイゼンハワーやマイヤー、カーのように人権尊重を訴えた人は、あくまで少数意見であった。連邦議会は一九四四年一月、ルーズベルト大統領にマイヤー長官を解雇する嘆願書を出していることからも、世論の意向がうかがえる(28)。しかしその後もマイヤーは解雇されることなく、一九四六年に同局が閉鎖されるまで局長を務め、その後も機会があるごとに収容所の早期閉鎖を訴え続けた。

日系人収容所での　集団生活

　収容所が設立された場所は、いずれも荒野などの自然環境が厳しい地域で、ツールレーク収容所やポストン収容所などはインディアン居住地内に建てられた施設だ。収容所の周りには有刺鉄線が張られ、番兵がライフルを構える監視塔が建てられたが、アリゾナ州南部のポストン収容所には柵はあったものの有刺鉄線も監視塔もなかった。それはポストン収容所が砂漠の真ん中だったためその必要性がなかったからで、夏には摂氏四六度を超えることも珍しくなかった。　同収容所は約二万人を収容した最大規模の施設で、三つの区画に分けて建設され、各区画間は三マイルも離れていた(29)。またここは唯一、WRAではなくインディアン局の管轄（四三年まで）となった収容所でもある。インディアン局では、農業

収容所の中のアダルト・スクール（成人教室）で初めて英語を学ぶ大人たち。Courtesy of the Bancroft Library. University of California, Berkeley.

に長けた日系人が来たからにはできるなら半永久的に定住してもらい、農業の促進に協力してもらいたいと希望していたが、軍事指定地域外への早期転住を奨励していたWRAの猛反対にあい、あきらめたという経緯がある(30)。農繁期には、各地の収容所から手伝いに出ており、一九四二年秋には合わせて約一万人が収穫作業に携わった(31)。

収容所によっては暴動事件が発生し、死者が出たところもあった。監視の厳しさは地理的な問題や責任者の方針によって差があったようだ。マンザナー収容所やツールレーク収容所はカリフォルニア州内にあったため、監視が厳しく、アイダホ州のミニドカ収容所は比較的おだやかであったといわれている。

また収容所に対する反応も、一世と二世では差があったようだ。学校で民主主義の教育を受けた二世たちの中には、自分たちが知る国はアメリカしかなかったという人も少なくない。それが4C（敵性外国人）の烙印を押され、市民としての権利を奪われたのだから、彼らが受けた衝撃は想像に難くない。

だが渡米以来、身を粉にして働き続けた一世の中には、収容所に入って初めて明日の食事の心配をせずにすむようになったという人がいたのも事実で、「私たちはもう外で苦労のありったけしていましたから、この三年のあいだキャンプがなかったら、アメリカへ来て楽することなかったんです。（中略）食物なんか外でしたら、あんなもの食べられないほど、たくさん出回りました。お米が足りないっていうのに、米もどんどん入ってくる。あれで文句言うたら、私罰があたると思いましたけど。人によったら、その受け取りようでしょうね。キャンプでは、いろんなもの習いたいと思ったら、書道でも絵でもね、何でも自分の習いたいものは教えてくださったしね。政府から先生にみな払ってくださるんですものね(32)」と語ったのは、和歌山県から一九二〇年に写真花嫁として渡米した仮谷小柳さんだ。当時、全米では食料の配給制度が導入されていた。

収容所内では裁縫や英語など数多くの成人教室が開講されていた。仮谷さんは「私たち夜学に行かしてもらって、ただでみんな先生つけて英語教えてくださるのにね。また、出てきてからに習うたって、あのとき、キャンプに入れてもらわなかったら、おそらく困ったろうと思うんです。日本人ということで、仕事はくれないわ、排斥されるわで、私ら子供が小さいでしょう。よう習いもできないのにね(33)」と語ったが、収容所内で初めて英語を勉強したという人も少なからずいたようだった。

収容所内で日系人は仕事に就くことを奨励され、一般職で月十六ドル、専門職で月十九ドル（見習いは月十二ドル）、そして家族分の被服費が支給された(34)。政府には当初、軍人と同等の給与を支給するという案もあったが、世論の反対にあったため上記の金額に落ち着き、その代わり衣食住と医療費が無料となった。「だからもう僕らキャンプに入ったときに安心しましたよ。これで衣食住、心配ないと思ってね。あのとき、キャンプに入れてもらわなかったら、おそらく困ったろうと思うんです。非常に困っていたんです(35)」と

ローワー収容所内でスペイン語の授業を受ける高校生。Students of Japanese Parentage of Grade 9-A in Spanish. Mrs. Marie McCullough, teacher. -- Photographer: Parker, Tom -- McGehee, Arkansas. 11/25/1942 Courtesy of the Bancroft Library. University of California, Berkeley.

極寒のワイオミング州、ハート・マウンテン収容所に収容されたカリフォルニアからの日系人は初めてのアイス・スケートを楽しんだ。 Residents of Japanese ancestry, at the Heart Mountain Relocation Center, were quick to grasp the recreational advantages of Wyoming's cold weather. For them, ice skating was a new sport. Photographer: Parker, Tom -- Heart Mountain, Wyoming. 01/10/1943, Courtesy of The Bancroft Library. University of California Berkeley.

前述のワダさんは語っている。収容に感謝する一世が多いのは、それだけ彼らが戦前は筆舌に尽くしがたい苦労を強いられていたからに他ならない。

特に西海岸では排日運動が過熱していたため、一世たちは生活に困っただけでなく、頻発する襲撃事件にもおびえていた。開戦直後に拘留された開業医の喜安都定さんは、「拘留所で家族は暴行加えられてないだろうか、どんな目に遭っているだろうか、食べていけるだろうか、そういう心配をしているときに、キャンプへ強制立ち退きをしてくれた」(36)と回顧しており、一般市民の反日感情が日系人に身の安全にまで影響を及ぼしていたことがわかる。「娘の学芸会で着る衣装を作るために、生地を許可を取れば収容所の外へ買い物に行くこともできた。

買いに出かけました。でもたいていの買い物はシアーズ・カタログ（通信販売）でオーダーしていました＊」と話したのは、アーカンソー州ローワー収容所にいた宇津見さんだ。アリゾナ州のヒラリバー収容所にいた開教師の妻の松浦さんも、収容所から出て東海岸で大学に通う息子と会うため、一度シカゴへ出かけているが、その際には旅費も支給されたという。(37)

強制収容を免れた
グラウンドゼロ

開戦後、米軍が頭を痛めたのが、約三千人いたハワイ統治領防衛兵のうち、約半数を占めていた日系兵の存在だった。一九四〇年の国勢調査による日系人はハワイ全人口の三七・三％で、白人の二四・五％を抜いて人口比率の最上位だった。先述のバーク＝ワッズワース法で兵役における人種差別が撤廃されたため、ハワイの第一回選抜制徴兵では、二世が六〇％を占めた。(38)開戦時にスコーフィールド基地で訓練を受けていた新兵は六〇〇人だったが、そのうち三五〇人は日系人だった。(39)新兵の日系人は開戦三日目に銃を取り上げられ、基地内のテントに集められた。だが二日後には銃は返され訓練は続けられており、軍部の困惑が読み取れる。

パールハーバー攻撃後、ハワイ大学でROTC（Reserve Officers' Training Corps: 予備士官養成部隊）に属していた学生たちが、ただちに防衛軍の中核となるべくホノルル軍本部に集められて、入隊の手続きを取っている。

学生たちの多くが日系二世だとの警告を受けたハワイ軍総司令官のウオルター・ショート中将は「日系人が忠誠を示す絶好の機会になる」(40)と、そのまま実施するように促した。攻撃の翌日、軍部は短波ラジオ、カメラ、花火などの戦時禁制品の提出命令を出し、邦字新聞社や日本語学校は閉鎖されたが、同時にショート中将は「日系人は法に従う限り配慮される扱いを受けるし、市民は日系人に友好的に接するように」(41)との声明も出している。

だが多くの新聞による扇動はアメリカ中の不安をかき立て、特にハワイや西海岸では日系人によるスパイ工作の噂や憶測が相次いだ。年が明けた一月五日には、徴兵サービスは日系人を4C（敵性外国人）扱いにして、新規の入隊を禁止した。この決定により、そのまま軍に残った日系兵もいるが、除隊あるいは雑務に回された二世も少なくない。

ROTCから入隊した二世たち三一七人も、ショート中将の後任であるデロス・C・エモンズ中将が総司令官として着任すると、一月二十一日、何の説明もなく解任された。(42)そのほとんどはハワイ大学の学生だったが、授業が行われていないに等しい状況の大学構内で、学生たちは連日議論を交わした。4C扱いの彼らは、ここで解任されると忠誠を示す機会を失うことになる。意気消沈する若い彼らの支えになったのが、当時大学内のYMCAの理事であったハン・ワイ・チンだ。チンは、中国系アメリカ人だが、シバ

＊2005年7月13日、敬老シニア・ヘルスケア中間看護施設にて取材

ズ支局長とともに日系人の擁護に務め、後にホノルル屈指の不動産業者として財界の実力者になった人物だ。除隊された日系学生の約半数にあたる一六九人がエモンズ中将あてに嘆願書を出し、「ハワイは私達の故郷で、アメリカは私達の国です。私達が忠誠を誓うのは星条旗以外にありません。どんな仕事でもかまわないので、アメリカに尽くす機会を与えてほしい（43）」と訴えたが、この嘆願書を陸軍情報部長のケンドール・フィルダー大佐に持ち込んだのもチンだ。

フィルダー大佐も日系人に信頼を寄せていた一人で、大佐の意見に促されてエモンズ中将は二月末日、日系学生に部隊編成の許可を与えた。この部隊は正式には技術予備労務隊と呼ばれ、陸軍工兵連隊所属となったが、実質的に彼らに与えられた仕事は一般市民が請け負う肉体労働だった。戦争特需に沸くハワイでは、肉体労働を必要とする仕事があふれていたのだ。彼らは自ら「トリプル・Ｖ・大学必勝義勇隊（Varsity Victory Volunteers）」と名乗り、学書の代わりに工具を手にして、兵舎や倉庫の建設や道路工事などに汗を流した。日系人が自分たちのことをＡＪＡ（Americans of Japanese Ancestry: 日本人を祖先に持つアメリカ人）と呼ぶようになったのはこのころだ。

一方、開戦前にあれほど忠誠心が疑問視されていたハワイの日系人は、皮肉にもそれが功を奏して強制収容は実施されなかった。一九四二年六月のミッドウェイ海戦までは強制収容を訴える声も多かった

が、政府が本土の日系人の強制収容で手一杯になっている間に、ハワイの軍情報部は「ハワイでは大型立ち退きは必要なし」という結論に達していた。それは調査の結果、スパイ工作は一件も立証されなかったためでもあるし、日系人たちが自主的に米戦時国債を買い、献血運動を展開するなどしてアメリカへの忠誠を示す努力を見せていたためでもあった。開戦前にはすでに市民であっても忠誠心を何らかの形で「証明」しなければならない立場だという自覚が、二世にはあった。一世も子供の将来を考え「自分は日本人だが、子供の国はアメリカ」の立場を取り、でき得る範囲の行動を起こしていた。ＦＢＩや軍情報部でも、長年かけて蓄積してきた「日系人には確固たる措置を取るが公平に」という政策が実を結んだという手応えを感じていた。

また軍事特需でハワイは好景気に沸いており、人手不足の状態だった。ある将校は後日「バラックを建てるにも日系人の労働力が必要だった（45）」と語っており、日系人が収容されるとハワイ経済が破綻する危険性もはらんでいた。また軍部も、これだけ大勢の日系人を本土へ輸送することは、兵士の輸送に船が必要な折に非現実的だとの結論を出した。六月末、エモンズ中将はハワイの治安が落ち着いていることを理由に、五千人だけの移送準備を依頼したが（46）、ミッドウェイ海戦で米軍が大勝を収めると、日系人立ち

グラウンドゼロであったハワイで、日系人が最終的に強制収容を免れたのは、物理的な諸事情もある。だがそれ以上に開戦前には「危険人物」に関する調査が完了し、シバース支局長やフィルダー大佐のように日系社会の忠誠心に信頼を置く白人の指導者が、ハワイにはいたという事情も大きい。結局、一九四二年十月から翌年三月までに本土へ移送されたのは九三〇人で、そのほとんどが開戦直後にＦＢＩによって逮捕され本土で拘禁されていた男性の家族であった（47）。

日系部隊の先駆け
「ワンプカプカ」

パールハーバー攻撃以来、ハワイがもっとも緊張に包まれたのは、一九四二年六月のミッドウェイ海戦前だ。多くの爆撃機がハワイから飛び立ち、ホノルル港沿いに住む女性と子供は内陸部への避難勧告を受け、ラジオはガスマスクの常時携帯を呼びかけた（48）。軍部ではミッドウェイでチェスター・Ｗ・ニミッツ提督が敗れるようなことがあれば、日本軍によるハワイ進行の可能性大だと見ていた。日本軍が米軍の軍服に身を包んで紛れ込んだら見分けがつかない。そこで軍部は、緊急対策として日系兵だけを集めて本土へ輸送することにした。
ラジオがミッドウェイ海戦を伝えた翌日の六月五日、ホノルル港からマウイ号が極秘で出航した。こ

れに乗船していたのが、日系兵一四三三人だ(49)。緊急命令であったため、彼らは行く先も知らされないまま、慌しく生まれ故郷を後にした。見送りに間に合った家族もごくわずかしかいない。日系兵たちがミッドウェイ勝利のニュースを聞いたのは、マウイ号の船上だ。日本軍ハワイ上陸という事態になれば家族はどのような扱いを受けるのかと心配していた彼らは、吉報にひとまず安心したものの、生まれ故郷の一大事に本土に輸送されることに対して不安を抱いていたに違いない。魚雷を避けるため二〇分ごとにコースを変えてジグザグ運航しながら、マウイ号がサンフランシスコ湾のゴールデンゲートブリッジをくぐったのは一週間後だ。多くの日系兵にとって、初めて見る本土の風景だった。

彼らが「第一〇〇大隊」と正式に名づけられたのはこのころだ。第一〇〇大隊という名称に、軍部の戸惑いが見え隠れする、通常、師団の下に連隊があり、一連隊は第一大隊から第三大隊で成り立つ。ところが彼らには所属すべき連隊や師団がなかった。前線に出すのが目的で結成された大隊ではなかったからだ。また一大隊はA中隊からD中隊までの四中隊で成り立つが、彼らは通常の大隊よりも人数が多かったため、さらにE中隊とF中隊が設けられた。「第一〇〇大隊」という聞きなれない呼称に、彼らは自分たちがいかに特殊な立場であるかを改めて思い知った。この時点では、まだ強制収容されると信じていた二世も多い。いつしか彼らは、自分たちのことを「ワンプカプカ」と呼ぶようになった。ハワイ

コラム

日系兵の知られざる戦功

太平洋戦線で活躍した MISの日系兵士たち

開戦前に極秘で設立

パールハーバー攻撃直前の一九四一年十一月、サンフランシスコのプレシディオ陸軍基地内に、MIS (Military Intelligence Service/軍事情報機関) 管轄の語学学校 (Military Intelligence Service Language School) が、極秘で開設された。日米間の緊張が高まる中、日本語教育機関の必要性を考慮して設立された日本語学校だ。日系の志願兵や徴兵の中から、ある程度日本語に長けた六〇人が第一期生に選ばれた。六〇人中、五八人が二世兵士だった(1)。 八人の民間人が教師として動員されたが、主任教師に選ばれたのは、後に米本土初の日系人裁判官となったジョン・アイソだ(2)。

西海岸の日系人に立ち退き命令が出ると、語学学校もミネソタ州キャンプ・サベジに移転になり、その後生徒数が増加したため、フォート・スネリングに移された。一九四六年六月、米陸軍語学学校 (U.S. Army Language School) と改名され、カリフォルニア州に移転されるまで、約六千人の卒業生を出したが、その八五％が二世兵士で占められていた(3)。

第四二連隊がヨーロッパ戦線で活躍し、その戦功が華々しく報道されたのに対して、MIS任務は極秘扱いであったため、長い間、その存在すら知られていなかった。日本語学校を卒業したMISの兵士たちは、アッツ島やガダルカナルの戦闘、フィリピン奪回や沖縄戦など、太平洋戦線の激戦地に配属された。日本兵捕虜の尋問や押収した日本語書類の翻訳、日本軍の通信傍受などを担当し、前線に出る時は、日本兵と間違って撃たれないように、必ず米兵と共に行動したという。「捕虜兵にはいつも、まずタバコをあげ、『日本では生きて帰ると恥だと言われるが、アメリカではヒーローなんだ。命を無駄にせず、生きて日本を再建するんだ』と説得しました*」と語ったのはジョージ・フジモリさんだ。戦後は進駐軍の一員として、日本の復興にも寄与したが、戦中・戦後を通して、米軍と日本人との架け橋として彼らが果たした役割は大きい。

MISの戦功が一般に知られるようになったのは、一九七二年、リチャード・M・ニクソン大統領が大統領命令一一六五二号を発令し、第二次大戦中の軍事情報の機密扱いを解除してからのことだ(4)。二〇〇〇年四月、陸軍は第二次大戦に従事したMISの兵士に対して、五五年遅れの大統領感状を授与した(5)。

※二〇〇五年六月二〇日、Go For Brok National Education Center にて筆者取材。

語で穴のことをプカというが、その延長でゼロもプカと呼ぶ。

第一〇〇大隊長となったのは、日系兵たちに「オールドマン（親父）」と慕われたファラント・ターナー大佐だ。ターナー大佐はハワイ島ヒロの生まれで、この時すでに四七歳。だが統治領防衛軍時代から日系兵士のことをよく知っており、日系部隊編成の話を聞くとすぐに大隊長に志願した。ターナーが右腕として副大隊長に任命したのはジム・ラベル大尉。「大尉」といえばラベルのことだというくらい、日系兵士たちの信頼を得た人物だ。ラベルはネブラスカ生まれだが、ホノルルの中学や高校で教鞭を執っており、運動部のコーチも多く引き受け、二世たちと親しんだ経験を持つ。ワンプカプカの兵士たちは、大隊長と副大隊長がターナーとラベルだと知って大喜びした。

ターナーは厳しい上官であったが、日系兵士を「マイ・ボーイズ」と呼び「マイ・ボーイズ」を不当な扱いから守ることに全力を尽くすと同時に、日系兵士が問題を起こすと、「日系部隊の評判は君達一人ひとりの行動にかかっているのだ。そして君達の肩には、親兄弟の将来がかかっているのだ(50)」と激励した。訓練で良い成績を残し、一日でも早く前線で戦功を挙げることが、彼らに与えられた任務だった。彼らはあえて「リメンバー・パールハーバー」をモットーに選んで訓練に励んだ。陸軍マニュアルによると、重機関銃の組み立てに要する時間は、一六秒で「軍基準を満たしている」に達し、幹部候補生学校のフォート・ベニングでも、一一秒で組み立てると「速い」と評価される。ところが第一〇〇大隊が訓練を出したキャンプ・マッコイでは、五秒という記録を出した日系兵が数人いた(51)。彼らの訓練ぶりを視察に来たある将校は「今までに指揮したどんな一〇〇人よりも、彼らのような一〇〇人を部隊に持ちたい(52)」と報告している。

ハワイ兵たちが話す言葉は、文法もめちゃくちゃなピジョン英語だ。ピジョン英語とは英語とハワイ語と日本語、時には広島弁などが混じったハワイ人が話す言葉で、慣れないと何を言っているのか理解できない。だが手紙を検閲した将校は、話し言葉に反して彼らの書く文章の高度さに驚いた。ワンプカプカの約九五％は日本人移民の息子で、約三五％が二重国籍、約二％が帰米二世、そして約八五％は日本語学校に通った経験を持ち、公立高校卒業にかかった平均年数は三年で、約十二％が大学に進学しており、約五％は大学卒業者だった。第一〇〇大隊の陸軍知能テストの平均スコアは一〇三。幹部候補生学校に進めるのは一一〇だから、平均が七ポイント下回っただけのワンプカプカには多くの幹部候補生クラスの兵士がいたことになる(53)。

だが彼らが訓練でどんなに素晴らしい成績を残そうとも、この時点で彼らが前線に出る可能性はゼロに等しかった。なぜなら米軍は開戦後、日系人の志願を禁止しており、軍部では「日系人の忠誠は信用できない」という意見が大勢を占めていたからだ。この不信感を覆したのが、ワンプカプカの優秀な訓練成績であり、ハワイ大学の学生たちが結成したトリプルVの活動であった。

アメリカのために
死ねる権利への道

年が明けて一九四三年一月、第一〇〇大隊はミシシッピ州のキャンプ・シェルビーに移動になった。それまでは軍部内でも日系部隊に対する意見は分かれており、日系兵士はあくまで内陸での労務に徹すべきで、戦闘部隊に回すべきではないという反対派と、優秀な人材は日系人であれ戦闘部隊として扱うべきで、二世の大部分は忠誠なアメリカ市民だと判断した賛成派があり、WRAは賛成派を支持していた。ニミッツ提督やエモンズ中将も同様に日系兵は前線で活躍すると見ていた。エモンズ中将はハワイに着任直後、日系人の強制収容を支持していた人物だが、トリプルVの学生たちの働きやキャンプ・マッコイでの訓練状況を知るにつれて日系人信頼派へと傾いている。その陰には、戦前から日系人をよく知るフィルダー大佐の働きがあった。陸軍省次官のジョン・マックロイがハワイの守備体制を視察に来たときも、フィルダー大佐はわざとコレコレ峠をルートに入れて、トリプルVの学生たちが岩を砕く作業に汗を流す姿を見せている(54)。

戦時情報局のエルマー・デイビス長官は、

一九四二年十月、ルーズベルト大統領あてに次の書簡を送った。「アメリカに忠誠を示す日系アメリカ人の志願兵を受け入れるべきです。（中略）立ち退きさせた人たちに徴兵令を出すのは正当ではありませんが、志願兵の受け入れなら士気の向上にも結びつくのはないでしょうか」(55)。戦時情報局には、日本政府が東南アジアで訴えていた「人種差別による戦争」という宣伝に利用されたくないという思いもあったようだ。ルーズベルト大統領はデイビスの書簡を陸軍省のヘンリー・スチムソン長官に回し、スチムソンはさらにそれをマックロイに回して意見を求めた。フィルダー大佐から何度も日系人に関する報告書を受け取っていたマックロイは、「日系人の多くは忠実であると強く確信している」(56)という注釈をつけて回答しており、スチムソンはそれを陸軍参謀総長のジョージ・マーシャル大将に送って意見を求めたが、「マックロイとデイビスの見解に強く賛同します。アメリカ市民を人種の理由で永久に排斥することはできません。彼らを強制収容したことでその極限までやりました。もう十分です(57)」と書いた非公式のメモを添えている。ちなみにスチムソンはルーズベルト大統領に日系人立ち退きを要請した人物だが、時間を経てエモンズ中将と同じように日系人信頼派に傾いたことがわかる。

本土の日系社会でも、JACLがソルトレイクシティーで総会を開いて、日系兵部隊の編成について協議している。総会では「収容状態を解いて、元の家に戻してもらってから決めよう」という至極当然

米国軍隊に入隊を許可された日系志願兵たち。
（ハワイ大学マノア図書館提供）

な意見も出たが、マイク・マサオカ事務局長は「戦からなる日系部隊を作って戦果を出せば、広く報道争に勝って平和な社会に戻った時、『勝つために戦地できるし二世にとっても有利になるはず、というもで戦った』と答えられなかったら、これからの社会のだった。第一〇〇大隊は白人将校を驚かせるだけの訓練成績を出していたから、この構想はマサオカに受け入れられて成功するチャンスは極めて少ないたちにとってもまさに忠誠を証明する絶好の機会にだろう。だから少なくとも選抜徴兵制を政府に要求なると受け入れたが、マサオカはさらに念を入れてたちに会いに行き、日系部隊の試みが成功すマックロイに会いに行き、日系部隊の試みが成功すれば、選抜徴兵制を二世たちに実施する約束を取り付けている(59)。

徴兵は据え置きされ志願兵のみを受け入れることになったが、次なる問題は日系兵を集めた日系部隊を結成するのか、それとも各部隊に散在させるのかであった。マサオカたちの窓口になっていたマックロイの補佐を務めるウィリアム・スコービー大佐がマサオカたちに説明した陸軍当局の構想は、二世たち

こうして日系人収容を管轄したWRA、第一〇〇大隊を送り出したハワイの総司令官、さらに戦時情報局や陸軍省の上層部が許可を出し、ついに一九四三年二月、ルーズベルト大統領は、日系志願兵からなる第四四二連隊の編成を発表した（日系兵の徴兵開始は一九四四年一月）。大統領は声明で「アメリカニズムは頭と心の問題であって、人種や祖先の問題ではない(60)」と演説したが、この文案はWRAが作成したものだ(61)。こうして二世たちは、晴れて「アメリカのために死ぬ権利」を得た。ただし将校は白人であることが条件だった。

政府では「収容されている日系人を徴兵するのは正当ではない」というデイビス長官の見解が通り、

忠誠登録と
日系部隊編成

日系部隊編成の発表と同時に、収容者対象に開始したのが「忠誠登録」だ。これは日系人の忠誠心を調べるための質問状だが、なかで問題になったのが、

「Q二七・米軍の命令であれば、戦地の場所に関わらずに兵役につく意思がありますか」「Q二八・米国に無条件の忠誠を誓い、意思を否定する外国政府や勢力に対する忠誠や服従を否定することを誓いますか」（中略）日本国天皇およびいかなる外国政府や勢力に対する忠誠や服従を否定することを誓いますか」(62) の二点だった。アメリカ市民になれない一世は、二つの質問に「イエス」「イエス」と答えると、日本へも背を向け、アメリカでも外国人という無国籍の状態になる。長い人種差別のあげく強制収容された彼らには、「なぜこんな仕打ちを下回ったこともあり、ハワイの募集枠は二六〇〇人する国に息子の命を託せられるのか」という思いもある。二世にすれば、市民なのに改めて忠誠を強制されることに深い屈辱を覚えた。

右の問いに「ノー」「ノー」と答えた人は、ツールレーク収容所へ転送され、そこから日本に帰国した人も多い。「イエス」「イエス」と答え、さらに志願までした人は、収容所内で裏切り者扱いされた。一世と二世、あるいは帰米二世のあいだでくすぶっていた意見の相違は、この「忠誠登録」によって家族をも対立させ、収容所内の混乱をよりかきたてた。志願兵募集に、ハワイでは募集人員の十倍近い若者が殺到したが、本土で収容されていた兵役年齢の二世男子のうち志願したのは、わずか約五％だった(63)。強制収容所にいた二世たちの、苦しい胸のうちも理解できる。

「志願したと伝えると、『お前はオレたちよりも偉いわけじゃないが、現にこうして収容されているじゃないか。そんなことをすれば、日本の家族はどう感じるんだ』と非難されました。でも私は言ったんです。

『今ここにいるのは、これまで何もしてこなかったからだ。今がチャンスなんだ。ここで志願して自分たちを証明しないと日系人の将来は来ないし、それは僕たちのせいになる。生きて帰って来れないかもしれないが、それでも価値があるんだ』」(64) と証言したのは、元MIS（陸軍情報局）のケン・アクネだ。

一方ハワイでは、一五〇〇人の募集人員に一万人以上の若者が殺到した。本土からの志願兵が予想を下回ったこともあり、ハワイの募集枠は二六〇〇人に増員された。収容所では家族から志願兵を出すと「イヌ」と罵られたが、ハワイでは反対に身体検査などで落ちると、「家の恥」と肩身の狭い思いをしたという。一九四三年三月二八日、ホノルル商工会議所主催の壮行会がイオラニ宮殿前の広場で盛大に開催され、二六八六人の志願兵たちはホノルル市内を行進している。この中にトリプルVの学生たちの姿もかったに違いない。ちなみに「本土からの徴兵」というのは、開戦前に徴兵されそのまま解任されることもなく宙に浮いた状態にあった本土出身の日系兵で、第一〇〇大隊と同様に軍が処遇に困っていた兵士たちだが、ハワイ兵が本土の軍の事情を知るはずもなかった。

出兵する前から英雄扱いだったハワイ兵と、裏切り者呼ばわりされた本土兵。本土兵とハワイ兵では、愛する人の晴れ姿をひと目見ようと、数万人の日系人が沿道を埋め尽くし、星条旗の手旗を振りながら「バンザイ」を叫んだといわれている。

訓練地で対立したのも無理はない。ハワイ兵が第四四二連隊の訓練地となったミシシッピー州のキャンプ・シェルビーに到達した時、下士官の地位はすでに本土からの徴収兵で占められていたのが、両者の間に溝を作った発端だといわれているが、これまたハワイ兵には、戦時特需に沸くハワイの親からの多額の小遣いが送金された。それに比べて、本土兵

話し言葉の違いも大きな原因になった。ハワイ兵の話すピジョン英語が本土兵には理解できない。ハワイ兵から見れば、本土兵は彼らが毛嫌いする白人のプランテーション主のような話し方をした。経済的な違いもあった。餞別として何百ドルも持っていたハワイ兵には、戦時特需に沸くハワイの親からの多額の小遣いが送金された。それに比べて、本土兵

442 部隊の訓練風景、キャンプ・シェルビー。（国立公文書）
442 nd RCT in training at Camp Shelby. Source: Archives and Record Administration.

の親は収容所の中だ。給料の中から親に仕送りをしていた者も少なくない。両者の対立に頭を痛めた首脳部は、ハワイ兵をキャンプ・シェルビーからもっとも近いアーカンソー州のジェローム収容所に見学に行かせることにした。その第一陣にダニエル・イノウエ議員がいた。初めて収容所内に足を踏み入れた時の感想を、議員は次のように語っている。

「ジェロームへ行くバスの中では、皆お祭り気分でウクレレを弾いて歌などうたっていましたが、帰り道は全員無言でした。おそらく皆同じ事を考えていたのではないでしょうか。もし自分がこの中に入れられていたとしたら、それでも志願しただろうかと
(65)
だった。

ハワイ兵と本土兵が日系部隊として団結した瞬間

評判を築いた イタリア戦線

第一〇〇大隊が極秘裏にホノルル港を出航してから一年三ヶ月、長い訓練を終えたハワイ兵たちは一九四三年九月二日、ついに北アフリカの戦地に着いた。

九月九日、イタリアは降伏し、ドイツ軍によって制圧され、翌日から連合軍によるサレルノ上陸作戦（なだれ作戦）が決行された。

第三四師団第一三三連隊の配属となった第一〇〇

大隊が、ローマ入城を目指してサレルノに上陸したのは、同月二二日のこと。日系部隊編成にあたって陸軍上層部が目論んでいた「戦果を出して広く報道を」という当初の目的は、初戦から予想以上の効果を生んだ。めずらしい日系米兵の活躍に報道関係者は興味を抱き、「前線で決して振り返らない兵」と好意的な報道がなされた。だが彼らが真の勇敢さを発揮したのは、モンテ・カッシーノの戦いだ。カッシーノはドイツ軍が連合軍のローマ侵攻を防ぐために死守せんとした要塞だったが、小高い丘の頂上には聖ベネディクトによって五二九年に設立された由緒あるカトリック寺院があったため、連合軍は空爆ではなく歩兵で突破しようとしていた。第五軍司令官のマーク・クラーク中将は「カッシーノ戦がイタリア戦線においておぞましく、もっとも悲惨で、ある意味ではもっとも悲劇の戦いだった」と戦後に回顧している。多数の師団を費やしても歩兵では突破できず、連合軍は一九四四年二月十五日、二五五機の爆撃機を投入して空爆をした。だが、カッシーノ陥落までさらに三ヶ月を要している。

第一〇〇大隊はカッシーノが落ちるのを見届けることもなく、連合軍のアンツィオ上陸作戦に参戦するため、アンツィオ前線に就いている。アンツィオを突破すれば、ローマを陥落したも同然で、このころ激化した東部戦線におけるドイツ軍兵力を分散するため、西部戦線を作り出そうと、連合軍は北フランスからの上陸を計画していた。これが「史上最大の作戦」と呼ばれる、総兵力三〇〇万人以上を投入

したノルマンディー上陸作戦だ。フランスを奪回するには、北フランスにあるノルマンディー上陸と、南フランスへの道を切り開くアンツィオ上陸が重要事項だった。ここでも第一〇〇大隊は、積極的な戦闘で多大な功績を残した。

アンツィオの陥落により、六月五日、連合軍は世界が注目する中、ローマ入城を果たした。第一〇〇大隊がローマに入ったのは夜の九時。「ローマへ一番乗り」の地点までは先陣を切っていたが、ローマ一番乗りを目前にして他の部隊を通すために『止まれ』の命令がかかった。「訓練では、戦車が装甲部隊として先に行き、歩兵は戦車に守られて前進するのだが、実践になるとそんなことは起こらない。戦車はいつも後ろからついて来るだけだ。（中略）ところが

イタリア　セシナ近郊で英国のジョージ国王の謁見を受ける442部隊。（ハワイ戦記局）

ローマ近郊で突然『止まれ』の命令が出て、戦車を先に進めた。ローマを解放した勝利者として報道陣の被写体にするためだ。戦車が僕たちの横を通り過ぎる時、大砲が撃ち込まれた。すると今度は、僕たちに先に行けという。大砲が収まるとまた『止まれ』の命令が出て戦車を先に行かせる。三度目に『先に行け』と命令が出た時には、誰も動かなかった(67)。

訓練を終えた第四二連隊に、イタリアへの出動命令が出たのはこのころだ。連隊のモットーは「ゴー・フォー・ブローク(当たって砕けろ)」。第四二連隊のノーマン・イカリさんは語る。「ナポリに到着したら、僕らを見つけた白人部隊が『ワンプカプカ』と手を振って喜ぶんです。それで先陣だった第一〇〇大隊が、日系部隊の評判を築いてくれたのだと知りました(68)」。第一〇〇大隊の戦功はすでに本国の軍関係者のあいだで鳴り響いており、引退したターナーの後任としてアンツィオから大隊長に就いたゴードン・シングルス中佐も、第一〇〇大隊配属命令を受けて「なんという幸運か」と口にしたという(69)。第四二連隊がヨーロッパ戦線の第一大隊となったが、第一〇〇大隊は第四二連隊の第一大隊に就くと、第一〇〇大隊は第四二連隊がヨーロッパ戦線に就くと、その後も「第一〇〇大隊」を名乗ることを許可されている。受け取り手がないために付いた大隊名は、いまや名誉の名称となった。第一〇〇大隊と第四二連隊がチームを組んで参戦したのは、ローマ北部のベルベデーレ戦からだ。ベルベデーレ突破には数日かかると見られていたが、第一〇〇大隊が背後に回る奇襲作戦でドイツ軍の戦死者一七八人、捕虜七三人、戦車二台などを押収し、ドイツ軍を壊滅状態にした一方、第一〇〇大隊の犠牲は戦死四人、負傷七人に留まった(70)。この戦闘で、第一〇〇大隊は、部隊としての叙勲では最高の第一回目の大統領殊勲感状を得ている。

叙勲式で第五軍司令官のマーク・クラーク中将は、「日本人を祖先に持つアメリカ人の諸君は、本日、誇り高いアメリカ人として戦ったのだ。もう一つ、諸君に思って良いことがある。それは諸君が米陸軍の高い水準に達したことだ。第三四師団は諸君を誇りに思っている。第五軍は諸君を誇りに思っている。アメリカは諸君を誇りに思っている(71)」と演説した。クラーク中将のワンプカプカの兵士に感動したというワンプカプカの兵士は多い。

九月末、彼らは連合軍が苦戦していたフランスのブリエア戦線に参戦するために、戦闘半ばでイタリアを離れた。アイゼンハワー元帥から「日系部隊を前線に出せ」との要請が入ったのだ。前線に出てから約一年で、日系部隊はすべての司令官が欲しがる部隊となっていた。

イタリアで降服したドイツ兵を警護する第100大隊の日系兵。German Soldiers being captured in Italy escorted by Japanese American Soldiers in the100th batalion. Courtesy of Go For Broke National Education Foundation.

米軍史に残る戦い

「失われた大隊」救出

第四二連隊は海路でマルセイユから上陸すると北上し、第三六師団に配属された。第三六師団はテキサス師団とも呼ばれ、イタリア戦線で第四二連隊が属した第三四師団とはサレルノからともに戦ってきた仲間で、カッシーノ戦では二個連隊がほぼ全滅するという犠牲を出した師団だ。激戦地を生き延びた彼らが再会を果たしたのは、ドイツ国境に近い

38

ボージュ山脈だった。ボージュ山脈は険しい山岳地帯ではないが、高い針葉樹がうっそうと森を覆い、森の中は日中でも日がささない。ドイツでこの辺り一帯を「黒い森」と呼ぶ由縁だ。

ボージュ山脈の山間の町ブリエアは、人口四千人の小さな町だったが、主要幹線が通っているためにナチ親衛隊SSが牛耳っていた要所でもあった。ボージュの森を越えればドイツに入るため、ヒトラーが「何があっても撤退は許さぬ。死守せよ」と命じていた。四年におよぶドイツの占領下にあって、町の人々は息を潜めて連合軍の到着を待っていたが、多くの師団がこの「黒い森」でドイツ軍の激しい抵抗に遭い足止めを食い、一九四四年八月二五日にパリ入城を果たした連合軍も、この地帯はいまだ突破できずにいた。

ボージュの森には無数の地雷が仕掛けられ、現在でも危険で中に入れない。しとしとと冷たい雨が降り続き、寒さと湿気で多くの兵士が塹壕足と呼ばれる凍傷になった。砲弾が頭上で炸裂すると、裂けた木片が武器となって降り注ぐ。敵は前だけでなく、左右後からも狙っており、どこから砲弾が打ち込まれるかわからない。そんな中、第四四二連隊は十月一九日、ついにブリエアに抜けた[72]。「米軍が来た！」のニュースは人々が隠れる地下室を這うように駆け巡ったが、森から姿を現した米兵の顔には度肝を抜かしたという。米兵は白人の大男だと思っていたのに、「OK」を連発しながら笑って近づく小柄な兵士は日本人の顔をしていたからだ。だが町の人々は米軍の軍服を着た日本兵の姿に歓喜した。

第三六師団長は、ジョン・ダールキスト少将。イギリスの司令部でアイゼンハワー元帥の下に長く居た人物で、第三六師団に着任してまだ二ヶ月足らずだった。終戦は時間の問題であったこの時期、師団長にドイツ入城一番乗りを果たしたいという野望がなかったとはいい切れない。ダールキストは前線に出て細かい指示を与え、無理な前進を要求した。ブリエアを解放した直後、捕虜と負傷兵を連れていた一部の第一〇〇大隊がビフォンテンを過ぎた森で敵に包囲されかけたのも、師団長の出した無謀な前進命令が原因だった。この時、十人以上が捕虜に取られている。

そのころテキサス兵からなる第一四一連隊の第一大隊が、やはりビフォンテンを過ぎたあたりで身動きできなくなっていた。ブリエアを解放した後、休息のためにベルモント村に入ったばかりの第四四二連隊に、その翌日さっそく救出出動準備命令が出た。

第一〇〇大隊のシングルス隊長は、なぜ彼らが敵地に紛れ込んでしまったのか手に取るように理解できたという。だがシングルス隊長が理解できなかったのは、充分な休息を取った部隊は他にもいたのに、なぜまた前線から戻ってきたばかりの日系部隊が、救出に借り出されるのか、ということだった。これに関しては、「他に十分な休息を取っていた連隊はたくさんいたのに人種差別だ」という意見と、「最も困難な状況では最強の部隊を出すもの」という声があるが、真相はわかっていない。

十月二十六日の早朝、まず第二大隊に出動命令が出て、翌日の午前四時、ベルモント村に残っていた第一〇〇大隊と第三大隊が出動している[73]。未明の森の中は、自分の手の先も見えないほどの暗闇だった。「前を歩く人の肩に手を置いて歩かなければばならなかった。誰が先頭なのかわからないし、そいつはどうやって行き先がわかるのかも不思議だった。野戦装備の荷物が肩に食い込み、疲れ切っていて、僕たちは彷徨う幽霊のようだった」[74]と述懐したのはジョン・ツカノさんだ。

テキサス部隊のニュースは、「失われた大隊」としてすぐさま全米に発信された。「失われた大隊」の救出には、ダールキスト師団長の軍人生命がかかって

'失われた大隊' 救出後、ブリエア、フランスで戦功をたたえる式典で整列する第442連隊。（国立公文書）442nd RCT color guards stand at attention while their citation are read in Bruyers, France. Source: National Archives.

いたといえる。これまでも前線に細かい指示を出し続けてきたダールキストだが、この時は自ら副師団長として前線に出向いて、塹壕で銃を構える日系兵をそこから追い立てている。絶叫しながら破れかぶれの突撃をする日系兵士の「バンザイ・チャージ」が登場するのは、この戦闘においてだ。

「突然血にまみれたゆがんだ口から『お母さん』という声が聞こえた。戦友もその声を聞いたというが、声が細くてはっきりとは聞き取れない。不安が走った。今までの経験から、戦場で重傷を負った日系兵士が死に際に口にするのは、たいてい『お母さん…』だからだ(75)」と振り返ったのはロバート・サトーさんだ。

炸裂する砲弾の中を駆け抜けること六日間。十月三〇日、第一〇〇大隊B中隊が最後の地雷原を突破して失われた大隊にたどり着き、第三大隊のI中隊とK中隊もほぼ同時に到着した(76)。だが日系部隊の任務はここで終わったわけではない。救出されて山を下りるテキサス兵とは裏腹に、日系兵士には「さらに前進せよ」との命令が師団長から出ていた。日系部隊にようやく「後退」命令が出たのは、それから約十日後のことだ(77)。こうして同じテキサス連隊の仲間でさえ助け出せなかった「失われた大隊」は、第四二連隊によって救出された。

「失われた大隊救出作戦」で出動した時点で、第一〇〇大隊A中隊第三小隊のうちキャンプ・マッコイから一緒だった同期は、すでに二人しか残っておらず、そのどちらも「失われた大隊」を見ることはなかった(78)。第一〇〇大隊全体で見ても、ヨーロッパ戦線最初の上陸地点である「サレルノから上陸した」といえる兵士は十人足らず。兵力のほとんどは後から送られた補充兵になっていた。一八五人で出陣した第三大隊I中隊は、わずか八人しか残っていなかった(79)。

三日後、戦功を讃える儀式に集まった日系兵士を前に、ダーキスト師団長は苦々しく言った。「連隊を全員集合させろと命令したはずだ」。中佐が師団長の眼をとらえてきっぱりと答えた。「彼らが連隊の全員です。残りは戦死したか、病院の中です(80)」。

ボージュの森に入って以来、ほぼ休みなしに戦い続けた三四日間で、日系部隊はブリエアを解放し、二一一人のテキサス兵を救出し、その後九日間におよぶ前進を続けた。この間に日系部隊が出した戦死者は二一六人、負傷者八五六人以上。兵力は半分以下になっていた(81)。現在ブリエアには、解放を記念して「リベラシオン（解放）通り」と名づけられた道は「第四四二連隊通り」だ。森の入り口に建つ記念碑には「国への忠誠とは、人種のいかんに関わらないことを改めて教えてくれた米軍第四四二連隊の兵に捧げる(82)」と刻んである。

ゴシックラインと ダッハウ強制収容所

一九四五年三月二五日、第四二連隊の主要部隊はフランスを離れ、極秘でイタリアに呼び戻された(83)。彼らがフランスで戦っていた八ヶ月間、連合軍はイタリア北部に張られたドイツ軍の防衛線「ゴシックライン」を突破できずにいた。ゴシックラインは、三千フィート級の切り立った山々を巧妙に利用したドイツ軍最後の砦といわれ、山頂の要塞から数キロ先まで見渡せたため、連合軍は近づくことすらできなかった。

そこで上層部は、第四二連隊を動員して、夜間ひそかに山を登り、夜明けと共に攻撃を開始する奇襲作戦に出ることにした。日系兵士たちは移動中に音を出さないように、胸に吊るした認識章まで軍服に縫い付けて*、四月五日の夜、敵の要塞を三方から囲むような形で登り始めた。数千人もの兵士が一切音を立てずに、傾斜の厳しい山を登るのは容易ではない。ある兵士は足を滑らせ三百フィートも転げ落ちたが、声ひとつ上げなかったという(84)。特に後方からの進行は、六〇度の傾斜を八時間も登り続ける険しい道のりであった(85)。

夜明け前、敵の背後に配置した部隊が計画通り攻撃を開始すると、周りで待機していた部隊も一斉に攻撃に加わった。奇襲作戦は見事成功し、三二分で要塞を占拠すると、その後も休みない攻撃を浴びせ続け、同日夜にはゴシックライン突破を果たした(86)。

*元４４２連隊のテツオ・アサトさん証言。2005年6月20日、Go For Broke National Education Center にて取材

クラーク中将から「日系部隊が来たからには、せめて一週間で突破できれば」という期待を背負って挑んだ戦闘であったが、第四四二連隊が要した日数はわずか一日であった。

ゴシックラインの戦功で第四四二連隊配属の第二三二戦闘工兵隊は、アイゼンハワー参謀総長から大統領冠状を受勲している。

第四四二連隊の本隊がイタリアに再上陸したころ、第五五二野砲大隊は第四四二連隊を離れ、連合軍の南ドイツ進行に加わり、必要に応じて各師団を移転しながら、ドイツ国内を進撃していった。

四月二九日、ミュンヘン東部を偵察していた彼らは、想像を絶する光景に遭遇する[89]。有刺鉄線の張り巡らされたゲートの中に、目が落ち込み、髪は剃

1946 年 7 月 15 日、トルーマン大統領より大統領感状を叙勲する第442 連隊。（国立公文書）　On July 15, 1946, 442nd RCT is awarded the presidential citation by President Harry S. Truman. Source: National Archive

られ、骨と皮になった囚人服姿のユダヤ人たちを見つけたのだ。そこは、計二〇万人以上が収容されたダッハウ強制収容所に付属する労働キャンプであった。キャンプの人々を保護した後、彼らはオーストリア国境近くで、ナチ親衛隊により「死の行進」に追い立てられ、瀕死の状態にあった人々も救助している[90]。

どの米軍部隊をダッハウ強制収容所の「解放者」とするかは、現在でも論議を呼んでいる。一九八五年、全米ホロコースト記念博物館がその栄誉を称えたのは、第四二歩兵師団などわずかであった。だが反論を含め、あまりに反響が高かったため、米軍史センター博物館は二年以内に「解放者」のガイドラインを定め、認定基準を師団レベルに限定した[91]。第五五二野砲部隊は師団ではないため、「解放者」とは認定されていない[92]。

ダッハウが解放された翌日の一九四五年四月三〇日、ヒトラーは自殺を遂げ、五月七日、ドイツは全面降伏し、ヨーロッパ戦線の勝利に全米が歓喜した。

第四四二連隊の「忠誠を証明」するための戦いは終わったが、日系社会には、まだ重要な使命が残っていた。アメリカ市民としての権利の獲得である。戦後、日系社会は新たな戦いに挑むことになる。

◆第三章

自由と平等の追求

一九四五年以降

終戦直後の1945年9月6日、ロスアンゼルスのパン・パシフィック博覧会でWRAと人種差別反対グループがスポンサーした "Americans All" のブースの日系女性たち。（カリフォルニア大学バンクロフト図書館）

CONTENTS

二世兵士たちの勇気と犠牲を無駄にしないためにも、日系社会は戦後すぐに日系部隊の功績を基盤にして、自由と平等を勝ち取るための運動を展開していった。数々の差別法を撤廃し、帰化権を勝ち取り、移民法改定を達成した陰には、日系人リーダーたちとともに闘った数多くの一般市民の支援があった。

日系兵の武勲を
伝えた人たち

終戦の翌一九四六年七月十五日、第四四二連隊はホワイトハウスの庭で、ハリー・S・トルーマン大統領から第七回目の大統領感状を授与された。この時、大統領は「諸君は敵だけでなく偏見とも戦い、勝ったのだ[1]」と演説した。第四四二連隊は、その戦力が四五〇〇人を超えたことはなかったが、死傷率は三〇〇％を超え、第四四二連隊と第一〇〇大隊の獲得した個人的勲章は一万八一四三個にのぼった[2]。日系部隊は、その規模と従軍期間では米軍史上もっとも多くの

犠牲者を出し、もっとも多くの勲章に輝いた部隊となった[3]。数ある帰還部隊の中で、大統領から直々に叙勲したのは日系部隊だけだった[4]。

終戦前年の一九四四年には、タイム誌など日系部隊の活動と犠牲を伝える報道が多くなり、それに比例して日系人擁護の意見が目立つようになっていた。ミネソタ州のウォルター・H・ジャッド下院議員やマサチューセッツ州のトーマス・J・レーン下院議員は、各誌の報道や日系部隊の記録を引用して下院議事録に掲載した[5]。第四四二連隊第二大隊司令官のジェームス・M・ハンレイ中佐は、「善良なジャップ・アメリカンがいるというが、どこに埋葬されているかわからない」とコラムに書いた彼の出身地の新聞、デイリー・パイオニア紙のチャールズ・ピーアス編集長に、抗議の手紙を送っている。「善良な日系アメリカ人がどこにいるか僕はよく知っている。本隊には五千人くらいいる。(中略)君やフッドリバー在郷軍人会支部、ハースト系新聞、その他の何人かの連中は我々がいったい何のために戦っているのかを疑わせる。まさか人種偏見の支援戦争ではないだろう。そうでないことを望む。ここに来てみろよ、チャーリー。『善良なジャップ・アメリカン』が埋葬されているところに案内するよ[6]」。この手紙は一九四四年三月三一日同紙に掲載された。

ハンレイ中佐の手紙にあるフッドリバー在郷軍人会支部とは、栄誉名簿から日系兵の名前を外して大問題になったオレゴン州にある支部のことだ。同支部は出兵したフッドリバー出身者を栄誉名簿に載せて、市庁前に大きく掲載したが、同地出身の日系兵一六人の名前を削除した[7]。また同支部は地元紙の広告欄を使って、収容所から出てくる日系人に対し「オレゴンに土地を所有している日系人は、土地を売って当地に戻らないように」と訴えた。その事実を指摘したのは、軍の報道機関であるスターズ・アンド・ストライプス紙だ。そして記事を読んで激怒したのは他でもない、第四四二連隊とともに戦った第三六師団や第四五師団の米兵たちだった。その中には日系兵によって救出された「失われた大隊」の兵士たちもいた。フランクリン・D・ルーズベルト大統領や議員、全米在郷軍人会本部へ抗議の手紙を出す運動が起こり、それがニュースとなって報道された[8]。すると全米各地の支部から非難が集まり、数週間後には全米在郷軍人会の会長が、フッドリバー支部に日系兵の名前を復活させるように指示を出す事態となった。

一般市民の中に染み込んだ反日感情はすぐに払拭されたわけではないが、日系部隊の活躍が伝えられるようになると徐々に、だが確実に、日系人を応援するアメリカ人は増えていった。特に日系兵と同様に命をかけて戦った軍人たちは日系兵への擁護を惜しまず、それがニュースとなって流れた。たとえばこんな事件がスターズ・アンド・ストライプス紙に掲載された。第四四二連隊の帰還兵が、テキサスのある街で軍服姿でバーに入ろうとした。するとバーテンダーは「ジャップは出て行け」と怒鳴り追い出そうとしたが、そこで飲んでいた客に元テキサス部隊の兵士たちがいた。彼らはバーテンダーをカウンターから引きずり出して袋叩きにすると、自らカウンターに入って日系兵の注文を受けたという[9]。

第四四二連隊の一員としてヨーロッパ戦線に参戦し、右腕を失ったダニエル・イノウエ上院議員は、軍服姿のままハワイの帰りに立ち寄ったサンフランシスコの理髪店で、「ジャップの髪は切らない」と断られた。帰還兵に対する同じような行為は各地で起こっていた[10]。だがそれが報道されると、今度は反対に日系兵を支援する同じような行為は各地で起こっていた。カリフォルニア州ストックトンで日本人墓地を荒らす反日勢力に対抗して、墓石を修復し、墓地を清掃したのは、太平洋戦線で戦った帰還兵二八人だ。彼らは大学に通いながら、「日系兵たちが帰ってくるまで続ける」と奉仕した。サンフランシスコ・クロニクル紙は、一面でこれを伝えた（一九四五年七月二〇日号）[11]。

ヨーロッパ戦線における日系部隊の功績は、それを語る者がいて初めて世間に知れ渡る。その役割を果たしたのが、日系部隊同様に戦場で生死を分け合った米兵であり、それを全米に伝えた報道機関であり、その報道を議事録に掲載した政治家であった。

パールハーバー攻撃を伝える報道に始まって、地元でありながら戦時中も「ジャップ」という言葉の使用を決して許さなかったのは、ホノルル・スターブルテン紙のライリー・アレン編集長だ。パールハーバー攻撃時、同紙には二人の日系編集者がいたが、開戦後も彼らは編集者として勤務し続けた。全米各紙が一面で彼らを「ジャップ」と伝える中、日系人を含む

最高裁に挑んだ
強制収容問題

終戦の前年、一九四四年十二月、「ジャップはジャップだ[13]」の発言で物議をかもした西部地区防衛司令官のデウィット中将が転任になり、プラット少将が後任に就くと、十七日には日系人立ち退き令の廃止を決定し、翌年一月二日より発効した[14]。これを受けてWRAは一八日に、一九四五年末を持って収容所を閉鎖し、WRAの任務は一九四六年六月末で終了すると発表した[15]。日系人収容に終止符を打つことが決定したこの日、日系人の強制収容に関する重大な判決が二件、最高裁判所で下されている。

一件はフレッド・コレマツ裁判で、立ち退きを拒否して逮捕されたコレマツが、日系人立ち退き令は違憲であると訴えていたものだ。この訴えに対し最高裁判所は「戦時においては市民の人権よりも国益が上回る」として、コレマツの訴えを退けた。だが最高裁は、もう一件のエンドー裁判については政府の違憲性を認めた。エンドー裁判は強制立ち退きを拒否して訴えたのではなく、法令に従った上で違憲性を訴えたもので、最高裁は「忠実な市民を公聴会なしに拘束した軍部は法律で許される範囲を逸脱し

てしまった。そこでパーセルは、民事の人身保護法

違反で訴えるのに最適な収容者探しに乗り出した。

当時二二歳のミツエ・エンドーは、サクラメント在住のカリフォルニア州DMV（陸運局）職員で、クリスチャンとして育てられ、日本語は話すこともミノル・ヤスイがやはり強制立ち退きや夜間外出禁読むこともできず、日本へ行ったこともなかった。さらに兄弟の一人がアメリカ兵として出兵していた。

パーセルはエンドーと会ったことはなかったが、書簡で起訴への同意を取り付けた。起訴の後、WRAは和解策としてエンドーに軍事指定地域以外への移住許可を与えた。だがエンドーは収容所に残って、最高裁によって収容に対する違憲性を問う道を選んだ。エンドー裁判は、強制立ち退き、収容の違憲性に挑戦して勝訴した最初の意義ある裁判となったが、エンドー自身は裁判所にも出頭せず、勝訴した後も

ている」との判断を下した[16]。エンドー裁判とコレマツ裁判の違いは、刑事事件か民事事件かの違いだった。コレマツ裁判以外にもゴードン・ヒラバヤシ、止令に故意に違反して大統領命令第九〇六六号やその他の法令の違憲性を訴える裁判を起こしていたが、この三件はいずれも刑事事件として裁かれた。だがエンドー裁判は違った。

エンドー裁判の発端は、カリフォルニア州人事担当局が日系職員に向けて質問状を送ったことに始まる。州職員は法律によりアメリカ市民でなければならない。にもかかわらず州人事担当局は開戦後、日系人職員に対して天皇への忠誠度、日本語の読み書き、日本へ行ったことがあるか、などの質問状を出して、日系職員の解雇を検討したが、それは州検事局長アール・ウォレン（後のカリフォルニア州知事で第一四代連邦最高裁判長）の警告により断念したという経緯があった。このころは州上院議員の間にも日系職員の解雇を求める声が出ており、二世の職員たちは不安な毎日を過ごしていた。

強制立ち退きが始まると、人事担当局はサクラメントの日系職員を全員停職にし、職務怠慢、不正就職、などの理由で起訴した。そこでJACLは、日系人に好意的なサンフランシスコのジェームス・パーセル弁護士に依頼して、停職になった職員たちの権利を奪回しようとしたが、計画を実行に移すよりも早く立ち退き、収容が実施され

編集員たちが「ジャップ」の使用を求める嘆願書をアレンに提出したときも、彼は「ジャパニーズ」と綴る方針を貫いた[12]。

強制収容問題で最高裁が初めて違憲性をみとめたエンドウ裁判の原告、ミツエ・エンドウ。（国立公文書）The Supreme Court found the government's actions unconstitutional in case with Mitsue Endo. Source: National Archive

人前に出ることはなかった。

コレマツ裁判など敗訴した三件も、一九四五年には早くもエール大学法律大学院のユージン・ロストウ教授が、最高裁の判決を「戦時中の最大の過ち」[17]と非難している。

戦後の平等への戦いにおいて、JACLの果たした功績は大きい。開戦時、JACLは一部の二世たちを会員とした日本人組織で、サブロー・キド会長をはじめマイク・マサオカ事務局長などのリーダーもほとんどがまだ二〇代という若い二世たちの集まりだった。指導者的立場にいた一世たちは開戦直後にことごとく検挙されたため、激動の歴史の中で若い彼らが日系人としての方針を決定せざるを得なかったのだ。強制立ち退きに従おうと日系社会に呼びかけた彼らの判断は、結果的には正しかったが、当時は必ずしも日系社会の全面的な支持を得ていたわけではない。だが彼らは信念を貫き、戦後は日系社会を主導して積極的な活動を行った。キドは有能な弁護士で、マサオカは優秀なロビイストであった。さらに日系人の人権を守るために貢献したパーセル弁護士、のちに国務長官となったディーン・アチソン弁護士などの協力を得て、JACLは次々に不正法改正に挑戦していった。

JACL会長、マイク・マサオカ。
（カリフォルニア州立大学サクラメント校図書館提供）

外国人土地法を廃案にした州民

JACLの支援で外国人土地法に挑み、勝訴したのはオーヤマ裁判だ。フレッド・オーヤマはカリフォルニア州に農地を所有していた。オーヤマが未成年の時に、一世である父親がオーヤマ名義で購入したものだ。ところが、土地購入時にオーヤマは未成年であったという理由で、この土地は州政府の没収の対象になった。第一章で述べたように、カリフォルニアには一世の土地所有を禁止する州法があったため、市民である二世名義で土地を購入する人が多かった。だが日系人が収容されている間に、二世が未成年の場合、事実上の所有者は一世であるとして土地を没収するケースが少なくなかった。

オーヤマ親子を支持することにしたJACLは連邦最高裁まで控訴し、弁護をアチソン（オーヤマ裁判に勝訴した翌年、国務次官に任命された）に依頼した。日系人は収容所から出たばかりで、オーヤマ自身もJACLも資金がなかったが、この件に違憲性を見出したアチソンは、無償で弁護を引き受けた[18]。オーヤマ裁判が連邦最高裁で勝訴したのは、一九四八年一月十九日のことだ。しかしこれはオーヤマ個人の勝利であって、外国人土地法はまだ存続していた。そこで「加州毎日」編集長の藤井整が、土地法に挑戦するためにロサンゼルスで使い途のない土地を購入して、政府に没収させた。藤井は一世だったが、没収は違憲であると訴え、一九五二年に州最高裁で勝訴した[19]。

だがJACLは当時、藤井の裁判は危険が大きすぎると考えていた。外国人土地法は住民投票によってできた法律のため、改正や発案を決定するにも住民投票によって決定されなければならず、JACLではこの法律そのものの効力を失効する廃止案を住民投票にかけようと動いていた。事務局長マサオカの作戦は、「失われた大隊」救出作戦で戦死した兄ベンの戦死支給金で土地を買って家を建て、それを彼の母親に贈ることだった。マサオカは土地譲渡の契約を済ませた上で裁判にかけ、「日本人であるがために、母親に土地を贈る行為が違法になるのは不当だ」と主張した[20]。一九五〇年、ロサンゼルス高等裁判所は外国人土地法は違憲であるとの判決を下した。

州政府は州最高裁に控訴したが、そこでも違憲であることが認められ、一九五六年、ついにJACLは州議会に働きかけて外国人土地法廃止案を提議十三として住民投票に持ち込んだ。大多数の賛成により廃案が決定したのは同年十一月のことだ[21]。一九一三年に最初の土地法が制定されて以来、廃案になるまで四三年もかかったが、住民投票で賛同を得たことの意義は大きかった。

四三年もの長い年月の中で、第二次世界大戦まで

の約三〇年間は、激しい排日運動が展開されていた。戦前、日系人は二等市民であり、戦時中は敵性外国人だった。それが戦後の約十年で、住民投票で大半の賛同を得るまで世論が変わったのだ。日系部隊の勇気と犠牲の上に成り立った実績が基盤になったのはいうまでもないが、それを世論に広めるためにWRAは、第四四二連隊やMISの帰還兵を派遣したり記者会見を開いたりして、一般社会に功績を認識させようと努力した。

日系人の強制収容を管理したWRAの歴代長官が、戦時中から日系人の社会復帰を支援していたことは第二章で述べたが、WRAは日系兵士の武勲を広めて一般社会の理解を促すと同時に、収容所閉鎖にともなう日系人の処遇にも心を砕いた。復帰に際して、一人につき二五ドルの支給金を支給したが、それ以外にも収容所内に福祉局の職員を置いて、帰る家のない人には最低限の家具を購入する費用や、最初の家賃の補助金などを支給した[22]。西海岸支部は、日系人に好意的な地元の教会や諸団体に働きかけ、主要都市に十箇所以上の簡易宿泊所を開設し、受け入れ体制を整えた。また収容所で余った日常生活品をこれらの施設に貸し出した[23]。

マイヤー長官は、終戦の一九四五年八月、日系兵に向けて以下のような声明を発信している。「転住センターにいる君たちの家族が、君たちの助けがなくとも無事に再定住できるように、我々はあらゆる努力を惜しまないことを知ってもらいたい。そして君たちが帰還する時には、家族はバラックを出て、君たちと呼べる場所に帰ることができるよう、でき限りのことをするつもりだ[24]。」収容を管轄するマイヤーのせめてもの思いやりが透けて見える。

スムーズな
復帰への支援

しかし政府の支援をもってしても、世論を変えるのは、時間のかかる地道な運動の繰り返しであった。収容所から戻ってきた日本人たちを温かく迎えてくれた地域があった一方、日本人の再定住に反対した地域も少なくない。

北イタリアで戦死したカズオ・マスダ軍曹の遺族は、ロサンゼルス近郊の家に戻ろうとして激しい排斥運動に遭った。様子を見に帰った姉のメアリーが、地元の人たちに「戻ってきたら殺す」と脅された直後のことで、マスダ軍曹の遺灰を埋葬しようとすると市は許可を出さなかった[25]。ヨーロッパ戦が終結した直後のこの姉弟二人がまだ軍に籍を置いていた。

マスダ軍曹は戦死する数日前に、四四二連隊の広報担当だったマイク・マサオカにこう語っていた。「四四二連隊の兵士たちが戦地でその価値を証明すれば、アメリカにいる家族の立場が良くなるはずだと確信している[26]」。マスダ軍曹のこの言葉は、日系兵

そこで軍部は脅迫事件を逆手にとって、マスダ軍曹への殊勲十字章の叙勲式に、ビルマ戦線などで活躍し国民に人気の高かったジョセフ・スチルウェル将軍を出席させて式典を行った。将軍はマスダ家の小さな農家の前で、メアリーの腕に勲章をつけた後、サンタアナボウルで行われた式典で、「アメリカニズムとは、金額や肌の色で測れるものではない」とスピーチした。将軍に続いて、映画俳優の若い将校が政治家人生において、これがレーガンの最初の政治色を帯びた演説となった。

ナルド・レーガンだった。この時レーガン大尉は、「海岸の砂を染める血の色は、同じ一つの色である[27]」と名台詞を残している。図らずもその後に続く長い政治家人生において、これがレーガンの最初の政治色を帯びた演説となった。

強制収容に踏み切った当時と相反して、軍部は日系人の復帰を積極的に支援した。この時、軍の最高司令官である大統領はトルーマンであった。トルーマン大統領は在任中、均等雇用法など人権問題に積極的に取り組んだ人権派で、日系人強制立ち退き令には批判的だったといわれる。一九四八年四月には、立ち退き令によって生じた損害を裁定するための立ち退き賠償委員会の設置案を議会に提出し、六月には大統領命令第九七四二号に署名して、WRA機関そのものを解散した[28]。

カリフォルニア州の検事局長として戦時中は日系人立ち退きに強硬派だったアール・ウォーレンも、州知事になると排日運動を非難する立場をとった。一九四五年一月二一日付のサンフランシスコ・エグ

47

ザミナー紙には、収容所から戻ってきた日系人が農地にダイナマイトを仕掛けられたり、放火や発砲された事件が紹介されている。また、同じ紙面にウォーレン知事が記者会見を開いて「善良なアメリカ人を主張する人がそのようなことをするなど考えられない」と反日運動を非難した上で、州に戻ってくる日系人を平穏に受け入れるように呼びかけた記事が掲載されている。(29)

一九四九年にロサンゼルスで開催された全米水泳選手権大会で、日本から特別に参加を許された日本人選手が世界新記録を出した。この時もウォーレン知事は、日本人選手に賛辞を贈ることを忘れなかった。この大会では、一五〇〇メートル自由形で日本人選手が金・銀・銅を独占した。予選で世界新記録を出し、本選でも優勝したのは、「フジヤマのトビウオ」と称して絶賛された古橋広之進だ。当時、まだ連合軍の占領下だった日本は、マッカーサー元帥の特別許可を得て選手団を派遣することができた。(30)ウォーレン知事は、のちに連邦最高裁長官になった。

外国人土地法と同様の趣旨を持つ規定に、漁業許可書の認可を規定する漁業法があった。戦時中、日本人を許可の対象から外す法律が制定されたが、戦後には「日本人」が「アメリカ帰化権を持たない人」と置き換えられて、一世たちの漁業再開を阻止していた。これをロサンゼルス郡高等裁判所に訴えたのは、トラオ・タカハシという一世だった。高等裁判所では勝訴したが、州政府は州最高裁に訴え、ここでは逆転敗訴してしまった。そこで連邦最高裁へ提

訴して勝訴したのは一九四八年のことだ。こうして戦後間もない時期に、次々と人種差別を違憲とする判決が連邦最高裁で出された。(31)

平等と個人の自由を謳うアメリカでも理想と現実の壁は厚く、建国以来、人権問題に関しては紆余曲折の連続だった。エイブラハム・リンカーン大統領の奴隷解放宣言まで百年近い年月を要し、マーチン・ルーサー・キング・ジュニア師が展開した公民権運動まで、さらに、百年を要している。奴隷解放宣言以降も南部諸州に根強く残っていた人種差別に関するさまざまな法律の中で、差別撤廃の大きな節目となったのは、一九五四年の最高裁の判決だったといわれている。これは、アフリカ系と白人を区別したものを連邦最高裁が下したものだ。人種差別は、アフリカ系あるいはアジア系だけの問題ではない。だがそれだけに根が深い。ただ白人が大多数を占める国で、一般社会の認識を変え、世論を変えていくことは、善意ある白人からの強力な支援なしには難しい。日系人が戦後、比較的早く多くの権利を勝ち取った陰に、そうした善意あるアメリカ人が多くいたことを知っておきたい。

親たちのために
勝ち取った帰化権

戦後、JACLが最優先課題として取り組んだのが、高齢の親たち、一世に帰化権を与える移民法の改正だった。そこでJACLは差別撤回委員会を設置し、マイク・マサオカが委員長に就任して、ロビー活動を行うことにした。(32)日系人に好意的だったミネソタ州のジャッド下院議員やペンシルベニア州のフランシス・ウォルター下院議員の協力を得て、一九四八年、ジャッド議員が人種に差別なく帰化権を与える法案を提出した。公聴会では第五軍司令官だったクラーク中将や、日系部隊設立に尽力したマクロイが二世兵士たちの戦功を讃え、犠牲を評価して、その親は帰化権を与えられるべきだとの考えを明白にした。(33)だがこの時は、本会議で表決されるまでには至らなかった。

翌一九四九年、ジャッド議員は再度法案を提出した。WRA長官であったマイヤーは七月十九日、「先の戦争で、太平洋戦での情報兵として、またヨーロッパ線での第四四二連隊として志願した日系兵たちは、戦死しても所有する土地を両親に遺すこともできないことを承知の上で戦っていた。収容所にいた一世の多くは三〇年から四〇年もアメリカで生活していた人たちだ。その中で忠誠宣言をしなかった人たちは、日本国籍を失うことを恐れていたに過ぎない。なぜなら彼らはアメリカに帰化できないことを認識していたからだ(34)」と訴え、法案を支持する書簡を

48

上院司法委員会に提出している。だがこの法案は、下院で可決されたものの上院では否決となった。

一九五〇年には、今度はウォルター議員が法案を提出した。この法案は、人種差別に関する一項を巡って上下院を往復した後、ようやく両院で可決されたが、トルーマン大統領に拒否されてしまった（35）。上下院を往復した間に盛り込まれた国家安全保障の条項に、トルーマン大統領は反対したのだ。五〇年代は冷戦に突入しており、マッカーシー上院議員のレッドパージ（赤狩り）が公然と行われていた時代で、移民にからむ国家安全保障の条項は微妙な問題だったが、トルーマン大統領はいかなる理由であろうとも、差別は撤廃すべきだと考えていた。

一九五一年、上院ではネバダ州のパット・マッカラン議員が法案を提出し、下院ではウォルター議員、ジャッド議員、イリノイ州のシドニー・R・イェーツ議員、カリフォルニア州のジョージ・ミラー議員が総合的な法案を共同提出した。ウォルター案は四月二五日に採択され、上院でもマッカラン案が五月二一日に採択された。その後、ウォルター案とマッカラン案の審議が両院の合同協議にかけられ、六月九日、HR五六七八号法案として採択された（36）。これが、ウォルター＝マッカラン法案だ。

この法案は、移民と帰化に関する人種差別を撤廃する一方で、破壊活動を行った移民を、帰化市民であっても強制送還できる権限を司法省に与える案だった（37）。移民割り当てが不均等で、日本人の新たな移民割り当ては年間わずか一八五人と少なく、（38）日系社会が望んでいた法案に比べると完全なものではなかったが、日系社会にとって何よりも急務だったのは、高齢化する一世たちに帰化権を与えることであった。そこでJACLはこの法案を支持することにし、活発にロビー活動を行った。その結果、法案は両院を通過したが、またしてもトルーマン大統領に拒否された（39）。人種間の移民割り当て率が不均等であること、また国家安全保障条項が複雑すぎることが理由だった。

だが一世たちに残された時間が少なく、休会を目前に控えて来期まで延期という事態を避けたかった。マサオカたちは、拒否権を覆すには、両院で三分の二以上の賛成票が必要だ。下院では、ウォルター議員をはじめ賛成派の議員たちがそれぞれ日系兵たちの武勲を持

1954年の民主党革命で選出された、統治領ハワイ下院議員たち33名中14名が日本人。Source: Hawaii House of Representatives.

ち出し、議会の賛成を求めた。下院は予想通り三分の二を上回る賛成票で通過したが、問題は翌日に予定されている上院での表決だった。最初の表決では半数をわずかに上回った程度で、三分の二を超える可能性は五分五分であった。ここでマサオカのロビー活動は頂点を迎える。マサオカは、日系人には好意的だが国家安全保障条項の件で大統領の拒否権を支持しそうな議員を回って、表決への欠席を依頼した（40）。結果は五七対二六で、辛うじて三分の二を確保し法案は通過した（41）。欠席して投票しなかった議員は十三人であった。

これによって一世たちにアメリカ市民になる権利が与えられ、少人数ながらも、一九二四年以来禁止されていた日本人の移民が認められたのだ。

一七九〇年に制定された最初の帰化法から、南北戦争を経てアフリカ系が帰化権を得るまで八〇年かかったが、日本人が帰化権を得るには、それからさらに八二年を要した。マッカラン＝ウォルター法が発効するや、一世たちはただちに帰化を申請した。同法が発効になった一九五二年には四〇人、一九五四年には六七五〇人、一九五五年には七五三人もの一世が市民権を取得した。一九五三年に市民権を取得した一世の在米平均年数は三八・六年だった（42）。ちなみにこの年は、日米関係にとっても新たな時代への第一歩を踏み出した年だった。日米講和条約の締結は前年の一九五一年だったが、連合軍の占領が正式に終わったのは一九五二年四月二八日で、同日、対日平和条約および日米安全保障

ハワイの州昇格がもたらした影響

一九五九年、日系社会にとって画期的な出来事が起こった。統治領に過ぎなかったハワイが、五〇番目の州として正式に合衆国に加えられたのだ。全米で唯一、アジア系が大多数を占め、なかでも日系人がもっとも多いハワイの州昇格に対して、連邦会議では慎重派も少なくなかった。この時、ジャッド議員など日系人に好意的な議員とともに州昇格に尽力したのは、戦後のハワイ社会で頭角を現していた日系二世の代議員たちだった。二世の代議員が戦後急増した理由に、GIビルと一九五四年にハワイで起こった「民主党革命」がある。

GIビルとは、退役軍人の恩給として支給される教育費のことで、戦後日系兵の多くがGIビルを利用して大学へ進み、ハワイで要職に就いていた。その現象を最大限に利用して民主党革命を起こしたのが、ジャック・バーンズだった(43)。

それまでにハワイ政界は、ビッグ・ファイブと呼ばれるプランテーション所有者の支持する共和党で占められていた。そんな金持ちに有利な政策に対して、長年ホノルル警察の警察官を務め、当時ハワイ民主党議長だったジャック・バーンズが、一九五四年の選挙に多数の日系人を立候補させて大改革を仕

人物コラム

揺れる日系社会の機動力になったJACL事務局長マイク・マサオカ

なかには差別をする人がいるかもしれません。だが私はそれで敵意を抱いたり、信念を失ったりはしません。なぜなら差別をする人が、大半のアメリカ国民ではないことを知っているからです。

（一九四一年五月十九日に上院議会で読み上げ、議事録に記録された「日系アメリカ人の信条」より）

一九四二年十一月、ソルトレイクシティーで開催されたJACL総会で、もっとも重要な議題は、日系人に対する選抜徴兵制の復活を政府に要求するかどうかであった(1)。強制収容や敵性外国人扱いなどで、人々の政府に対する不満が鬱積していた時だった。それを承知の上で、差別的な対応のすべてに目をつぶり、国のために死ねる権利を要求しようと呼びかけたのが、JACL事務局長のマイク・マサオカだった。

マサオカは一九一五年、カリフォルニアのフレスノで生まれ、ユタ州ソルトレイクシティーで育った。同三七年、ユタ大学を卒業すると、二五歳でJACL事務局長に就任した(2)。志願兵による日系部隊の設立を聞いたマサオカは、その場で志願兵第一号に名乗り出ている。広報に配属されると、戦闘に出る直前のイタリアで彼は、各大隊から人材を選び、次の任務を託した。第一線で戦っている兵士について表彰の申告をすべて書くこと、それをアメリカの新聞社に送ること、部隊の歴史を記録することであった。

「もしわれわれが優秀な記録を残すことができたら、戦後、政治的に役立つことになる(3)」マサオカはこの時すでに、この戦争は戦後の自由を勝ち取るための戦争なのだと確信し、そのためには組織立った計画が重要だと考えていた。

日系兵の獲得した一万八千個以上の勲章の数は、そのまま彼らの犠牲の数だ。だが日系兵の死を無駄にせず、戦後、その武勲を武器にできたのは、マサオカの先見の明と政治的見解によるところが大きいのではないだろうか。現に二〇〇〇年、最高勲章の採決に人種差別があったと認められた(4)。日系兵たちが当時、どんなに勇敢に戦い、どれほどの犠牲を出していても、マサオカの計画がなかったら、これだけの武勲を記録できたかどうかは疑わしい。

一九六三年にはJACLを代表して、マーチン・ルーサー・キング・ジュニア師と共にワシントン大行進にも参加している(5)。強制収容に同意したことや徴兵制の再導入を要求したことなどで、マサオカに対する反感を払拭できない人がいるのも事実だ。だが、その結果得た功績は、評価に値するのではないだろうか。アメリカへの忠誠を示すために、「二〇〇%」アメリカ人(6)であろうとしたマサオカは、一九九一年、ロビイストとして活躍したワシントンDCで他界した。

掛けた。投票が開票されてみると、統治領下院三〇議席のうち二三議席を民主党が占め、現職の下院議長まで落選するという大逆転を果たした(44)。この選挙で統治領議員に当選した人に、のちに上院議員になったダニエル・イノウエ、スパーク・マツナガ両議員、日系人初の知事となったジョージ・アリヨシなどがいる。バーンズとともに彼ら日系人政治家が大きな牽引力となって、ハワイは州昇格を果たした。バーンズはのちにハワイ州知事になり、一九七四年の選挙で副知事だったアリヨシが後を引き継いだ(45)。

ハワイが州に昇格すると、イノウエ議員は日系初の連邦下院議員に選出された。イノウエ議員がワシントンの議事堂に初登庁した日、議員たちは真新しい州であるハワイ選出の日系議員の宣誓式を、息を潜めて見ていた。「右手を上げて、宣誓の言葉を続けてください」とレイバーン議長が言った。イノウエ議員が上げたのは左手だった。

「イノウエ議員が『議長、右手はありません。第二次大戦で、若きアメリカ兵として戦場で失いました』と答えた途端、会場に重苦しく漂っていた偏見がすっと消えた(46)」と、ニューヨーク州のレオ・オブライエン下院議員は議事録に掲載した。

一九六二年の選挙では、マツナガ議員も連邦下院入りを果たし、イノウエ議員は連邦上院議員に選出された。ハワイからは中国系二世のハイラム・フォングも上院議員として議席を確保しており、JACLはこの三議員に働きかけて、マッカラン=ウォルター法の移民割り当てを是正するための改正に乗り出した(47)。改正案は一九六五年、リンドン・B・ジョンソン大統領によって署名され、ついに人種別割り当てを廃止する移民法が成立した(48)。最初の法案成立後、十年近く改正されなかったマッカラン=ウォルター法の改正案は、日系人政治家の登場で瞬く間に議会を通過し、大統領の署名を得て発効された。日系人の声がワシントンに速やかに届くようになったのは、戦前では考えられない大きな進歩だった。

ハワイの日系人の台頭が目覚ましく、一九六五年にはパッツィー・ミンクが、アジア系女性として初めて連邦下院議員になった(49)。終戦から二〇年で、ハワイから三人の日系政治家が生まれ、カリフォルニア州などでも裁判官や検事、地方自治体、大企業などで日系人が多くの要職に就くようになった。

一方、日本にも大きな変化が起こるようになった。この二〇年で日本は敗戦から立ち直っただけでなく、朝鮮戦争によるいわゆる戦争特需を踏み台にして、一九五五年からの世界的好況の波に乗り、六〇年代には驚異的な高度経済成長を遂げた。一九六四年には、東京オリンピックが開催された。東京の市街地が整備され、東京・大阪間を三時間十分で結ぶ東海道新幹線が開通し、戦後の高度成長に拍車をかけた。そのオリンピックの東京招致に尽力したのは、ロサンゼルス在住の二世、フレッド・ワダだ。前述の全米水泳選手権大会で日本人選手を世話したのがきっかけとなって、のちに東京都知事となった東龍太郎に招致の票集めを要請された。ワダは青果店を何軒も手広く経営しており、メキシコ人の従業員も多かったせいでスペイン語が話せた。そのスペイン語を武器に、夫婦で中南米諸国をすべて自費で各国の政府高官を訪問し、オリンピックの東京招致への協力を要請して回った(50)。

日本は経済力をつけ、六〇年代になると商社や銀行、そして家電や自動車などのメーカーが、アメリカ進出を果たすようになった。だが移民法が改定されていなければ、日本企業は幹部や社員をアメリカに派遣できなかったはずだ。外国人土地法が撤廃されていなければ、倉庫を構え、工場を建てることはできなかったはずだ。マッカラン=ウォルター法や外国人土地法の廃案が、日系企業の進出を可能にしたといっても過言ではない。しかし、日本企業の繁栄の陰に、何年にもわたって差別法撤廃と闘った日系社会の努力があったことを認識していた人は少ない。

三世が促した
謝罪と補償問題

一九七一年、日系人に対して行われたような収容・拘留が二度と起こらないように、マツナガ議員が発起人になって、国内安全保障法に含まれているスパイや工作活動をする可能性がある人を収容・拘留する権限を廃止するための法案を提出した(51)。この法案は圧倒的多数で議決され、リチャード・M・ニクソン大統領の署名によって成立した。

二世リーダーが設立した 敬老シニア・ヘルスケア

コラム

ロサンゼルスのリトルトーキョー東部に、日系シニア用施設がある。池には鯉が泳ぎ、食堂では和食が楽しめる。敬老シニア・ヘルスケアが管理する高齢者用施設だ。日系社会に数々の貢献をしてきた二世たちだが、敬老シニア・ヘルスケアの設立も彼らの功績の一つだ。

きっかけになったのは、二世のフレッド・ワダ夫妻が東京オリンピック誘致の票集めのために、自費を投じて敢行した南米諸国の訪問だった。一九五九年、ワダ夫妻はサンパウロ郊外で病院風の白い大きな建物を見かけた。それがユダヤ人専用の老人ホームだと知ったワダの脳裏に浮かんだのは、高齢化する親の世代、一世たちの姿だ。当時、日系社会にそのような施設はなかった。夫妻は後日、日本領事館に頼んで改めて施設を見学した(1)。

ワダは帰国すると、実業家のジョージ・アラタニなど二世リーダーたちと力を合わせて、一世のために高齢者用施設を設立しようと立ち上がった。非営利団体の日系社会福祉財団を組織し、一九六九年、介護施設の敬老ナーシング・ホームを開設した。同ホームの建築費用として五〇万ドルの融資を受けたが、融資が可能になったのも、ワダやアラタニが自宅を担保として提供したからに他ならない(2)。

敷地三エーカーにあるユダヤ系老人ホームが居抜きで売りに出たのは、ちょうど彼らが、健康な高齢者向け居住施設の建設を検討していた一九七三年の秋だった。ボイルハイツにあるユダヤ系老人ホームの敷地三エーカーに大小十三棟の建物があり、売値は六〇〇万ドル。建物は老朽化していたため、ワダたちは一〇〇万ドルで交渉するつもりだった。それでも

一九七四年当時、一〇〇万ドルもの寄付を募るのは容易ではない。彼らは率先して多額の寄付をし、募金活動に乗り出した。目標達成までにかかった期間は、わずか五ヶ月だった。寄付金集めに無料で奉仕した人数は六〇〇人。

買収の最終交渉の日、ワダは交渉の場にアナウンサーの日系女性を伴った。ユダヤ系老人ホームの理事には、交渉が決裂した場合、寄付してくれた人たちにテレビで返金の旨を伝えるためだと説明した。十七軒の食料関連店を経営し、東京オリンピック誘致やロサンゼルス港湾委員会として数々の交渉を実現してきたワダの最後の賭けだった。作戦は功を奏した。一〇〇万ドルで合意しただけでなく、ワダはこの時ユダヤ系老人ホームの理事から、当初の運営費用として十五万ドルの無利子融資まで取り付けている(4)。

一九七五年、敬老引退者ホームが開館した。その二年後には中間看護施設、さらに五年後には、ガーデナにサウスベイ敬老ナーシング・ホームを開設。現在では、アルツハイマー及び認知症患者専用の施設など数多く有し、高齢者の世話に当たっている(5)。

一九八三年、ロサンゼルスに着任したばかりの松田慶文総領事と面談したワダは、印象深い言葉を残している。「昔苦労した老人たちが安心して住める場所を確保するために、われわれは頑張ってきたつもりです。しかし、老人たちを救うだけが目的ではありません。三世、四世の若者たちに後顧の憂いなくアメリカ社会で仕事をしてもらうためにも、引退者ホームは必要なんです。（中略）おまえたちが失敗しても大丈夫なように、おまえたちの年寄りは全部面倒見てやる、だから失敗を恐れずに思い切って仕事をやれとおまえたちが言うとるんです」(6)。ワダの言葉は、敬老シニア・ヘルスケア設立に尽力した二世リーダーたちの、日系社会にかける情熱を代弁したものに違いない。

※高杉良 著作「祖国へ、熱き心を―東京にオリンピックを呼んだ男」（新潮文庫二〇〇一年十月一日出版）から引用

建国二〇〇周年を迎えた記念すべき一九七六年二月十六日に、ジェラルド・R・フォード大統領は「記念すべき年に、国家の繁栄を祝うだけでなく、国家が犯した過ちを認識することにより、再び同じ過ちを繰り返さないようにしなければならない」(52)と声明を発表して、存続していた第九〇六六号の廃案を宣言した。

フランクリン・D・ルーズベルト大統領が、日系人の強制収容を可能にした大統領令第九〇六六号を発令してからちょうど三四年目だった。強制収容の象徴であったこの法令の廃案により、戦時中の苦い体験の記憶も風化したかに見えたが、実はまだ重大な戦後処理が残っていた。政府による正式謝罪と補償の問題だ。

それが日系社会で形となって現れたのは、一九七八年のJACL全国大会においてだった。同大会でJACLは、強制収容に対する正式謝罪と一人あたり二万五千ドルの補償金を政府に求める決議を採択した(53)。戦後、三〇年近くも補償問題が棚上げされた背景には、一世や二世たちが、収容された事実を「恥」と受け止めて多くを語らなかったという事実があった。親から収容所の話を聞いたことはなかったという三世は少なくない。ところが六〇年代に入って公民権、女

性人権運動、反戦運動などが起こり、社会の風潮が反体制に傾いていくと、若い世代の三世たちは、「なぜ黙って収容されたのか」と親の世代を非難するようになった。そういう社会の流れの中で、補償問題が必然的に持ち上がってきた。時代は三世の世代になり、ワシントンでも若い日系人政治家が頭角を現していた。

一九七五年、ノーマン・ミネタ前運輸長官が、サンホゼ市長から連邦下院議員になった。ミネタ前長官は、日系初の全米主要都市の市長で、本土で選出された連邦議員としても日系初だ。二〇〇〇年にはウィリアム・J・クリントン大統領に任命され、アジア系で初めて官僚入りを果たした。ミネタは十歳の時、ハートマウンテン収容所に送られ、ゲートで野球のバットを没収されたことを覚えていた[54]。翌年、ハワイの上院二議席は日系人で占められ、同州の上院二議席は日系人で占められ、同州下院二議席のうち、一議席をミンク議員が確保していた。

一九七七年には、生後六ヶ月で収容所に入った経験を持つロバート・マツイがカリフォルニアより下院議員に選出された。これで日系人は、上下両院併せて五議席を確保した。この五人のうち、マツナガ議員は第一〇〇大隊編成時の兵士で、二度負傷し、青銅星章を叙勲しており[55]、他の二人は収容所体験者で、あと二人は第二次大戦の退役軍人という顔ぶれだった[56]。

だが補償問題に対する日系社会の反応は賛否両論だった。戦後三〇年が経ち、日系人の生活水準は戦前とは比較できないほど向上していたため、「当時のことは思い出したくないから済んだことは水に流そう」という意見と、「補償金は要らないが謝罪してほしい」という意見、そして「謝罪した上で補償してほしい」という三つの意見に分れた。「謝罪だけでてほしい」という三つの意見に分れた人たちには、「失ったものに値段をつけることは不可能だ」という思いがあった。また補償金を要求するにしても、個人で受け取るのか、日系社会として受け取るのか、という問題もあった。結局JACLは、アメリカ社会では損害を受けたら補償を要求するのが慣例で、罰金には懲罰の意味も含んでいるため、生存する収容者全員に、一人につき二万五千ドルの補償金を請求することを決定した。

委員会では多くの人が証言し、戦時中のFBI報告などによって、日系人によるスパイや破壊工作は一切なかったことが立証された。その結果、強制立ち退きおよび収容は、軍事上の必要性からではなく、人種差別、戦時の異常反応、政治的リーダーシップの失敗による戦時の不法な処置であったと委員会は結論を出した[58]。そして政府の正式謝罪、被害者一人当たり二万ドルの補償金の支給が決定した。ところが委員会でそのような結論が出ても、一人当たり二万ドル計十五億ドルもの補償金を予算に組み込むには、議会で承認されなければならない。このため下院では、HR四四二法案が共同で提出された。四四二法案は第四四二連隊を記念してつけられた番号だ[59]。この時の議会は、奇しくも第一〇〇議会であった。上院でも四四二法案に対応する上院法案が共同提議され、法案の両院通過は確実になった。だがまだ問題があった。この時期のアメリカは、レーガン政権のレーガノミクスというユニークな経済政策にもかかわらず、財政赤字と経常収支も赤字の双子赤字が大幅に悪化していた。また保守的なロナルド・W・レーガン大統領は、最初からこの運動に賛成しているわけではなかったため、署名に至るかどうかは疑問視されていた。日系社会は何

レーガン大統領に送った手紙

イノウエ議員が議会に調査委員会の設置を提案した。この法案は両院を通過し、ジェームス・E・カーター・Jr大統領の署名を得て、正式に調査委員会が発足した[57]。委員には、アーサー・ゴールドバーグ元最高裁判事、エドワード・ブルック元上院議員などの公職経験者が選ばれ、日系人はウィリアム・マルタニ判事一人だけだった。JACLはまたもや大々的な募金活動を行い、多数の証人を動員して公聴会で証言するように働きかけた。この広報活動に

とかして大統領に署名してもらう手段はないかと考えた。そこで思いあたったのが、故マスダ軍曹に贈られた勲十字章の叙勲式のことだった。あの式典にレーガン大統領は若き大尉として出席し、人種差別を非難する演説をしていた。そこで故マスダ軍曹の妹ジューンがレーガン大統領に手紙を出し、式典で当時のレーガン大尉が述べた声明の内容を書き綴った(60)。

HR四四二号法案が下院を通過したのは一九八七年九月だったが、レーガン大統領が署名するまで約一年かかった。翌一九八八年八月十日、ついにレーガン大統領は正式謝罪文書、HR四四二法に署名した(61)。この法案は、現在では「一九八八年の市民自由法」として知られている。

市民自由法は成立しても、双子の赤字を抱える財政状態で十五億ドルの予算を組むことは難しい。そこで日系両院議員が中心となって、十五億ドルが確保されるまで、毎年十五億ドルを既得権予算とする法律を制定した(62)。収容者が最初の補償金と謝罪状を受け取ったのは、一九九〇年十月九日のことだ(63)。ワシントンDCにある法務省のグレートホールで、高齢者から先に授与された。

過ちを認めて　未来へつなぐ

一九八三年、戦時中に敗訴となったコレマツ、ヒラバヤシ、ヤスイの三人は続けて、連邦地方裁判所に誤審の訴えを起こした。まず、コレマツ裁判に人種差別があったことが認められてのち戦時中の審議が行われ、裁判長は「最高裁の見解を覆すことはできない」としながらも判決の過ちを認識し、四〇年ぶりにコレマツに対する有罪判決を無効にした(65)。

一九九八年、ウィリアム・J・クリントン大統領はコレマツに、市民として最高勲章である大統領自由勲章を授与した。式典で大統領は、「絶え間なく正義を追求してきたわが国の長い歴史の中には、何百万人もの魂を代表する一般市民の名前がある。その名誉ある名簿に今日、フレッド・コレマツの名前を追加する(66)」と演説した。

コレマツに続いてヤスイ裁判の審理が始まったが、ヤスイは審理の途中で他界し、審理そのものが立ち消えた。翌年始まったヒラバヤシ裁判に関しては、四年に及ぶ長い審理の結果、コレマツ裁判と同様にすべての有罪判決が無効になった(67)。

一九八七年、憲法成立二〇〇周年を記念して、ワシントンDCのスミソニアン・アメリカ歴史博物館が、「さらにパーフェクトなユニオンへ」と題した日系人史の展示を公開した(68)。この展示では、憲法で保障された人権の重要性を訴えている。一九九九年にはロサンゼルスのリトルトーキョーに、一万六千

人以上の退役軍人の名前が刻まれた「ゴー・フォー・ブローク・モニュメント」が完成した(69)。

ロスアンゼルス国際空港近郊に、戦時中、もっとも栄誉ある議会最高勲章を受けた唯一の日系兵士、サダヲ・ムネモリの功績を讃えて、彼の名前を付けたインターチェンジがある。だが、最高勲章の選別に人種差別があったことが認められてのち戦時中の最高勲章の選別に人種差別があったことが認められたのち、二〇〇〇年に、クリントン大統領はイノウエ上院議員も含む、二二人のアジア系退役軍人に最高勲章を授与した。その二二人のうち二〇人が、第四四二連隊と第一〇〇大隊の元兵士だった(70)。五五年遅れの最高勲章である。

一九九二年に議会で成立した法律により、全米日系人メモリアル基金が制定され、ワシントンの国会

クリントン大統領より議会最高勲章を叙勲するダニエル・イノウエ上院議員。Senator Daniel Inouye receiving the congressional medal of honor from President Bill Clinton. Courtesy of Jeff Timsley National Museum of American History.

1990年10月9日、司法省のホールで最初の謝罪文と保証金が渡された。受領者の1人、マモル・エトー牧師は107歳だった(64)。
（アメリカ司法省提供）

議事堂近くに「愛国記念碑」が設立された。この記念碑では、戦時中における日系人の勇気と愛国心を伝えるとともに、過ちを認めて正式謝罪した国家にも敬意を払っている。パネルには八〇〇人以上の戦没者の名前が刻まれ、石碑には全十ヵ所の強制収容所の名前が記されている(71)。「愛国記念碑」は二〇〇一年六月、一般公開された(72)。

二〇〇四年四月、マンザナー収容所跡が国立公園局の管轄で、マンザナー国立歴史遺跡として設立された(73)。翌二〇〇五年九月には、取り壊されていた監視塔も復元された(74)。

戦後六〇年を通して人権を追求し、人種差別に取り組んできた日系社会は、一九九二年、リトルトーキョーに全米日系人博物館を開館し、日系人のみならず全人類の人権擁護に乗り出した(75)。二〇〇一年九月十一日の同時多発テロで真っ先に「アラブ系市

民を差別することがあってはならない」と声明を発表したのも、全米日系人博物館だった。アイリーン・ヒラノ館長は「アラブ系社会に、彼らの他にも支援するコミュニティーがあると知ってもらうことは重要だ＊」と語っている。

日系人の歴史は日系人のものだけでなく、移民の国アメリカで生活するすべての人が共有すべきアメリカの歴史だ。二三〇年の決して長いとはいえない歴史の中で繰り広げられた自由と平等への闘いは、若いアメリカが成長する際に避けて通れない「成長の痛み」だともいえる。同時多発テロ事件は人権尊重の危うさを再認識させる事件でもあった。同じ過ちを二度と繰り返さないためにも、歴史を振り返ることは重要だ。過ちは過ちとして認め、それを糧に前進する勇気をこの国は持っている。このアメリカの歴史が、永遠に語り続けられることを願いたい。

＊2005年6月7日、全米日系人博物館にて取材

「一世が築き上げてきたものは戦争で失った。成功したらからこそ日系社会を助けたい」

ミカサ及びケンウッドの創業者

ジョージ・アラタニ

1917年生まれ。ガーデナ出身。サンタマリア高校を卒業後、慶応大学を経てスタンフォード大学へ。父他界で大学を中退し農場経営を継ぐが、太平洋戦争勃発で強制収容所へ。戦後貿易ビジネスに着手し、ミカサ、ケンウッドを創業。63年より日系社会へ貢献し、故フレッド・ワダさんなどとともに敬老引退者ホームの設立に尽力。全米日系博物館や日米文化会館など日系団体多数に貢献。2001には「アラタニ基金」を設立。UCLAにも長年にわたって寄付を続け、2003年、UCLA勲章を受賞。2004年、氏の寄付によりUCLAアジア系アメリカ人研究センターに日系人強制収容所の歴史研究の講座が開設。

人物コラム

戦後、政界や法曹会で活躍し日系社会に貢献してきた二世は多い。だがビジネスマンでこれほど日系社会に愛され、親しまれてきた人はこの人をおいてほかにいるだろうか。大農場主の跡取りから一転して強制収容所へ連行。戦後は一からビジネスを立ち上げた。成功した後には日系社会への援助を惜しまない日系社会のリーダー、ジョージ・アラタニさんの素顔に迫る。

一九歳で母が、二二歳で父が他界
大学中退して事業を継ぐ

高校時代は一年中、野球やフットボールなどのスポーツをしていて、将来はプロの野球選手になりたかったし、ピッツバーグ・パイレーツから誘いもあったのですが、フットボールの試合中にひざを故障してしまい、過激な運動ができなくなりました。でもその時は「人生スポーツばかりではない」と自分を励ましてがんばることができました。

しかし、母が亡くなった時は、本当にショックでした。一九三五年、両親の願いで日本の大学を受験するために日本に行ったのが七月。住み込みの家庭教師について猛勉強をしていたのですが、母が突然亡くなったのが十二月でした。私はもともとスタンフォードに行きたかったし、そうでなくても当時は「受験地獄」と言って皆ハチマキを締めて勉強するような状況で、私は土日も休みなしで猛勉強しなければならなかったのですが、母が亡くなると精神的に参ってしまい、「アメリカに帰った方がいいのでは」とヤケを起こしそうになりました。でも母は、「がんばって日本語も日本の文化もわかるようになってほしい」と言っていたのです。それを思い出してがんばりました。荒谷の祖母などいろいろなサポートがあったおかげで、何とか乗り切ることができたのです。

慶応大学三年生の時に今度は、父が結核になったと報せが入りました。どの程度悪いのか様子を見にアメリカに帰ると、父は私の日本語が達者になったのに驚いて、「それくらい日本語ができるのなら、もう日本はいい。慶応に入っただけでうれしい。スタンフォードに行きたいと言っていたのだから、日本に戻らずスタンフォードに編入してはどうか。そうしてくれ」と言いました。当時父はロサンゼルスのサナトリウムに入っていましたが、今にして思えば、余命の短いことを知っていたのかもしれません。スタンフォードの三年に編入して三週間で医師から電話があり、あわててロサンゼルスに戻った時にはすでに意識不明で、十日後に他界しました。

父が残した農場の規模は五千エーカーもありました。いずれはそれを私が見なくてはいけないのはわかっていましたが、父が病気で伏している時から同郷の広島県人三人がビジネスを切り盛りしてくれていたので、「卒業までの二年だけ見てくれないか」と三人に頼んで大学に戻りました。ところが、父が亡くなると三人が権力争いを始めたんです。それで大学を辞めて故郷のグアダルーペに戻りました。

強制収容所にいる間に農場も他人の手に

朝は五時に起きて農場、午後は出荷に回ってビジネスを勉強しましたが、規模が大きすぎてなかなか把握するのは難しかった。そうこうしているうちに日本軍がパールハーバーを攻撃しました。一世たちが次々とFBIに逮捕されていきましたが、私はアメリカ市民なのでまさか私にま

で影響があるとは考えてもみませんでした。ところが一九四二年、ルーズベルト大統領令で、日系人は市民でも強制収容されることになりました。でも戦争は永遠に続くことはないので、出荷会社で使っていた製氷会社の白人四人に戦争中の経営を、マネージメント費を払って見てもらうことにしたのです。製氷会社も出荷する野菜がないと仕事ができなくなるからです。

ところが、立ち退きをして一年半経った頃に彼らから「日本人の農場ということで偏見が厳しく、このままでは経営を継続できない」と連絡がありました。驚いて地元の友人に連絡すると「そんなことはない」と言う。「地元では反対に大規模な農場維持を喜んでいる」と言うのです。

そのうち彼らが収容所にやってきて、「日本人のビジネスというのでは維持できないから譲渡のサインをしろ」と書類を出しました。「会社を乗っ取るつもりだろう」と反論しても、サインをしないのならマネジメントはもうやらない、と言う。そう言われると、私にはどうしようもありません。相手の魂胆はわかっていましたが、仕方なしにサインしました。

その頃、陸軍から毎週のように「情報部語学学校のインストラクターとしてぜひ協力してほしい」と電報が来ていました。それでミネソタで日本語を教えるようになりました。終戦後はモントレーに配属になり、カリフォルニアに帰ってきましたが、一年後、リトルトーキョーでデスクが一つだけのオフィスで貿易ビジネスを始めました。戦争が終わって皆就職するか自分でビジネスを決めなければなりませんでしたが、私はファミリービジネスもなくなったし、スタッフも散らばって、農場のような仕事はもうできなくなっていました。終戦になったら何か日本と貿易関係の仕事ができないか、という気持ちだけで新しいビジネスを始めたのです。

私名義の土地が四〇エーカーあったのです。それを担保に銀行で五万ドル借り、魚の干物で商売を始めました。その後干しあわびも取り扱っていましたが、実は冷凍マグロを後で、陶器の輸入を始めました。それがミカサです。

目標はメーシーズへの納品
ブランドイメージ確立を優先

父が経営していた農場でも、農産物はブランドで売れるようになっていたので、とにかく最初はブランドイメージを確立したいと思いました。そのためには百貨店に入り込むのが一番です。百貨店は新聞広告で一ページ使って食器の広告を出します。ここにミカサを載せたい、と思ったのです。ある人に「百貨店に出荷するにはニューヨークにオフィスとショールームが必要だ」と言われ、五〇年にニューヨークにオフィスを開きました。

当時、一番評判の良かった百貨店がメーシーズで、メーシーズのジェリー・ストーンは、彼を知らないともぐりだと言われるほど有名なバイヤーでした。そこで食器販売で経験のあるアルフレッド・フナバシを誘ってセールスを強化しました。ずっと断られ続けた後、「二年も通ってくれているから、そろそろ商品を見せてくれ」と、ストーンがオフィスに来ました。五二年のことです。ショールームもなかったので、ちっぽけで小汚いオフィスの壁に棚を作り、即席で食器を並べました。そこでストーンは四点注文してくれました。ここまで来た、と思ったのはその時です。

百貨店ビジネスは、在庫を切らすということができないのでリスキーなのですが、とにかくミカサを育てなくてはと思い、他のビジネスは利益を生み出しているものもすべてやめて、ミカサに全力投球しました。反対意見もありますが、結果的にはそれが良かった。メーシーズで売り始めると、全米の百貨店から注文が来ました。

ミカサもケンウッドもメーカーだと思っている方が多いのですが、メーカーではなくブランドです。でもメーカーだと思っている人が多いのは、どの家庭にもあるなじみの名前になったからで、それが私のやりたかったことなのです。

戦時中は十二万人の日系人が立ち退きになり、強制収容されました。私も損害が出ましたが、多かれ少なかれ皆損害があったはずです。一世ががんばって築き上げてきたものが戦争で失われ、戦後は皆がゼロからの出発になりました。私は幸いにも成功したからこそ、日系社会を助けている。チャリティーは六三年から続けています。敬老ヘルスケアは、一世の親たちが高齢になった時、二世の私たちは休む暇もなく皆が共働きで働いていましたから、必要なケアをすることができない状態だったので設立することになったのですが、これもまさに手探りでした。

※ライトハウス「人物名鑑」（二〇〇五年二月一日号）より抜粋

スペースシャトル・チャレンジャーの乗組員。（NASA 提供）

CONTENTS

千変万化する時の流れの中で、人種の壁を乗り越えて様々な分野で活躍する少数民族が激増し、アメリカ社会は多様性を尊重する時代になった。日系社会にも、自分たちのルーツを求めてその歴史を伝え、文化を継承しようとする若者たちが現れた。

陸軍最高位に立った

シンセキ参謀総長

マーチン・ルーサー・キング・ジュニア牧師ほか、多くの指導者の下で展開された社会運動によって、六〇年代以降、一般社会の公民権に対する認識は劇的な変化を遂げた。さまざまな分野であらゆる人種に門戸が開かれ、政治の世界でも選挙のたびに「初の○○系」という表現がメディアに登場するようになった。現ブッシュ政権には、アフリカ系、アジア系、ラテン系など多様な顔ぶれが閣僚に並び、社会の変化が如実に現れている。

前ミネタ運輸長官が閣僚入りをしたのは、ウィリアム・J・クリントン大統領によって商務長官に任命された二〇〇〇年だったが、クリントン大統領はその前年にも、重要ポストに

退官式で閲兵する米国34代陸軍参謀総長、エリック・シンセキ。（国立公文書館）

初めて日系人を任命している。それが第三四代陸軍参謀総長となった日系三世のエリック・シンセキだ。シンセキがハワイのカウアイ島で産声を上げたのは、パールハーバー攻撃からほぼ一年後の一九四二年十一月だ。そのころ日系人は軍部によって「敵性外国人」とみなされ、本土だけでも十二万人の日系人が強制収容されていた。

地元のカウアイ高校からウエストポイント陸軍士官学校に進学し、一九六五年に同校を卒業すると、デューク大学大学院で英文学の修士号を取得した。さらに陸軍司令参謀大学と国防大学で教育を受けた。

後、ベトナム戦争に二度出兵し、二度負傷した。そのうち一度は地雷を踏んで、足の先を吹き飛ばされている。

ヨーロッパに十年以上駐在したシンセキが、破竹の勢いで出世街道を邁進するのは九〇年代に入ってからだ。一九九六年、中将に昇進して、作戦・計画担当の参謀次長補となり、翌九七年にはクリントン大統領によって大将に任命され、ヨーロッパ中央司令官に就任した。一九九八年には第二八代参謀次長に任命され、翌九九年、ついに日系人として初めて陸軍最高位の第三四代参謀総長に就任した。

同年六月に行われた就任式でウィリアム・コーエン国防長官は、「彼が生まれた日、リックは国敵とみなされました。そして今、私たちは彼を第三四代陸軍参謀長官に任命できることを名誉に思います」(1)と講演した。シンセキの叔父二人は第一〇〇大隊、一人は第四四二連隊で、子供のころには夕食のテーブルを囲みながらよく戦争の話を聞いたという。シンセキは当時の思い出を披露すると、「私が疑惑を持たれることもなく、すべての権利と特典を享受して生きることができたのも、彼らの功績のお陰です」(2)と先達の兵士たちを賞賛した。

上院国軍委員会でイノウエ議員は、参謀総長に任命されるのは、アメリカならでは(3)」と語ったが、第四四二連隊に属していたイノウエ議員にすれば、感慨もひとしおだったに違いない。シンセキの成功は、彼の努力を物語さることながら、アメリカという国の懐の広さを物語っているといえる。シンセキ任命の承認を得る上院議会でイノウエ議員は「この日、何年もの間、私たちの肩にのしかかっていた恥辱のすべてが、完全に払拭されました(4)」と日系社会の喜びのすべてを代弁した。

フロリダの空に散った
オニヅカ宇宙飛行士

空軍将校からアジア系初の宇宙飛行士になったのは、エリソン・オニヅカだ。オニヅカは戦後間もない一九四六年に、ハワイ島コナで生まれた。彼の祖父母は一八九〇年代に福岡県から移住して、ハワイ島でコーヒー栽培に携わっていた(5)。

オニヅカも幼いころ、日系部隊の武勇伝を聞いて育ったという。コナの公立高校を卒業した後、コロラド大学で四年間、ROTCを学び、大学院卒業後、空軍に入隊した。一九七四年から一年間、空軍テストパイロット学校で正式に訓練を受け、カリフォルニア州エドワーズ空軍基地の空軍飛行テストセンターの飛行テスト技術者となった。

オニヅカがNASAの宇宙飛行士候補に選ばれたのは、一九七八年のことだ。一年間の訓練と査定期間を経て、ケネディ・スペースセンターで補佐官となった。一九八五年一月、国防省による初のスペースシャトル任務でディスカバリー号に搭乗し、アジア系として初めての宇宙飛行を成し遂げ、七四時間の宇宙飛行時間を記録している。

オニヅカに二度目のスペースシャトル任務が訪れたのは、翌年の一九八六年一月だ。チャレンジャー号のミッション・スペシャリストとして、再び宇宙に向かうことになった。ケネディ宇宙センターでチャレンジャー号が轟音をあげて発射したのは午前十一時

三八分。そのわずか一分十三秒後に、シャトルは一瞬にして大きな炎に包まれ、空中で爆発した。世界が息を呑んで見守る中、民間人二人を含む宇宙飛行士七人全員の命は、炎とともに地上十六マイルの空に散った。約十八マイル沖の大西洋には、火だるまになった破片が一時間も雨のように降り続けたと、翌日のニューヨーク・タイムスは伝えている。アメリカの宇宙プログラム史上、最悪の事故となった。

同機にミッション・スペシャリストとして搭乗していたのは、オニヅカ、ロナルド・マックネアー、ジュディス・レズニックの三人だ。マックネアーは一九八四年、アフリカ系アメリカ人として二番目に宇宙飛行を達成した経歴を持ち、ユダヤ系アメリカ人のレズニックも同年、ディスカバリー号の処女飛行に搭乗して、女性として二番目の軌道飛行に成功している。また民間人二人のうち、シャロン・マックオーリフは「教師を宇宙に」というNASAのプログラムで、当初から、初の教師宇宙飛行士として報道機関の注目を集めていた。

女性の高校教師で、一万二千人の応募者の中から選ばれたチャレンジャー号事故の後、遺族が集まって、殉死した宇宙飛行士を記念するものを何か作ろうということになった。こうしてできたのが、チャレンジャーセンターだ。遺族が選んだのは一般的な記念碑ではなく、広く共有できる宇宙科学教育センターだった。一九八八年、ヒューストン自然科学教育センター内に、チャレンジャー教育センター第一号が開館した。現在ではバージニアを本拠に、全米三一州、カ

ナダ、イギリスに計五〇のチャレンジャーセンターがあり、毎年のように新しいセンターを開設して、子供たちの宇宙教育に力を入れている。

オニヅカの墓は、オアフ島のパンチボール国立墓地にある。太平洋を見下ろす小高い丘にある墓地で、オニヅカとともに永眠するのは、彼の子供のころのヒーローだった日系兵士たちだ。

ハワイ島のコナ空港には、オニヅカの功績を讃えて一九九一年、「宇宙飛行士エリソン・S・オニヅカ宇宙センター」が開設された。ロサンゼルスのリトルトーキョーには「宇宙飛行士エリソン・オニヅカ通り」があり、福岡県の先祖の家近くにある橋は「エリソン・オニヅカ橋」と名付けられている。

NYのツインタワーを設計したヤマサキ

ミノル・ヤマサキは、シアトル生まれの二世だ。両親は富山県出身で、シアトルでは靴職人として生計を立てていた。一九一二年生まれだから、ヤマサキが幼少期から青年期を過ごしたシアトルは、激しい排日運動が吹き荒れていたに違いない。鮭の缶詰工場で働きながらワシントン大学を卒業したヤマサキは、三〇年代にニューヨークに移住して建築学科の夜学に通って建築学科の修士号を取得した。卒業後、エンパイアステートビルを手がけた建築事務所やロックフェラーセンターを請け負っ

た建築事務所など、有名事務所で経験を積み、一九四五年、大手設計事務所スミス・ヒンチマン・グリルス事務所の主任デザイナーに就任した。

興味深いのは、ヤマサキが各事務所で修行していた期間は、第二次世界大戦の真っ只中であったことだ。シアトルを含む西海岸の日系人は、全米十箇所に集められ強制収容されていた。ニューヨークに住む日系人は強制収容の対象にはならなかったが、敵国日本に対する反日感情は少なくなかったはずだ。そんな環境の中で、彼が有名事務所に、次々に勤務出来ていたことは、日系人が軍によって敵性外国人と指定されていた時期に、彼の才能を認め、それを受け入れる一般アメリカ人がいたということに他ならない。しかもそれがごく一部の人間に限られていたわけではなかったことは、注目に値する。

一九四九年、ヤマサキはスミス・ヒンチマン・グリルス事務所の同僚と共同経営で設計事務所を開設している。一九五五年に手がけたセントルイス空港で脚光を浴び、同年、在神戸アメリカ総領事館の建

ヤマサキの代表作となったワールドトレードセンター。Yamasaki's most famous project, the World Trade Center in New York. Source: National Archives

築は、日本建築学会作品賞を受賞した。一九五九年、ヤマサキ＆アソシエイツと改名し、その後、アメリカ建築家協会賞を四度受賞している。

彼の代表作となったのは、後年世界中の注目を浴びることになるニューヨークのワールドトレードセンターだ。ワールドトレードセンターはローワーマンハッタンの再開発として、ニューヨーク・ニュージャージー港湾管理委員会の開発事業企画で、全七棟からなる集合建築には約五万人が勤務し、毎日約二〇万人が訪れた。独自の郵便番号を有するほどの規模だった。

なかでもニューヨークの名所となったツインタワーは、タワー一（北タワー、一一〇階建て四一七メートル）、タワー二（南タワー、一一〇階建て四一五メートル）の二棟からなり、一九七二年にタワー一が完成した当時は、エンパイアステートビルを抜いて世界でもっとも高いビルとなった。タワー二が完成した翌七三年にはシカゴのシアーズタワー（四四二メートル）が工事に入っており、「世界一高いビル」の栄冠に輝いたのは二年間だけだったが、一九八〇年代に入り金融関係の入居会社が増えると、ウォール街に近い場所柄もあり、世界金融の象徴として君臨した。

一九九三年に同ビル地下で起きた爆破テロでは、ビルの独特な構造が幸いして被害を最低限に抑えたと伝えられた。だが悲劇は、二〇〇一年九月十一日に起きた。午前八時四六分、アメリカン航空十一便が北タワーに激突し、九時三分にはユナイテッド航

ローワーマンハッタン開発の設計模型と主任設計者、ミノル・ヤマサキ。（Yamasaki Associates, Inc 提供）

型ジェット旅客機を武器にしたテロを想定したものではなかった。

当初の設計段階から、飛行機が激突する可能性とその衝撃は計算済みであったという。だがそれは大

空一七五便が南タワーに突っ込んだ。イスラム原理主義者のオサマ・ビン・ラディンとテロリストネットワーク・アルカイダによると言われている世界中を震撼させた同時多発テロだ。

全世界が生中継で北タワーの崩壊を目撃したのは九時五九分。それから約三〇分後の十時二八分、南タワーが崩壊したのは激突から約一時間後。一〇〇分後、一一〇階建てのビル二棟は相次いで、砂の城が崩れるように多くの人を飲み込んだままニューヨークの摩天楼から姿を消した。救助活動に当たっていた消防士三四三人、警官二三人を含む約三〇〇〇人が死亡した(6)。

型ジェット旅客機を武器にしたテロを想定したものではなかった。

ツインタワーの崩壊は、ジェット機の激突以上に大きな衝撃を与え、事件直後はビルの構造が疑問視された。崩壊に問題があったのではないかという疑惑だ。だが二〇〇二年に発表された緊急管理局（FEMA）の報告書によると、この独特な設計デザインがビルの崩壊を遅らせ、その結果、激突から崩壊までに避難できた数千人の命を救っていたことが明らかになった(7)。一方、全米規格テクノロジー協会（NIST）は二〇〇五年、「航空機が激突した衝撃で耐火材料が外れていなければ、崩壊しなかった可能性が高い(8)」と結論づけ、ビルの構造の是非に関しては関係者の間で、現在も賛否両論が交わされている。

ヤマサキ自身は一九九三年の爆破テロも、九・一一での無残な最期を見ることもなく、一九八六年、癌のため他界している。

NBCのニュース・アンカーとして活躍するアン・カリーは、一九五六年、グアム島に生まれた。父は海軍兵士で、母は日本人で農家の出身だ。母親が渡米した当時のアメリカは、日本人にとって居心地のいい場所ではなかったと、カリーはインタビューで答えている。「人々はまだ日本に対して怒りを抱いていた時期で、そのため母は私をアメリカ人として

育て、日本語すらしゃべらせてくれませんでした(9)。日本人であることに誇りを持てと教えてくれたのは、意外にも白人の父だったという。「父は『どちらも見捨ててはいけない。もしどちらかを選ばねばならないとしたら、日本人を選べ』と言いました。父はサムライの持つ強さを崇拝していました」。

カリーは子供のころに見たテレビジョンの印象を、「TVに出ている女性は皆白人で、男性も白人ばかり。しかもほとんどが金髪で、私の居場所があるとは思えませんでした」と語っているが、「子供心にも、自分と同じような顔をした人はTVで活躍していなかったので、自分にできるとは考えもしませんでした」という思いは、アジア系の子供たちが感じていた現実であったに違いない。

五人姉弟の一番上として生まれ、各地を転々としたカリーは、一つの学校に二年以上続けて通ったことはないという。オレゴン州のアシュランドに落ち着いた時も、一家に経済的なゆとりはなく、カリーにとって大学進学など夢のまた夢の話だった。だが両親に励まされ、わずかな奨学金と数え切れないほどの仕事をしながら、オレゴン大学に進学した。時にはレイクタホのカジノホテル「ハラス」のメイドとして、風呂場を磨いたこともあった。「大学の費用を稼ぐためにあらゆる仕事をしましたが、それだけの価値があると思っていました」という。

一九七八年、ジャーナリズムの学位を取得したカリーが大学で得たものは、インタビューの技術だけではなかった。「ケン・メツラー教授は私に自信を与え、努力すれば夢は叶うと信じさせてくれました(10)」と、二〇〇三年のオレゴン大学パイオニア賞の授賞式で、恩師に感謝の辞を述べている。

一九八四年にロサンゼルスのKCBSのレポーターとなり、一九八七年にロサンゼルス地震、またサンバーナディーノのガスパイプライン爆発の報道で、二度エミー賞に輝いた。そして一九九〇年、ついに三大ネットワークの一つ、NBCニュースのキャスターとなり、一九九七年、人気番組『トゥデイ』のニュース・アンカーとして、視聴率競争の激しい朝の顔になった。二〇〇五年五月には、報道番組『デート・ライン』で、ストーン・フィリップスのパートナーとしてアンカーに抜擢されている。

二〇〇二年、オレゴン大学スクール・オブ・ジャーナリズム・アンド・コミュニケーションの殿堂入りを果たすと、放送業界を目指す後輩のためにアン・カリー奨学金を設立している。また母親を胆嚢癌で亡くし、妹が乳癌を患ったことから、カリーは乳癌に関する報道も多く取り上げ、乳癌関連の運動も積極的に支持している。

邦楽とジャズを融合したヒロシマ

シノダがヒップホップという分野で日系人の歴史を語っているのに対して、ジャズ・フュージョンと邦楽という分野で日本の伝統楽器をアメリカの音楽界に広めたのはヒロシマだ。ヒロシマは、ジューン・クラモト、ダン・クラモトなど日系人を中心に結成したバンドで、ジャズに琴や尺八、和太鼓などの邦楽器を取り入れて独特の音色を作り出している。

バンド名をタイトルにした曲、『ヒロシマ』でデビューしたのは一九七九年。バンド名をヒロシマと決定した時、レコード会社はあまりにも暗い印象に難色を示したという。だが彼らは日系人のイメージに、あえて論議を呼ぶような名前に固執したと口を揃える。「原爆が投下されて壊滅状態にあった広島は、戦後見事に復興しました。ヒロシマという名前には、そういった前向きな思いが込められています*」とリーダーのダン・クラモトは命名の理由を語った。

東西文化の融合であるヒロシマの中でも、特に印象的なのは琴の音だ。琴奏者の第一人者であるジューン・クラモトは埼玉県生まれで、バンドの中で唯一の日本生まれだ。父親は日系二世で、母親は日本人。六歳でロサンゼルスに移住してきたが、当初は日本が恋しくて仕方なかったという。ジューンが移住してきた一九五〇年代半ばには、渡米間もない人を対象にした二世運営のソーシャル・サービスがあった。「さくら会」もそうしたサービスの一つで、ジューンが初めて琴の演奏を聴いたのは、「さくら会」においてだ。日本的なものに飢えていた六歳の少女は、琴の音に魅了され、自らレッスンを受けるようになった。

＊ジューン・クラモト宅にて筆者取材

一方ダンは、カリフォルニア州立大学ロングビーチ校で、芸術や法律を学んだのち、初めてのアジア系アメリカ人研究室の室長として教鞭を執っていた。時代は、アース・ウィンド・アンド・ファイヤーやサンタナ、ジミー・ヘンドリックスなどが、R&Bやジャズ、ラテン音楽などをミックスして新しい音楽を形成していたころだった。「音楽を通して、日系人も同じようなことができるのではないか」と考えていた時に出会ったのが、ジューンだ。ジューンは当時でによく知られた琴奏者で、県人会のピクニックや敬老ホームなど日系のイベントでもよく演奏していた。

一九八〇年に発表した二枚目のアルバム『オドリ』はグラミー賞の候補に選出され、一九八五年の『アナザー・プレイス』で初のゴールドディスクを達成した。一九八七年の『ゴー』はビルボードのコンテンポラリージャズ部門の一位を三ヶ月維持し、ソウルトレイン賞のベストアルバム賞を受賞した。また坂本九のヒット曲『上を向いて歩こう』の複製で、人々の心のよりどころとなった。戦時中の収容所生活テイスト・オブ・ハニーが歌って全米ナンバーワンを飾った『スキヤキ』では、ジューンが琴を担当した。『ブラックレイン』や『ラストサムライ』など映画音楽も手掛け、『レッド・シン・ライン』ではアカデミー賞候補に選出された。また毎年各地で慈善コンサートを開催しており、日系社会へも貢献している。

海外渡航自由化で
始まった文化の交流

第一章でも述べたように戦前、ほとんど英語を話さなかった一世たちの娯楽の場となったのは、県人会や文化会館などの集いだった。彼らは懐かしい故郷の踊りや歌を通して遠い祖国に思いを馳せ、二世も幼いころから自然と日本文化に親しむ機会を得た。柔道や剣道、空手などの武道も、日系社会では戦前からすでに盛んであった。全米日系人博物館発行の日系史事典によると、最初に柔道がアメリカに紹介されたのは一九〇三年のことだ。翌年にはセオドア・ルーズベルト大統領も門弟に入り、一躍全米に広まるかに見えたが、一九〇七年ころからいつしか衰退の一途をたどる(11)。理由は軍国主義に突入した日本帝国に対する不信感の高まりに他ならない。一方日

本では、体鍛科の一環として武道が学校の授業に組み込まれ、その結果、アメリカの日本語学校でも武道を教えるところが急増した。戦時中の収容所生活の文化であった。無料で実施された成人教室には生け花や茶道の教室もあり、演芸場では娯楽に日本舞踊が披露された。

日本文化が日系社会の壁を飛び越えて、アメリカ全土で知られるようになったのは戦後のことだ。最初のきっかけを作ったのは、進駐軍として日本に駐屯した軍人やその夫人たちであった。終戦直後に彼らが足を踏み入れた東京は、度重なる激しい空襲を受けた焼け野原だった。そこで初めて彼らは、食物も充分でなく精神力のみで戦っていた日本人の本質を目の当たりにした。武道や茶道、華道など、技術だけではなく精神的な向上が求められる日本文化の存在は、彼らにとって未知の世界であったに違いない。またPX（Post Exchange: 軍人用の両替・購買所）で販売された日本製の良質な陶器、漆器や真珠等、日本の伝統文化を軍人の間に広めただけでなく、食うや食わずだった終戦直後の日本産業の活性化にも一役買った。多くの軍人やその夫人が日本に駐留中、いわゆる日本文化に触れる機会を得て、任務終了後それまで刀ば剣道の良質な陶器、漆器や真珠等、スキヤキ、てんぷら、鮨などの食文化も含めてあらゆる日本文化に触れる機会を得て、任務終了後それをアメリカに持ち帰った。

一九五〇年に勃発した朝鮮戦争によって日本経済が特需景気の波に乗り始めた一九五二年、対日平和条約および日米安全保障条約が発効され、日本にお

64

裏千家沼野宗美社中の稽古風景。

ける連合軍の占領は終わりを迎えた。一九五五年下半期から始まった世界的好況の追い風も受けて、翌五六年、日本政府は経済白書で「もはや戦後ではない」と宣言し、日本は飛躍的な成長期に入った。そのころアメリカの映画産業は黄金時代を謳歌しており、銀幕のスターは日本人をも魅了した。一九五四年にハネムーンで訪日したマリリン・モンローとジョー・ディマジオは熱狂的な歓迎を受けた。また、映画『ローマの休日』で主役オードリー・ヘップバーンのヘアスタイルを真似たヘップバーンカットは日本中で大流行した。五〇年代後半にはロックンロールブームが日本にも飛び火し、一部の富裕層に早くもアメリカを目指す若者たちが出現している。彼らの中には、アメリカにおける日本文化の振興に貢献した人も少なくない。

六〇年代に入ると日本の一般家庭にもテレビの普及が広まり、『サンセット七七』(一九六〇年)、『コンバット』(一九六二年)『ルート六六』(一九六三年)などのアメリカの番組が相次いで放送開始になった。

「豊かなアメリカ」のイメージが急速に日本の茶の間に広まったころ、日本人の本格的な海外渡航がアメリカ文化の浸透に影響したのと同様に、アメリカにおける日本文化の広まりも映画やテレビが大きく関与している。主演のマーロン・ブランドが日本人役を演じた『八月十五夜の茶屋』(一九五六年)は、米軍占領後の沖縄が舞台だ。同じくブランド主演の朝鮮戦争時に駐屯した日本で日本女性と恋に落ちる兵士の物語『サヨナラ』(一九五七年)はアカデミー賞四部門を受賞した。この作品で助演女優賞に輝いた梅木美代志は、アジア系として初めてオスカーを獲得している。またショーン・コネリー主演のジェームス・ボンドシリーズ『〇〇七は二度死ぬ』(一九六七

年)も日本が舞台で、六〇年代の日本ブームを裏付けている。

八〇年代に再び日本ブームが到来するが、そのきっかけになったのはテレビ番組だった。一九八〇年、ジェームス・クラベル原作のベストセラー『将軍』がNBCテレビでのミニシリーズで高視聴率を得て放送された。瞬く間にアメリカ全土で、サムライブームとともに寿司ブームまで巻き起こり、日本の文化はいつしかアメリカ人の日常生活の一部になって

ぞって日本製品の輸入に乗り出した。アメリカで最初の日本ブームが起きたのは、六〇年代で、日本の海外渡航自由化とアメリカにおける日本ブームは期を同じくしているのが興味深い。

アメリカの映画やテレビが、日本におけるアメリカ文化の浸透に影響したのと同様に、アメリカにおける日本文化の振興に貢献した人も少なくない。

一連の海外渡航自由化により多くの日本人が夢を求めて渡米した(12)。一方通行だった文化の流通は、ここに来てようやく相互的な交流を始めることになる。

海外渡航の自由化に伴い、高度経済成長の波にも乗って、六〇年代は日本のエレクトロニクス系企業やカメラ会社が本格的にアメリカに進出した時代でもある。一般的に五〇年代のアメリカでは「Made in Japan」といえば「安い粗悪品」の代名詞だった。そのイメージを根底から覆したのが、これらの企業が低価格で売り出した高性能な製品だ。アメリカのエンジニアたちは、日本製品の性能の高さと価格の低さに目を見張った。最初に日本の製品を取り入れたのはハリウッドだ。映画やテレビの撮影所、レコーディングスタジオなどが一斉に日本製品に切り替え始めると、それに目を付けたビジネスマンたちがこ

ろアメリカの映画産業は黄金時代を謳歌しており、銀幕のスターは日本人をも魅了した。一九五四年にハネムーンで訪日したマリリン・モンローとジョー・ディマジオは熱狂的な歓迎を受けた。また、映画『ローマの休日』で主役オードリー・ヘップバーンのヘアスタイルを真似たヘップバーンカットは日本中で大流行した。五〇年代後半にはロックンロールブームが日本にも飛び火し、一部の富裕層に早くもアメリカを目指す若者たちが出現している。彼らの中には、アメリカにおける日本文化の振興に貢献した人も少なくない。

と宣言し、日本は飛躍的な成長期に入った。そのこ

幕を開けた。戦中から戦後にかけて外貨保全のため外貨持ち出し規制されていた海外渡航は、一九六三年に外貨持ち出し年間総額五〇〇ドル以内の業務渡航が承認され、翌六四年には観光渡航も年一回五〇〇ドルまでの持ち出しが自由になった。一九六六年には、依然として外貨の枠は抑えられていたものの「一人年間一回限り」という回数制限も撤廃され、これら

65

日系人の歩んできた道は決して平坦ではなかったが、それは紛れもないアメリカ史の一ページであった。苦難を乗り越え、逆境に立ち向かった先達の努力は、次世代のために語り継がれるべきアメリカ史に違いない。だが大きな社会の変化の陰には、時には安泰した生活を犠牲にして支援を惜しまなかったアメリカ人がいたことも忘れてはならない。第三章で紹介しきれなかったそんなヒーローたちを、最後にここで紹介したい。

先述のコロラド州ラルフ・カー知事、ジェームズ・パーセルやディーン・アチソンの両弁護士などの他にも、できる範囲の行動で日系人を支援した人は少なくない。収容所では、白人専用住居施設に入ることを拒んで、日系人と同じようにバラックで寝起きした白人教師がいた。親友が強制収容されるのを知って、日系人ではないのに一緒に収容所に入った若者がいた。このような草の根の抗議が、日系社会の心の支えになったのはいうまでもない。

ホノルル・スター・ブルテン紙は「ジャップ」の使用を禁止し、あくまで「ジャパニーズ」と書く方針を貫いたことは第三章で記述したが、ひときわ排日運動の高かったカリフォルニアで強制収容に反論した編集長がいた。オレンジカウンティー・レジスター紙創設者のR・C・ホイルズだ。ホイルズは日系人の強制収容実施に傾く軍部に対して、「異国の地で生

人物コラム

坂東三津拡師

ロサンゼルスを中心に三七年間、日本舞踊の普及に努めた女流日本舞踊家。一九二八年愛媛県八幡浜市に生まれ、四歳から日本舞踊を始め、のちの人間国宝、八世坂東三津五郎家元の直門師範となる。

一九六九年、観光でロサンゼルスの親戚を訪れ、滞在中、ある催しのため地元の子供たちに日本舞踊を教えることになった。子供たちの愛らしい踊りの評判がとても良く、ぜひ教えてほしいと大勢の人から望まれたため、三年間のつもりで再渡米し、稽古を始めた。

その三津拡会は現在すでに三九年になるが、日米文化交流の功績を讃えられ、シュワルツェネッガー・カリフォルニア州知事、ロサンゼルス市長、その他、数々の団体から多くの感謝状を授与されてきた。また、日本においても、二〇〇三年には師匠の功績を称え、十代目坂東三津五郎家元より名誉ある幹部師範の称号を与えられた。

日本と違って英語社会の子供や大人に日本舞踊を教えることの難しさは並大抵なことではない。日本語の唄の意味も理解できず、役の心や感情を説明するには、師匠自らが何回も踊って身体で伝えなけれ

ばならない。

「日本舞踊は役によってある時には娘になり、ある時には男になり、年齢もさまざま。その時々違った感情と表情を持った人間になりきることが舞踊の魅力であり、難しさでもあります。小さな弟子たちが上達していくのを見ると、涙が出るほど嬉しいですね」と三津拡師は話す。これまでに三津拡会の門をくぐった日系人、アメリカ人は六〇〇人を越えるという。

現在、師範十名、名取三五名、弟子八〇名余りを抱え、カリフォルニア州ではロサンゼルス、オレンジ郡、サンディエゴ、モントレーおよびワシントン州のタコマにも稽古場を持ち、七九歳とは思えぬ若々しさで意欲的に活動している。

取材・水口まみ

坂東三津拡師の若い弟子。

まれ、その地で何年も善良な市民として生活してきた人たちの忠誠心に懐疑的になるべきでなく、彼らが危険だとは信じがたい[13]と同紙で訴え、市民的自由のあり方を問いかけた。また強制立ち退きが強行されると、立ち退き令の撤廃と強制収容の再考を促すコラムを掲載した。世論が戦争の恐怖でヒステリックな排日感情に陥っていた時に、もっとも排日気運の高かった激震地区で新聞として反論を掲げるのは勇気のいる行為だ。購買者からの反発が明らかな状況で、なおかつ信念を貫いたホイルズの記者としての良心に敬意を表したい。

戦後、差別法撤廃のため議会で証言し、日系兵に惜しみない賛辞を送ったのは、日系兵とともに前線で戦った数多くの白人将兵たちだった。だが日系兵、とともに戦場で傷を負い、ともに戦死して、議会で証言できなかった多数の将兵がいたことも覚えてお

きたい。日系部隊がたてた輝かしい戦功は、日系兵だけのものではなく、多くのアメリカ軍人たちの勇気ある行動によって支えられて成し得た功績だ。戦後、日系人が真のアメリカ人として活躍できる基盤を手に入れられたのも、彼らの支援があったからに他ならない。

第一〇〇大隊の将校としてキャンプ・シェルビーから参加し、戦場では飛び抜けた指導力と戦闘能力を見せて、日系兵の多大な信頼を得たのは、韓国系のヤング・オーク・キムだ。キムの父親は、日本軍支配下にある韓国からアメリカに亡命してきた。筋金入りの日本人嫌いだったという。子供のころに育ったロサンゼルスでキムが受けた人種差別は、日系人のそれと変わらなかったはずだ。ベニング幹部候補生学校の卒業生同期で、最後まで配属先が決まらなかったのもキムだった。

キム少尉は、キャンプ・シェルビーに到着してすぐに配置換えを言い渡された。「到着したばかりですが」と怪訝そうに言うと、第一〇〇大隊のターナー大隊長は「君は知らないかもしれないが、ここは日系兵の部隊だ。日本人と韓国人が折り合わないのは知っている。すぐに別の隊に変わる手続きを取ってあげよう」と説明した。このころ日本軍は東南アジア諸国を占領しており、アメリカ各地で東南アジア系による日系人を狙った暴行事件が多発していた。この時のキムの返答が際立っている。「それは誤解です。私もアメリカ人で、私もアメリカ人です。私たちはアメリカのために戦うのです[14]」。

ゴーフォーブローク記念碑。

ヤング・オーク・キム大佐。（Go For Broke 国立博物館提供）

キムは戦場でヘルメットを着用したことはない。いつもニット帽だけで、眠るときは塹壕も掘らなかった。見かねた日系兵が代わりに掘ってやっても入ろうとはしなかったという。それは、日系兵たちの恐怖心を軽減するためにとったキム独特のポーズであった。第一〇〇大隊のアービング・アカホシは「キム中尉と一緒なら地獄からでも生きて帰れると確信していました。彼となら、どこへだって迷うことなくついて行ったでしょう[15]」と回顧している。朝鮮戦争では、アジア系で初めて部隊の司令官となった。一九七二年に大佐として退役した後は、韓国系コミュニティーだけでなく、ゴー・フォー・ブローク・ナショナル・エデュケーションセンターや全米日系人博物館の設立など日系コミュニティーにも積極的に関与した。二〇〇五年の二世ウィークでは名誉グランドマーシャルを務めたが、同年末に癌のため他界した。

移民の国アメリカは、ある意味で世界の縮図だと

いえる。異なった価値観を持つ多民族が共存していくのは容易ではない。アメリカの歴史がなによりもそれを如実に物語っている。それでもアメリカは多くの過ちを繰り返しながら、一歩ずつ共存の道を模索してきた。現在も人種差別が完全になくなったわけではない。移民の問題も、今に通じる問題だ。だがお互いの歴史を知り、文化を共有することで、異なった価値観を理解し合えるのではないか。そうすることで世界中の人が、いつかお互いを尊重し合える日が来るのではないか。ひいては全人類の平和に繋がるのではないか。そう願ってやまない。

人物　コラム

アメリカ市民として、誇り高く生き抜いた人

John E. Kashiwabara M.D.（ジョン・カシワバラ医師）

スポーツ選手として活躍していた大学生活から、両親が日本人であるという理由だけで、強制収容所へと追い立てられた若者は、その経験を苦いものとせず、自分の生まれた国、アメリカの善意を信じ、地域社会への貢献を惜しまない市民として人生を捧げた。その若者こそ、半世紀にわたってロングビーチ市の医学会、教育界、スポーツ界、経済界、および多人種で構成される地域のために貢献し、優れた指導者の一人として高い評価を得、二〇余りの功労賞に輝いた日系アメリカ人、ドクター・ジョン・カシワバラである。

ジョンは、一九二二年十一月三〇日カリフォルニア州フローリンで六人兄妹の三番目に生まれた。父、マツオは一九〇五年に渡米し、鉄道員として働いた。一九四一年十二月、彼がプレイサー短期大学に在学中に、日本軍の真珠湾奇襲攻撃によって太平洋戦争が勃発し、一九四二年五月、彼はカリフォルニア州ツールレイクの強制収容所に両親、兄妹と共に収容された。

「後に収容所を出た私は、四四二部隊の兵隊としてヨーロッパで負傷した兄のケイが、Gービル（軍人に与えられた奨学金）を使って大学にいくということで、一緒にイリノイ大学に入学しました。兄は歯学部に進み、私は医学部に進みました。その後、アメリカ空軍の軍医として日本にも駐留していました。退役後、一九五四年カリフォルニア州、ロングビーチ市で family practice（一般内科）を開業し、一九九〇年まで開業していました」と、彼は語った。

経済面では、日系人初のロングビーチ港「Board of Harbor Commissioner（港湾委員）」として港の発展に尽くすと共に、スポーツ振興のためにも協力を惜しまず、大学スポーツ部の専属医師として、ドクター・ジョンの愛称で親しまれてきた。その他、長年に亘って、米国赤十字ロングビーチ市支部の理事もつとめていた。

彼は、教育分野においても、一九八六年カリフォルニア州知事によって任命された、カリフォルニア州立大学の「Board of Trustee（評議員）」の一員に任命された、ただ一人の日系人である。評議員とは、全二三校におよぶカリフォルニア州立大学の管理政策の作成、財源の管理、予算決定、学長、総長の審査、および任命等を行う要職である。彼は、JACLロングビーチ支部にJohn E. Kashiwabara 奨学金を設け、次世代を育てる事にも力をいれている。

「ある時、デンバーでの試合の帰り、子供たちに食事をさせようと小さな食堂に入ったのです。食事の注文をして座っていると、カウンターに腰掛けていた白人の男が、食堂の主人に向かって『ジャップの子供たちを追い出せ』と、何度もわめきました。主人はたまりかねたように『もう一度言ったらお前こそ出て行け』と遮ったのですが、その男は止めず、遂に、主人はドアを指さして『出て行け』と彼を追い出しました。怖がっていた子供たちは、漸く、ほっとして食事をすることができましたが、あのような時代に、こうした勇気ある善意のアメリカ人もたくさんいたのです」と語った彼の声には、アメリカ市民としての誇りが溢れていた。

後にコロラド州アマチ収容所に移されたジョンは、収容所内の子供たちにバスケットボールを教え、チームを作り、外部の一般アメリカ人の子供たちとの試合にも出られるようにした。

しかし、その後、日系人学生は、収容所を訪れ、プレイサー短期大学の学生だった日系学生一人ひとりに卒業証書を手渡してくれた。

壁を超えた人間の暖かな面を強調し、このように言葉を続けた…「日本軍の真珠湾奇襲攻撃の直後、対日感情が急に悪化したなかで当時プレイサー短期大学のバスケットボールの選手だった私は、日系人の自分がいたらチームメートに迷惑がかかるので、バスケットボール部をやめようと、それをいつコーチに話そうかと悩んでいました。そんなある日、学長室に呼ばれて行くとそこには学長の他、理事たちやコーチが並んでいました。学長が、『ジョン、君は今まで通りバスケットボールを続けなさい。心配する事はないよ』と言ってくれたのです。コーチは私が進退について悩んでいたのを知っていたのです。私はそのままチームに残り、以前と変わらず他校との試合にも出場しました」。

たが、この学長は、一九四三年二月、収容所を訪れ、プレイサー…

取材・水口まみ

「私がしてきたのは社会のため」

アメリカ名誉市民

浅見紳太

1925年埼玉県生まれ。45年東京高等商船学校航海科卒業、川崎汽船に入社。1972年ITS（インターナショナル・トランスポーテーション・サービス）社長に就任し渡米。90年同社会長就任、95〜99年名誉会長。86〜98年埼玉県人会会長、98年県人会協議会会長、2004〜06年パイオニアセンター会長を歴任。1993年に外務大臣章、95年には勲五等双光旭日章を受勲。また2006年5月に第1回カスロフ財団日系パイオニア賞を受賞。

ニュージャージー州、ポート・エリザベス。
Port of Elizabeth, New Jersey.

ロングビーチ港をアメリカ最大のコンテナターミナルに成長させ、全米東西を結ぶ内陸運送をふまえたコンテナ輸送に次々と革命を起こした「キャプテン浅見」。アメリカに赴任した企業戦士でありながら、アメリカの物流界そして経済に貢献してきた。海に憧れ、海とともに歩んできた生涯を聞いた。

海なし県で育ち憧れの船乗りに

私が生まれ育った埼玉県は海なし県ですので、余計海に惹かれたということもあるんでしょうね。船に乗りたい、海外に行きたいという思いがあり、旧制中学卒業後、東京の商船学校に入りました。卒業までには通常六年半必要なんですが、終戦時で繰り上げ卒業となり、終戦後は当時国が作った組織「船舶運営会」に就職することになりました。

戦争で多くの船が海底の藻屑と化していたため、ほとんど乗船の機会はなかったのですが、ある日突然ダグラス・マッカーサー元帥より、引揚船の業務に従事せよという電報が来ました。行き先は満州・韓国・ソ連・中国などで、アジア全域に残された数百万人の日本人を送還する、という大変な仕事でした。引揚者の方々は悲惨な思いで港までたどり着いた状態でしたので、皆できるだけ親切にして差し上げたいと努力しました。

引揚船の仕事が終わり、川崎汽船に入社した後は、日本の近海で資材運搬などの業務に就き、航海士としての経験を積みましたが二年を過ぎた頃、過労から胃潰瘍になり、手術と自宅療養を余儀なくされました。その間に人生のことをゆっくり考え復帰する頃には、良い船乗りになろうと決心していました。

一九五一年から外国航路にも出るようになり、タイやカ

ンボジア、フィリピンなどの近海を中心に、日本からは建設資材としての鋼材を運び、各地から材木・米などを運搬しました。五二年に結婚し、その後アメリカやアフリカ航路にも携わりましたが、一度出港すると四ヶ月から七ヶ月かかることもあり、たまに帰宅した時子供に「おじちゃん、今日泊まっていくの？」と聞かれて面食らったものでした。

州の発展を唱えアラスカ航路開設

一九六〇年一月、まだ航路の開けていないアラスカ行きを命じられました。航路開設の是非を調査するためです。極寒の街を毎日歩き回るなか、ある人から州知事と話をしてみてはと進言され、会いに行きました。知事から「実は悩んでいる。アラスカの発展についてあなたの意見を聞きたい」と言われ、私が「日本とアラスカが航路を開くことで、州民のために住み良いところにしようではありませんか」と提案すると、翌日の新聞には、アラスカと日本の交易が進む可能性が大きな見出しで報じられ、積荷の問い合わせが殺到しました。

潮の速さや地形上入港が困難な点については、知事が紹介してくれたコーストガードが、詳細な海図を使って的確に教えてくれ、入港の目処が立ちました。三五歳の時でした延長でアラスカ航路の船長となりました。ところが二度目の航海で日本に帰る途中、ニューヨーク勤務を命ぜられ、六一年五月からは海務監督という立場で駐在することになったのです。

ニューヨークで見たコンテナ輸送に確信

当時、海運会社は代理店制度を取っており、私は現地責任者として代理店の監督・指示を行いました。その頃に出会ったのがコンテナ。コンテナ船を作ったシーランド社のマルカム・マックリーン氏から、披露パーティーに招待されたのです。コンテナ船とは、トラックをコンテナ化して、そのまま船に積むという、当時考えもつかない発想でした。従来は積荷をバラしていったん倉庫に入れ、トラックに積み直していましたが、コンテナだと雨や風雪に左右されず、安全に効率的に運搬できます。それがいずれ海運界の主流になるとは誰も予想できませんでしたが、私はこれからの海運はこれだという確信を得ました。

日本に帰任した後、海務部付で運搬の効率化を研究する役につきました。徐々にコンテナ輸送導入の波が押し寄せるなか、六八年にはコンテナ室の課長に命じられ、その推進役になりました。ところが私は四面楚歌。コンテナ船だけでなく大きなクレーン、ヤード（コンテナ置場）なども必要で、膨大なコストがかかる。「お前は会社を潰す気か?」と会議で詰め寄られる一幕もありました。

しかし、当時は海運業界の経営不振もあり、政府からコンテナに対応するため、六社あった船会社が二社と四社のグループに分かれて提携するように指導がありました。川崎汽船は商船三井、山下新日本、ジャパンラインの四社と組むことになり、私はターミナル関係を主に担当し、七一年には港湾事業室長として尽力するようになりました。

ロングビーチ港にコンテナ埠頭を開設

川崎汽船では、国内のコンテナターミナルに加えてロングビーチに自社のターミナルを作ることになり、私はロングビーチ港湾局との交渉や、ターミナル建設準備に奔走しました。そして運営に当たる現地法人ITSを作り、私は二代目の社長として七二年に再び渡米しました。ロングビーチ港のコンテナターミナルはそれまで五エーカー程度の規模でしたが、そこに一〇〇エーカーもの広大なコンテナターミナルを作ったのです。「なんてバカでかいものを」と非難されましたが、初めに大きなものを作らなければ、後からでは修正できないと思って決断しました。ターミナルも完成し本格的な運営がスタートしましたが、日本の船会社は様子見の状態でロングビーチ港を使用してくれない。「せっかく精魂込めて作った港に顧客を集めたい」と、私は妻と二人で港を使ってくれる船会社を探して、イギリス、ドイツ、フランス、ノルウェー、イスラエルなどヨーロッパ中を回りました。各地の船会社を訪ね、コンテナターミナルのことを説明して回りました。崖っぷちの営業活動でしたが、一社二社と契約が取れ、どんどん船が入り、そして数年のうちにITSは全米最大のターミナル会社に成長しました。

さらに、港から出すコンテナを二段積のDSTにすれば、荷物を倍運ぶことができる。これが「オン・ドックDST」です。それにあわせて、必要箇所の修理を行うなど、インフラの整備も強いられましたが、私がこれを始めてから他社も追随しました。特許を取るとその普及を遅らせることになるので、特許は考えませんでした。また一つの港に頼っていては危険だと、西海岸ではワシントン州タコマにコンテナターミナルを作り、また東海岸でニュージャージーのエリザベスにも作りました。タコマの小さな港は次第に大きなコンテナ港に発展し、タコマ市から感謝され、開設の九月十一日を記念して「キャプテン・アサミズ・デー」が設けられました。

アメリカ物流を変えた革命へのチャレンジ

次に取り組んだことは、アメリカ東西の流通改革です。当時、東西の大型物流はパナマ運河に頼っていました。ロングビーチでコンテナの輸送が始まり、将来物流が増加することを考えると、西と東を鉄道で結ばなければならないと確信。それを根底に打ち出したのが「オン・ドック・ダブルスタック・トレイン（DST）」という構想でした。

これは、コンテナターミナルへそのまま列車を引き入れ、コンテナ輸送を合理化することでした。湾岸局や市の説得には数年かかりましたが、新しいレールを敷設することができました。

長期的で大きなビジョンを持つ

若い人にいつも言っているのは、「夢を持ってほしい」ということです。何事もなせばなるものですから。将来のビジョンをしっかり持って生きてほしい。レールを港に敷き、二段積のコンテナ列車を走らせることに対して、ロングビーチ市との交渉には三、四年かかりましたが、それがアメリカには必要だという信念を持ち、必死で説いて回りました。すごく時間と忍耐がいることでした。私はいつも、「会社のため、自分の」ではなく、「みんなのため、社会のため」を考えてきました。それは結果的には日本のため、アメリカのためにもなります。可能性があることに対しては、信念を持って、粘り強く続けることが大切だと思います。

※ライトハウス「人物名鑑」（二〇〇六年九月一日号）より
抜粋

人物コラム

全米日系人博物館　館長兼専務理事
アイリーン・Y・ヒラノ

一九四八年ロサンゼルス生まれ。一九七〇年、南カリフォルニア大学公共行政学科卒。七二年同大学院卒。T・H・E・クリニック専務理事などを経て、一九八八年、全米日系人博物館の館長兼専務理事に就任。現在は全米日系人博物館と並行して、スミソニアン・アメリカ歴史博物館理事、芸術・人間性振興のための大統領諮問委員会委員、ロサンゼルス観光局理事などを務める。アジア太平洋月間市長賞（一九九六年）など数多くの賞を受賞している。

全米日系人博物館

中学生の頃からコミュニティーに関与

父方の祖父は一九〇〇年代初期に渡米し、私が子供の頃は一緒に住んでいました。母は東京生まれなので、父方から見れば私は日系三世ですが、母方から見ると二世になります。三歳の時に母と一緒に東京に行き、数ヶ月過ごしたことがあるので、日本の家族とも親しんでいました。

父は大戦前から米軍情報部に所属しており、パールハーバー攻撃後もそのまま米軍に残ったので強制収容所には行きませんでしたが、祖父や叔父などはアーカンソーのローワー収容所に行かれました。病弱だった祖母は、収容所に行く前にサンタアニタのアセンブリーセンター（集合所）で亡くなりました。多くの日系人は収容所の体験を語りたがりませんし、私の家族も詳しい話はしなかったので、大学生になるまで収容所のことはあまり知りませんでした。

実態をいくらか理解できるようになったのは、大学の時でした。収容所体験をテーマに期末レポートを書いたので、その時初めて叔父や叔母などに話を聞いたのですがやはり詳細を知ったのは、戦後補償運動が開始され、多くの人が体験談を語るようになってからでした。

中学や高校の頃から多くのコミュニティー・サービスグループに参加しており、その頃からコミュニティーに関連する仕事に興味がありました。南カリフォルニア大学では公共行政学を専攻しました。通常、卒業後の就職先は政府関連か非営利団体の選択なのですが、今でも非営利団体を選んで良かったと思っています。

大学院を卒業して最初の仕事は、アジア女性センターの副理事で、次に連邦保険教育厚生省（当時）のエイジング管理局・中高年支援プロジェクトのリサーチのためにワシントンDCで勤務しました。その後、非営利団体であるT・H・E・クリニックに戻り、そこで専務理事を十三年間務めました。

同クリニックはクレンショーにあるのですが、おかげで多くの公共医療サービス機関と仕事をしたり、さまざまな家族と接することができました。多言語で情報を提供したり、民族の文化に基づいたサービスを築く機会に恵まれました。

たとえば、アフリカ系とヒスパニック系では食事療法しても違ってきます。民族の文化によってアプローチが変わるという認識を自分の中に定着させることができたのは幸いでしたし、アジア系医療プログラムを立ち上げるなど、多くの機会に恵まれました。

日系人の体験は人種を超えたもの

全米日系人博物館の仕事は、それまでの仕事と比べるとずいぶん違う印象がありますが、非営利団体を運営する点、またコミュニティー教育という点では類似点も多くあります。特にコミュニティー教育の観点から見ると、博物館はもっと多くの人々を対象に長期間にわたるサービスを提供

72

できます。それまで全米規模のさまざまなサービス機関と仕事をしてきたので、経験を活かせる素晴らしい機会だと思いました。

どんな組織も、創設にはまず基金が必要です。博物館の仕事は、その必要性など博物館のビジョンを人々に認識してもらうところから始まりました。ニューヨーク、ハワイ、シアトル、シカゴなどでは、全米日系人博物館を他地域ではなく、ロサンゼルスに設立することの意義を説いて回りました。

開設にあたってのもうひとつのチャレンジは、所蔵品がなかったことです。通常、何かのコレクションがあってそれを公開するために博物館を開設するのですが、同館の場合は展示する品がありませんでした。特に日系人のストーリーがテーマの博物館なので、収容所体験者に話を聞き、それを録音して保存する作業などが必要でした。私が理事になったのが一九八八年で、ちょうど市民の自由法が署名された年だったので、補償運動が起こる前に比べると多くの人が体験談を語ってくれましたが、今でも当時の話をしたがらない人は少なくありません。もっと時間が経てば、さらに多くのストーリーを分かち合えるのではないかと思っています。

さらに日系人以外の人にも興味を持ってもらい、関与してもらうにはどのようにすればいいか、というのも課題でした。多くの人に博物館を訪れてもらうには、日系人の歴史が日系人だけのものでなく、アメリカの歴史の一端として心を引きつけるものでなければなりません。現在、来

て展示しました。この展示は、広島、沖縄、大阪、新潟で日系人の歴史を展示しました。多くの日系人以外の人にも興味を持ってもらい、関与してもらうにはどのようにすればいいか、というのも課題でした。その一環としてスミソニアン研究所にも加盟しており、一九九八年にはスミソニアンで「弁当からミックス・プレートへ・多文化社会ハワイの日系人」

館者の多くが日系人以外の人たちで、この進展に関しては博物館者として誇りに思っています。

日系人の体験は、人種を超えたものです。毎日のように課外授業で若い世代が来館していますが、若い人たちはここで学んだものを自分たちの経験に照らし合わせることができます。たとえばヒスパニック系の移民の子どもたちは、日系一世が経験したことを自分の親が経験しているのでいかに人種が融合した文化であるかを展示したストーリーは、彼らのストーリーでもあったのです。

九・一一テロ後、同館がすぐに「アラブ系が人種偏見に遭うべきではない」と声明を出したのもそのためですが、「戦後五〇年以上経って、今では民主主義が徹底し、人種偏見はもう起こらない」と思っていた若い世代の日系人も、歴史は繰り返されると認識できたのではないかと思います。四〇年代には日系人差別に対して異論を唱えた人はごくわずかでしたが、九・一一テロ後には多くの人が立ち上がりました。アラブ系の人に、彼ら以外にも人種差別に反対するコミュニティーがあるのだと知ってもらえたことは、私たちにとっても重要でした。

日本人と日系人の絆を太くしたい

私の仕事のひとつに、多くの博物館や文化機関と協力関係を築くことがあります。その一環としてスミソニアン研究所と連携し、一九九八年にはスミソニアンでも大好評を博し、巡回展示会を記録しました。「弁当からミックス・プレートへ」はハワイで始まったものなので、スミソニアンに展示した時は、ワシントンDC界隈に住むハワイにゆかりのある約百人がボランティアをしてくれました。多くが日系人ではありませんでしたが、ハワイに住んだ経験のある彼らにすれば、ハワイがいかに人種が融合した文化であるかを展示したストーリーは、彼らのストーリーでもあったのです。

私のゴールのひとつに、日本人と日系人の間に強い絆を築くことがあります。博物館には、アート、教育、日系二世の歴史、そして国際の四つのプログラムがあります。ここ数年は国際プログラムに力を入れています。もっと多くの日系人、特に三世や四世、五世たちが自分たちの日本におけるルーツを知ることは重要だと思いますし、日本人と日系人の絆を太いものにするのは博物館の役割のひとつでもあります。幸い私は母が日本生まれなので、日本の家族とも親しくしていますが、父方のルーツはほとんど知りません。博物館として、将来の日系人リーダーたちが自分たちの伝統を誇りに思い、日米関係さらには国際関係の理解を深めて支援できるように、またルーツを知ることによって日系アメリカ人としてより広い視野が生まれるようにサポートするのも、博物館の重要な役割だと思います。

※ライトハウス「人物名鑑」（二〇〇五年八月一日号）より抜粋

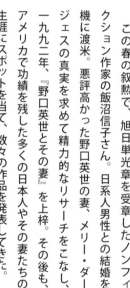

「真実を知りたいと思ったのです」

ノンフィクション作家

飯沼信子

1932年静岡県生まれ。53年、実践女子大中退後、日系2世の男性と結婚し、渡米。84年、高知新聞『ロスの日系家庭から』の連載で、文筆業に入る。代表作の『野口英世とその妻』のリサーチでは、野口英世の遺言状の発見など、多大な功績を残した。著書に『高峰譲吉とその妻』『黄金のくさび』『彫塑家　川村吾蔵の生涯』など多数。ロサンゼルス日系婦人会、ロサンゼルス市など、数多くの団体から表彰され、2006年、旭日単光章を受勲。

この春の叙勲で、旭日単光章を受章したノンフィクション作家の飯沼信子さん。日系人男性との結婚を機に渡米。悪評高かった野口英世の妻、メリー・ダージェスの真実を求めて精力的なリサーチをこなし、一九九二年、『野口英世とその妻』を上梓。その後も、アメリカで功績を残した多くの日本人やその妻たちの生涯にスポットを当て、数々の作品を発表してきた。

日系男性と結婚で渡米人種差別を目の当たりに

実践女子大二年生の時のことです。寮生活だったのですが、日系米兵が同室の同級生を訪ねて寮に来ました。女性ばかりですから、皆「二世の人が来た」と大騒ぎです。彼はUCバークレー大学の学生だったところを、朝鮮戦争で徴兵されて東京に駐屯しているとのことでした。出発前にロサンゼルスの友人から「東京に妹がいるから、会いに行ってやってくれ」と頼まれており、その妹というのが私の同級生だったのです。その時、映画に誘われてお付き合いが始まり、一九五三年、私はその米兵と結婚して渡米することになりました。

渡米の第一印象は、決していいものではありませんでした。シカゴに行く予定でしたが、船でシアトルに着いた後、彼の親戚がいるロサンゼルスに立ち寄ることにしました。グレイハウンド・バスで南下したのですが、道中入ったレストランで、店の人が見向きもしてくれないのです。初めは訳がわからなかったのですが、主人に「差別だよ」と教えられました。結局、その時はランチを食べられませんでした。

シカゴで主人はイリノイ大学に入り、三年半で卒業した後、イリノイ工科大学に入りました。主人はあるエレクロニクスの会社でバイトをしていたのですが、ブルーカラーとホワイトカラーでは、乗るエレベーターでさえ違っていたそうです。一九五四年でしたから、まだ人種差別がまかり通っていた時代です。主人は差別の実態を目の当たりにして、「日本人は頭脳で秀でるしかない」と発奮し、優秀な成績で卒業しました。エンジニアは引っ張りだこの時代でしたので、航空機のノースロップ社に高給で就職することができました。当時は、成績によって給料にも差があったのです。それが一九五七年ですから、四年前にランチを食べられなかったのとは雲泥の差でした。

手紙の文面から察した誠実なメリーの人柄

ものを書くのは、子供の頃から好きでした。著述業に入ったきっかけは、山崎豊子著『二つの祖国』が原作の大河ドラマがロサンゼルスで放送されるということで、高知で育った主人に高知新聞の社長から「感想文を書いてくれ」と依頼されたのが発端です。その時、主人が、私に「書かない？」と振ったのです。それで私が考察をまとめ、書簡を送りました。それを読んだ社長から「連載しよう」との話があり、一九八四年より『ロスの日系家庭から』の連載が始まりました。

その後、ある一世の生涯を紹介したいと思い、出版社に打診したところ、「移民して苦労したなどという苦闘の歴史は、誰も聞きたくないから見向きもされませんよ」という返事が返ってきました。日本はちょうどバブルの真っ只中だったのです。そこへ郡山にある福島テレビのプロデューサーから「福島といえば野口英世ですが、妻は大変なひとだったらしいね。ひとつ書きませんか」と話がありました。

そこから、『野口英世とその妻』のリサーチが始まり

ました。国勢調査の記録を掘り返し、妻のメリー・ダーがわかると飛んで行き、ロックフェラー大学のアーカイブから野口の孫弟子を探し出すと、インタビューに行きました。ロックフェラー大学のアーカイブは、ニューヨークから汽車で一時間半ほど離れた大学所有の別荘内にあります。天皇陛下も泊まられたというその別荘に、アーカイブの館長を訪ねました。メリーさんの手紙を見つけたのはその時です。文面から察するメリーさんは、誠意があり、几帳面で、世間に伝えられてきたようなふしだらな印象とはかけ離れていました。

野口は、ガーナで黄熱病にかかった時、長文の電報をメリーさんに打電したのですが、メリーさんは返事を出していません。それが、出せなかったのではなく、出せなかったからだということもわかりました。メリーさんの弟三人は全員が塵肺で死亡したのですが、野口が打電した時、上の弟が余命いくばくもないという状態で、彼女は弟を特別列車に乗せてニューヨークの病院に入院させたところだったのです。「ニューヨークのロックフェラーで仕事を完成させる」が、野口からの最後の電報でした。

何もないはずの丘陵に野口の別荘が健在

野口はアフリカに行くまで、ニューヨーク郊外にある小さな町の別荘に住んでいました。行く前に関係者から「今、日本では、山内一豊の妻がカカア天下でテレビで放映されていますが、これらの日本人男性を夫に持ったアメリカ人女性たちが、いかにして夫を助け、アメリカ社会に押し出したかを書き出したいと思っています。

今までもずいぶん講演を行ってきましたが、これからも

ジェスさんの弟三人がペンシルベニアの炭鉱の町にいたこらい、泊まらせていただきました。別荘の近くには、ボーイスカウトのジャンボリーもあり、それは素晴らしい場所です。

今回、日本政府より旭日単光章を叙勲いただいたのは、こういった功績が認められたのだと思います。結局、同作の信頼を築いたのです。

野口の眠る墓地を訪ねた時のことです。野口には立派なお墓があるのですが、メリーさんは墓石もありません。墓地の人に聞くと、野口と一緒に埋葬されているとのことでした。でも名前が刻まれていないと、無縁仏と同じです。そこでメリーさんの名前を列記して刻んでもらう手筈を整えました。メリーさんの弟たちの墓は、野口とはかけ離れた一般人向けの墓地にありましたが、墓石だけで名前も入っていません。こちらは実費で名前を刻んでもらいました。

日系人の祖国はアメリカでもルーツは日本

現在、メリーさんなど、日本人男性と結婚したアメリカ人妻六人ほどを題材にした本の執筆に取り組んでいます。日本人妻をカカア天下なわけではありません。これらの日本人男性を夫に持ったアメリカ人女性たちが、いかにして夫を助け、アメリカ社会に押し出したかを書き出したいと思っています。

に建っており、敷地内に川も流れており、部屋を見せてもらい、泊まらせていただきました。別荘の近くには、ボーイスカウトのジャンボリーもあり、それは素晴らしい場所です。

今回、日本政府より旭日単光章を叙勲いただいたのは、こういった功績が認められたのだと思います。事実を知りたい、という思いに駆られたわけですが、いろいろと調べているうちに、あまりにもメリーさんに対する誤解が多かったことがわかりました。ちっぽけな正義感ですが、「それなら私が誤解を晴らしてみよう」という気になったのですね。

日本人は国際性がないと言われますが、自分の文化で計るから受け入れられないのです。今アメリカには、大勢の日本人が留学しています。せっかく留学しているのですから、その人たちが改善していってほしいですね。

アメリカンドリームは自分で作るもので、人に与えてもらうものではありません。それを手に入れる方法は努力以外にないのです。

戦後、日系人はアメリカナイズしようとけなげな努力をしてきました。ですがどんなに同化しようとしても、日系人の親を持つことに変わりなく、どうやってもアングロサクソンにはなれません。彼らの祖国はアメリカですが、ルーツは日本なのですから、日本文化を伝えていくのは大切だと思います。

より多くの人に偉業を成し遂げた日本人のことを紹介していきたいですね。日本からの講演依頼の題材として多いのは「今、日本人はアメリカでどのように受け入れられているのか」というものです。歴史というのは、昨日、今日で判断できるものではありません。積み上げて、時が経って、初めて評価できるのです。昔からの蓄積が、今ある日本人の信頼を築いたのです。

※ライトハウス「人物名鑑」（二〇〇六年八月一日号）より

抜粋

「人間は自由」という信念を貫き日本食を全米に普及した寿司ブームの仕掛け人

共同貿易社長

金井　紀年

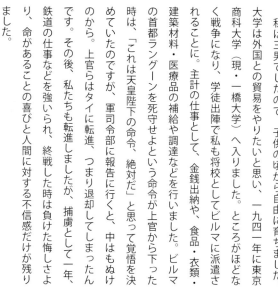

1923 年、東京・新宿生まれ。1964 年に渡米し、食品会社・共同貿易（Mutual Trading Co. Inc）の社長に。以後、日本食のアメリカ輸入にとどまらず、日本酒、味噌、海苔、麺類の製造を行う。また、寿司をはじめとする日本食の全米普及に貢献。ロサンゼルスを本社とし、ハワイ、ニューヨーク、ボストン、サンフランシスコ、アリゾナ、東京、神戸を拠点に展開。従業員約 250 名、年商 1 億ドル。

外国貿易への憧れから東京商科大学に入学するも、一九四三年の学徒動員で第二次世界大戦の激戦地・ビルマに出陣、上官の失踪に人間への不信感を抱く。戦後の焼け野原でビジネスを始めるが、一生かかっても返せない額の借金を抱える。しかしその後、自動車部品の流通で借金をすべて返済。縁あって四一歳で渡米、あるユダヤ系アメリカ人との出会いから全米の寿司ブームの仕掛け人となる。年商一億ドル以上の食品商社を経営し、日本食普及の使命をかける金井氏に、その半生を振り返ってもらった。

一橋大の新自由主義に共感

私は三男でしたので、子供の頃から自由に育ちました。

大学が外国との貿易をやりたいと思い、一九四一年に東京商科大学（現・一橋大学）へ入りました。ところがほどなく戦争になり、学徒出陣で私も将校としてビルマに派遣されることに。主計の仕事として、金銭出納や、食品・衣類・建築材料・医療品の補給や調達などを行いました。ビルマの首都ラングーンを死守せよという命令が上官から下った時は、「これは天皇陛下の命令、絶対だ」と思って覚悟を決めていたのですが、軍司令部に報告に行くと、中はもぬけのから。上官らはタイに転進、つまり退却してしまったんです。その後、私たちも転進しましたが、捕虜として一年、十年ほどして石井さんが脳溢血で倒れてしまい、跡を継ぐ人がいなかったので、妻と子供二人を連れて渡米を決めました。一九六四年、四一歳の時です。

鉄道の仕事などを強いられ、終戦した時は負けた悔しさより、命があることの喜びと人間に対する不信感だけが残りました。

若かったので悩みました。本をたくさん読んで、到達したところは「自由であることが人間の幸福である」という、一橋の学長でもあった上田貞次郎先生の言葉。「自由という

当時、日本人町にグロッサリーストアは四軒、日本食レストランも四、五軒。売られていたのは、海苔などの乾物、かまぼこなどの缶詰、そして漬物やたる詰めのしょう油く

のは自分で考えて選択できること」、それを私も実践しようと決意し、自分でビジネスをすることに決めました。

友人らが企業に就職していく中、私は自分で二、三ビジネスを立ち上げますが、いずれも失敗。卒業の数年後には一八〇万円もの借金を負います。当時、一生かかっても返せない額です。死のうかとも思いましたが、「自由だなんて言っておいて、返せないというのは情けない。好意で貸してくれたお金だから、何が何でも返そう」と思い直し、三浦半島に沈んだ特攻部隊のモーターボートに目を付け、そのディーゼルエンジンを再生してトラックを作って売るなどして、二年で借金をすべて返しました。

寿司を食べたアメリカ人

それから、母の知り合いで戦前にアメリカに渡り、サンタマリアでスーパーを成功させた石井さんにお会いしました。財産は没収されてしまい日本に引き上げてきた彼でしたが、アメリカに帰り食料品のビジネスをやりたいと、私と一緒に一九五一年、共同貿易のエージェント・東京共同貿易をスタートさせました。ロサンゼルスの共同貿易は一九二六年に創業した会社ですが、オーナーの星崎さんのリタイヤを機に、石井さんがアメリカに渡り同社を買い取りました。その後、私は日米間を往復していたのですが、十年ほどして石井さんが脳溢血で倒れてしまい、跡を継ぐ人がいなかったので、妻と子供二人を連れて渡米を決めました。一九六四年、四一歳の時です。

らい。日本食のマーケットは小さく、将来性などないと

言われていました。しかし、本格的な日本食はもっと美味しいものだ、美味しい日本食ならアメリカ人にも売れる、ならば可能性は無限だと私は考えたのです。何を持ってくれば売れるか。最初、万国共通のお菓子ならと思い、東鳩のハーベストクッキーを売り出しました。クリスピーさがうけて売れましたが、中国や韓国の工場が安い類似品を作り、市場を壊してしまいました。次にアメリカの家庭用品を日本に売ることを考え、シカゴの展示会に出かけたところ、あるアメリカ人に出会います。「アメリカで成功するには、いいユダヤ人と友達になることだ」と彼。物知りな彼をコンサルタントとして雇い、貿易のヒントを求めて一緒にアジアを旅することにしました。

最後に日本を訪れたとき、彼は神田の「新之介寿司」で寿司を食べ、「寿司は米国にない独創的な食べ物だ。これをやれ」と言う。私にはない発想でした。でも、ヨーロッパでも生魚は食べるし、これは当たると彼は言うんです。やってみようと決意しました。

第二次日本食ブームに対応

まず、日本人町の「川福」に寿司カウンターを作ってもらい、始めたところ白人の客が来るようになりました。二号店は栄菊、三号店の東京会館では真下さんという人がカリフォルニア・ロールを発案しました。センチュリーシティーの白人専門の寿司店を発案しました。そして、ニューヨーク、シカゴと全米へ広がっていきました。寿司だけでも、米、酢、海苔、魚、酒、食器など、調達する食材や商品はたくさんあります。私はそのロジスティックを整え、普及を進めていったわけです。

一九八〇年には映画『将軍』がヒットして日本ブームに。日本の車や家電も進出し始め、日本に対するイメージが変わってきました。貿易摩擦やバブル経済、バブル崩壊と時代は移りますが、寿司の人気は高まるばかりです。

そして現在は、第二次日本食ブーム。居酒屋スタイルの店が流行り出しました。第一次ブームの寿司はロサンゼルス発でしたが、今度はニューヨークから。高級居酒屋「MEGU」などは、魚をすべて空輸しています。そんな要望に応えるため、我が社ではマイナス六五度の大型冷凍庫を設置しました。地酒も百種類以上揃え、酒のソムリエを置くなど本格的な店も登場しています。

私は四〇年前に来た時に会社の方針を三つ作りました。人間は自ら立つのだから社員が自社株を持つ、病気になってはいけないので健保部門を自社で作って社員に入ってもらう、そして定年を作らず社員で利益を分け合うということです。

これからの目標は、本物の日本食を供給できるロジスティックを確立し、日本食文化をもっと広めること。社員が自由で楽しく働ける雰囲気を作っていくこと。そして、コミュニティーにも貢献していきたい。これらを実現するために、日々努力していきます。

※JBA NEWS 二〇〇四年九月号企業家シリーズより抜粋

年　表

年	日系社会	年	アメリカと世界	年	日本
1834	尾張の千石船、宝順丸の乗組員音吉、久吉、岩吉、イーグル号でハワイに行く。その後、英船。	1837	オバリン大学、初の女子学生入学を許可。	1837	日本人漂流民(音吉ら7人)を乗せて来航した非武装の米国商船モリソン号に日本側が発砲し入国を拒否。(モリソン号事件)
1838	インディアンに捕らわれイギリス人に救われる。その後、マカオに渡る。英船。	1840	米国人口、17,069,458。		
1841	漁師ジョン万次郎漂流し、無人島(鳥島)に漂着、アメリカの捕鯨船ハウランド号に救出される。	1845	アイルランドからの移民が始まる。その後15年でアイルランドの人口の半分に当たる1,500,000人が米国に移住。	1846	米国の使節ビドル提督来航、開国を要求。日本拒否。
1843	音吉、日本に入国できずニューヨークに戻る。	1846	メキシコ・アメリカ戦争(〜48)勝者、米国はカルフォルニア、ネバダ、ユタなど15,000,000ドルで購入。	1853	7月8日米国の使節マシュー・ペリー提督来航、横浜浦賀沖に上陸し米国大統領の親書を幕府に手渡す。久里浜に上陸し米国大統領の親書を幕府に手渡す。開国を要求。7月14日
1851	ジョン万次郎マチュー・ペリーにフェアヘブンで船長の好意で学校教育をうける。	1848	女性の権利集会ニューヨークで開催(エリザベス・スタントン女史指導)。カルフォルニアでゴールドラッシュ始まる。	1854	ペリー提督再び来航、函館の2港を開く。日米和親条約を結ぶ。鎖国の終焉。
1854	彦蔵、他16人漂流中、米国船オークランド号に救助されサンフランシスコに上陸。カルフォルニアで滞在した最初の日本人達。	1854	ペリー提督日本を開く。日米和親条約を結ぶ(ピアース大統領)。	1858	井伊直弼大老、米国と修好通商条約を結ぶ。その後イギリス、ロシア、オランダ、フランスとも条約を結ぶ。日本6港を開く。
1858	彦蔵、アメリカの好意でボルティモアのカトリック新宿学校に入学。洗礼を受け、ジョセフ・ヒコとなる。	1859	ブルックリン無人島ミッドウェイ島をより所所得。日本人権利を獲得。	1860	初の米国軍艦ポーハタン・ハリス下田に着任。77人の幕府使節、正史新見豊前守、副使村田泡淳渡米、護衛艦咸臨丸、艦長勝海舟。豊後丸でパナマを経由でワシントンDCに到着。サンフランシスコまで同行。
1860	ジョセフ・ヒコ、日本人最初の米国市民権を取得。	1861	アブラハム・リンカーン大統領就任。南北戦争勃発。奴隷制度廃止。		
1865	新島襄(安中藩の子弟)、米国船の乗組員として渡米し、ボストン大学、アンドーバー神学校卒業、同志社大学の前身となる学校を設立。	1862	解放奴隷、200,000人北軍兵士として参加、連邦政府自営農地法施行。西部開拓推進。		
1866	海外渡航が解禁されると多くの藩が子弟を留学の為米艦でサンフランシスコに渡り、パナマを経て東海岸の都市を訪れたりジョンソン大統領に謁見。その後ニューヨークを経由し、各地で大歓迎される。	1863	リンカーン大統領奴隷解放宣言に調印。4,000,000人の奴隷が解放される。	1866	小栗上野介忠順、慶応大学の前身となる学校をつくる。フランス人フリュリ・ヴェルニー横須賀最初の製鉄所、造船所を建造。後に横須賀港に整備。
1867	森有礼、鮫島尚信(薩摩藩)日下部太郎(福井藩)横井佐平太(肥後藩)後の総理大臣高橋是清。彼らは米国の文化、思想、教育制度、技術などの知識を日本に持ち帰った。	1865	南部軍敗北し、憲法改正13条を追加(奴隷制有禁止)。リンカーン大統領暗殺。KKK創立(旧南部軍兵士を中心に黒人弾圧目的の結社)。	1867	大政奉還、徳川慶喜政権を前将軍。
1868	長沢鼎(薩摩藩の子弟)15才でニューヨークに留学、7年後カルフォルニアに移住し、ワイン製造業として成功した。	1867	米国、ロシアからアラスカを買収(7,200,000ドル)。ミッドウェイ島を併合。	1868	王政復古(明治天皇)明治元年、五箇条の御誓文、江戸を東京に改名。明治新政府。
1869	この頃までに渡米でした米人の為新島襄、知識となる技術を習得し日本に帰国する留学生だった(元年者)。	1868	カーネギー製鋼会社創設。	1869	首都を東京に移す。東京招魂社建立、明治維新で尊王側のために死亡した人々を祀った(1879年に靖国神社と改名)。
1870	シュネール、会津藩士たち数十人を連れて渡米。カルフォルニアワインと絹の生産のための若者を松に渡った。初のコロニーを開設。	1869	大陸横断鉄道開通。東西からユタ州で結合。	1872	学制を定め全国に小学校をつくる。義務教育の開始。東京・横浜間に鉄道開通。
1873	日本政府ワシントンDCに日本公使館、サンフランシスコに領事館を開設。	1870	スタンダード石油会社設立(ジョン・ロックフェラー)。	1873	太陽暦導入。新貨幣制度(円を貨幣単位とする)。郵便制度ができる。
1880	ジュンジウ・マツムラ 初の日本人としてアナポリス海軍士官学校に入学。	1871	ペリー・バブ・マンスフィールド米国初の女性弁護士となる。大陸横断鉄道開通、東西からユタ州で結合。	1879	ユリシーズ・グラント大統領来日訪問、明治天皇と会見。
1884	安本貞之進、兼太郎兄弟渡米しフォルニーア花園薬で成功、後にカルフォルニアで土地を購入。日本人として初めて土地を購入。	1876	アレキサンダー・グラハム・ベル電話発明。	1881	大隈重信早稲田大学の前身となる学校を設立。
1885	初の国勢調査、日本人148人。	1877	トーマス・エディソン蓄音機発明。	1882	日本銀行発足。
1890	米国移民944人がサンフランシスコに到着(3年契約)。初の官約移民。	1879	トーマス・エディソン電球発明。	1885	内閣制度発足、初代総理大臣・伊藤博文。
	米国国勢調査、日本人2,039。この頃から米国本土に移住した日本人は殆どが農業、漁業、鉄道、成航で働く出稼ぎ労働者だった。	1882	米国議会、中国人排斥法を可決。	1887	東京に電灯がつく。
		1885	クリーブランド大統領、ニューヨーク港自由の女神の序幕。	1890	第一回衆議院選挙、帝国議会開催。人口40,000,000。
		1886	クリーブランド大統領、ニューヨーク港自由の女神の序幕。		
		1890	米国人口62,947,714。		

年　表

年 ／ 日系社会

年	日系社会
1894	ハワイの日本人、29,000人になる。ハワイへの官約移民禁止。
1895	アメリカ本土の日系人、6,000人に達する。
1898	スパニッシュ・アメリカン戦争で日系一世も人戦死（USS Maine の乗組員）。米国ハワイ併合。
1899	西本願寺布教師、北米仏教団創設。
1900	米国国勢調査。日系人24,326（女性410）。日本政府、日本人労働者のハワイ旅券を制限する事に同意。
1901	高橋謙吉博士（消化剤ジアスターゼの発明者）、ジョン・ロスアンゼルスでパスポートでドレナリンの抽出に成功。
1902	ホテルト日系市開業。
1903	シアトル日系市開業。
1905	西原清東（同志社大学総長、衆議院議員、農学者）、ヒューストン商工会の招きで日本から種米を持参し渡米。ヒューストン近郊で農園を経営し、米の生産業に貢献。
1906	サンフランシスコで東洋人排斥連盟結成。「羅府新報」創刊。
1907	サンフランシスコ大地震。日系社会の中心が南カリフォルニアに移る。我採種子太郎"大和コロニー"を開設、白人と協調関係を築き農業に従事し栄えた。
1908	38,000人の日系移民、ハワイから米国本土に移転、ルーズベルト大統領令によりハワイ、メキシコ、カナダからの移民を禁止。日本政府、日本人労働者への移転禁止。
1909	日米紳士協定成立。日本政府、一般の観光客、商人、学生など以外の日本人にアメリカ行き旅券を発行しないと約束。
1910	南カリフォルニアで日米協会「JAS」発足。
1913	アーサー・オキタ（ハワイ出身の日系二世）、日系人初の弁護士免許を取得。米国国勢調査、日系人72,157。
1917	カルフォルニア州議会、"外国人土地法"（米国籍を持てない者の土地所有を禁止）を可決。
1920	第一次世界大戦に日系一世出征。
1922	日系排日移民、写真花嫁の渡航を禁止。米国国勢調査、日系人111,010。
1924	連邦最高裁判所、オザワ訴訟の判決、日本人一世の帰化権を拒否（小澤孝雄、帰化権拒否）1952年まで続く。
1927	クーリッジ大統領、"1924年移民法"に署名。事実上、日本からの移民停止。
1930	最高裁判所、全員一致でハワイの日本語学校に対するラロウ・ウッズ抗議のため辞任。南カリフォルニア議会、日系市民協会（JACL）設立。

年 ／ アメリカと世界

年	アメリカと世界
1891	ジェームス・ネイスミス、バスケットボール考案。
1892	ニューヨーク沖のエリス島、ヨーロッパからの移民検査のために開設。1954年までに20,000,000人が通過。
1898	スパニッシュ・アメリカン戦争、勝利国米国はプエルトリコ、グアム、フィリピンを20,000,000ドルで購入。マリアナ諸島、ハワイを併合。
1903	フォードモーター社設立。ライト兄弟、飛行に成功。
1906	サンフランシスコ大地震。
1909	N.A.A.C.P.（黒人公民権運動）発足。
1910	米国国勢調査、人口91,972,266。日本朝鮮半島侵略、軍支配下とする。
1912	タイタニック沈没、1500人余り死亡。
1913	連邦準備制度（米国中央銀行）創設。
1914	パナマ運河開通、第一次世界大戦勃発。
1917	第一次世界大戦米国参戦（～1919）。ロシア革命。
1918	インフルエンザ大流行、死者500,000人。
1920	米国議会、婦人参政権（改定案19条）承認。ラジオ放送開始。
1922	ベニト・ムッソリーニ、イタリア独裁支配。
1924	ワイオミング州、デキサス州、女性知事輩出。
1927	チャールス・リンバーグ、ニューヨークからパリまでの飛行に成功。
1929	米国株式市場暴落、世界経済恐慌はじまる。
1932	英国の科学者ジェームス・チャドウィック、中性子発見。
1933	フランクリン・ルーズベルト大統領就任（～45）、ニューディール政策開始。ヒットラー、ドイツ首相に就任。日本に中国、満州からの撤退を勧告。

年 ／ 日本

年	日本
1894	日清戦争、中国—日本（～1895）。日本国内で戦い日本勝利。
1895	下関講和条約締結。台湾日本の統治下となる。
1897	八幡製鉄所創設。
1904	日露戦争（～05）、日本ロシアに勝利。
1905	ポーツマス条約締結、ロシア日本に韓国、サハリン北部の統治権を譲渡。
1906	日本、満州に南満州鉄道設立。
1907	ブラジル移民協約締結。
1908	日米紳士協定（日本、労働者の移民廃止を約束）。
1910	日本、韓国を併合、軍支配下とする。
1912	明治天皇死去、大正天皇即位。
1914	第一次世界大戦に参戦、日本、中国に21ヶ条の要求を出し、満州にも手を伸ばす。
1915	第一次世界大戦勃発、日本、好景気となる。
1917	第一次世界大戦参戦。
1920	国際連盟加入、常任理事国となる。人口56,666,000。
1921	ワシントン軍縮会議調印（日本、米国、英国、フランス）。
1923	関東大震災。
1925	普通選挙法―25才以上の男子のみ参政権、ラジオ放送開始。
1926	大正天皇死去、昭和天皇即位。
1929	日本経済の悪化。
1931	満州事変、日本軍奉天占領、南満州に侵攻、国際連盟。
1932	上海事変、日本軍上海空襲、ハルビンに侵攻。満州国建国宣言をする。日本軍奉天、満州国建国、5.15事件、犬養首相暗殺、国際連盟。
1933	中国、日本の満州侵略を国際連盟に提訴。非難し満州、中国からの撤退を要求。日本、国際連盟を脱退。

年表

日系社会

年	日系社会
1934	二世ウィーク開始。
1935	フランクリン・ルーズベルト大統領ナイ法案に署名。第一次世界大戦に出征した500人のアジア人に市民権を与える。
1940	米国政府、在米の日本財産を凍結。JACLの指導者たちが忠誠である事を伝えた。
1941	12月7日、日本軍の真珠湾奇襲攻撃、FBIはハワイと米国西海岸の日系人リーダー1,291人を拘束。12月18日から24日にかけて8隻の米国商船が攻撃され2隻が沈没。西海岸全域が第一区軍事地域となる。
1942	ルーズベルト大統領"行政命令9066"に署名。特定地域に居住する権限を軍に与える。第一区軍事地域であった110,000人余りの日系が、退去するように命ぜられた。退去したものは5,000人らずで、他の110,000人余りオレゴン州西部・カリフォルニア州サンフォアキン・スティーブンスとケース・フレンソ、カリフォルニア州サンタバーバラが含まれた。
1943	ルーズベルト大統領の日系二世の442戦闘部隊が編成された。日本の潜水艦によりオレゴン州フォート・スティーブンスと、海岸近い州で戦果をあげた。彼らは主にニューヨーク軍線を戦い抜いた日系二世の。
1944	日系二世徴兵資格回復。
1945	日本、連合軍に無条件降伏。第二次世界大戦終結。
1946	4,724人の日系人の希望者が、交換船で日本へ帰還(その後、多くは米国に再移住)。
1948	トルーマン大統領、日系人立ち退き損害賠償法に署名。
1949	二世ウィーク再開。
1952	マッカラン・ウォルター法案(新移民法)可決。日本人にも。東京ローズ(イヴァ・トグリ)反逆罪で有罪判決。
1953	南カリフォルニア御工会議所(JCC)設立。移民割り当て、日本人にも、市民権取得可能に。
1955	第二次世界大戦中最高位の日系ジョン・アイソ、日系初のカルフォルニア州検事に就任、後に連邦控訴裁判所判事に就任。日本人一世1600人帰化宣誓式。

アメリカと世界

年	アメリカと世界
1934	ブラジル排日移民法成立。ルーズベルト大統領、年金法に署名。日本国際連盟脱退。
1935	ルーズベルト大統領、中立法に署名。イタリア軍エチオピアを侵略。
1936	日、独、伊 軍事同盟締結。中国侵攻。
1939	ドイツ軍のポーランド侵攻によりチェコスロバキア侵略により6,000,000人のユダヤ人が虐殺される(1935~45)。
1940	ドイツ軍、ノルウェー、デンマーク、オランダ、ベルギー、ルクセンブルク、仏領、ロンドンを空爆。
1941	日本へのガソリン、同鉄の輸出禁止。米軍、民間人2,403人死亡。日本軍、香港、グアム島、フィリピン、ウェーキ島、マレーシアを侵攻。米国と日本の交渉を承認。
1942	ルーズベルト大統領、西海岸在住のイタリア系米国人120,000の抑留をギリシャを侵略。イタリアとドイツがエジプトとギリシャを侵略。'バターン死の行進'フィリピンで55000人の日系米軍兵。10,000人。フィリピン駐在の日本軍兵下192キロの捕虜を死亡させた。
1943	イタリアのムッソリーニ首相失脚。ビルマ独立。ドイツとイタリア軍。
1944	連合軍156,000人、フランスのノルマンディー上陸。ドイツ軍大敗。連合軍に大敗。
1945	国際連合誕生(50カ国)。ドイツ、連合軍に無条件降伏(5月)。米国、原子爆弾実験(7月)。ソ連日本宣戦。広島、長崎に原子爆弾投下(8月)。日本連合軍に無条件降伏。
1946	インドネシア、フィリピン独立。
1947	対ソ連、冷戦時代始まる。
1948	米国、イスラエル建国承認。NATO発足。大韓民国成立。
1949	ソ連初の原子爆弾実験成功。中華人民共和国(共産党政権)。中国人民共和国(共産党政権)成立。
1950	朝鮮戦争始発(~53)。米国の人口、150,697,361(中国人)。
1952	英国、オーストラリア西海岸モンテベロ島で初の原子爆弾実験。
1953	エドモンド・ヒラリー卿、エヴェレストに征服。
1954	フランス軍、北ベトナムでベトミンに敗退。
1955	ベトナム内戦始まる。ローザ・パークス、フランスベトナムモンテゴメリーの市のバスボイコット始まる。この結果、黒人差別法的に廃止になる。男性に席を譲らず逮捕。黒人のバスボイコット始まる。この結果、黒人差別法的に廃止になる。

日本

年	日本
1934	日本、ワシントン軍縮条約破棄。ブラジル排日移民法施行。日本人のブラジルへの移民を禁止。
1936	日本、ロンドン軍縮会議脱退。内蒙古、華北に自治政府を作る。
1937	盧溝橋事件をきっかけに日中戦争勃発。中国北部への物資、労働力の統制、運用。日本満州州の。
1938	国家総動員法制定。政府による各種の物資で戦う。各党を支配。
1939	日、独、イタリア同盟締結。ノモンハン事件。ソ連軍と満蒙の国境で戦い大敗。
1940	東条英機内閣。アジア各地に侵攻。御前会議で決定。各党の解散。人口、71,930,000
1941	日本、真珠湾奇襲攻撃。太平洋戦争。タイ、ウェーキ島、フィリピン、ボルネオ、マレーシアを侵攻。太平洋戦争。(大東亜戦争と呼んだ)に突入。
1942	大東亜省設置。シンガポール占領、ガダルカナル。日本軍初の空爆。
1943	東京ローズ、太平洋で戦っている米兵向け英語放送開始。サイパン島、ガダルカナル敗退、アッツ島玉砕。
1944	サイパン島、レイテ島海戦大敗。米機、東京、横浜、大阪、北九州等空爆。
1945	日本軍沖縄戦上陸。東京大空襲。米、英、中国、原子爆弾投下(無条件降伏)。日本は無条件、米機、広島、長崎に原子爆弾投下(8月)ソ連日本宣戦。日本を占領(マッカーサー元帥)。財閥解体。
1946	昭和天皇、神格を否定し'人間宣言'をする。日本国憲法の公布(国民主権、基本的人権の尊重)女性参政権の獲得。神道制廃止。第二次農地改革の施行。
1949	湯川秀樹、日本人初のノーベル賞受賞(物理学)。
1950	人口、83,200,000
1951	サンフランシスコ平和条約締結(吉田茂首相、米国等48カ国と)。第二次世界大戦正式に終結。日本、独立を回復。日米安全保障条約。
1952	テレビジョン放映開始。
1953	防衛庁、自衛隊ができる。

年表

日系社会

年	日系社会
1956	難民救済法に基づき、鹿児島から戦後最初の移民団到着。外国人土地所有禁止法廃止。
1960	スパーク・マツナガ下院議員に当選。米国国勢調査、日系人、260,877。
1964	パツイ・タカモト・ミンク初のアジア系女性下院議員に当選。
1965	ジョンソン大統領、新移民法法案（89 236）に署名、初めて世界各国からの移民が同等に扱われる事になった。
1970	米国国勢調査、日系人373,983。
1971	ノーマン・ミネタ、サンホゼ市長に当選。
1975	ロスアンゼルスに日系敬老ホーム開設。
1978	日米市民協会、戦後補償活動を開始。
1980	ユニス・サトウ、女性、及びアジア系初のロングビーチ市長に当選。
1985	スペースシャトル・チャレンジャー爆発事故。エリソン・オニズカが殉職。
1986	Dr.ジョン・カシワバラ、アジア系初のカリフォルニア州立大学評議員に任命される。(1986〜1994)
1988	ロナルド・レーガン大統領、日系アメリカ人への強制収容補償法に署名。（各20,000ドルの補償金及び日系社会に12,500,000ドルの教育資金）
1990	米国政府、謝罪状と共に補償金、支払い開始。
1992	日系5世、クリスティーナ・ヤマグチ、オリンピック、フィギュアスケートで金メダル受賞。
2000	第二次世界大戦の日系兵士へ勲章授与。ワシントンDCに日系記念碑建立。

アメリカと世界

年	アメリカと世界
1956	イスラエル軍、シナイ半島侵攻。イギリス、フランス軍エジプトを空爆。
1959	革命軍フィデル・カストロ、ハバナでバチスタに勝利。キューバ共産国となる。
1960	米国食品薬品局、避妊薬（ピル）発売許可、（第50州）。ジョン・ケネディ大統領当選。フランス、サハラ砂漠で原子爆弾実験。
1961	ロシアのユリ・ガガーリン、人間宇宙飛行に成功。東ドイツ、東西ベルリンの間にコンクリートの壁建設。
1963	ケネディ大統領暗殺される。米国ベトナム戦争に突入り、リンドン・ジョンソン大統領。
1964	中国、南太平洋で原子爆弾実験。
1967	サーグッド・マーシャル初の黒人最高裁判所判事に任命。
1968	マーティン・ルーサー・キング牧師、暗殺される。
1969	米国の宇宙飛行士、ニール・アームストロング人間初の月面ウォークに成功。
1971	憲法改訂第26条成立により選挙権18才となる。米国人口、203,211,926。
1974	リチャード・ニクソン大統領、ウォーターゲイトスキャンダルで大統領辞任。
1975	ベトナム戦争終結。インドで原子爆弾実験。
1979	マーガレット・サッチャー女史、英国首相に就任。
1981	サンドラ・オコーナー、初の女性最高裁判事となる。IBM、家庭用コンピューター発売。
1988	国際テロ集団アルカイダ発足（オサマ・ビンラーデン）
1989	中国、天安門事件—中国軍、民主化を望む若者多達数千人殺害。東欧諸国共産政権崩壊、ベルリンの壁、撤去。
1990	東西ドイツ合併。イラク軍クウェート侵略、殺戮、放火始める。港湾戦争終結。
1991	米国、西欧諸国、アラブ諸国、イラク軍と交戦、イラク軍撤退。ソビエト連邦崩壊、冷戦時代終わる。
1993	ウィリアム・クリントン大統領就任。北米自由市場発足（NAFTA）。
1996	初の動物クローン成功（羊のドーリー）。
1997	ヨーロッパ、新通貨、ユーロ導入。
1998	パキスタン、原子爆弾実験。
2000	科学者、人間のゲノム解読に成功。
2001	ニューヨーク、ワールドトレードセンター、ワシントンDCのペンタゴン、同時多発テロ事件。3,025人死亡。国防省等、アフガニスタン空爆。地上作戦開始。タリバン政権崩壊、
2003	米国主導のイラク戦争始まる。フセイン政権崩壊。

日本

年	日本
1956	国際連合加入、ソ連と国交回復。日本経済上昇。
1960	日米安全保障条約の改定。人口、93,419,000。
1964	東京オリンピック開催。
1965	大韓民国と国交回復。
1972	沖縄諸島日本復帰。
1973	円為替変動相場制に移行。貿易の自由化。
1980	人口、117,063,000。
1989	昭和天皇死去。平成天皇即位。消費税実施。
1990	日本経済バブル崩壊と不況。
1995	阪神・淡路大震災。死者6,000人。東京地下鉄サリン事件、オウム心理教、麻原ら逮捕。
1996	米国大統領ウィリアム・クリントン来日。
2000	人口、126,284,000。
2001	ハイブリッド車、トヨタ、ホンダが発売。
2004	新潟中越地震。

■ 編集後記

「Bridge of Hope　日系アメリカ人の辿った道」の出版が多くの方たちのご協力と励ましをいただき出発してから二年半かかり、やっと現実になりました。

日系史に深い知識もなく、まして本の出版には未経験の私たちですが、この二年余り、本の編集にあたって新しい発見に驚き、感動し、感謝しこの日系史を語り継ぐことの意義を更に自覚させられました。

群馬県高崎市、東善寺住職村上泰賢様。神奈川県横須賀市、横須賀自然・人文博物館。東京都千代田区一番町、日本カメラ博物館。高知県土佐清水市天神町企画広報室。カルフォルニア大学バークレイ校、バンクロフト図書館。

多くの貴重なコレクションの中から絵画、写真などの資料の提供ならびに、ご親切なアドヴァイスをいただき、ありがとうございました。

北村崇朗著、「一世としてアメリカに生きて」からの引用許可をくださいました北村光世様にお礼を申しあげます。

英文の編集をしてくださったセントルイス・ワシントン大学日本文学助教授、マーヴィン・マーカス博士、校正と適切なアドヴァイスをしてくださったアイリーン・ウィロビー先生、ナンシイ・ジェイコブス先生、パム・アイゼンバーグ様、キャレン・コープランド様、ありがとうございました。

日本語ライター	三谷由美
日本語・英語年表	水口まみ
日本語DTPデザイン	伊藤秀記
表紙・デザイン	ボサノー雅子
歴史ギャラリー製作	水口まみ
	中森明美
英語翻訳者	ジョセフ・ドレーハー
	アーロン・ヘイムス
	シホ・タカイ
英語編集者	マーヴィン・マーカス博士
編集者	藤村富士美
	水口まみ
	西川裕子